BEHIND THE PICTURE

BEHIND THE PICTURE

ART AND EVIDENCE
IN THE ITALIAN RENAISSANCE

Martin Kemp

1997
Yale University Press
New Haven and London

Set in Adobe Garamond by SX Composing DTP, Rayleigh, Essex
and printed in Hong Kong through World Print Ltd., Hong Kong

Library of Congress Cataloging-in-Publication Data

Kemp. Martin.
    Behind the picture : art and evidence in the Italian Renaissance /
Martin Kemp.
      p.   cm.
    Includes bibliographical references and index.
    ISBN 0-300-07195-7 (cloth)
    1. Art, Early Renaissance—Italy—Sources.   2. Art. Italian-
-Sources.   I. Title.
  N6915.K46   1997
  709'.4509'024—dc21   97-26267
                                         CIP

Contents

Announced to the friend pictured on p. 177, by anagram

The raw materials with which the historian of Renaissance art works are of two kinds: the artefacts which are the central subjects of study; and written evidence which may provide indications of why the artefacts look like they do. In the standard histories of Renaissance art, the 'simple' business of juxtaposing the works with the documentation has become overlain with heavy veils of modern interpretation – most recently by incestuous discussions of theory and methodologies. I am not suggesting that artefacts and documents can simply be left to speak for themselves. Rather I will be asking what we may consider to be the relevant sources and how their nature as cultural products in their own right can be respected. Or to express my aim at its most basic level, the central question of the book asks what kinds of things the documents which we use to help our interpretation of Renaissance art actually are. It is my experience of years of teaching and using existing books to introduce students to the primary sources for the study of Renaissance art, that this fundamental question is rarely given a high priority. Indeed, it is seldom asked at all in a direct way.

The immediate origins of the book can be recognised in two courses taught to students who were preparing to embark on research while I was Benjamin Sonnenberg Visiting Professor at the Institute of Fine Arts in New York in 1988 and Dorothy Ford Wiley Visiting Professor in Renaissance Studies at the University of North Carolina in 1993. The students who gave me such pleasure in both institutions will recognise the central core – the naggingly insistent theme of this book – and some of the case studies, but the book itself is necessarily different from a syllabused course aimed at a specific group of students. In particular, I have aimed to speak to anyone who wishes to broach the question of what criteria we can use to interpret Renaissance art given the documentation that is available to us. Moreover, I hope the way I seek entry to this issue – and I certainly do not intend it to be a method, even less accord it that much-abused and pretentious description 'methodology' – will be of assistance to anyone who looks at how contemporary written sources may be brought to bear on visual creations in any period, particularly those in which the notion of the individual artist stands in the foreground. It is intended above all to be a useful book, though I hope it avoids the dull and pedestrian quality that 'useful' might imply. It is also intended to stand on pragmatic and relatively restrained ground, in contrast to what I regard as the self-promotional and ill-founded excesses of much recent cultural theory. It is my conviction that the establishing, or re-establishing, of a well-provisioned base camp is essential before launching more speculative expeditions into unexplored territories. I have tried to avoid the obscure jargon that is too often used to give an air of professional profundity to commonplace thought. Not the least of the arts of historical writing is the analysis of complex issues in clear and systematic language. If I have failed, it is not for want of trying.

Covering such a wide territory of Renaissance art, the potential size of the apparatus of the book – the documentation, the footnotes, the bibliography and any historiographical discussions – is enormous, and I have certainly not attempted to provide a comprehensive introduction to the literature, which has been considered to contain some of the finest art-historical writing on any period. I say 'has been', since studies of Renaissance art have recently been criticised for remaining conservatively insulated from the 'New Art History', with its incorporation of techniques derived from anthropology, social studies, linguistics, psychology and some branches of the philosophy of culture. I think the accusation of insularity may in some measure be justified, but many of the broader cultural aspirations of recent art history had already been met by the wide range of approaches adopted during the long history of ambitious writing about the Renaissance. A new technique only becomes worthwhile if it delivers a new result, otherwise there is a danger that all we are doing is to switch jargons for the sake of apparent modernity. My own approach has relatively little to do with structuralism, post-structuralism, deconstruction and such-like, but neither does it aim to align itself comfortably with the more traditional kinds of writing about the Renaissance. Broadly speaking, I suppose that my emphasis upon a functional approach, always asking what role a document or work of art was meant to perform (advertently or inadvertently), carries a strong flavour of my training as a biologist, and of my increasing involvement with the history of science – though my concentration on written evidence means that the evidence of the scientific examination of paintings is only glimpsed in passing. I am in effect practising a kind of historical ecology.

Recently I have been involved with the construction of what I am rather grandly calling a 'new history of the visual', in which the visual products of other cultures are examined without using our prior classifications of 'fine art', 'applied art', 'scientific instrument', 'book illustration' or whatever. In as much as I am here concerned with 'art', as the title of the book immediately signals, the chapters that follow are not specifically directed towards my new endeavour. However, in that I am concerned throughout to highlight many of the problems that arise from the imposition of our notions of 'art' and 'artists' on any earlier period, my arguments are consistent with my history of the visual – and I have endeavoured to acknowledge that the sources often suggest that the priority we give to the masterpieces of the great geniuses in the realm of 'fine art' does not necessarily correspond to the systems of value at work in the period itself.

The bulk of the material is drawn from the period *c.*1400 to *c.*1520, with a strong emphasis upon the era before 1500. Only with the career of Michelangelo do we venture into the mid-sixteenth century. I have concentrated upon the main centres of cultural activity (as conventionally designated), and I am conscious that there is a distinct weighting in favour of Florentine art, in which my own area of expertise chiefly lies. I am not, therefore, providing a challenge to the conventional geographical biases in the writing about Renaissance art, although I recognise the validity of such a challenge. My main excuse is that this book is seen as a complement to the publication and analysis of primary sources in forms that are reasonably accessible to readers. I am therefore reliant upon the path of the existing mainstream for published documentation, not least because I cannot devote extensive space to full transcriptions of all the many kinds of source I wish to examine. Since I am mainly intending to look at how we might deal with *types* of sources, and not giving an outline history of Renaissance art, the biases are perhaps of less consequence than they might otherwise be. Although I am not intending to provide an introductory overview of art in the Renaissance, I have deliberately tried to choose examples which give a fair idea of the range and quality (and I do still believe in quality) of the works produced by those who have been recognised as artists of significance.

In citing documents I have tried to concentrate on sources that are available in high quality transcriptions and (preferably) translations in publications that are either in print or available in good libraries. Two translated anthologies have proved especially useful in this respect: Creighton Gilbert's *Italian Art, 1400-1500* in the 'Sources and Documents' series, which has subsequently been published in Italy with texts in the original language; and David Chambers's *Patrons and Artists in the Italian Renaissance*. The present book might in some way be seen as a companion to these anthologies. I have also seen André Chastel's *A Chronicle of Italian Renaissance Painting* as a natural partner in juxtaposing art and documentation in a suggestive manner. After the completion of the present text I was fortunate to read the proofs of Evelyn Welch's valuable *Art and Society in Italy 1350-1500*, which contains a wealth of documentation, particularly for art outside Florence, Rome and Venice, though it is not specifically concerned with source material as such. In terms of approach, the obvious comparison is with Michael Baxandall's highly influential *Painting and Experience in Fifteenth Century Italy*, and there are clear parallels with what we have both been attempting to accomplish. However, I intend my text to be at once more wide-ranging and systematic than Baxandall's in the types of source it discusses and more constrained in its functionalist approach. In particular, I have not attempted the inferential setting of texts beside pictures – like the suggestive juxtaposition of gauging of size techniques and three-dimensional depictions of objects – since the status of such inferences in the generation of the relevant works is open to misinterpretation. I certainly do not wish to align myself with the way that Baxandall's inferential methods have been (I believe incorrectly) taken to demonstrate mechanisms of social causation. I should be happier if he were seen as providing evidence for fields of potentially fertile viewing, in which the makers of artefacts *might* sow their seeds, rather than providing explanations of why works inevitably came to look as they did. By contrast, I am arguing that if we understand the sources in terms of what they were intended to do we can begin to establish a firmer base from which to embark on a whole range of more speculative interpretative strategies, of which inferential juxtaposition is just one.

In the text I have limited my system of references to the primary sources, or, rather, to publications in which the sources may be read either in part or (preferably) whole. Where a publication is used on a number of occasions, an abbreviated reference is given to the bibliography, using the number of the item in the bibliography. The bibliography itself is designed functionally for this book, to suggest some general reading on its themes and to provide references to all sources that have been directly cited. I have not, therefore, attempted to provide sets of comprehensive references to the main literature on the artists and works discussed. The inclusion or exclusion of a secondary source does not therefore imply any judgement about its overall worth. There are therefore omissions which will appear surprising, particularly to the authors themselves. All I can do is to ask forbearance in the light of the restrictions I have placed on what it is practical to do in this book.

As the fruit of many years of researching and teaching Renaissance art, my list of people who deserve thanks is potentially of very considerable length. To many generous colleagues, helpful curators, conservators and librarians I offer collective gratitude, as I do to the generations of students who have been the recipients of some of the ideas. Not a few of the specific topics will be recognised by particular students who essayed papers on them, and I have benefited consistently from seeing both the successes and difficulties which arise when able students confront primary sources – and when undertaking one of my favourite exercises, the invention of 'fake' primary sources for the period. My graduate assistants, including Kathryn Smith, Lila Yawn, Cheryl Kramer and Ioanna Christoforaki have responded to the often routine tasks they were asked to perform with friendly and invaluable efficiency. Ioanna has played a vital role in seeing the text and its apparatus through to a publishable state. Very direct personal encouragement has been provided by Kathleen Weil-Garris Brandt and Pat Williams, whose conversations on related and apparently peripheral questions has given me more food for thought than they might guess. My former colleague in the University of St Andrews, Peter Humfrey, has always provided a ready response to enquiries and has set scrupulous standards to which I have not always been able to adhere. Paul Crowther, who has joined me in Oxford, has offered partnership in a way that has made my life more manageable than it would otherwise be, and Sheila Ballard has striven to protect my time from terminal erosion, as did Dawn Waddell while I was in St Andrews. During the course of the writing of the book, I have shared eyes and ears with Marina Wallace, without whose inspiration the protracted completion of the text would have been prolonged indefinitely. To John Nicoll, I owe unstinted patience and creative support. It is not their fault that the book is not better than it is, but it is to their credit that it is better than it would otherwise have been.

Summer 1996

I PRELIMINARY HEARINGS
Apelles Post Tabulam Latens

THE ROMAN AUTHOR Pliny tells the story – well known in the Renaissance – of the famed Greek painter Apelles hiding behind one of his pictures to overhear the comments of spectators:

> It was his custom to expose his finished works to passers-by in a loggia and he would remain hidden behind the picture [*post tabulam latens*] to overhear its faults, regarding the public as a more discerning judge than himself. There is a story that when he was faulted by a cobbler for putting one strap too few in a sandal, he corrected it. The next day, filled with pride about the correction of the error, the cobbler found fault with the leg, at which Apelles angrily stuck out his head and admonished the cobbler to stick to his last.[1]

There may be a conscious echo of this story in Leonardo's account of 'how in the course of his work the painter should eagerly receive all men's opinions of it':

> Certainly while a man is painting he should not refuse anyone's judgement. For we know that one man, even though he may not be a painter, still knows what another man looks like, whether he is hunchbacked or has one shoulder higher or lower than the other. . . Therefore be eager to lend a patient ear to the opinions of others and think long and hard whether whoever finds fault has reason or not to censure you.[2]

If anything, Leonardo allows the lay judge even more scope than Pliny granted to his cobbler, in as much as Leonardo would have assumed that the cobbler was capable of recognising a good leg when he saw one.

The motif of *Apelles post tabulam latens*, or even *Leonardo ante tabulam audiens* (. . . listening in front of the picture), provides an effective point of entry into the problem of what lies behind the business of picture-making and picture-viewing in the Renaissance. It raises the questions of the role of the artist and of the function of works of art in relation to their various kinds of audience. The story of Apelles, who heeds the critical comments of a cobbler, reflects a very different conception of the relationship between the artist and his public than that which prevails today. Apelles and his Renaissance successors were making images that communicated to the spectator within a framework of the naturalistic depiction of more or less familiar objects – even if the totality of the image might depict something which none of the viewers had actually seen or normally expected to see (like the *Birth of Venus* or the *Last Supper*). The Renaissance artist, following his ancient and medieval forbears, emerged from a context in which visual images had traditionally been functional objects which played specific, representational roles in religious, political and domestic life.

In Pliny's story, the cobbler is encouraged by his critical success over the question of the shoe to extend his 'connoisseurship' into other aspects of Apelles's painting. He is roundly scolded by the painter, who tells him (in the oft-repeated phrase) to 'stick to his last'. This rejoinder suggests that there are elements in the discrimination of what is good in 'art' which lie beyond the untutored or uncultivated eye, and that the artist is not merely bound to satisfy an aggregation of public opinions or some common denominator in vulgar taste. However, should we think that understanding of art was simply a matter of class and education, Pliny also tells us that 'Alexander the Great, who was a frequent visitor to the workshop' was wont to pontificate on matters in which he was 'not expert', and that Apelles gently warned him that the 'lads who ground the colours were laughing at him'.[3] When Leon Battista Alberti in his pioneering book *On Painting* (*De Pictura*) in 1435 recalled the story of Apelles hiding behind his picture, he specifically concluded that the artist should pay greatest attention to 'expert' judges.[4] This conclusion is in keeping with Pliny's praise of Apelles's equestrian portrait of Antigonos and Artemis, which was preferred amongst all his works by those who were 'expert' judges – expert we may assume in matters of painting rather than in horseflesh.[5] The rise of the 'experts', the connoisseurs, was closely linked to a series of other issues, including the fame accorded to an artist of true and enduring quality, and the material rewards that might be appropriate. When Apelles himself was in Rhodes, he boosted the reputation of the neglected Protogenes by buying his pictures for very high prices and threatening to sell them as his own – an anecdote which also raises nice questions about attitudes towards authorship.[6]

All the issues about artistic excellence, types of viewers, connoisseurship, rewards, fame, social status, relations with patrons, and authorship raised by Pliny's account of Apelles – of which only a few incidents have been cited here – were in the Renaissance becoming newly germane to those who thought and wrote about the visual arts. In part this was because they avidly devoured Pliny's account of the ancient masters, but Pliny could only become fully relevant in a context in which these issues assumed a fresh urgency.

The Renaissance saw the rebirth of a written literature specifically devoted to the criteria of excellence in the visual arts, criteria which implicitly or explicitly advocated the severing of the artist from a humble artisan, such as Pliny's cobbler. This severance occurred on two fronts: the first, in keeping with the story of Apelles, relied upon the conviction that the uncultivated viewer could not ultimately provide the artist with a discriminating audience on all matters of 'art'; the second, embedded as an assumption behind Pliny's account of the great artists of Greece, was that the makers of everyday objects of a utilitarian kind did not provide suitable role-models for the artist, particularly with respect to social and intellectual status. For all his willingness to listen to the lay judge, Leonardo intended to leave his readers in no doubt about the cerebral nobility of painting and of its practitioners. For him, as for other artist-authors of the Renaissance, the painter was no vulgar mechanic.

The whole business of a specialist literature devoted to the visual arts – of which modern art history is the heir – is founded upon the belief that there is something special about the visual image (or about certain types of visual image) which requires articulation through the intellectual medium of words. The modern rebirth of such a specialist literature most conspicuously involved two related genres of writing, treatises on the intellectual foundations of painting, and biographies of artists. The authors of the innovatory texts, such as Alberti (a prolific humanist author) and Lorenzo Ghiberti (the sculptor who wrote a set of *Commentaries*, which included his autobiography), openly looked to classical antiquity for inspiration. However, the actual writings that had survived from Greece and Rome provided very incomplete models for what the Renaissance authors felt they needed to say about painting and sculpture. Most of the key specialist texts, including the writings of Apelles, were lost. The major exception was the treatise on architecture by the Roman author, Vitruvius, but this provided limited guidance for writers on the figurative arts. The pioneer authors of Renaissance texts which focused exclusively on the arts of painting and sculpture were virtually starting from scratch. Not only did they need to forge a vocabulary from the disparate legacies of Antiquity and the Middle Ages, but they also needed to establish what it was they were addressing – and to whom they were addressing their remarks. We can witness in Renaissance writings the founding struggles of our modern attempts to bring words to bear in an effectively critical manner on visual images. These struggles provide us with an unrivalled opportunity to examine the relationship between word and image – to question the interpretative adequacies and inadequacies of verbal formulas in the face of the special operations of visual communication.

With respect to the critical evaluation of works of art – whether dealing with 'value' in the sense of aesthetic worth or with 'values' in a social framework – the modern art historian stands as a successor to Alberti and company, though we now have a huge platform of existing vocabularies, aspirations and literary genres on which to stand. In the period I will be covering, we will encounter some works of art on which most ink has been spilt over the ages. I would not care to estimate the hours of collective writing that have gone into the exposition of works like Masaccio's *Trinity*, Piero della Francesca's *Flagellation*, Leonardo's *Last Supper* and *Mona Lisa*, the sculpted Davids by Donatello and Michelangelo, and Michelangelo's Sistine Ceiling. This is to say nothing of the hours any one person might consume in reading only a representative sampling of the literature which continues to pour forth in the popular and specialist publications. A high proportion of the literature is repetitive. At best I suppose we might take this as testimony to some kind of consensus which does genuinely relate to the nature of the works under discussion and their ability to retain some kind of stable meaning, or at least a power of continuing attraction. However, the fact that the consensuses represented by the repetitions have undergone substantial transformations in different eras and places might well lead us to suspect that they tell us more about the prejudices of successive observers and the conditioning of attitudes than the works themselves. Indeed, there is a school of thought that nothing is observable other than the interpretations of the observers, and even those only dimly and ambiguously.

Where there are radical differences in what postmodern, modern, traditional

3

and Renaissance writers say about Renaissance artefacts, and in what it is believed can be said about art at all, we often seem to be dealing with sets of incommensurate dialogues in which the purposes of writing about art are defined in ways that cannot be reconciled. The reader who is not a party to the academic field sports of semiotics, structuralism, poststructuralism, deconstruction and reception theory, or feels little sympathy for the recherché skills of connoisseurship, the scientific technicalities of pigment analysis and interminable disputes over dating, may well feel that the whole business of bringing words to bear on images has got badly out of hand. There is a clear sense in which the academic industry of art history can be seen as serving the aspirations of the authors within their institutional and broader professional frameworks rather than performing the function of elucidation in the clear and non-exclusive way that ought to be the historian's duty.

The present book cannot avoid being a part of the present industry of writing and publishing about art, and stands the obvious danger of establishing yet another set of criteria which stands in a closer relationship to current debates about art history than to anything that would have made sense in the period itself. However, I propose to cut this Gordian knot by adopting a strategy that builds towards interpretation from within the written material which has survived from the era in which the art was made and first viewed. This is not to say that such material is somehow automatically 'given'. Indeed, our model (or rather my model in this instance) of what is significant in a visual product of the Renaissance will determine what body of surviving written material may be considered as providing the most relevant evidence in our quest to understand the products in terms of their own context. Thus, a social historian might well assume that a contract is more relevant than a treatise on the geometry of perspective, while a cultural historian might see a humanist text as more compelling than a set of payments for artists' materials – though I happen to think that neither of these assumptions is necessarily justified. However, although the documents on their own can neither establish their own credentials nor speak for themselves in the absence of purposefully directed enquiries being made of them, the selection of documents that can be fruitfully brought into play is not a matter of arbitrary choice from an almost limitless set of possibilities. The range of potentially relevant material is finite and non-arbitrary in two important respects: in the theoretical terms of the number of conceivable types of written evidence which can actually be placed in an effective and historically productive relationship to the works of art; and in the practical terms of the historical production of different kinds of written sources and their survival. By 'historically productive' I refer to the uses of primary materials in ways that satisfy two criteria: the sources should stand in a demonstrable relationship to contemporary concerns about the production and reception of art; and, more subjectively, they should be capable of stimulating insights which affect our perceptions in a manner which is intuitively satisfying and communicable to others.

In building this study around the types of written testimony that have come to us from the Renaissance itself, I will not be claiming that the available documents tell the whole story. The problem is not simply a matter of survival. We cannot assume that the types of written source generated in the period cover

1. Joanna's Teddy Bear

everything that was then significant in visual intention and response, to say nothing of values that lay outside conscious intentions and critical criteria. Thus the absence in the Renaissance of, say, a substantial literature on brushwork, does not *necessarily* mean that it was of little consequence to makers and viewers. And, even if a particular feature of the works seems not to have been a matter of conscious interest at the time, this does not mean that it should necessarily be excluded from the historian's purview. There is much to be gained from using our position of historical distance, which carries advantages as well as manifest disadvantages, to draw out aspects of the works and ways of looking at them that could not have been articulated verbally in the period – providing we are clear about what we are doing. What in our eyes seem to be particularly characteristic visual features of an object or group of objects might simply not have been apparent or worthy of comment in the period itself.

The situation is not unlike that of a child with a long-owned and much loved toy – let us say a well worn teddy bear (fig. 1) that has over the years lost much of its fur and facial features. The child shows no awareness or discomfort with what to an adult observer appear to be obvious mutilations. As adults, our position of remove from the child's perceptual and emotional priorities gives us the strength to make observations to which the child would be unwilling to give any kind of weight. But our remove also means that we have to make a leap of imaginative reconstruction to understand how the threadbare teddy stands whole and complete in the child's eyes, when considered in terms of the demands the child makes on it. A significant facet in the historian's art consists in drawing our attention to the equivalent of the loss of the teddy's features – that is to say heightening our own perceptions in ways that the visual and conceptual frameworks of the original users and viewers might not have accomplished or been able to accomplish in themselves – but this awareness needs to be accompanied by at least as powerful a sense of why the teddy's 'patron' was oblivious to its impairments. The trick consists in adjusting our

5

looking in modes which are both engaged with and disengaged from contemporary criteria, with a full awareness of the nature of the interacting processes involved. The present study takes as its starting point the engaged mode.

In looking at the demands we can make on written sources, I hope not to lose sight of what to me is a central truth of the visual arts; that is to say there is something irreducibly *visual* about them, and that however comprehensively we can reassemble intentions and viewings in the period, the written sources inevitably leave us short of the visual experience – anyone's or everyone's visual experience. And, however much we may bring our full panoply of present-day machinery of visual analysis to bear upon our perceptions of the work, we are still coming up short – albeit in a different kind of way. I was going to say 'frustratingly short', but on reflection I do not think the shortfall is 'frustrating'. It is this very shortfall between what can be accomplished in words and in a visual image that gave the impetus for the making of the image in the first place, and it is this same shortfall that permits the object to enter into such a rich and sustaining visual exchange with a range of viewers. I believe that such exchanges are immeasurably enriched when we achieve an awareness of the many explanatory mechanisms which can be brought to bear upon accounts of the making and viewing of the objects – or what we take to be such accounts. This does not mean to say that all explanatory strivings are of equal validity. Each approach needs to be examined critically for its historical credentials.

What we will find when we look at the variety of actual sources which have survived from the Renaissance, and which have in past historical practice been found to operate with some kind of interpretative leverage on the visual material, is that different types of source paint quite different and even contradictory pictures of what artistic activity was like. The extremes are represented by, on the one hand, those documents which relate to the business of art – its ordering, its manufacture, its purchase and the subsequent assigning of financial value – and, on the other, the literary texts that promote the claims of art and its practitioners to high virtue in aesthetic, intellectual and social terms. When we find in an inventory of the possessions of the Medici family in fifteenth-century Florence that three very large and innovatory paintings of the stories of Hercules by Antonio Pollaiuolo were valued at only 20 florins each (including their gold frames), while a classical gem of really good quality would have cost Lorenzo de' Medici between 500 and 2,000 florins, and the *Tazza Farnese* (fig. 2) was estimated to be worth no less than 10,000 florins, we may wonder about how we can interpret a scale of values that seems so very different from our own.[7] When we realise that a *lettuccio* (a large decorated bed or couch) in the same Medici inventory was valued at 40 florins, and a damask robe lined with sable at 30 florins, well over the book price of a Pollaiuolo, the question of value becomes all the more starkly highlighted.[8] On the other hand, if we look to the arguments for the supreme worth of painting used by Leonardo, who grew to artistic maturity in Lorenzo de' Medici's Florence, we find that the painter is valued as the supreme philosopher of visual causes and effects, whose representations surpass those of the poet and whose ability to summon up harmonic beauty triumphs over the transient beauties of music. The inventorist values the products of the painter less highly than the manufactures of the

2. *The Tazza Farnese (Allegory of the Fertility of the Nile?)*, agate-sardonyx bowl of 2nd – 1st century BC, Naples, Museo Nazionale di Capodimonte

furniture maker and the tailor – or in much the same league as the fanciest products of the cobbler. Leonardo, however, denies that painting is a manual craft, insisting that the artist is a gentlemanly intellectual deserving of fame and not subject to the vulgar constraints of trade. At least, such appear to be the contrasting implications of inventories and Leonardo's *Treatise on Painting* when read at their most obvious level.

However, the most obvious reading might not be the best one we can make. The inventorist was not writing to inform the modern historian about how the Medici regarded the works of art in their palaces and villas, and, even if Leonardo was more consciously writing with an eye on posterity, he was writing for a particular purpose within a contemporary frame of reference in which 'art' was a very different kind of thing from what it is taken to be today. What I will be arguing consistently throughout this book is that each kind of source needs to be respected for what it was; that is to say judging the reasons for its own production, what its originator was aiming to communicate, and who was the intended recipient of its message. Each source needs to be evaluated not only with respect to the kind of information it can legitimately be expected to yield

3.   Alessandro Botticelli, *Primavera*, Florence, Uffizi

to the enquiring historian but also with respect to the kinds of questions which it is illegitimate or at least unreasonable to ask of a particular type of written account. For example, inventorists were not notably interested in the authorship of paintings and sculptures, and they were only interested in subject matter in as much as they needed a way of identifying a particular work in the collection of objects that they were dealing with at that time. Thus, what appears to be Botticelli's *Primavera* (fig. 3), now one of the most revered treasures of the Uffizi, is first described to us in an inventory of 1498 as 'a painting on wood attached above a *lettuccio*, on which is painted nine figures of men and women' – with no mention of its author or precise subject.[9] This particular bed was about 3.2 metres wide, and the painting was either built into its structure or the two components were installed in the room as a decorative ensemble in a relatively permanent manner. At least in this instance the painting is worth more than the bed (100 *lire* compared to 84), although there were more highly valued items of furniture in the same inventory.

A comparable case of an inventorist's disconcerting failure to share our priorities occurs in a document of 1525 which lists the possessions of Gian Giacomo Caprotti, known as Salaì. It seems that this apparently rascally pupil and companion of Leonardo had come into the possession of a clutch of his master's most important paintings, including the *Mona Lisa* (fig. 4).[10] Although the paintings are in this instance accorded very high values, the name of their author is nowhere mentioned – a problem to which we will return. We can, I believe, only make sense of what to us appear to be unaccountable omissions or lapses of interest if we understand the nature and function of the documents

4. Leonardo da Vinci, *Mona Lisa (Portrait of Lisa del Giocondo?)*, Paris, Louvre

5. Leonardo da Vinci, *Virgin of the Rocks*, Paris, Louvre

with which we are dealing. For us, the documents are historical sources. For their authors and original readers, they were doing a specific job in a circumscribed way.

My manner of reading texts functionally will be complimented by a way of viewing works of visual art according to their functional types. However, I will not be trying to define works of art as falling neatly into unitary or clearly defined functional categories – each painting or sculpture within one watertight category. A classification is itself a functional system, directed not least by the needs and interests of the classifier, and any complex human artefact can be studied within numerous effective taxonomies in response to numerous legitimate interests. Thus to classify Leonardo's *Virgin of the Rocks* (fig. 5) as an altarpiece – that is as a member of a recognisable group of paintings to be set above altars – is obviously correct, but it could also be classified within a number of alternative categories that are not simply imposed on the period from without. One example would be as a painting for the Confraternities of the Immaculate Conception. Another would be as 'a Leonardo', and, lest we think this category is too redolent of the modern art market, we should note that a number of contemporary patrons are recorded as wishing to lay their hands on a painting by Leonardo for the prime reason that it *was* by the master. There were, for example, prospective purchasers for a painting of the *Virgin of the Rocks* by Leonardo in addition to the Milanese Confraternity who generated the initial commission. One classification which we take for granted, and indeed is embedded as a 'given' in what has been said so far, is that of 'art' itself. Yet this category would not have been recognised in anything like its modern sense during the Renaissance. There was no concept of such an overarching category of objects uniquely created for aesthetic contemplation. For the moment, I am using 'art' as a convenient label – in as much as *we* know more or less what type of thing we are talking about – but we should not assume that it relates to a given reality in the period itself, and we will see repeatedly that it can be very misleading. We will not find, for example, anyone in the Renaissance whom we can adequately describe as a 'patron of art'. Nor can we assume that our categories of the 'Fine Arts' and 'Applied Arts' be directly and automatically appropriate. The frame of Leonardo's painting, it is worth noting, was a grander and more expensive item than its pictorial elements.

If an individual picture is viewed within different classificatory categories, it can actually 'look' different to a greater or lesser degree. An analysis of Leonardo's picture in the light of his theories of light and colour will almost certainly mean that we will notice different things about it than if we are trying to understand why the Virgin, Child, St John and an Angel are kneeling and sitting in a rocky landscape. To some extent, art history is about providing visual insights through the adjustment of our way of looking. I think the point can be made by reference to a mundane analogy. When I am expecting visitors to my house, I become uneasily aware in a heightened way of how much the rooms need redecorating or the furniture reupholstering. What I specially notice is directed by my interests and concerns at the given moment. I normally fail to notice the increasingly dowdy paint, because it is a constant feature of my environment, and as such is taken for granted. My attention is normally directed to other matters in such a way that I do not actively 'see' the paint.

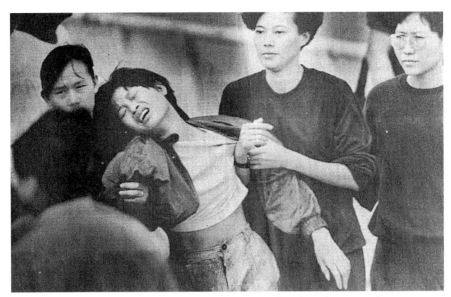

6. 'Vietnamese Refugee Seized for Repatriation', *The Daily Telegraph*, 9 November 1991

This argument about directed looking might seem to be leading inexorably towards the conclusion that all looking is arbitrary and particular to the individual viewer at a particular moment, or at best to groups of viewers in particular places at particular times, and that the specificity of any individual's or group's experience is irredeemably inaccessible to anyone else or another group. In one sense I can never prove incontrovertibly that my experience of a work of art has any point of contact with yours. I cannot take my visual experience out of my head and implant in it in someone else's. However, over the years that I have been looking, reading and writing about the visual arts I have been struck intuitively not with the inaccessibility of other people's modes of looking but with the remarkable robustness of the parameters within which visual communication has occurred over the ages, and with the robust way in which the communication of visual experience can be enhanced by words for a wide range of viewers. Let me take as an example a modern news photograph, which flitted briefly across the stage in that most ephemeral of illustrated texts, the daily newspaper. I am deliberately taking an image from a British context, conscious that its background is fully accessible to me in a way that will not be the case for all readers of the book. The selection of an image within my immediate experience will help highlight the problems of interpretation for viewers who are not 'insiders' with respect to the circumstances for its immediate generation and interpretation. On Saturday 9 November 1991 the Associated Press Agency supplied *The Daily Telegraph* in Britain with an image of a woman in obvious distress in the company of at least four other people (fig. 6). Let us for a moment detach the image from the 'story' it was illustrating and see what we can make of it.

I said that the woman was in 'obvious distress', which is already an act of interpretation. No doubt it would be possible to force other interpretations, but I think they would be forced. This central facet of the image sets parameters on

12

7.   Raphael, *Entombment of Christ*, Rome, Galleria Borghese

what we subsequently can do with it. This is not to say that our perception of her distress means simply that we are responding to the photograph as an untranslated 'act of nature'. Our familiarity with instantaneous snapshots clearly plays a role in our ability to work effectively with the image. And our viewing of other representations of suffering people in a state of near collapse helps determine the interpretative frame within which we make our response. As an art historian, prone to rather arch visual cross-referencing, the image rang particular bells for me. It summoned up the fainting Virgins in Renaissance pictures of Christ's passion, of which Raphael's *Entombment* (fig. 7) provides a superb example. Raphael's Virgin does not give vent to such overt grief as the woman in the photograph – the decorum required of a Renaissance altarpiece would have prohibited an uninhibited cry of anguish – but the essential meaning of both portrayals communicates itself with considerable robustness, within and outside their own frames of reference as photograph and religious painting respectively. The format of the photograph carried with it less focused memories of a class of narrative paintings in the Renaissance in which biblical stories are depicted on a relatively small scale on horizontal canvases in which

13

8.   Titian, *Christ and the Adulteress*, Vienna, Kunsthistorisches Museum

the figures are no more than half length. A quick survey of a collection of illustrated books produced a *Christ and the Adulteress* in Vienna, attributed to Titian (fig. 8), as a suitable example. Again, the woman at the centre of the other figures' attentions appears to be characterised in such a way as to elicit our sympathy.

However, the stories of the fainting Virgin and of the woman accused of adultery have quite distinct elements to them, and the representations would hardly have assumed full efficacy unless the painters had achieved a good measure of differentiation between them. This point is where the reading of the other figures and their interaction becomes crucial. And it is at this level that the simple robustness begins to prove inadequate and to require further interpretative clues of a more refined kind. The Virgin's supporters can be read relatively readily as just that – as sympathetic supporters. It probably requires more knowledge of the specific story to be certain that those surrounding the adulteress are wholly unsympathetic, with the exception of the bearded man on the left. And to make adequate sense of both images as communicative tableaux we need at least to know the biblical narratives – that is we need access to relevant texts. We really need to know that Christ is rescuing the woman from stoning by her accusers, with the famous words, 'He that is without sin among you, let him cast the first stone'.[11] No stones were cast. What now happens when we turn back to the photograph and try to assemble the story in a fuller form?

Our understanding of the relationship between the distressed woman and those surrounding her is not easy to read unambiguously. The woman holding her left arm is hardly participating in her grief, but neither is she obviously the prime agent of that grief. She is perhaps more readily aligned with the accusers of the adulterous woman than the supporters of the Virgin, but the image does not seem to be decisive in itself. We need more direction. Once we reattach the photograph to its context on the front page of the newspaper, the necessary direction is provided. The distressed woman is one of the unfortunates who fled Vietnam by boat, risking a perilous sea journey in an inadequate craft, and seeking access to a new life via the British Crown Colony of Hong Kong. The refugees were held in reception camps, and eventually a process of repatriation was agreed by the British and Vietnamese authorities. The woman is one of the first fifty-nine refugees to be returned against their will, and the picture shows her in the grip of camp employees who were preparing to expel her. That much is reportage. But of course much more than reportage is involved. A series of complex motivations surround the genesis of such an image, and complex clusters of attitudes become part of its viewing.

There are almost endless questions that can be asked about the 'causes' behind its production and printing. There are issues concerning the Associated Press Agency itself – its manner of operation, its relationship to photographers and so on. There are the actions of the particular photographer, the reasons for the choice of shot and the broader issues of regarding the photographer as voyeur or participant. There are the editors who chose this story as the lead item, who determined that this particular photograph of a woman was a 'good, strong image', and who decided that it should be cropped in a certain way and printed to fit across five columns of text. There is the setting in a paper which stands decisively to the right of the political spectrum in Britain, and which could generally be expected to promote the policies of the then incumbent Conservative government – though in this case the image seems to evoke more sympathy for the 'victims' of government policy than to lend it support. This is not even to begin to think about the broader issues of the production, marketing and readership of newspapers, how 'stories' become important, the role of visual images in the dissemination of knowledge about world events, photographs as 'truth', and so on.

When we come to think about the viewing of the image, we have to allow for a huge variety of responses, each potentially coloured by a variety of predispositions. An inveterate critic of the government might well feel rage at the result of the policy of repatriation, combined with a sense of bitter pleasure that the picture serves the anti-government cause so nicely – even in a government-oriented newspaper. The relevant government minister's rage, by contrast, might well be directed to what is seen as a slanted and atypical representation of a difficult but successfully conducted exercise. With friendly newspapers doing this, the minister may think, who needs enemies. A resident of the already crowded community of Hong Kong might look on the distressed woman with little sympathy, feeling that the boat people were not welcome anyway and had brought their troubles on their own shoulders. The Vietnamese authorities might have envisaged the picture with a quite different caption: for instance, 'Traitors returned home for re-integration'. Other viewers might claim that there are 'bigger', more significantly structural issues than those involved in the reading of the immediate political circumstances of the event. A feminist, for example, might well claim that the 'central' issue is one of gender, and involves such factors as the use of women as the coercers and the choice of a woman victim for illustration.

15

Inevitably, this brief list of viewers has tended to deal with stereotypes rather than with the complex mix of sentiments with which we often respond individually and collectively to events in the mobile flux of world politics. However, this relatively crude sampling of a few of the varieties of potential response should provide a reasonable indication of the plurality of considerations involved when we think about the intended and actual reception of an image.

We can, I think, begin to see how even such an apparently simple image, of the kind which we devour daily in enormous quantities – without apparent difficulty or sustained reflection – brings in its train a huge number of potentially relevant questions about how it may be regarded as significant, both within its immediate historical context and within broader frames of reference. Each question brings in its train its own documentary sources. Someone looking at the role of photographic agencies may depend on quite different primary sources from someone who is researching the depiction of women as victims in modern photography. Each of the questions will in turn determine which nexus of evidence becomes relevant. None of the bodies of primary written and visual sources comprise the 'right' groups of sources, because there is no single 'right' line of enquiry – unless we are prepared to say that the only truly worthwhile thing to understand is, say, the operation of capitalism with respect to the market for images, or, say, the issue of gender representations. Of course, if we are prepared to adopt such prescriptions and exclusions, anyone following any other line of investigation is deemed to be reprehensible or at least misguided. But if we allow such exclusions to rule, we lose the greater purpose of what I would like to call the perceptual generosity of history as a humane discipline. We will be in danger of disqualifying ourselves from any understanding of the child's love for the defaced teddy bear – and we may logically see no reason why it should not be thrown away and replaced with an example that meets our standards of wholeness.

When we turn to more elaborately synthetic, obviously constructed images, into which a series of knowing allusions have been deliberately built, virtually every aspect of the potential questions becomes even more complex. Again I think it will be helpful to look at a relatively recent image, because the range of circumstances which lead to its production are more readily accessible to me than for any Renaissance painting or sculpture, even though detailed memories of the circumstances are already beginning to dim, and a viewer in a different culture will find many of the visual references inaccessible. In this instance, let us begin with some knowledge of the story – such as the readers of the British newspaper, *The Guardian*, would have been likely to have possessed on the morning of 23 November 1990 (fig. 9).

As the result of a series of events and political manoeuvres, Margaret Thatcher, the long-serving Conservative Prime Minister of Britain had resigned the day before. The immediate catalyst for her resignation was a challenge for the leadership by Michael Heseltine – depicted as 'Tarzan' at the head of Steve Bell's bizarre procession – but he was not *the* 'cause' of her decision to go. That decision was compounded from many factors and judgements, ranging from the most specific – like a damaging speech a few days earlier by Geoffrey Howe, her ex-deputy prime minister, who is recognisable as the sheep – to the most

16

Let sleeping dogs cry freedom

freedom of information, free-dom of expression, and freedom to build up a business.
Some of these freedoms are socialist expressions for equal-ity looked at another way. Others are openly and even provocatively laissez-faire. Both kinds would give the state the task of enabling people to do things, on every front. By adopting them, socialism could take a new and vital turn, unit-ing left-wing libertarians and socially reasonable critics of

That's why the lady was a champ

Commentary

dominated by women inter-viewers, women cabinet minis-ters and women Opposition front-benchers, barely occa-

of hers, your knees just turn to jelly." And the men (invari-ably) in the room with them would nod sympathetically and

9.   Steve Bell, 'The "Bagging" of Margaret Thatcher', *The Guardian*, 23 November 1990

general, such as the reluctance of ambitious politicians in a democratic system to tolerate any single, unshiftable leader over a prolonged period. The cartoon drawn by Bell for the 'Comment and Analysis' page of *The Guardian* on one of the more memorable days in recent British politics exploits a notable density of political and cultural reference. This density would have presented little obstacle to the average reader of the paper on that morning. Indeed, its essential features and allusions would generally have been scanned and absorbed in a few moments. But even after a short interval of time, some of the references become obscurely arcane, and, for an English-speaking reader in another country, a number of the allusions would from the first have required an elucidating commentary.

The well-informed *Guardian* reader – and *The Guardian* is the kind of newspaper that openly prides itself on its well-informed readership – would have recognised the deposed prime minister being transported like a piece of 'bagged game' by two weeping crocodiles who have been given the features of two of her senior ministers, Douglas Hurd and John Major. The hints of exotic vegetation are just enough to evoke the kind of imperial location in which big game has traditionally been hunted. But why are the four men so transfigured? The portrayal of Heseltine as Tarzan alludes to an incident some years earlier when he had breached parliamentary decorum by seizing the Speaker's mace and whirling it round his head with such muscular vigour that he earned the nick-name Tarzan, the famous jungle hero of children's films. Howe is a sheep by allusion to a witty remark by Dennis Healey, a politician in the opposing Labour Party, who compared being attacked by his rival to being 'savaged by a dead sheep'. The crocodiles require a different mode of explanation, since the allusion here is to the common expression 'crying crocodile tears'. Our *Guardian* reader would have no difficulty in knowing that crocodile tears are notoriously

17

insincere, and that Bell is echoing the common if cynical perception that none of the 'Iron Lady's' lieutenants were wholly saddened by her departure, whatever their public protestations of grief.

There are elements in this image which exhibit the same kind of robustness as the photograph. Again, I think the 'Lady's' basic distress requires little contextual reading, though the bagging of the big game does require some cultural knowledge of an imperial heritage. Similarly the tears are readily recognisable as such, though not their ironical function. If we imagine that in later centuries Bell's original drawing is discovered by a historian with no indication of its proper context, we can readily envisage how complex the task of decipherment would become. The more local and specific the clue, the more ephemeral the reference, the harder the task would be. One of the less potentially prominent allusions for the 1990 reader, the crocodile tears, might well for the later historian become the most accessible, since the conundrum of their meaning yields to a knowledge of common sayings. Even if the saying is no longer current, it is the kind of matter that can be elucidated by a rapid search of the standard reference material. An obvious source to which to turn would be the *Oxford English Dictionary* for the period, assuming that the investigator is able to make a reasonable guess about the date of the drawing. The *OED*, as it is known in the profession, tells the historian that the crocodile was, according to ancient and medieval legend, supposed to weep to attract sympathetic people, whom it then devoured, still weeping crocodile tears. The references take our imaginary researcher back into the Mediaeval Bestiary, a collection of legends of animal behaviour, or to a literary source, such as Shakespeare's *Othello*: 'If that the Earth could teeme with a woman's teares, Each drop she falls, would prove a Crocodile'. The cunning interpreter decides that the drawing plays on an ingenious inversion of Shakespeare's text, giving the men the tears of insincerity. If it so happens that the main focus of the investigation is on the art of Steve Bell, we may imagine that the researcher is able to attribute the drawing convincingly to that master. Subsequently, the documentation of Bell's life discloses a school visit to a performance of Othello while studying the play for an A-level examination. The conclusion seems obvious, and indeed it is. Bell's drawing alludes to Othello. And the conclusion might not be utterly wrong, in as much as some echo of Shakespeare's lines may have been lurking in the back of Bell's mind when he was casting around for the theme for his cartoon. However, in terms of an explanatory mechanism for the meaning of the image, something has gone badly awry. The interpretation might result in a learned article, but it will have missed the central point of the image in terms of its function.

It is also worth noting in passing, the rich field of allusion and metaphor in the headlines immediately beneath the image. The term 'sleeping dogs' refers to the popular proverb, 'let sleeping dogs lie'. Even the 'cry freedom' may have been designed to resonate with the title of what was then a recent film about the life and death of the black South African, Steve Biko. The introduction to the article below informs us that Thatcherism is 'on the rocks', which is of course a nautical analogy, though the careless historian of a later era might think it alludes to the American habit of serving whisky with great lumps of ice. The other headline parodies the well-known song, 'That's why the lady is a tramp'.

The ease with which we navigate our way through such a forest of allusions tends to make us overlook that our imagery operates on a level of symbolic allusion which is no less complex than that of the Renaissance, and no less open to misreading at a historical distance.

Obviously my proposed misreading of the cartoon (or of the 'rocks') is artificially staged, and asks you to accept the apparently improbable premise that the historian has not realised that the drawing was for *The Guardian*, and accordingly has not undertaken a trawl of the newspaper over the possible range of years. But his hypothetical trawl is itself dependent on the survival of copies of the newspaper. In the Renaissance, we are faced with the very incomplete survival of even the main bodies of the types of evidence that stood some chance of being preserved, and many of the more local and immediate circumstances behind the making of a work may never have entered the historical record at all. I suspect that we are all too often in the position of the researcher into the cultural history of crocodile tears; that is to say that we are fooled by the accidents of the survival of sources into thinking that what we can actually discover corresponds to what might be discovered if we could be transported back to the equivalent of the privileged position of *The Guardian* readers on that 23rd day of November. There is of course no certain remedy for lost evidence, other than to try to find it – which is precisely what many historians try to do. Inevitably we need to accept that many of the lacunae are simply not fillable, however diligent the search. What we need to do in these circumstances is to try to determine, by direct demonstration and analogy, what kind of object we are dealing with, and what kind of analysis will yield what kind of results. This is where the definition of the functions of the object becomes crucial, since it will allow us to regulate and limit the kinds of historical enquiry that will operate in a non-arbitrary way with the meanings of the image. Such a definition of functions, setting parameters for interpretation, applies to the written sources to which we have recourse, as I have already indicated, no less than to the works of art themselves.

It may be objected that the interplay of general robustness and specific meanings which I have been trying to establish is at best valid only in the context of a certain kind of image-making within specific societies – especially those which operate with European and European-based values. Obviously there are substantial portions of the meaning of the images which are highly specific to the society in which they have arisen. Even the language of gesture, both formalised and spontaneous, may be quite radically divergent in another society. The interpretation of images is also heavily influenced by what the viewer knows about images and representations in general. A viewer who has never seen a naturalistic representation in the Western manner, let alone a newspaper photograph, would obviously not be able to articulate his or her act of looking with anything like the range of interpretative contexts available to the *Guardian* reader. But this is not to say that an observer from another society would be incapable of gleaning anything coherent from the photograph in perceptual terms. Recognition of objects in complex depictions seems to operate strongly even for viewers from what used to be called 'primitive' societies. Nor can we assume that what is gleaned exhibits no central points of contact with the robust response I have been describing. The less the familiarity with the type of image and its setting, the more the interpretation is forced back towards a minimal core of robustness, but I firmly believe that this robustness never dwindles to nothing. This is not to say, however, that all art (least of all 'good' art) necessarily has to follow this perceptual model. I am simply saying that this way of making images, which arose in a particular region of the world in a particular era, and in relation to certain circumstances, does exhibit a visual potency which is not explicable entirely in terms of some arbitrary factors that are unique to that society. I suspect that certain kinds of symmetry in formal pattern-making, such as that developed to a supreme level by Islamic decorators, exhibits a robustness of its own kind – but that takes us too far from our present line of enquiry.

I have concentrated so far on relatively recent images because of the relative ease with which their ostensible function can be determined and because of the ready availability of a wide range of information which I can automatically bring to bear on their interpretation. This is not to say that we could solve all the important historical issues arising in the Renaissance if we could somehow put ourselves in a position of comparable closeness to the images. The very closeness brings problems associated with a lack of historical perspective, which may well lead us not to be able to see some of the issues at all – not being able to see the wood for the trees. There are also obvious problems when we try to transpose lessons learned from the study of modern newspaper imagery back into a period when the majority of the surviving visual images were significantly different in more than one of the many respects we may care to consider – function, production, setting, scale, medium, subject matter, style, audience . . . But let me begin by looking at one Renaissance example that does seem to have some points of contact with the cartoon of the 'bagged prime minister', namely the painting by Botticelli which is generally called *Minerva and the Centaur* (fig. 10), which is proudly displayed in the galleries of the Uffizi in Florence. Its most obvious point of contact with the cartoon is that it associates a recognisable image of a woman with a fantastical creature, in which animal and human parts are compounded. The other main point of contact, as will become clear, is that Botticelli's painting has also been taken to refer to political events.

The *Minerva and the Centaur* is less famous than the *Primavera*, but as one of the renowned mythologies by Botticelli it has been the subject of many and varied interpretations. According to whom you read, it is an allegory of the senses and intellect (based on Neoplatonic philosophy), a philosophical meditation on Platonic love, a political allegory of the alliance of Lorenzo de' Medici with either Naples or Pope Innocent VIII, a celebration of Lorenzo's escape from the murderous conspiracy of the Pazzi family, a representation of Lorenzo's Minerva emblem, a picture of Camilla with a satyr, an image of the armed Venus (and therefore belonging to the series of Venus pictures by Botticelli), or the painted equivalent of vernacular love poetry with direct allusions to contemporary personages. Each of these interpretations brings contemporary texts to bear on the painting, sometimes from the same written sources interpreted differently and sometimes from entirely different sources. Assuming that the painting cannot be simultaneously working with all the writings, how are we to determine which text or group of texts has the highest probability of being relevant to its interpretation?

The first move, in keeping with what I have already argued, is to determine

10.   Alessandro Botticelli, *Minerva(?) and the Centaur*, Florence, Uffizi

what kind of object the painting was intended to be. In its current habitat, it is for much of the year hemmed in by pressing throngs of cultural tourists, to be consumed (however passingly) as a glorious masterpiece of Florentine painting in the golden age of Lorenzo il Magnifico. The attitudes which lie behind its modern viewing owe much to the romantic image of Botticelli and his ambience which was cultivated by his 'rediscoverers' in the nineteenth century. None of this modern cultural baggage helps us much in our present quest. Let us return to basics. Although it was for many years assumed that the great Botticelli mythologies were painted for Lorenzo il Magnifico, and most probably for one of his country villas, the same Medici inventory of 1498 that describes the *Primavera* so laconically, also indicates that the *Minerva and the Centaur* was in the town house of Lorenzo and Giovanni di Pierfrancesco de' Medici, who were cousins of il Magnifico.[12] The painting is listed in the 'ground-floor room which adjoins the room of Lorenzo' as 'a painting on wood above the door from the antechamber on which is painted Chamilo [Camilla] with a satyr'. It was valued at 40 *lire* (less than 10 florins). This Lorenzo – or Lorenzino ('*Laurentius minor*', 'little Lorenzo') as he was called – had been born in 1463. A ward of Lorenzo il Magnifico, he was tutored by the intellectuals in his older cousin's orbit, although later the relationship between the Lorenzos showed signs of strain. Since the picture appears to have been in his suite of apartments, he has not unreasonably, if not invariably, been identified as its patron or its first recipient.

The reference in the inventory is clearly fundamental, not so much because it tells us everything we might want to know or legitimately expect to discover about the painting, but because it does serve to set parameters of probability on the kind of interpretation which will work effectively in relation to its likely patron, its location, its function and its viewing. Assuming that the location of the picture in 1498 was the same or essentially similar in type to that for which it was acquired from the artist (probably less than twenty years earlier), we can say that Botticelli's painting is a decorative panel of the newly fashionable kind of pagan subject, painted for the domestic apartments of a young man. I was going to add, 'a young man who was in close contact with the particular kind of culture that Lorenzo il Magnifico cultivated'. But such a rider already begins to load the interpretative scales in a certain direction. The minimal interpretation would be that Lorenzino wanted an attractive painting to decorate his room, and asked Botticelli to come up with something appropriate – 'you know the kind of thing, a pretty woman in one of those rather naughty Roman dresses, like the one you did for my uncle, but not as wide because it's got to fit above the door'. Put in these terms, the brief seems much too crude, but it is not too remote in tone from letters written by Titian to Philip II of Spain about the famous mythologies he was supplying to the king on a relatively regular basis. In 1554 the painter wrote about his plans for the series:

> Because the figure of Danae, which I have already sent to your Majesty, is seen entirely from the front, I have chosen in this other *poesia* [*Aphrodite and Adonis*] to vary the appearance and show the opposite side, so that the room in which they are to hang will seem more agreeable. Shortly I hope to send you the *poesia* of Perseus and Andomeda, which will have a viewpoint different from these two.[13]

Titian's concentration on whether the nudes are to be frontal or not lends support to recent styles of minimalist interpretation of the subject matter of such pictures. According to this line of thought, there was no elaborate programme formulated by or on behalf of the commissioner and communicated to the painter.

However, even if this minimalist interpretation corresponds to the nature of the surviving exchanges between patron and artist, the argument about the subject matter and its choice does not go away. The argument just shifts to another point in the sequence of events that gives rise to the picture. The more specific of the unanswered questions concern the identity of the figures and why they were chosen. The most pressing general issue is why large paintings on these kinds of pagan themes were favoured at this time. As we will have noticed in the inventory, one of the problems is that our assumed identity of the woman as Minerva (or the Greek Pallas Athena), a goddess of might and wisdom, does not correspond to the inventorist's title. We have already noted that inventorists were often casual about subject matter, and the compiler of the lists of Lorenzo's and Giovanni's possessions certainly did not go to much trouble to record the content of the *Primavera*. But Camilla is hardly an obvious or casual choice. She was a martially inclined heroine of Virgil's *Aeneid*.[14] If we wish to support the identification as Camilla, we might ask why should the inventorist make a relatively obscure mistake, when he was not much concerned with obvious truth in other instances? There was obviously some reason for his choice. On the other hand, his identification of the centaur as a satyr hardly boosts our confidence in his judgement. The problem is that in speculating on the reasons for his choice in terms of his knowledge and inclinations we are entering territories in which various explanations – pertaining to various imagined scenarios – begin to float free from any foundation in available evidence, either in this case or in parallel cases.

We might reasonably hope that internal evidence in the painting itself would clarify the identification. Were the picture a straightforward narrative, based on a single text, the problem would be greatly simplified. But it appears likely that the woman and the centaur have been brought together in what the Renaissance called a *fabula*, that is to say an allegory, a synthetic composition designed to carry some kind of poetic, philosophical, political or social message. The ancillary 'clues' with which she has been adorned – her weapons, the trailing plant and the linked rings – do not look like casual ornaments, and they ought to help. But they prove to be surprisingly ambiguous. The shield and halberd seem to point clearly to Minerva, but one type of image of Venus, sanctioned by antiquity, depicted her as armed. Venus's sacred plant was myrtle, and the woman is here 'wreathed in myrtle', as described by Filarete in his Renaissance treatise on architecture (fol. 148v).[15] Or is she? Attempts have been made to identify the plant as laurel, for which there is no shortage of possibly relevant meanings. Laurel was especially associated with victory and eternity, and as *laurus* could well have made allusion to the patron, *Laurentius*. However, myrtle (*myrtus communis*) and laurel (*laurus nobilis*) are distinct plants, the former displaying an opposite arrangement of leaves and the latter an alternate pattern. Unless Botticelli has muddled his plants, the woman in the picture is indeed 'wreathed in myrtle'. In the third of her 'clues', the linked diamond rings, we can confidently recognise an emblem primarily associated with the Medici, even if there is still some uncertainty as to when it came into use and who used it.

Camilla, Minerva or Venus? Plausible arguments can be summoned for all three identifications, and in themselves the arguments do not seem to differ greatly in historical plausibility and efficacy. My own inclination would normally be to favour the identification which it is likely that most viewers would have made in the period – that is to say Minerva – but this preference has to fight against the myrtle and the inventorist. I am inclined on further consideration to take the myrtle as the most reliable label, but the issue is by no means closed. The centaur, thank goodness, is clearly identifiable as a centaur. If we wanted a specific name, we might think of him as Cheiron, the leading centaur, but this hardly seems necessary. The meaning of the centaur in the Renaissance was reasonably stable, and relied upon the legendary creature's obvious compound of the more noble parts of man with the body of a beast. Dante set the tone in his *Divine Comedy (Divina Commedia)*, in which the centaurs are sadly aware of their bestial tendencies, and we may reasonably think that Botticelli's submissive hybrid shares their awareness. The general polarity which is emerging is of virtue and vice, albeit softened by an air of consent on the beast's behalf – providing we are correctly interpreting the figures' actions and expressions on the basis of the kind of communicative robustness I have already advocated.

What this process of inching forward from the inventory does not tell us is where we should go next, or even if we should try to go anywhere at all. Do we look to political texts and events? After all the woman is adorned with at least one Medicean emblem. Or do we turn to ancient writings about the classical gods? Perhaps the Neoplatonic philosophy of Marsilio Ficino, who is known to have written educative letters to Lorenzino, holds the key. Or is the vernacular culture of jousts, feasts and plays the immediate source for Botticelli? There is also the further problem of what features of the painting require interpretation. Is the boat in the background significant? What about the picket fence? Are the bow and arrows crucial? We may do well to recall Veronese's no-nonsense reply when quizzed by the Inquisition as to why he put so many supporting figures, such as 'Germans, buffoons and similar types' into his *Last Supper* (later retitled, *Feast in the House of Levi*).[16] He began by informing his Inquisitors that 'we painters share the licence that is taken by poets and madmen', an equation which may not seem at first sight to be designed to instil confidence, until we realise that the idea of an affinity between poetic inspiration and lunacy had become something of a commonplace in the sixteenth century. He then answered the specific charge about the irrelevant intruders by saying that 'the commission was to adorn the picture according to how it seemed best to him, and the painting is big and capable of containing many figures'. The ancillary figures were invented 'ornaments' to fill up the space.

A fuller review of how we might deal with such problems will be left to chapter V. For the moment I want to re-emphasise my intention to understand what functions such paintings can be shown to have performed in the Renaissance. I should like to support this emphasis with an insistence that any explanation must pass the 'whiff of reality' test. That is to say, our explanation must be reconcilable with a credible scenario for the work's conception,

24

production, and reception taking into account what is documented about the relationships of patrons and artists, about artists' own levels of knowledge and ways of proceeding, and about the way people viewed the paintings. If we can find or generate no credible model for a certain mode of interpretation from contemporary sources about the visual arts, we should regard such an interpretation as at best hypothetical and at worst wholly unsafe. With respect to Botticelli's mythologies and comparable paintings in this period, it has to be said that there is no evidence that they were interpreted as referring to specific political events, and anyone advocating such a message takes on substantial burdens of general proof as well as the making of specific associations. More generally, if we are faced with a number of texts which make similarly approximate matches to the subject of the painting, we would do well to prefer the most accessible, in terms of such criteria as its language, availability, diffusion and regularity of use in the visual arts. Indeed a string of artistic precedents might mean that we do not need a text at all as an immediate source, though the text cannot ultimately be eliminated from the explanatory process.

The case of Botticelli's *Minerva and the Centaur* poses the problem of relevant sources in something of an extreme form. On one hand we have the mundane listing and valuation in the inventory – a document which does not aspire to perform an intellectual function on our behalf – and on the other we have the kind of abstract philosophical text concerning Neoplatonic notions of transcendental love, which have regularly been seen as providing the conceptual foundations for Botticelli's mythologies. Somehow we have to bridge the gap between the levels of circumstantial specificity and philosophical generality. The greater part of this book will consist of the study of direct and contextual sources for precisely this purpose; that is to say attempting to understand the realm of competence of each kind of source in itself and in relation to the spectrum of sources we might legitimately expect to tell us something about the making and viewing of the works of art. The range of direct sources – those which directly deal with works of art – extends from business documents to high-flown theory. We will be looking at a sample of inventories, contracts, letters between the various parties involved in the generating of works of art, accounts by differently placed observers, literary works that deal with art and artists, biographies of artists, and writings on the theory of art. These direct sources will provide a basis for asking how they might be used to bring the contingent sources into play – how we can know where to look amongst the vast range of documentation relating to the domestic, communal, cultural, religious, and intellectual lives of those who are involved in the establishing of the context in which the works perform their functions. We will also need to be alert to the way in which our present manners of viewing, including the whole industry of what is called 'cultural heritage' (in which this book is a participant), give priority to certain questions over others, in a way that may not correspond to the priorities which ruled the original context or may rule in the future. Our present interests inevitably skew the asking of the individual questions and may even give rise to questions which cannot be brought to bear in a non-arbitrary fashion on the surviving historical material. The final chapter of this book will aim to heighten our alertness to the kinds of skewing that may be involved.

The whole enterprise of the chapters which follow is based on the conviction that a study of contemporary documents and texts is essential if we are purposefully to direct our looking in such a way as to produce that thrill of insight which comes when there is a special resonance between a verbal account and a visual object. It is of course possible that excitement can be produced by a pseudo-insight – the apparently telling heightening of awareness that proves on closer scrutiny to be without sustainable foundation – and it is not easy to distinguish the genuine from the spurious. I should like to think that the emphasis upon foundations and functional relevance in the present study will act as something of a protection mechanism against pseudo-insights.

It is inevitable that my quest is conducted in words and that the raw material I will be using comprises Renaissance words through which the viewing of images may be broached. How the Renaissance viewed (and how I now view) the relationship between word and image will obviously be crucial in determining the nature of the enterprise. The Renaissance itself became notably concerned with the relationship between the written and the visual. To some extent that concern came with the heritage of the Middle Ages, in which the problematic role of visual images in Christian devotion in the face of Biblical proscriptions had been a continued matter for anxiety and theological debate. The oft-cited idea of painting as sacred 'books for the unlettered' stood implicitly behind a huge number of the regular and routine works of art produced during the Renaissance. Probably a larger majority of the works fell into that category than most books on Renaissance art would lead us to believe. An exceptional work, like a Botticelli mythology, is more likely to be illustrated in a text-book than a humdrum regional altarpiece. However, there was perhaps from the first something slightly disingenuous about the notion of the 'unlettered' spectator as the prime beneficiary of works of religious art. The great majority of commissions were under the control of relatively well-informed clerics and, increasingly in the Renaissance, of demanding private patrons, who expected and received works with more sophisticated content than the stock formulation might suggest.

To the standard text-related function of religious images, the Renaissance added a developing involvement with the relationship of painting to literary texts of a secular kind, particularly the poetic and mythological writings of antiquity and their modern equivalents. This interest is neatly encapsulated in the phrase of the Roman author, Horace, *ut pictura poesis* ('as poetry, so painting'), which signalled that in a series of fundamental properties – including the conveying of meaning, the use of imaginative licence, and the higher purposes of fictional depictions – the natures of painting and poetry were essentially similar. In the Renaissance, the exemplar of a poetic painting which was invariably cited whenever the art-poetry question was discussed was the *Calumny of Apelles*, known through Lucian's description (fig. 11).[17] Apelles's painting told the story of the calumnious denouncing of an innocent youth by a league of evil-doers, including Ignorance, Envy, Treachery and Deceit, using a series of personifications of the vices and virtues in a tableau assumed to be rich in gesture and expression. The *fabula* was occasioned by a calumny perpetrated on Apelles himself by a fellow artist and which had led to Apelles's condemnation to death. His brilliant conception was taken to justify the role of poetic invention and expression in painting. Pliny indicates that in his painting

11.   Alessandro Botticelli, *The Calumny of Apelles*, Florence, Uffizi

of Antigonus and Artemis, Apelles was even considered to have surpassed the magisterial text of Homer himself. Painting can both serve and be served by the author's pen.

The kind of descriptive writing used by Lucian for the *Calumny*, termed *ekphrasis* (or *descriptio* in Latin) was eagerly adopted by the Renaissance, and provides one of the main bodies of evidence as to how paintings were viewed in the period. Such writing stood in a symbiotic relationship to the images. It endeavoured to evoke the nature of the work through word-painting, delighting in passages of naturalistic detail and busy story-telling. In turn, the style of the writing influenced how educated patrons viewed pictures, affecting their taste, and perhaps also exercised an impact on the artists themselves. The great sculptor, Lorenzo Ghiberti, an intellectually ambitious artist in close contact with the humanist authors, wrote about his own reliefs for the Baptistery Doors in Florence in the style of the *ekphrasis*, and it is reasonable to think that the *ekphrastic* manner of writing and viewing affected how he devised his compositions.[18]

Increasingly in the Renaissance we will hear the voices of artists asserting their status as at least the equal of masters of the written word. Indeed voices were raised in favour of visual representation as inherently more powerful and noble than the writing. Leonardo was the most insistent of these advocates. Like other Renaissance theorists he was fully alert to the need to invent subject matter in a way that was analogous to the stories of the writers. In his so-called *paragone*, the comparison of the arts, he specifically cites the by now obvious precedent: 'the

27

poet may say , "I will make a story that signifies great things"; the painter can do the same, as when Apelles painted the *Calumny*.[19] However, Leonardo was convinced that the medium of visual representation and communication used by the painter was in all other respects superior to that of the poet. If the poet says 'I will describe hell or paradise, or other delights and terrors', Leonardo replies that 'the painter will surpass you, because he will place things before you that will silently tell of such delights or terrify you or turn your mind to flight'.[20] The painter's representation is more vividly true to life, does not require sequential and laborious description, displays its harmonies at each and every moment, does not rely upon a specific language (e.g. Italian or French), and, above all, nourishes sight, the noblest sense of all.

The germ of a reply to Leonardo occurs in a letter written by Pico della Mirandola, an aristocratic member of il Magnifico's philosophical luminaries in Florence. In answer to the question as to whether a painted portrait or a letter conveys a better impression of someone's soul, Pico writes, 'it seems to me that between a portrait and a letter there is the following difference, that the former represents the body and the latter the mind'.[21] A letter can give a direct account of a person's inner thoughts, ideas and emotions in a way that is impossible in a painted image. However, this line of reasoning is not quite as dismissive of painted portraiture as it might at first sight seem, since the Neoplatonic philosophy, to which Pico subscribed in his own particular way, deemed that the soul was the 'form' or *figura* of the body – not in the sense that the 'form' was identical with the body's external appearance but that it acted as the agency through which the immaterial soul could impress itself upon matter to give rise to the body. This concept probably explains Pico's conclusion that a portrait and a letter played complementary roles in conveying the essence of an individual.

Leonardo's own arguments that the power of visual representation embraces fields of perception that the written word cannot enter so effectively depend not a little upon a misrepresentation of the aspirations of poetry – which he takes as necessarily aspiring to affect the spectator through the evoking of visual sensations. But his assertions do serve to focus our attention upon the existence of realms of the visual that cannot be simply subordinated to language. The vast acreage of writing on his own *Mona Lisa* (fig. 4) suggests, at the most basic level, that the visual artist is capable of making an image which has an apparently limitless potential to attract words and yet ultimately remains resistant to definite verbal formulation. But, even if we allow the ultimate ambiguity of the visual experience of an artefact like the *Mona Lisa*, it may be argued that we each rely upon predetermined categories of an essentially verbal kind to control our way of looking, so that we can give our own personal sense of cognitive structure to the subject of our scrutiny.

The *locus classicus* for the verbal category as the master of the visually-perceived has been the account of the way that Eskimos have many different words to distinguish between a multitude of different types of snow. We have been told repeatedly that the naming of categories is responsible for the Eskimos being able to see many kinds of snow, whereas with our one word 'snow' we are not able to make such fine discriminations – verbally and, hence, visually. In fact, the evidence on which this *locus classicus* has been founded melted away, like snow itself, when it was subject to proper scrutiny, and it seems that Eskimo language only discriminates between 'snow in the air (snowflake)' and 'snow on the ground'.[22]

On one level, the farce of the serial repetition of the Eskimo's mythical vocabulary for snow illustrates the vital point that evidence should always be checked, however often it is asserted as fact and however much it may appeal to a particular historian's favoured modes of interpretation. Yet, at a deeper level, the question of naming and seeing will not go away quite so easily. There is plenty of evidence that different languages – including some that are traditionally defined as 'primitive' – do operate different levels of discrimination within objects which we only name by class, and also devise collective nouns on the basis of quite different systems of classification. In Arabic, for example, it is possible to distinguish by name many different types of camel, according to age, gender, varieties of use and so on. One Arabic-English Lexicon lists some twelve distinctly descriptive words and compound words.[23] And if we return to the business of naming snow, I can remember as a child being able to distinguish between the kind of snow that would stick together to make good snowballs, the kind that could be compacted to make the best slides, and the irritating kind that would do neither. In this instance, the visual and tactile discrimination was accompanied by a simple form of naming, in that we could differentiate between what we called 'snowball snow', other 'good snow', 'crumbly snow' and nasty 'slush'. My parents would hardly have considered 'snowball snow' as high on their list of priorities for naming, while the differentiation between snow compacted into slippery ice and snow which was less hazardous for bicycles would have been of more consequence to them. Even their interests as cyclists did not, however, lead to specific naming of the dangerous and safer snows. Snow falls were not very common and the problem not all that urgent . A few well chosen adjectives, like icy or slippery, rutted or compacted, would suffice to make the necessary point about whether it was safe to cycle.

In general it seems to me that the basic act of naming and classifying objects is primarily driven by a visual-cum-tactile system which is dedicated to functional requirements. The highly specialised skills different peoples have devised for living in their variously demanding environments provide the incentive, even the necessity, for making detailed discriminations in certain important areas of experience, and having some way of articulating those discriminations through the spoken word, so that they can be communicated on a general basis and taught to the young. The centrality of camels to the Arabs' ability to thrive in hostile deserts provides quite different incentives for understanding, recognising and communicating about types of camel that exist in a temperate country, whose camels are imported subjects of zoological curiosity. However, evidence from the new study of ethnobiology (which studies the biological knowledge of different ethnic groups) indicates a large measure of central robustness in how animals and plants have been classified in traditional societies. The highly differentiated way that organisms have arisen within their environmental niches appears to work strongly against anarchy and arbitrariness in biological classifications.

Not the least of the problems with a model which dictates that visual experience is always dictated by the verbal is that it cannot readily cope with a developing response to new visual phenomena. If we imagine, for instance, that some intentional act of breeding or unwanted mutation resulted in a type of camel that exhibited different characteristics and could not be embraced within the existing categories, the Arabs would need a way of devising a fresh category in response to the new phenomenon – just as we have devised the term 'acid rain' to denote the kind of rain that is damaging trees. Or to return to the Eskimo's snow, it may be worth noting that our modern access to microscopic means of viewing snowflakes permits the devising of elaborate classifications based on different types of crystalline structure. The new tool for seeing does not in itself cause the new form of naming, but it sets new parameters for what can be discriminated and enables us to satisfy our classificatory needs in a new way. These needs may be differently motivated – an artist concerned with the order of nature might make different demands on images from a scientist researching crystalline structures – but the range of possibilities is neither infinite nor arbitrary.

I accept that our existing and deeply ingrained forms of verbal categorisation act as one of the powerful filters through which we strain visual experience to make it intelligible, and that our system of naming will predispose us to see certain things and not others, but the interplay of visual perception and verbal formulation is so complex and reciprocal that the imposition of a linguistic model will not suffice to analyse our handling of visual experience – any more than Leonardo's visual model provided adequate criteria for the characterisation of poetry.

The reader may have noticed that I have not once used the word 'reading' with respect to visual images. This omission is entirely conscious, not so much because there are no similarities between the reading of a text and the viewing of a picture – indeed it would be surprising if that were so when many pictures were illustrative of texts – but rather because accounts of the act of 'reading' have been used as part of a strategy to designate pictures as texts in such a way as to suppress the peculiarity of the visual experience. Since I have journeyed this far without finding the need to use 'reading' or to propose a direct substitute, perhaps I would be best advised to say that we can make our approach to the visual without satisfying any such need. However, since historical analysis, like any other form of analysis, thrives on a kind of shorthand to designate its procedures, I think I may need to offer a hostage to fortune. In place of reading, I should like to proffer 'prospecting', without really expecting that it stands much chance of being adopted on a universal basis. There is both an academic and popular dimension to this preference. In his book on perspective in 1569, the Venetian author Daniele Barbaro distinguished between two kinds of vision, 'aspect' and 'prospect'.[24] The former involved simple seeing by glancing at something, while the latter consisted of purposeful scrutiny in which certain things were understood in the act of looking. What the historian of the visual is trying to accomplish is the transforming of 'aspect' into 'prospect'. The other sense of prospecting which I want to echo is that evoked by the phrase 'prospecting for gold'. The prospector looks searchingly amongst the debris sieved from the rushing stream to see if there is any trace of the glitter that might indicate the fulfilling of long-held dreams. The prospector's visual attention is highly directed, filtering visual experience even more finely than the sieve has strained the debris from the water. In as much as the prospector has to be as alert as the historian for 'fool's gold' – something that appears to be as bright and shiny as the real thing – the parallel has a validity even beyond the sense of perceptual sieving.

In the final analysis, I am convinced that the act of prospecting in the field of complex visual images involves perceptual processes which are at once language-like and distinct from linguistic structures. When we look at something like the photograph of the boat person being restrained, we make an incredibly rapid set of clustered perceptual shots which are accompanied by a cascading mixture of impressions and associations in which possibilities are paraded and reviewed in a non-linear manner. At the centre of this fluid process is the essential robustness of recognition which I have discussed earlier but around or within this robustness there may be few, if any, aspects of the image which communicate their significance in the systematic way that words accomplish. This is not of course to say that verbal expression is unambiguous, but the inherent logic of meaning that words combined in a recognisable grammar can achieve is of a quite different kind from even the most carefully contrived visual image. When it comes to giving some kind of coherent form to the melange of perceptions and associations which accompany our basic acts of visual recognition, words do of course play a crucial role, as we saw when we needed to make sense of how the figures in the photograph related to each other. But even with the act of captioning and detailed verbal commentary, neither the complex fluidity of the initial response nor the continuing power of the image to bring other trains of thought into play are wholly constrained by the verbal acts. In a sense, the whole of this book is an endeavour to analyse contemporary sources in such a way as to provide captions and commentaries, collaborating with the Renaissance voices that the artist *post tabulam latens* might have heard. The aim is to enrich rather than constrain our subsequent visual responses. And, at the end, we may be better placed to find out what is left over when we have done the best we can with verbal sources and resources.

31

II   ORDERING ARTEFACTS
The Framework for Agreements and Disagreements

THE PROVISION OF artefacts in the Renaissance was a business – or, rather, involved a number of types of business. Like other professionals in the growing urban economies of the late Middle Ages and early Renaissance, any artist with an established practice would have been involved in various kinds of transaction of a more or less formal kind with those who wished to acquire the kinds of product on offer. Many of these transactions would have involved written records, and the most important – in terms of complexity, significance or cost – would have involved the due processes of the law. Certain of them specifically required the service of a lawyer or notary, who would have been schooled in the formulas and formats appropriate to each type of transaction. These kinds of records provide one of our main bodies of evidence for the production of works of art in the Renaissance. They can potentially yield different types of information – about the names of artist and patron, about date and intended location, about sizes, materials and costs, about subject matter (to a limited extent), and generally about the business and legal frameworks within which artists and clients conducted their dealings. Given their specific function within the legal processes of the law, the more formal types of record each have their own particular nature, and cannot be properly interpreted without an understanding of what information they were intended to convey to whom – and, by implication, what we *cannot* legitimately expect them to tell us.

Clearly, there were large areas of the relationship between client and artist that were not likely to be covered by written records, even in cases where a notarial record was involved. Indeed, the drawing-up of the contract may have been the climax of a series of contacts between the parties, involving discussions of subject matter and format of the kind that were rarely handled in any detail in the legal agreements. The spoken interchanges between artist and client are clearly the most elusive components in the transactions behind the making of a work, yet they may involve matters in which the historian has the highest interest. We can gain occasional glimpses into the nature of such interchanges in letters, such as might occur when the parties are so geographically separated that they have to resort to correspondence. We can also occasionally look to anecdotes in other kinds of written account, such as the biographies of artists that Giorgio Vasari published in 1550 and 1568. All of these sources need to be examined critically in terms of their own natures and functions if we are to know what weight to place on the evidence they apparently provide. The writers of all kinds of literary account – including Vasari in this literary category – were trying to achieve particular kinds of effect in relation to their perceived readership, and they did not conceive their primary aim as providing us with precisely the kind of information we might want from our standpoint as modern historians. The same caution applies to letter writers.

In addition to those sources which relate directly to the making of works of art, there is a huge body of other documentation which becomes potentially relevant for understanding the worlds of patron and artist. The artist, his household and his family would inevitably have been involved in a whole series of transactions, such as legal separation from a parent or guardian, marriage, the provision of dowries, the witnessing of legal documents, the granting of the legal power to act on someone else's behalf, standing as guarantor, acting as a valuer for other artists' works, and the business of inheritance (most notably the drawing up of wills, and serving as executor of the deceased person's wishes). A few artists, such as the notoriously violent Florentine sculptor and goldsmith, Benvenuto Cellini, might feature in legal proceedings for less savoury reasons. Such records may give us a good idea about artists' wealth and status, and generally about their general interplay with the society in which they pursued their business. Probably the most complete picture for the complex legal framework within which an artist worked, particularly one with a large and diverse professional practice, can be seen in the published documents relating to the Lombard sculptor and architect Giovanni Antonio Amadeo, starting with the will of his father in 1450 and finishing with his own death in 1522.[25] The 1,550 documents indicate just how intricate the business of a successful all-round artist could become. The clients of artists, inevitably, would feature in similar kinds of records – particularly since they are likely to have been amongst the more prominent and richest individuals and organisations in the society. The art historian can hardly be expected to conduct primary research on an extensive scale into the social and economic history of the artists' clients, but the research into such histories by other historians clearly yields a body of material which is important to art history, especially in comparative terms if we are dealing with such issues as wealth and status.

Such broader issues are to feature to varying degrees in later chapters; for the moment we are chiefly concerned with the question of the kinds of direct agreement between patron and artist that brought the works into being, and with other aspects of the formal and less formal records that shed light on the framework of obligations within which artists pursued their careers. I intend to concentrate firstly on the legal framework, most notably contracts, before looking at the position of artists in court, and at some of the more complex procedures involved in large-scale projects for sculpture. Finally, we will hear the artists' voices in a few letters which provide more personalised insights into the relationships between artists and patrons. As well as the formal contract and other forms of binding agreement, there were other forms of legal proceedings which played a vital role in an artist's career. It will, I think, be worth outlining a few of the other kinds of proceedings to give some kind of context for our more sustained analysis of the direct contract.

In order to set up as an independent master, able to receive commissions and remuneration on his own account, the young artist might need to achieve formal separation (an *emancipatio*) from parent or guardian. The length of time that a child remained under parental jurisdiction varied from place to place. In Milan, for example, a son was not legally independent for full contractual purposes until the late age of thirty-five. Bernardo Zenale, Milanese painter and architect, was thirty years old when he finally gained the consent of his father to his independence.[26] The precociously talented Andrea Mantegna had been legally adopted by the Paduan artist, Squarcione, who apparently prided himself on teaching the most up-to-date ideas, but in 1448, after a dispute over remuneration for 'the making of pictures of great price' under his master's aegis, the seventeen or eighteen year-old Mantegna was effectively granted his independence by two arbiters.[27] The final legal word on their separation did not occur until 1455, when the Venetian Consiglio dei Quaranta ruled against Squarcione, on the grounds that the consent of Mantegna's natural father had not originally been obtained.

A young artist might find it easier to obtain work if an older parent or guardian was legally responsible for any default. It may well be that the obscure Evangelista di Pian di Meleto was included primarily as a guarantor in Raphael's contract at the age of seventeen for the now dismembered *St Nicholas of Tolentino Altarpiece*. The two may have still been operating under the aegis of the workshop of his father, Giovanni Santi, who had died six years earlier.[28] Although Raphael is, remarkably, named as *magister* at this tender age, the partnership with the older Evangelista probably provided the authorities with some comfort that a mature attitude would be taken to the commission.

Formal partnerships of varying duration between artists were more common than we might expect, given our modern image of the artist as individual author. Partnerships of any significance would be the subject of a *pacta* or *societas*, in which the terms would be clearly established. One major reason for entering into such an agreement would be to take on a complex commission, involving extensive work of a varied nature, such as might not be possible if the artist acted on his own or even with his own band of assistants. Donatello's partnership with the highly skilled and apparently business-like Michelozzo is a conspicuous case in point.[29] Michelozzo had previously collaborated with Lorenzo Ghiberti, but in the mid-1420s, apparently to Ghiberti's irritation, he allied himself with Donatello, bringing considerable expertise in bronze casting into the partnership. In 1427 Michelozzo was even responsible for completing his partner's tax declaration so that the *catasto* could be levied on Donatello's possessions.[30] The records of this innovatory Florentine tax, first levied in that year, provide a rich source of information about the households and businesses of artists, and about related professionals and patrons – though then as now, we would be unwise to expect tax returns to reflect an entirely accurate picture of someone's income and assets. Michelozzo, on Donatello's behalf, listed moneys owed to him – including a sum of 180 florins due from the administrator of Siena Cathedral, 'on account of a narrative scene in bronze [the *Feast of Herod*, fig. 12] which I did. . . some time ago' – as well as his debts, which include no less than 'two years' back rent on the house I live in' (30 florins). One suspects that the Florentine authorities came to regard ritual declarations of poverty and ailing relatives with due scepticism, but it is clear that the unmarried Donatello

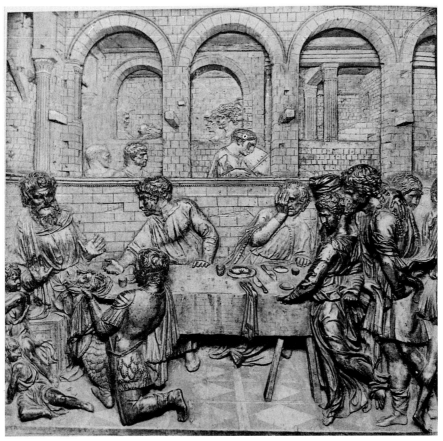

12.   Donatello, *The Feast of Herod*, Siena, Baptistery, Font

in his early forties had not made a conspicuous fortune from his art – or if he
had, he had disposed of it.

   Perhaps the most unlikely partners were Fra Bartolommeo and Mariotto
Albertinelli, who had once been fellow pupils in the workshop of Cosimo
Rosselli.[31] In 1500 Baccio della Porta had entered the Dominican convent of
San Marco as Fra Bartolommeo, having ceased his career as a painter and leaving
unfinished a fresco of the *Last Judgement*, which Albertinelli was commissioned
to complete. As part of his payment, Albertinelli received thirteen barrels of
wine, a large quantity which was in whole or in part intended for resale.
Albertinelli's own inclinations certainly did not seem to lead in the direction of
the cloistered life of a monk. In or before 1505 he married a wine merchant's
daughter, and subsequently invested in two taverns, one of which was bringing
in an income of 65 florins a year by his death. If Vasari is to believed, Albertinelli
had at one stage become so fed up with the need to master 'muscles,
foreshortenings and perspectives' that he decided to concentrate on his
hostelries, saying that in his earlier profession he 'imitated flesh and blood',
whereas his new business 'made flesh and blood'. Other documents indicate that
he was granted his *emancipatio* from his father in 1506, at the age of thirty-one,
and that in 1507 his wife converted the currency of her dowry which had been

35

deposited in the state bank, the Monte. Some years after Fra Bartolommeo had resumed his career as a painter, these apparently disparate characters entered into an agreement to set up a *compagnia* under the auspices of San Marco, in which all commissions and all profits would (as normal in formal partnerships) be considered as joint products of their business, regardless of which artist actually undertook the execution. The formal dissolution of the partnership in 1513, recorded in a copy from the *Libro debitori et creditori et ricordanze* of San Marco, evaluated Albertinelli's share of the profits as 212 florins.

The remuneration of Albertinelli in commodities was far from exceptional. An extreme example is provided by Mino da Fiesole's commission for the monument to Marchese Ugo in the Badia, which he undertook between 1469 and 1471.[32] In payment he received a large quantity of wheat, enough for about two dozen people for a year, and sufficient wine for about the same number, with other provisions and cloth worth 294 *lire*. The woollen cloth was consigned to him by a dealer who rented his own shop from the Badia, and the appropriate sum offset against the dealer's rent. How Mino realised the value of the commodities is unclear, but it is possible that he never physically took possession of them and that he in turn used all or part of them as credits. Under one third of his payment was in cash.

Complex commissions often involved various kinds of subcontracting and supervisory work. The provision of an altarpiece, for example, could be an elaborate undertaking, potentially involving carpenters, specialist wood carvers, gilders and polychromers, as well as the actual painter of the image. Today it is the painter who generally attracts our attention, and many of the paintings now exist outside their intended ensembles. However, the production of the framework ornamented with sculpture could sometimes involve greater expenditure of money, and sometimes of time, than the painting of the picture. For example, the frame by Giacomo del Maino that was to contain Leonardo's *Virgin of the Rocks* (fig. 5) cost 710 *lire imperiali*, and it was only after a protracted dispute that Leonardo and his partner Ambrogio da Predis were offered a greater sum (1,000 *lire*) for the painted adornments of the altarpiece.[33] (The *lira imperiale* was the standard currency of account in Milan, with an exchange rate of about 4 to the gold ducat at this time.) The carvers of what we now regard as the 'frames' for great paintings were often accorded considerable status in the proceedings, and could be required to undertake skilled carving in the round and in relief. In the document of 1488 commissioning an altarpiece from Pietro Perugino in the coastal town of Fano, the notary unexpectedly appended a poetic eulogy of the painter, who is described as another Parrhasius (one of the revered masters of ancient Greece), while the framemaker, Joachim, was identified with the Greek sculptor, Lysippus, and accorded praise no less effusive than that directed at Perugino.[34] Joachim was to be paid 80 ducats for the frame, which was to be made in accordance with the *designia* he had submitted, while Perugino was to receive the high sum of 300 ducats, but this was to cover the provision of the main panel, lunette and predella, together with the costs of 'gold, ultramarine blue and fine colours and everything else necessary and appropriate' for the enrichment of whole structure. On the majority of occasions the painter was given responsibility for the *ornamento* as a whole, which would have included the design and provision of the frame and subsidiary sections. On average, the structural work seems to have amounted to 20 per cent of the total cost in an altarpiece with framing elements which did not include substantial sculpture.

The gilding and polychroming of an altarpiece frame generally involved significant costs in materials, and could in some cases have absorbed as much as 40 per cent of the overall expenditure.[35] The gilding might be contracted out to a specialist, a *metodoro*, and require the transportation of the wooden frame to the gilder's workshop. On occasion, it was only at a relatively late stage that the painter took over what was already an elaborate structure which had involved the work of many skilled hands and had not involved direct design input from himself. In North Italy, in particular, the carved structure might be highly elaborate, decoratively and figuratively, although there was an increasing tendency during the fifteenth century for altarpieces to be dominated by a large central panel painting and for the frame to be designed (sometimes by the painter himself) to serve the needs of the central image. The painter himself might order the making of the frame, as in 1456 when Neri di Bicci provided a design and commissioned Giuliano da Maiano to carve the structure of an altarpiece for Poggibonsi 'in the antique style', for which he paid Giuliano 60 florins.[36] A frame 'in the antique style' was, paradoxically, of the most modern kind, built primarily to accommodate a dominant single image rather than being arranged as a polyptych. Not infrequently in earlier altarpieces the panel or panels which were to receive the painted images were already built into the structure. The raised and ragged lips of paint visible inside the margins of many Renaissance panel paintings bear witness to their harsh removal from integral frames in later ages. In the sixteenth century, especially in Venice as canvas became more common as a support for altarpiece paintings, there was a greater tendency for the painting and frame to be united only in the final installation, although the designs were often carefully co-ordinated from the beginning.

In such an intricate operation as the provision of an altarpiece or decoration of a chapel, potentially involving more than one contractor, the control of quality obviously became an important issue for the commissioner. Not only did this involve the quality of the materials – specifying the grade and quality of gold leaf and of other valuable items, such as the blue pigment, ultramarine (*lapis lazuli*) – but also the standards of craftsmanship. Many painted items were expected to be durable, especially in an ecclesiastical setting where the donors were hoping to establish posthumous credit in the eyes of people and the mind of God, and contracts might well include some kind of assurance about the enduring qualities of the artefact. Increasingly, there is also an overt sense that the less quantifiable qualities of artistry needed to be ensured. If a patron chose a master because of the admired appearance of a work he had done for someone else, he or she would hardly tolerate a slippage in standard because of casualness or because the painter had not undertaken the work himself. Sometimes the standard was directly set by reference to an admired work by another master, requesting that the new painting should be made in the 'form and manner' or 'similitude' of the exemplar. The provision of a fully-worked design before the signing of the contract obviously helped guarantee the results. We also find clauses to the effect that the work must be undertaken by the master's 'own hand'. This requirement does not necessarily mean precisely what we may now

13.   Andrea Verrocchio, *The Pistoia Altarpiece (Madonna and Child with St John the Baptist and St Donatus)*, Pistoia, Cathedral

think – that all the painting must be wholly 'autograph' – but rather it was intended as a guarantee against the farming out of substantial parts of the work, either to apprentices or even to subcontractors in other studios. Some workshops employed senior assistants who were capable of providing work up to a fully acceptable standard. The highly skilled Lorenzo di Credi worked as a painter and general 'foreman' in Verrocchio's *bottega* until his master's death, when Lorenzo was in his late twenties. Verrocchio's amanuensis appears to have been largely responsible for the painting of one of the finest of the 'Verrocchio' paintings, the altarpiece for the oratory of Donato de' Medici beside the cathedral in Pistoia (fig. 13), about which we will be hearing more in this chapter. It is likely that Leonardo's continued presence in Verrocchio's workshop in 1476, four years after the Company of St Luke requested his dues as an independent master, involved a similar arrangement.

Although partnerships, collaboration, studio teamwork and subcontracting were designed to increase productivity while maintaining acceptable quality, problems could occur. In 1476 the widow of Augusto de Beccaria, Zaccharina, who was responsible for the commissioning of the painting of the life of Christ by Vincenzo Foppa and two partners in the church of S. Jacopo outside Pavia, petitioned the Duke of Milan about what she considered to be the unsatisfactory results of the associates' collaboration.[37] The duke in turn wrote to the painters insisting that they meet their obligations to ensure that 'the painting is not done by so many hands as it would seem to be done, so as not to make the work ugly'. He instructed that one of the artists should alone be responsible for finishing it, adding a rider to the effect that this requirement should not be used as an excuse for delaying 'the work on the chapel of this our Castle of Pavia' for which the artists were directly obligated to him.

There is probably no single transaction which is so well documented that it can on its own provide a wholly comprehensive account of how the business of ordering and obtaining a painting proceeded. To overcome this problem, and to avoid having to cite excerpts of many different contracts, I have invented a fictional scenario which will cover all the main processes when a notarial contract was specifically required. The story that follows probably involves more of the possible procedures than any single episode is likely to have included in practice, but each of the stages and actions may be recognised from documented events. Let us suppose that a well-off, land-owning notary dies. We will call him Ser Giovanni Doio. ('Ser' is the prefix for a notary.)

Ser Giovanni dies, leaving a widow, Lucia. His will stipulates that 200 florins are to be devoted to the provision of an altarpiece and the saying of masses and prayers for his soul and members of his family once a week in a chapel over which he had acquired rights in the church of S. Francesco. A property is to be sold by his executors to raise the necessary sum. The chapel is not a separate structure, but a bay in the northern aisle of the Franciscan basilica and carries an existing dedication to the *Annunziata* (the Virgin Annunciate). Although Lucia has no legal powers to act independently of a male member of the family, it is accepted that she assumes the practical responsibility on behalf of the heirs for seeing that the adornment of the chapel is undertaken without unnecessary delay.

In consultation with the prior of S. Francesco, she calls in the painter known as Il Imbrattatore (real name Tomaso di Ser Benedetto da Lucca). Imbrattatore, himself the son of a provincial notary, is somewhat better educated than the general run of artisans, and is a member of the rising generation of intellectual artists who are aspiring to move in the circles of humanist authors. The painter is already known to the family, since he rents a workshop in one of the properties owned by the late Giovanni, and he had already supplied an image of the Virgin and Child when their first son had been born. Additionally, he had already painted a lunette of St Francis in the cloister of the church, and had won the confidence of the prior. Imbrattatore agrees to provide a *disegno* or developed drawing to show how he is intending to compose an image of the *istoria* of the *Annunciation*, in keeping with the dedication of the altar, with the need to portray St John the Baptist, as the deceased man's name-saint, St Francis, in honour of the church and monastery, and St Lucy, a requirement of the widow in deference to her own saint. With some skill, Imbrattatore produces a design which shows the Virgin Annunciate at the centre of the composition, flanked by the Angel Gabriel on the left. On the right, decorously separated from the Virgin by the bench from which she has risen, Sts John and Lucy appear rather as if witnesses – though, strictly speaking the altarpiece is a devotional image of the Virgin Annunciate rather than a narrative. On a hill in the landscape visible over the wall of the garden (the wall of the *hortus conclusus*, the enclosed garden, which was a customary symbol of the Virgin's inviolate nature), St Francis can be seen receiving the stigmata.

Satisfied with the painter's ingenious solution, Lucia, Lorenzo Doio (the deceased man's brother, as an executor of the will), Imbrattatore and the prior meet at an appointed time at the office of the notary, Ser Giusto da Fiesole, who has in the past acted as the monastery's procurator. The parties discuss the nature of the agreement into which they wish to enter, and the notary produces a rapid summary, an *imbreviatura*, of the salient points in Latin using a hasty hand which is later destined to test the inadequate palaeographic skills of a modern doctoral student. Ser Giusto emphasises that the *imbreviatura*, which he will place in chronological sequence in his current file of such documents, is legally binding on all the parties whose names are listed. He also enters a note or *rubrica* of the act in his consolidated chronological index of documents. It is agreed that a fuller, neater version of the contract, an *extenso*, will be produced on Lucia's request. Appended to the contract is the *disegno*, together with a copy of a list in Italian of the painter's obligations. Although neither artist nor commissioner have actually signed any of the documents at this stage, the agreement has full contractual status.

The contract, in notarial Latin and using all the normal formulas and abbreviations, begins with standard protocols and the recording of the date and naming the parties. It is then noted that the 'said Master, Tomaso di Ser Benedetto, painter and worthy master [using his real name] of the quarter of Sto. Spirito has agreed to make and paint and decorate at his own expense an altarpiece in the Cappella dell' Annunziata in the Chiesa di San Francesco in which is to be an image of the Annunciation of the Most Holy Virgin with Sts Giovanni Battista, Francesco and Lucia, according to the design which the painter has provided. There are also to be five small scenes of the life of Our Lady in the predella.' The main panel and all the other parts of the altarpiece are to be decorated in gold (of a specified grade and quantity), ultramarine (of a specified quantity) and other such colours as would be deemed appropriate, and the various tasks are to be undertaken according to a *lista* in Italian appended to the contract and supplied to the painter. The arms of Ser Giovanni are to be prominently displayed, as are the arms of Lucia's family. The whole must be undertaken 'by the hand of the said master Tomaso' and he is to undertake no other commission until the present work is finished. 'The whole is to be as large and fine as the altarpiece in the neighbouring chapel of St Jerome, painted by the hand of Fra Filippo Lippi, and everything is to be undertaken according to the wishes of the Prior.' It is to be finished in eighteen months, and the painter is responsible for its installation and the rectifying of any faults. Additionally, the painter is responsible for any defects appearing within ten years.

A total sum of 120 *fiorini larghi d'oro* is set aside, with 20 to be paid in advance. The painter is to receive board and lodging in the monastery for himself and one assistant (including laundry expenses and wine). On delivery, a remaining sum between 80 and 90 *fiorini* is to be paid. The exchange rate of one florin as equivalent to 80 *soldi* (or 4 *lire*) is noted and guaranteed. The price is broadly in line with other commissions for altarpieces, but there was nothing that could be called a 'standard' price in the Renaissance, since the sums agreed between artists and patrons varied in a surprising manner, even under apparently similar circumstances, as will be seen in chapter IV. Top Florentine artists could generally command the highest fees, but the financial aspects of each contract seem to have been agreed individually on an opportunistic basis in relation to a variety of factors and market pressures. Additional provision in our contract is made for an estimate (a *lodo* or *stima*) to be provided by parties named below. In the event of a *lodo* being required, the painter names Alessandro Amico as his 'friend', while Ser Jacopo de' Ciechi is charged with acting on behalf of the heirs of Ser Giovanni. The painter additionally appoints Niccolò Abbondanza as his guarantor, should he default on the contract, and penalty clauses are agreed, covering both painter and patron. The contract ends with a few standard protocols, which no one bothers to read.

Subsequently, the advance payment of 20 florins is handed over, as recorded in the *Libro dei debitori e creditori* (the ledger of debtors and creditors) of the monastery. The account is recorded in florins, and in the standard book-keeping currencies, *lire*, *soldi* and *denari*. It was possible for the painter to be paid in gold coinage (florins, ducats, *scudi* etc, depending on locality), but payment in silver *denari*, the normal coinage for daily transactions, was more common. Since the relative value of silver coinage decreased over time and varied in different places, the guaranteeing of payment in the equivalent of the more stable gold units ensured that any downwards revaluation of the *lira* against the gold *fiorino* would be beneficial to the painter. The same book of debtors and creditors also records two further down-payments (totalling 30 *fiorini*) passed to the artist for the carver of the frame and for the *metodoro* to undertake the gilding, although such interim payments were not specifically envisaged in the contract. Although work starts on time, and some progress is made, the painter is in great demand and he is commanded by the local marchese to undertake a number of tasks, including the designing and painting of street and theatre decorations to celebrate the marriage of his daughter to a French duke. Eighteen months pass, and another year. Loosing patience, the prior and Lucia require Ser Jacopo, acting as their procurator, to bring the artist to heel. The procurator reports that the panel has been inspected in the painter's workshop and remains unfinished. Under threat of sequestration of the unfinished panel, the artist duly promises to finish it within six months, promising that it will be as beautiful as anything to be seen in the city, but he protests that his expenses for gold and other materials mean that he will be out of pocket. Eventually, eight months later, the altarpiece is installed, and estimated by mutual agreement and without recourse to outside parties to be worth a further 60 florins (over and above the advance payments of 50 already received), which is duly handed over to Imbrattatore in the equivalent amount of *denari* according to the stipulated rate of 80 *soldi* per florin.

I should be very surprised if any actual episode corresponded to all the complex mix of details in the narrative of this fictional account, but the great majority of agreements can be seen to have worked various permutations on the component parts of my invented commission – problems and all. Surviving documentation also indicates that disputes over completion and payment were far from uncommon, though it may be that a dispute occasioned a larger body of documentation and resulted in a greater chance of its survival and publication. Impatience with artists was expressed with some regularity, and almost seems to have been an expected part of the process. Documented incidents which lie outside my fictional scenario can be considered unusual to greater or lesser degrees or specific to the particular circumstances which pertained in an individual commission. Although there would also be variations from city to city, since contractual law varied, and the stock notarial formulas and procedures were not necessarily the same, the general framework for contracts was similar throughout Italy. Parallels can also be found outside Italy. For instance, the contract signed between John Thornton and the Dean and Chapter of York Minster for the great East window in 1405 requires that within three years the glazier should use his '*scientia*' to 'portray with his own hands in the best manner and form . . . the historical images and other painted work'.[38] In addition to his remuneration of 4 shillings a week and payments of 100 shillings for each year, he would receive 10 silver pounds if the Dean and Chapter were fully satisfied.

Formal contracts drawn up by a notary were not the only kind of contractual agreement by which an artist might be legally bound to produce a work. Very occasionally, as when Cima da Conegliano and a frame carver contracted in 1513 to make a polyptych for Capodistra (Koper), the legal obligation was recorded in a memorandum in the artist's own hand and signed by witnesses.[39] More commonly, the record of an official body to the effect that agreement had been reached with a supplier served as a binding record of contract. If a guild noted in its minutes or *ricordanze* that a certain sculptor had agreed to provide a statue on certain terms, this agreement would have contractual status, whether or not the artist was recorded as present and had actually signed anything. Thus on 26 August 1418 the Arte del Cambio (Money Changers' and Bankers' Guild) recorded that designated officials, 'after holding a diligent and secret scrutiny among themselves and taking a vote with black and white beans' decided to commission a statue of their patron saint, St Matthew, from Lorenzo Ghiberti (fig. 14).[40] In this instance, Ghiberti was actually present and the record was formally signed. The sculptor agreed that his new figure should be 'at least as large as the present figure of St John the Baptist' which he had previously made for the Arte di Calimala (Cloth Merchants'), that it should not exceed in weight 2,500 pounds, that the extent of gilding would be decided in due course, and that it should be delivered and installed within three years. His salary was to be at the discretion of the consuls, regardless of what he had been paid for the St John.

A comparably binding record of a contractual agreement in an organisation's record-book occurs in the minutes of the Scuola di S. Marco in Venice.[41] The Venetian Scuole were influential associations of citizens established for religious observance, mutual support and charity. As one of the prominent Scuole Grandi, the Scuola di S. Marco played an important role in the life of the maritime republic. In 1492 'Messer Gentile Bellini (at present our most worthy

14. Lorenzo Ghiberti, *St Matthew*, Florence, Or San Michele

Guardino da matin) and his peerless brother Messer Giovanni Bellini' agreed to provide paintings on canvas to decorate the hall of the Scuola. The new paintings had been necessitated by a destructive fire, and the brothers were additionally motivated by devotion to the memory of 'their late father Messer Jacopo Bellini, who worked in the said Hall before the burning of the Scuola'. The long-term family association with the Scuola and Gentile's official position as *guardino* (a largely honorary position) helps explain why 'no arrangement is made concerning the fee, nor shall any other arrangement be made, save with reference to their work, their conscience and the discretion of experienced and intelligent persons'. The very large painting on which they were commencing for the upper hall was to contain 'such stories and works as shall be detailed by the Scuola, though in accordance with the advice and opinion of the two brothers'. The building up of such trust between a Venetian Scuola and the workshop of a favoured 'house artist' or favoured partnership seems not to have been uncommon, and Tintoretto achieved a comparable position with the Scuola di S. Rocco in the second half of the next century. Such relatively stable relationships were less common in Florence, but organisations such as guilds, confraternities and religious orders did build up effective working relationships with particular artists, and Ghiberti achieved a position of considerable power and trust at Or San Michele as the campaign of decoration of the interior and exterior progressed.

The provision of stable income for painters was rare outside the courts, but a

43

few civic authorities did see the advantage of securing the residential services of a major master, in the face of possible outside competition. The official 'painter to the state' in Venice in the fifteenth century was accorded the handsome annual salary of 300 ducats, with all-round responsibilities for paintings, mosaics and other visual manifestations of the Republic's ambitions.[42] In 1474 and 1478 Gentile and Giovanni Bellini each received appointment from the Greater Council in Venice as a 'broker to the Warehouse of German Merchants' (*Sanseria del Fondaco dei Tedeschi*), an income-bearing sinecure, in return for which the painters were to be responsible for the continuing repair and provision of paintings of the Great Council Hall.[43] Dürer, who visited Venice for the second time in 1505-6, claimed to have been offered a salary of 200 ducats to stay.[44] In 1513-14 the ambitious Titian petitioned to move alongside the aged Giovanni as the officially favoured painter of the Republic, having, as it happens, already been responsible with Giorgione for exterior wall paintings on the Fondaco dei Tedeschi.[45] Titian's references to offers from Pope Leo X and 'other Signori' carry the clear threat that he might be lost to the city. In the winter of 1515-16 Titian renewed his bid for the next available *Sanseria*, offering in a petition to Doge Loredan to undertake a major canvas for the Great Council Hall for no advance payment, other than for paints and for one of his two assistants, and for a final fee of 400 ducats, 'half of that which was once promised to Perugino'.[46] Perhaps alert to the Venetian precedent, the town of Brescia agreed in 1489 to the petition of their native son, Vincenzo Foppa, who had made a name for himself in Milan, that he should be granted 50 ducats annually for teaching and practising the 'honourable' art of painting in the city, 'especially in public buildings'.[47] The arrangement continued until 1499, when the Council voted by a substantial majority to cancel his salary. Generally, however, most of the income that painters outside courts could expect came as the result of fees for specifically contracted tasks.

In the cases both of notarial contracts and of other contractual arrangements, disputes between artist and commissioner could exceptionally reach the point at which outside parties became involved, either by their own volition or at the request of one of the parties. In 1483 Leonardo and the Milanese brothers, Evangelista and Giovanni Ambrogio de Predis, contracted with the Confraternity of the Immaculate Conception in Milan to provide the painted adornments for the large carved altarpiece which was being made for their chapel in S. Francesco Grande in Milan.[48] The *lista* appended to the contract detailed all the gilding and polychroming, such as the brocade cloak of God the Father in ultramarine and gold, as well as the middle panel on which 'is to be painted on a flat surface Our Lady with her son and the angels all done to perfection with the two prophets painted on the flat surfaces in colours of fine quality as specified above'. The incomplete documentation shows that a tangled dispute ensued and dragged on for a dozen years. At some point, probably in 1494, the painters appealed to their 'Most Illustrious and Excellent Lord' (presumably Duke Ludovico), claiming that the commissioners had valued 'the said Our Lady done in oils by the said Florentine at only 25 ducats, whereas it may be valued at 100 ducats, as is seen by the petitioner's list, and this price of 100 ducats has been offered by persons who wish to buy the said Our Lady' (fig. 5). The painters scathingly informed their Illustrious Lord that the members of the confraternity were not expert judges of painting, since 'the blind cannot judge colours', and asked that expert valuers, one for each party, should be appointed. The result of the appeal is unknown, but it did not result in the rapid resolution of the problems, since as late as 1503 the son of the original notary summarised the legal position, noting that Evangelista had died, that Leonardo was not in Milan and that the altarpiece remained unfinished. Leonardo's surviving partner had submitted his own appeal, which implies that he was trying to detach his interests from those of the absent master. A procurator was duly appointed to bring the matter to a satisfactory conclusion, but three years later two arbiters confirmed 'with their own eyes' that the picture remained unfinished, and they decreed that Leonardo must complete it within two years in 'his own hand'. This time, the legal requirements were met. By August 1508 the altarpiece was in place and the artists were granted permission to take it down temporarily to make a copy. The financial settlement of 1,000 *lire imperiali* (250 ducats) for all the painted work appears to have been significantly better than that previously offered by the confraternity, and the artists could at least see some reward for their intransigence. Additionally they had generated a second version which would command a good price. How the tangle of documentation relates to the two surviving versions is not my concern here.

Leonardo's master, Andrea del Verrocchio was no stranger to disputes which eventually dragged in outside authorities. Probably in 1466, Verrocchio had been commissioned by the Mercanzia, the guild which had overall responsibility for the regulation of Florentine trading and which had come to be dominated by the Medicean faction, to make a group in bronze of Christ and St Thomas for their niche on the exterior of Or San Michele (fig. 15) – the niche that had previously been assigned to the Parte Guelfa and had held Donatello's *St Louis of Toulouse* (fig. 16).[49] By 1480 a disagreement had arisen about the payment, and was only resolved in 1483 following a *provisione* by the Florentine government, who had a long-standing interest in the filling of the niches in the prestigious guild hall. Although the magnificent bronze group was unveiled on 21 June 1483, there were still payments outstanding in 1487, when the Signoria responded to the artist's petition. What may have been the final act of settlement was the payment of dowries for the sculptor's nieces in 1487 into the Monte di Dote (the state-sponsored dowry bank). The involvement of dowry payments in the settlement may seem strange to us, but the provision of dowries played important social and financial roles. When Leonardo was commissioned to undertake the panel for the main altarpiece for S. Donato a Scopeto in 1481, payment was offered in terms of property in Valdelsa, and the artist himself was to deposit money in the Monte to provide a dowry for the 'daughter of Salvestro di Giovanni'.[50] As it transpired, Leonardo met neither of his obligations. The panel of the *Adoration of Magi* remained unfinished, and the monks themselves deposited 28 gold *fiorini larghi* in the Monte so that interest would accrue and the young lady could receive her dowry in due course.

Verrocchio had himself earlier been involved in a dispute about an incomplete altarpiece which involved the civic authorities. He had been asked to provide a large panel with predellas of the *Madonna and Child with St John the Baptist and St Donatus* (fig. 13) for an oratory adjoining the cathedral of Pistoia which had been founded by Bishop Donato de' Medici in honour of a

15. Andrea Verrocchio, *Christ and St Thomas*, Florence, Or San Michele

16. Donatello, *St Louis*, Florence, S. Croce, Museo

miracle-working Madonna on the exterior of the cathedral. Verrocchio was almost certainly involved in other decorative work in the oratory, including the design of Donato's tomb marker, but it was the altarpiece that caused trouble.[51] The contract has not survived, but in 1485 the Pistoian Council recorded that the painting had not been supplied, although it was 'said to have been made or to lack little' more than six years previously. Since the continued absence of the altarpiece in a prestigious site was considered to be to the dishonour of the city, the council decreed that payment should be authorised by the Opera di San Jacopo (the overseers of the works of the cathedral), including customs duty and tolls, for the completion and transport of the picture. Payments during November testify that the council's intervention had the necessary effect.

Although contracts, contractual records and payments are probably the most widely cited pieces of documentary evidence in the history of Renaissance art, we would be wrong to imagine that formal written contracts were the norm for all types of painting and sculpture. Some small-scale domestic terms, such as devotional images of the Virgin and Child for a domestic setting, or the kind of terracotta busts of holy infants deemed suitable for nurseries, may well have been ordered verbally from the painter or sculptor. Some standard items, such as painted crucifixes, might well have been available on an off-the-peg basis, priced according to size and the lavishness of the materials. We should also

17. Follower of Apollonio di Giovanni, *Forziero (Cassone) with the Conquest of Trebizond*, New York, Metropolitan Museum

remember that most artists, including those we now recognise as major masters, undertook a wide range of humble decorative work in their studio, and that such work was unlikely to justify a notarial agreement on grounds of significance and cost. Lesser transactions are unlikely to be recorded in formal records, unless an account book of an unusually business-like artist survives through a series of happy chances. The records which the busy, if unremarkable, Florentine painter, Neri di Bicci, maintained between 1453 and 1475 provide an unusually clear insight into the standard business of a well-established and versatile workshop.[52] His *ricordanze* deal not only with the provision of designs and works in various media but also with other aspects of his finances, such as taking on apprentices, subcontracting, his wife's dowry and the wine produced by the country property at Ghanghalandi, in which he had apparently invested. Images of the Madonna with Saints (more than fifty) comprised the staple item in his substantial production. Neri systematically notes the agreements with customers in summary form, listing the main components, subjects, materials, sizes and prices, and subsequently records delivery and payment. His generally expeditious fulfilling of his obligations confirms that he ran his business in an orderly manner. A comparable *bottega* book covering the period 1446 to 1462 is known for the partnership of Marco del Buono and Apollonio di Giovanni, and records the painting of *cassoni* (or, more regularly, *forzieri*), the richly decorated chests which were often presented as prestigious gifts at weddings (fig. 17). No less than 173 such orders were met, such as the chest decorated for a Rinuccini-Rucellai wedding at a cost of 25 florins, or the pair made for Pierfrancesco de' Medici in 1455 together with an 'Our Lady in a round picture' for a 'high price'.[53] Apollonio's personal skill in painting *cassone* panels with Homeric subjects acted out by fashionably dressed figures earned a humanist eulogy from Ugolino Verino, in which the painter was accorded the title of the

18. Michelangelo, *The Doni Tondo (the Holy Family)*, Florence, Uffizi

'Tuscan Apelles' – rather contradicting any assumptions we might make about the humble status of 'furniture painters'.[54]

For the most part, smaller commissions or purchases are elusive. Vasari tells a revealing story about Michelangelo's involvement with the provision of a picture for the home of a patron. Although the story may be apocryphal – and, if real, any incident involving Michelangelo cannot be taken as wholly typical – the general tenor of the verbal agreement and subsequent haggling would presumably have rung true to his sixteenth-century readership. Angelo Doni, a distinguished young Florentine who was to be portrayed with his wife by Raphael, asked Michelangelo to make a round painting of the Madonna (fig. 18).[55] The round shape alluded to the *desco da parto* (birth-plate) presented to the mother of a first-born son, and its intention may have been commemorative. When the picture was finished Michelangelo wrapped it up, and it was delivered to Angelo with an 'invoice' for 70 ducats (about three-quarters of what Angelo might have been expected to pay for a full-scale altarpiece). The patron dispatched payment of 40 ducats, which was promptly returned by the painter with an enhanced request for 100 ducats. Angelo decided to settle on the original 70, but by now, ' because of Angelo's breach of faith', Michelangelo 'demanded double of what he had asked first of all, and this meant that to get the picture Angelo was having to pay 140 ducats'. What is likely to be exceptional in this incident, or in Vasari putting it forward as credible, is Michelangelo's self-proclaimed and increasingly recognised status as a 'super-artist' who could begin to dictate his own terms. Prices for works of a certain type and size by recognised masters tended to move within well-established parameters, and Vasari's Michelangelo was breaking the mould in trying to alter the financial parameters so radically.

Even many large and expensive projects would have been subject to a verbal assent or spoken *pacta* and an official delegated to watch over progress, payments etc. This situation was most likely to occur in a court context, where secretaries and treasurers oversaw the business arrangements on behalf of their lord. It is, for example, possible that when Michelangelo embarked on the ceiling of the Sistine Chapel in 1508 (fig. 19) he never entered into the standard notarial contract of the kind we reconstructed earlier, but rather that the terms were agreed with the pope and instructions issued to court functionaries, who might or might not involve a notary at some point in the process. When a team of painters, Cosimo Rosselli, Botticelli, Ghirlandaio and Perugino, was engaged in the chapel by Sixtus IV in 1481, the superintendent called in a notary to record the undertakings made by the artists – but only some time after the work had already been started on agreed terms.[56] In Michelangelo's letter of 1523 to Giovanni Francesco Fattucci summarising the financial implications of his dealings with the Julian projects, he specifically records that he 'entered into a pact [*facemo e' pacti*] for three thousand ducats' with the pope for the ceiling frescoes.[57] Thereafter, instructions to such officials as the superintendent of the fabric and treasurers would serve to control the business aspects of the undertaking. Subordination to the court functionaries could prove irksome. One of the reasons for Michelangelo's flight from Rome in 1506 was his extreme frustration at being unable to get past the officials to speak directly to Pope Julius himself about the problems he was having with the project for the pope's tomb.

When Leonardo was painting the *Last Supper* in the refectory of S. Maria della Grazie in Milan, Duke Ludovico Sforza instructed his secretary by memorandum in the summer of 1497 to press the tardy painter to complete the wall on which he was working and to turn to 'the other wall'.[58] Courts ran according to hierarchies and chains of command, and one senses that as leading painters like Leonardo increasingly harboured social and intellectual ambitions, they found being under the thumb of a plenipotentiary rather demeaning. In 1470, when Francesco del Cossa was one of a team of artists undertaking the interior decorations of the Palazzo Schifanoia in Ferrara for Borso d' Este, lord of Ferrara (fig. 20), he wrote a vigorous complaint to Borso that he was being paid at the same miserly rate per foot as 'the sorriest assistant in Ferrara'.[59] Clearly, the Ferrarese ruler did not concern himself with the day-to-day administration of the artists, and an official was handing out payment on the standard basis. We may well imagine that Francesco had been told by the official that if he had any complaint, he should set in down in writing. The petition was brusquely dismissed by the duke, and, no doubt, the relevant official bore the ill news back to the painter.

20.   Francesco del Cossa, *The Months of May, April and March*, Ferrara, Palazzo del Schifanoia

The position of artists in courts could vary greatly from that of their colleagues in urban contexts, and not all courts provided the same kind of environments and terms of employment. The most obvious model of court employment was for the artist to be designated as one of the *stipendiati*, that is to say those who received a regular emolument (if the lord's finances were in a solvent state), in return for being at the court's beck and call for all kinds of artistic and sometimes sub-artistic tasks. Some part of the income might be assured through the provision of an incoming-bearing sinecure or the granting of rights to an established money-making venture, as we will see in chapter IV. As leading Italian courts increasingly saw the value of grandly fashionable decorations, stylish portraits etc., so the demand for the few renowned masters increased, and the terms began to be more favourable than those offered to Cossa. Court households in centres of major political and economic power could be very large. In the 1470's Galeazzo Maria Sforza's immediate household in Milan comprised over one hundred members, not to mention the households of his wife and children. When he and his brother, Ludovico, visited Florence in 1471 a huge entourage of richly attired retainers accompanied them. Courts with a number of castles and palaces in their territories moved *en masse* from one property to another. A painter's traditional status in the internal pecking order of such complex and populous households was probably not all that high. Captains of the lord's forces and those responsible for his stables (particularly in Mantua where horse-breeding was a passion of the Gonzaga) were likely to have performed roles of more day-to-day prominence than the painters. Other less 'functional' *stipendiati*, most notably the rising band of humanist authors (at least those who were not primarily employed as secretaries) were obvious

19.   Michelangelo, *The Sistine Ceiling*, Rome, Vatican, Sistine Chapel

51

competitors for the ruler's attentions, and Leonardo's diatribes about the low status of painting and its inherent superiority to poetry can be read in a context of such competition. Panegyrics of rulers, especially those composed for special occasions, and laudatory dynastic histories, little read today, played important roles in the boosting of the individual ruler's status, confirming the pedigree of his rule and broadcasting the regime's virtues across a broader geographical canvas. When Raphael's father, Giovanni Santi, composed his rhyming *Chronicle* in praise of Duke Federigo da Montefeltro, ruler of Urbino, he was endeavouring to exploit one of the established routes to the courting of favour, perhaps having failed to establish himself decisively as the duke's favourite painter.[60]

In one respect, however, the artists had a distinct advantage over the poets. Their products, particularly large-scale wall paintings, potentially benefited from being highly visible at all times. The provision of a major suite of internal decoration, such as the cycles of famous men (and sometimes women) which became so fashionable, may not have cost a great sum of money in terms of total court expenditure, but they would be highly conspicuous to visiting dignitaries, who would, according to their relative status, be progressively admitted to public and more private rooms adorned with appropriate imagery. The increasing tendency for rulers to commission large-scale pieces of public art, such as fountains and equestrian memorials, which were more expensive, also gave visual artists a significance greater than that of a simple court functionary. The inclusion in Giovanni Santi's chronicle of a section on modern artists – occasioned by his account of Federigo's visit to Mantua and the duke's admiration for 'the marvellous painting and exalted art' of Mantegna, that 'high and famous talent' – is indicative of the complementary trends during the second half of the fifteenth century for patrons to accord greater importance to modern pictorial glories and for a few leading painters to claim more exalted status.[61]

Modern research has inevitably focused on a few centres which were spectacular for the scale, expenditure and quality of their patronage, and, inevitably, the presence of a major master has ensured special attention to that particular court. Thus, for Mantegna working for the Gonzaga at Mantua, there must have been dozens of lesser and now virtually unknown masters at more obscure courts who undertook interior decorations and other routine tasks by the yard. Not only has the focus of research tended to skew our attention towards the exceptions rather than the norms, but there has also been a severe attrition of secular decorative schemes. They were particularly vulnerable to changes of political regime and to the vagaries of fashion. However, since one of the major concerns of this book is the overt use of the historical record by patrons and artists in order to establish a special position for themselves, a concentration on the conspicuous cases is more than a matter of convenience.

A few artists seem to have founded their careers on their ability to satisfy the demands of courts for masters of visual effects, with a special emphasis on grand decorative schemes. Pisanello provides the first well-documented example in the fifteenth century. Having proved himself on a large scale in the extremely prestigious setting of the Doge's Palace in Venice, continuing the cycle of Venetian histories by Gentile da Fabriano that the Bellini brothers were later to be responsible for replacing, he gained major employment in the courts of Mantua, Ferrara and Naples. Diplomatic and dynastic relations between courts undoubtedly helped in transmitting an artist's reputation and gaining additional employment, much as the careers of certain painters seem to have been furthered by becoming known to a particular order of monks. In 1441 Pisanello was recorded as a *stipendiato* of the Gonzaga court in Mantua, in receipt of a salary, and in 1449 he was granted a very handsome annual income of 400 ducats as one of the royal 'familiars' at the Aragonese court of King Alfonso in Naples.[62] He had been preceded in this position at the Neapolitan court over a century earlier by Giotto, who was granted a charter as '*prothopictor familiaris et fidelis*' having been judged to possess the *probitas* and *virtus* expected of a 'familiar'.[63] Alfonso's *privilegium* for Pisanello indicates in extravagant terms that he has heard 'of the many outstanding and virtually divine attributes of Pisanello's matchless art in painting and sculpture, from the testimonies of many people'. The king now confirms with his own eyes the painter's unique 'talent and art' (*ingenium atque arte*) by means of which he seems to 'fabricate nature herself'. An ancillary advantage of employment in such a context was that the artist and his products might be caught up in the literary industry of court eulogies, and the poem on Pisanello by Guarino, the leading humanist educator in Ferrara, set in train a series of literary compositions in honour of Pisanello's particular kind of sumptuous naturalism – as we will see in chapter VI.

The Mantuan 'Sala del Pisanello' (as it was termed in 1480, when the roof had collapsed) gives a good idea, albeit in a very incomplete and damaged state, of the ambition and flavour of the kind of large-scale decorative schemes which

21.   Pisanello, *Arthurian Battle Scene*, Mantua, Palazzo Ducale, Sala del Pisanello

warranted a good salary (fig. 21). The subject matter is not drawn from classical antiquity in a humanist manner but is based on Arthurian legends, the chivalric tales in French which featured so conspicuously in the libraries of Renaissance courts, including that at Mantua. Pisanello's wall paintings would originally have presented a rich tapestry of incident painted in lavish detail, with silvered elements built up from the surface to evoke the glittering armour, and they still bear witness to his dazzling inventiveness. Along the top runs a frieze of heraldic motifs incorporating the Gonzaga marigold and the 'SS' collar of the English Royal house of Lancaster, reflecting a long-standing alliance which was confirmed in 1436 when Henrÿ VI granted Gianfrancesco the right to distribute gold 'SS' collars to fifty persons of suitable nobility. It is characteristic of the dearth of written agreements between patrons and painters in such a court context that we have no documentary evidence about the commissioning, progress or completion of the wall paintings.

If from our present-day perspective, the great Sala del Pisanello seems to provide the best indication of his significance to the court, we should not assume that our priorities necessarily match those of the original patrons. It is perhaps salutary to recall that in 1471 the Sala was adapted from a courtier's dining hall to become a kitchen for the visiting Niccolò d'Este. More positively, we can point to other aspects of Pisanello's activity as having notable and innovatory importance for his patrons. Medals are today likely to be segregated into cabinets of coins, or at best displayed in cases as supporting material for paintings, but Pisanello's pioneering role in the establishing of the medal as a prestigious and fashionable genre in humanist courts would have been a significant claim to fame, not least because the medal was seen as a very direct emulation of the revered civilisation of Rome. The cast list of Pisanello's noble 'sitters' reads like a role call of leading courtly rulers and their families – Gianfrancesco and Ludovico Gonzaga, Lionello d'Este of Ferrara, Sigismondo Malatesta of Rimini, Federigo da Montefeltro of Urbino, King Alfonso V of Naples, Filippo Maria Visconti and Francesco Sforza of Milan. A portrait medal possessed special advantages over a painting in that it was portable, could be produced in multiples, and the reverse permitted an elegantly compact image of the subject's proclaimed virtues. It was therefore eminently suitable as a diplomatic gift. Typically, a ruler would be shown in military guise on the reverse, often with strongly chivalric implications, while the humanist, Vittorino da Feltre, who ran a famed school at the Gonzaga court, was accorded the reverse of a phoenix pecking its breast to succour its young (much as the pelican was reputed to do).

A particularly impressive example depicts Cecilia Gonzaga (figs. 22-3), Gianfrancesco's daughter and an especially gifted pupil of Vittorino, who entered the convent of S. Paola in 1445, with much pomp and circumstance. Two years later the medal by Pisanello broadcast her virtues on a wider stage, through an inscription which identified her as 'Cecilia, the Virgin daughter of Giovanni Francesco first Marquis of Mantua' and an allegory on the reverse of the capture of the elusive unicorn, which could only be accomplished by an immaculate maiden. Since the marquis had earlier sought to coerce Cecilia into a dynastic marriage with the house of the Montefeltro of Urbino, his subsequent trumpeting of Cecilia's chaste virtue has something of the flavour of

22. Pisanello, *Medal of Cecilia Gonzaga (obverse)*, London, British Museum

23. Pisanello, *Medal of Cecilia Gonzaga (reverse)*, London, British Museum

opportunism, and the portrait image reveals her beauty in the kind of secular costume she wore before taking her vows. No documents of commission for such medals survive, and they were likely to have been occasioned by agreements which were not formally preserved. However, we do know that the medal of the humanist, Pier Candido Decembrio, was specifically made as a present at the behest of Leonello d'Este, who sent it to the writer with a letter on 19 August 1448: 'at last we have wrested from the hands of Pisano the Painter the coin with your likeness, and send it to you herewith, keeping a copy thereof, in order that you may understand how highly we esteem you and all that concerns you'.[64]

Pisanello's successor in Mantua, Andrea Mantegna, is the best documented of all the court artists of the fifteenth century – which is not simply an accident of survival, since he was the most famed. Like Giotto in the previous century, he was accorded such praise by writers that he became famous for being famous, and there is every indication that he worked assiduously on his own behalf to cultivate his status. When Mantegna entered the service of Ludovico Gonzaga in 1460, it was the culmination of three years of persuasion on the marchese's part. Although still young, the painter had acquired a considerable reputation, and at the age of eighteen he had painted a double portrait of Leonello d'Este of Ferrara, Ludovico's brother-in-law. A letter of 1458 sets out the marchese's terms.[65] Mantegna was to receive the decent stipend of 180 ducats a year on a monthly basis, a house, grain to feed six and supplies of firewood. His removal expenses, by boat along the Po, were also to be met. The letter also hints at further 'rewards', and in 1470 Ludovico mentions 'other privileges' granted to the artist. If the experiences of Mantegna in Mantua and Leonardo in Milan are typical, the payment of salaries tended to be erratic in courts living at the limits of their finances, but gifts of income-generating property and other concessions smoothed the problems. Mantegna received two estates, as well as investing in properties on his own account. Leonardo was given a vineyard, and granted concessions to draw a measured amount of water out of the Lombard irrigation

24.   Andrea Mantegna, *Ludovico Gonzaga and Barbara of Brandenberg with Members of their Family and Court*, Mantua, Castello di San Giorgio, Camera degli Sposi, west and north walls.

system for potential resale to other users.[66] Gifts of property were almost certainly not regarded by artists as poor replacements for unpaid salary, since property promised both capital assets and income independently of the vagaries of patronage and the patron's fortunes. Leonardo's Milanese property remained his throughout his life, in spite of repeated changes in the rulership of the city between the Sforza and the French kings. The accumulation of income from property is a topic to which we will return in chapter IV.

What did three successive Gonzaga marquises gain from what Ludovico called the 'great expense' of sustaining Mantegna's ambitious life-style? Looking at the masterly wall paintings of the Gonzaga family in the Camera degli Sposi (fig. 24), the answer seems obvious to us, and in this instance our reaction is not entirely misleading. Ludovico's father had been the dedicatee of Alberti's *On Painting*, the first humanist treatise on the worth of painting, and, even if Gianfrancesco himself may not have spent much time on bookish pursuits, the text fell on fertile ground in Vittorino's school, the Ca' Giocosa, where Ludovico and a number of the next generation of patrons were to be educated. There is every reason to think that Ludovico took good note of Alberti's statement that painting possesses a truly 'divine power', not least because of its ability to represent 'the dead to the living many centuries later'.[67] The example he cites (from Plutarch) is of Alexander, whose painted likeness caused one of the late emperor's commanders to 'tremble all over'. Ludovico's grandson, Francesco, issued a decree in 1492, donating property holdings to the painter, with effusive praise for the ability of a great artist to confer immortality on his subjects.[68] The parallels were all drawn from antiquity: King Hiero of Syracuse enhanced his fame by his friendship with Archimedes; Alexander gained glory from his favouring of Apelles and Lysippus; while Augustus is honoured for his recognition of Vitruvius. There is, of course, a caution to be applied in taking such evidence of Mantegna's status too literally. The decree is a nice piece of humanist rhetoric which brandishes ancient precedent in a stock manner in order to reward the artist with inexpensive words rather than immediate cash. As always, the nature of the document needs to be recognised in terms of the role it was designed to perform. There was a tradition of flowery praise in the charters for court 'familiars' which should not be taken too literally. If the overt puffery of the decree is set beside Mantegna's typical letter of 1479 moaning about inadequate remuneration and inferring that he was looking elsewhere for patronage, the image and the reality are put into more realistic perspective – although Mantegna clearly had well developed propensities both for spending money and complaining.[69]

During the Renaissance, the Albertian power of the painter was increasingly recognised in terms of inherent significance, if not always in direct remuneration. There is a nice piece of evidence to suggest that Mantegna's inclusion of likenesses in settings such as the Camera degli Sposi was more than a local matter of interest. In 1475 the Duke of Milan wrote in high dudgeon about his omission from the scene of the 'Meeting', when the King of Denmark and Emperor Frederick III – 'the two most wretched men in the world' – had been included.[70] Mantegna became a noted point of attraction for prestigious visitors to the court. We have already noted Giovanni Santi's record of Federigo da Montefeltro's keen inspection of Mantegna's paintings, and when Lorenzo de' Medici went out of his way to visit the city in 1483 to see its glories, he

25.   Andrea Mantegna, *The Triumph of Caesar* (Canvas IX, *Caesar on his Chariot*), Hampton Court Palace

'visited Andrea Mantegna where he looked with great pleasure at several paintings by Andrea and certain sculptures of heads with many other antique pieces'.[71] Lorenzo was subsequently the recipient of at least one precious cabinet picture by the master. Small-scale, immaculately executed paintings of ancient and religious subjects, which became one of the specialities of Mantegna's workshop, were suitable gifts for diplomatic and other purposes. In the case of the picture which Lorenzo received in 1481 and which he acknowledged by letter, the presentation seems to have been made directly by the painter, rather than from the Gonzaga.[72] The gift may be viewed in much the same light as a humanist sending the manuscript of his latest composition to a nobleman in order to curry favour and to attract potential patronage.

    One of the problems in judging the way that works were generated in a court context, is that even major projects were not subject to contractual documentation. Mantegna's great series of canvases of the *Triumph of Caesar* (fig. 25), on which he worked for a number of years, were viewed admiringly by important visitors, such as Ercole d' Este in 1486, but we do not know for whom, for where or even why they were begun. The idea that they were begun

26.   Andrea Mantegna, *Madonna della Vittoria (Madonna and Child with Saints Michael, George, Andrew, Longinus, Elizabeth and John the Baptist, with Francesco Gonzaga)*, Paris, Louvre

at the artist's own volition, as spectacular demonstrations of his power to surpass the ancients, is probably anachronistic, but the project seems to have proceeded in a different way than a commission on a straightforward contractual basis undertaken by an artist not in court employ. One factor that undoubtedly affected the progress of any single project was the likelihood of the court artist suddenly being diverted on to another task, such as decorations for a feast, or the need to make drawings of peacocks and peahens for a planned tapestry, as Mantegna was commanded to do in 1469. Just as humanist authors objected to the diversion of their energies into the production of 'occasional' pieces, we may imagine that Mantegna, like Leonardo, sometimes regretted the diversion of his time into the production of trivia and ephemera.

The best documented of Mantegna's Gonzaga commissions is the result of exceptional circumstances – in a way that stresses both that the best documented incidents may be the least typical and that the kind of opportunism which prevailed in individual projects makes it hazardous to generalise about means and motives behind even apparently comparable works. In 1496, Mantegna provided a magnificent votive altarpiece for Francesco Gonzaga (fig. 26), to celebrate the more-or-less victory at Fornovo, where the marchese had been the leader of the Italian coalition against the French and attributed his personal survival to the Virgin. On first sight, the painting appears to be a standard if unusually glorious *sacra conversazione* with a portrait of the donor. Although Mantegna has used a much lower viewpoint, the picture is in general terms comparable to the great altarpiece now in the Brera in Milan in which Piero della Francesca had portrayed Federigo da Montefeltro kneeling in armour beside the Virgin. However, the financial means behind the commission introduce a quite unexpected factor, and draw us into the anti-semitism which was not uncommon in Italian cities, whether tyrannies or republics.[73]

A wealthy Mantuan Jew had destroyed a frescoed Madonna on his house, with due permission, but a fevered and hostile atmosphere was generated, not least by the marchese's brother, Sigismondo. The legal proceedings and Sigismondo's zeal in writing to Francesco result in a remarkably full account of the motives and progress of the project. The Jew was coerced into paying for a church on the site of the destroyed image and to meeting the cost of 110 ducats for Mantegna's painting. An elaborate scheme for the painting devised by Sigismondo was revised by Francesco to focus on his relationship to the Madonna. On the first anniversary of the battle, the picture was borne triumphantly from Mantegna's house to the new church, accompanied by a *tableau vivant* of God the Father, two prophets, three little angels and the Twelve Apostles, perhaps designed and costumed by Mantegna himself. The celebration set a deadline for the completion of the picture in a way that was very different from the protracted execution of the Camera or the canvases of Caesar. There is no obvious trace of the anti-semitic motives in the painting itself, unless the presence of the prophetic St John is designed to underline that Christ was indeed the King of the Jews, to whose coming John was a direct witness by proclamation (*ecce agnus Dei*, Behold the Lamb of God) and baptism. However, knowing the anti-semitic component in its origins, we can align the genesis of the picture with the Corpus Domini altarpiece for Urbino, in which the *Institution of the Eucharist* by Justus of Ghent and Uccello's predella of the

27. Paolo Uccello, *The Jew Attempts to Destroy the Host (*Scene 2 from the Predella of the *Profanation of the Host)*, Urbino, Galleria Nazionale delle Marche

bloody story of a Jewish pawnbroker who attempts to destroy the host (fig. 27) allude to similar hostility to unconverted Jews. Indeed, viewed in this light, the Mantuan and Urbinate altarpieces are symptomatic of efforts in many Italian centres to combat Jewish usury, a theme which runs prominently through Italian culture in this period and which has subsequently become best known through its English manifestation in Shakespeare's *Merchant of Venice.* The most tangible result of the Italian campaign was the establishment of sponsored banks, the Monti, some of which still survive today. Without the chance survival of the documentation, we would stand virtually no chance of reconstructing the chain of Renaissance anti-semitism which connects the two altarpieces with each other and with present-day institutions.

Rulers of courts were, of course, involved in many dealings with artists outside their own immediate orbit. Indeed, it was probably unusual for many courts, particularly smaller ones, to be able to call on the services of the same resident artist over a number years. Members of leading courts corresponded with each other when they were seeking masters to perform specific tasks, as when Ludovico Sforza wrote to Lorenzo de' Medici in 1489, asking if he could suggest two specialist masters to undertake the great equestrian monument he was planning in honour of his father.[74] Apparently, the duke had lost confidence in Leonardo's ability to complete the daunting task of casting his colossal model in bronze. There was even a kind of export trade in good masters for diplomatic purposes. When Lorenzo was courting favour in Rome to obtain the cardinal's hat for his teenage son, Giovanni, his dispatch of Filippino Lippi to decorate the chapel of the influential Cardinal Caraffa in S. Maria sopra Minerva with frescoes and altarpiece of the most fashionable kind (fig. 28) certainly did his cause no harm. In 1488 Caraffa wrote with pleasure that he had acquired the services of the painter whose commendation by Lorenzo places him 'above Apelles', although he noted impatiently that Filippino still had to report to him.[75] The artist deemed it prudent to write a placatory letter to Filippo Strozzi,

28. Filippino Lippi, *Altar Wall of the Caraffa Chapel*, Rome, S. Maria sopra Minerva

whose chapel he had abandoned in Florence. Although apologetic, Filippino cannot resist telling his Florentine patron that his 'good Lord' in Rome is paying him 250 large gold florins 'for my mastery alone', in making marble adornments for the altar, in addition to normal costs. Cosimo de' Medici had earlier used architects' services as diplomatic gifts, sending Luca Fancelli to Mantua and Filarete to Milan. Mantegna's move to Rome in 1488 resulted from Francesco Gonzaga's lending of his services to Pope Innocent VIII in Rome, where he undertook an influential and much admired chapel decoration, which was destroyed in 1780. Francesco's correspondence reveals considerable anxiety that his prized painter might settle permanently in the Holy City.[76]

More typical than the actual dispatch of an artist, was the employment of a master in another city by remote control. Needless to say, such employment at a distance could cause problems. Not only was direct pressure for speedy delivery difficult to sustain, even with someone local detailed to act on the patron's behalf, but there were also difficulties in controlling the form, quality and content of the work. The correspondence of Francesco Gonzaga's wife, Isabella d' Este, one of the most highly motivated patrons in the Renaissance, illustrates both the nature of the problems and the exceptionally assertive vigour with which she personally attempted to exercise effective control.

Isabella's most notable projects involved the decoration of her successive suites of small rooms in the palazzo at Mantua. Amongst these, her *studiolo* involved the commissioning of a highly innovatory suite of paintings, initially from the ageing Mantegna and subsequently from 'the most excellent artists in Italy'.[77] Perugino in Florence was one of the painters she had talent-spotted, and he was commissioned to undertake a canvas of the *Battle between Lasciviousness*

29. Pietro Perugino, *Battle between Lasciviousness and Chastity*, Paris, Louvre

and Chastity (fig. 29). Poor Perugino was shackled with the most pedantic and detailed instructions about content, which worked against any pictorial coherence. Her 'poetic invention', which she sent to the painter in the form of a drawing and written description in 1503, involved a 'fundamental' group of Pallas and Diana fighting against Venus and Cupid, together with a host of secondary motifs, including the rape of Europa, Polyphemus and Galatea, Phoebus and Daphne, and Pluto and Proserpina. Perugino was granted the licence to reduce the number of secondary motifs, but still found it necessary to inform Isabella at the end of the year that the consequence of her instructions would be that the height of the figures would be too small for the picture. In reply, he received a length of string to ensure that the size of the largest figures would be consistent with Mantegna's neighbouring canvas. When she heard that Perugino was 'perverting the whole sentiment of the fable' by departing from the drawing 'to show off the excellence of his art', she instructed Agostino Strozzi to impress upon the painter that he should in no way depart from her instructions. When the picture was eventually supplied, for the standard price of 100 ducats, she received it rather coolly, criticising its finish and his failure to employ oils rather than tempera.

30.   Giovanni Bellini, *Baptism of Christ*, Vicenza, S. Corona

The impression which emerges is very much that of the Isabella who threatened to imprison the painter and intarsia makers who were working on her second 'grotta' (another smallish room for cultural treasures). However, she was capable of recognising that some artists needed to be humoured rather than pushed around. When her agent in Venice, Michele Vianello, was pestering Giovanni Bellini on her behalf to provide a painting for the standard sum of 100 ducats, he informed her that the painter had reacted very adversely to the 'story' she provided, since 'he cannot devise anything good out of the subject at all'. She eventually reconciled herself to receiving what Bellini himself wanted to supply, if anything at all. She also dealt with the recalcitrant Leonardo with some deference, when she repeatedly encouraged her representatives in Florence to obtain a picture painted 'with that air of sweetness and suavity in which your art peculiarly excels' – though without apparent success.[78] It is symptomatic of the problems of patronage-at-a-distance that Florimond Robertet, a French patron of substantial diplomatic clout, seemingly had to wait for eight years for the resumption of direct contact with Leonardo in Milan to obtain the *Madonna* he had requested from the artist in 1499.

Against these well documented problems, we must probably set a large number of more routine export transactions which did not occasion agitated correspondence. Venetian masters seem to have made almost as many altarpieces for dispatch to the regions and other territories as for the city itself. Cima da Conegliano, for example, working in Venice supplied an altarpiece of the most polished and professional standard for a city as far off as Parma.[79] When Giovanni Bellini undertook his great painting of the *Baptism* (fig. 30) for the altar founded by Battista Graziani, Count Palatine, in the church of S. Corona in Vicenza, less than two years appear to have elapsed from its ordering to its installation in its extremely grand stone frame.[80] The transport of such a large picture was a considerable undertaking, not without hazards. The most famous mishap involved the Raphael painting of *Christ Carrying the Cross*, known as the *Spasmo di Sicilia*. Vasari tells how the picture was intended for S. Maria dello Spasmo in Palermo, but the ship delivering the picture was driven off course by a storm and wrecked. Miraculously (in the literal sense, according to Vasari) the picture in its crate was washed up undamaged on the beach at Genoa.[81] It took the intervention of the pope to release the picture from Genoan clutches, so that it could be delivered to its proper destination.

If the ordering of paintings from distant centres caused difficulties, it is probably true to say that sculpture caused even greater problems. The authorities in charge of the works in the Sienese cathedral and baptistery endured eighteen years of frustration in attempting to obtain prestigious works from various permutations of resident and Florentine artists to complete their new font (fig. 31). The story can be followed in a substantial series of documents, including letters, legal proceedings and most notably in three types of account book kept by the cathedral Opera, the *memoriale* (the bursar's annual records), the *entrata-uscita* (the incomes and outgoings) and the *Libro dei debitori e creditori*.[82] The project involved payments to numerous individuals: local stone cutters, quarriers and transporters (including the settling of necessary taxes and duties); various craftsmen and suppliers specialising in different materials; the Sienese sculptor, Jacopo della Quercia, and the goldsmiths,

31. *Baptismal Font*, Siena, Baptistery

Turino di Sano and Giovanni Turini; the noted Florentines, Ghiberti and Donatello; and the various assistants and specialists employed by the main contractors. The complex business involved much coming and going between Siena and Florence, with Ghiberti being paid expenses and offered generous hospitality for at least three visits to Siena, and various Sienese being reimbursed for journeys to Florence to visit the Florentine sculptors and to purchase bronze. As time dragged on and completion seemed forever elusive, the authorities took various measures to force the sculptors to meet new deadlines. Indeed, Donatello, who was assigned one of the reliefs originally commissioned from Jacopo, seems to have been brought into the project specifically to expedite matters. As we have already noted, Donatello's *catasto* return of 1427 records that he is owed 180 florins for his *Feast of Herod* (fig. 12). Amongst his debts he notes that he is due to pay 'Jacopo di Piero, carver, of Siena' 48 florins and Giovanni Turini 10 florins for work on the 'narrative scene', while the cathedral administrator is owed '25 florins for gilding'.[83] At one stage, intended payments to the Florentines were rescinded, and a formal condemnation of Jacopo della

Quercia was issued, together with a fine. The notably detailed documentation does not cast the main sculptors in a happy light, but it does vividly illustrate the complex management and finance required for a collaborative project involving workers in different centres.

We have already mentioned the difficulties with Verrocchio's altarpiece for Pistoia (fig. 13), but at least these were satisfactorily resolved. His more important sculptural project for the marble monument to Niccolò Forteguerri in the cathedral at Pistoia remained incomplete at his death in 1488, which must have been all the more frustrating for the commissioners, since they had gone through a lengthy procedure to ensure that the right artist was selected.[84] Forteguerri was a prominent cardinal in Pius II's Rome, and a patron of some importance who had endowed a charitable college, the Pia Casa di Sapienza, in Pistoia. Following his death in 1473, his native city decided to honour the cardinal with a memorial, and a group of commissioners was set up to supervise the operation. Five sculptors submitted models, but the quoted price of 350 florins for the preferred scheme by Verrocchio exceeded the available sum. The Pistoian council decided to levy a customs tax to meet the higher price and the commissioners confirmed Verrocchio's contract. Meanwhile, the Sapienza and their allies had asked Piero Pollaiuolo to provide an alternative design which they favoured on the grounds that 'it appears to us more beautiful and of more artistic worth, and more pleasing to the wishes of Messer Piero, brother of the said Monsignore, and of all his family, and similarly to us and to all the citizens of our city who have seen it'. In 1477, to resolve the conflict of opinions, the cathedral authorities, the Sapienza and the elected citizens jointly wrote for arbitration to Lorenzo de' Medici, whom they knew to be 'most full of intelligence' in such matters and whose status in Tuscany would shield them from further aggravation. Il Magnifico decided in favour of Verrocchio, and by 1483 the memorial was said, with some exaggeration, to have been 'in large part brought to a conclusion'.

After Verrocchio's death, Lorenzo di Credi contracted to complete the monument, having taken charge of seven of the marble figures that Verrocchio had made in their Florentine *bottega*. In 1489 the Pistoians were told that 'it is said to be finished', and all the carved figures were subsequently dispatched from Florence. However, the final assembly still involved some extensive work, especially of an architectural nature, and only in 1514 was a contract for its erection agreed with another sculptor, Lorenzetto Lotti. In the event, the monument did not assume its final form until the eighteenth century. The difficulties caused by the commissioning of a monument to a Roman cardinal who had lived in Viterbo for the Pistoian cathedral from a sculptor in Florence stand in sharp contrast to the relatively expeditious completion of the bronze and marble tomb of Pope Innocent VIII in St Peter's in Rome between 1492 and 1498 by the Pollaiuolo brothers and their workshop. The pressure for completion of a papal project from the cardinal who commissioned it, Lorenzo Cibo, and the available moneys – some 4,000 ducats – lent greater urgency to the project than the Forteguerri commission had for Verrocchio, who had become heavily committed to the bronze equestrian memorial for Bartolommeo Colleoni in Venice.[85]

The protracted nature of the Forteguerri project unhappily anticipates

32. Michelangelo, *Tomb of Pope Julius II*, Rome, S. Pietro in Vincoli

significant aspects of the story of Michelangelo's planned tomb for Julius II (fig. 32).[86] We have already noted Michelangelo's precipitate departure from Rome in 1506 through frustration in failing to gain direct access to the pope, and when he did return it was to be charged with the painting of the Sistine Ceiling. The original project of 1505 is described in some detail in 1553 in the biography of the artist by his pupil, Ascanio Condivi, but there is no original document describing the nature of the agreement. When Michelangelo drafted a letter in December 1523 to Giovanni Francesco Fattucci, who was a chaplain of the Florentine cathedral and who was in Rome attempting to unscramble the sculptor's financial dealings with Julius and his executors, he recalled that he had made 'many designs' to show Julius, who approved one of them, and 'we struck a deal' (*facemo el mercato*) to undertake the tomb for 10,000 ducats. Drawings by Michelangelo or from his workshop of the type submitted in conjunction with a contract have survived. The example in New York (fig. 33) has been claimed as autograph and identified with the 1505 project – and, in any event, it does show the type of drawing that was produced for such contractual purposes. The agreement, the *mercato*, would have been legally binding, and may have involved a notary at some stage, but probably was not recorded in precisely the same kind of standard contract as was subsequently agreed with Julius's executors on 13 May 1513 after the Pope's death. Michelangelo told Fattucci in 1523 specifically that 'a contract was made' (*si fece uno chontratto*) in this second phase. Late in 1505 Michelangelo had himself already entered into contracts for the shipment of substantial 'cartloads' of marble from Carrara and with two stonemasons for the provision of marble blocks.

The contract of 1513 with Julius's executors, Cardinal Aginensis (Lionello Grosso della Rovere) and Cardinal Santiquattro (Lorenzo Pucci), to produce a tomb with forty statues, was accompanied by 'a drawn model or figure' (*unum designum modellum seu figuram*). He was to be paid 13,000 ducats in addition to the 3,500 he had already received and was to finish the tomb in seven years, undertaking no other work which would interfere with its execution. The payments were to be made monthly at the rate of 200 ducats for the first two years and 136 thereafter. In an appended undertaking in Italian, Michelangelo certifies his obligations, with respect to the dimensions, form and sculptural adornments of the tomb – 'as is seen in a little model in wood' – but with no mention of the identity of the individual statues, with the exception of the image of Julius himself which was to be accompanied by four angels. It seems that the sculptor set vigorously to work, and on 9 July Michelangelo subcontracted Antonio da Pontassieve to make the front face of the tomb, 30 *palmi* wide and 17 high, which appears to be larger than either the 1505 scheme (12 *braccia*, i.e. 24 *palmi*) or that agreed earlier in 1513 (20 *palmi*). However, in spite of the best efforts of the executors and the political leverage exercised by successive della Rovere Dukes of Urbino, more powerful forces intervened. The new pope, Leo X, was a member of the Medici family, who were recently reinstated as effective rulers in Florence, and in 1516 Michelangelo entered into a contract for the facade of the Medicean church of S. Lorenzo in his native city. This contract was preceded by a renegotiation with Julius's heirs, and a new agreement stated (with undue optimism) that Michelangelo was now to work on the tomb project to the exclusion of all others of 'major moment'.

33. Michelangelo (?), *Design for the Tomb of Pope Julius II*, New York, Metropolitan Museum

To facilitate work, a house in Rome was made available by Cardinal Aginensis. Realising that the huge amount of work required by the figurative sculpture for the tomb was now unrealistic, the executors and Michelangelo settled for a grand wall tomb with twenty-two statues rather than the more temple-like structures earlier envisaged. Inevitably, the Medicean facade project tended to take precedence, given papal pressure, and matters were not helped by the deposing of Francesco Maria della Rovere in 1516 as Duke of Urbino in favour of Lorenzo de' Medici. Briefly, with the reign of Pope Adrian VI (1521-3), the tomb again assumed priority. The new pope, having reconfirmed Francesco Maria as Duke of Urbino, authorised a *motu proprio* binding the sculptor to return the moneys he had received with interest 'if Michelangelo is unwilling to execute the tomb'. However, the advent of a second Medici pope, Clement VII, meant that Michelangelo was again hauled into Medicean employ, this time to work on the funerary chapel (the New Sacristy) in S. Lorenzo rather than on the abandoned facade project. Some years of inconclusive haggling followed between Michelangelo and Julius's executors, with a threat of legal action in 1525, which induced Michelangelo to consider the return of some of the money so that others could complete the work. Matters dragged on inconclusively until 1531, when Pope Clement issued a brief to the effect that Michelangelo was to work exclusively on both the tomb and the chapel. The executors resigned themselves to the signing of a contract for an even further reduced scheme on 29 April 1532, which stated that Michelangelo should finish in three years *di sua mano* [by his hand] six statues already begun, and that five statues would be contracted out to other masters. The sculptor 'promises to make and supply a new model or design . . . as he pleases [*ad suo piacere*]'. The pope was to release the sculptor for two months a year for the work on the tomb. Michelangelo was to contribute 2,000 ducats, *in lieu* of the house and the value of the marbles he already held, and, in the event of default, he would be held liable under the terms of the 1516 contract.

In 1536, with completion still apparently distant, Pope Paul III, who was no less keen than his Medici predecessors to retain Michelangelo's services, issued a *motu proprio* freeing the sculptor of his obligations to Julius's heirs. Strained negotiations with Guidobaldo della Rovere, now Duke of Urbino, resulted in Michelangelo's petition to the pope in 1542 indicating that he was proposing to produce one statue wholly by his own hand, the *Moses*, and to subcontract all other work, including the completion of figures already begun. The duke, however, was insistent that the three statues, the *Moses*, the *Active Life* and the *Contemplative Life*, should be 'entirely undertaken and finished by your hand', and ratification of the contract was delayed until Michelangelo had acquiesced. Various subcontracts were subsequently issued, most notably to the sculptor Raffaello da Montelupo to complete five statues, and Raffaello in turn contracted the herms on the pilasters to 'Jacomo my pupil'. One of the contracts with stonecarvers was signed on Michelangelo's behalf by three of his friends, Gianotti, Bracci and del Riccio.

During all this wearisome process, of which I have provided only a simplified outline, Michelangelo was well aware that he was vulnerable to the charge that he had broken contracts and received substantial payments for little return, but he was at the mercy of power games that were beyond his control. Dead popes exercised less muscle than living ones – at least on earth. He wrote wearily that 'labour and trust have ruined me, and it's still going from bad to worse. It would have been better if in my early years I had set myself to making matches.' The tomb in its final form in Julius's titular church of S. Pietro in Vincoli, as finally erected on Michelangelo's behalf in 1545, is no less heterogeneous in effect than the Forteguerri monument, and falls far short of the grandiose ambitions with which the pope and sculptor embarked on the project. The Medici, in their turn, were to encounter similar frustration, when Michelangelo departed from Florence for good in the summer of 1534 to enter long-term papal employment, leaving the sculptures in the Medici Chapel in S. Lorenzo incomplete and scattered across the floor.

The saga of the Julius tomb is unusually full of grand vicissitudes, but the underlying problems are not atypical of complex undertakings requiring many hours of labour, involving many other workers and conducted over a time-scale which leaves them vulnerable to fluctuations of political and economic fortune. Although it has been popularly assumed that Michelangelo worked in heroic isolation even on large-scale projects, the production of the Julius tomb, which was originally intended to involve a large, free-standing architectural structure and bronze reliefs, could not but have involved a large team of diverse craftsmen and dealings with various suppliers and subcontractors. It has been estimated that Michelangelo's labours on the unfinished New Sacristy at S. Lorenzo in Florence involved his relationship with some three hundred persons on an occasional or regular basis. The financial complications were legion, and a series of different legal instruments were employed during the course of the tomb project – a *mercato*, various *contratti*, a *motu proprio* (on two occasions), an action to sue, a papal *breve*, and a formal petition.

The documentation of the Siena fonts and the Julius tomb, though differing in their immediate circumstances, tell not dissimilar stories in legal and administrative terms. What is exceptional in the primary sources available for Michelangelo's project is the group of vivid letters written by the artist, which not only provide some evidence about the progress of the statues but also give an unrivalled insight into his personal feelings at key moments. To some extent the survival of Michelangelo's letters is a reflection of the pious preservation of his legacy, but it seems improbable that any earlier artist, say Donatello, was involved in a comparable campaign of personal correspondence. Michelangelo's letter-writing, at least as far as some of the set-piece communications are concerned, reflects a self-conscious desire to establish his position and set down his thoughts in writing. A certain portion of his correspondence may be viewed as a humanist phenomenon, since letter-writing had become a consciously cultivated art. The impulse behind his more studied letters is related to that which gave vent to his poetry. The nature and implications of the written records produced by artists will be examined in a later chapter, but we need to be alert at this stage to the fact that a letter is not simply a neutral record. If we wish to interpret evidence in artists' letters about dealings between them and their patrons, we need to take into account what kind of letter we are reading. A complaint to his father in Florence, explaining why he had limited money to send home, was (and is) to be read in a different manner from a communication addressed to one of the Medici. The famous letter of December 1523 to

Fattucci, who was acting on the sculptor's behalf to resolve the financial entanglements with the della Rovere, needs to be read in the light of the function of that letter, the questions which had previously been asked by its intended recipient and Michelangelo's desire to present his case in the most favourable light.

It is relatively rare to find a series of letters shedding such revealing light on earlier commissions. The much quoted nature of the examples that do survive, most notably Isabella's lively exchanges, give a rather misleading impression of the likelihood of sustained correspondence providing significant insights into the processes by which the form and content of works were determined in the earlier phase of the Renaissance. However, those letters which were occasioned by particular circumstances, and which have chanced to survive, do give valuable evidence of the relationship between clients and artists and of the kind of issues they more normally settled face-to-face. Geographical separation between the artist and patron provides the motive for most of the known interchanges of this kind. A group of four particularly nice letters involves Piero de' Medici, who was a substantial patron in Florence well before the death of his father, Cosimo, in 1464.[87]

Piero particularly liked works of a rich and sumptuous kind on both large and intimate scales. Tapestries and illuminated manuscripts gave him particular pleasure. In 1441 Matteo de Pasti, illuminator and medallist who was later to become Alberti's architectural associate, was in Venice providing the illustrations for a manuscript of Petrarch's *Trionfi*, the allegorical poems which were particularly favoured subjects for sumptuous illuminations. Matteo writes enthusiastically that he has found a new way of painting with ground gold which allows him 'to enrich it so that you have never seen the like'. He follows this piece of encouragement with a request for 'your instructions for the other fantasies (*fantasie*), so that I can visualise them'. He has specific questions about the *Triumph of Fame*: 'I don't know if you want the seated woman in a short gown or in a mantel, as I would like. For the rest, I know what is to go into it, that is, the chariot with the four elephants. And I don't know if you want shield bearers and maidens behind, or famous men of the past, so tell me all of it.' Matteo clearly expected his patron to take the same kind of detailed interest as Isabella was to do, but we cannot take such concern as typical of all commissioners.

Piero's detailed oversight of commissions is confirmed by a letter written in 1459 by Benozzo Gozzoli, when he was painting the brilliant cavalcade of the kings in the chapel in the Medici Palace, for which Filippo Lippi provided the altarpiece (fig. 34). The letter was sent to Piero in his country villa of Careggi. The painter had been informed by letter that 'the seraphs . . . are out of place'. Benozzo argues that they are largely obscured by clouds and do not 'deform the picture at all'. However, he agrees to add 'two little clouds' to 'take them away'. After complaining about the effect that the hot weather was having on his plaster – Piero had retreated to the more pleasant air of the country – he drops a hint that his master should come to inspect his work, since he 'cannot improve it without knowing what is wanted'. We also learn that he has received 2 florins from Roberto Martelli, who was acting as paymaster, which was 'enough for the time being'. Money, as always, was a significant concern of letters written by artists. Ten years earlier, Fra Filippo Lippi had written a whining letter to Piero explaining that he was 'one of the poorest fathers in Florence', and that 'God has left me with six nieces to find husbands for, all sickly and useless'. If, as Piero had insisted, he was unwilling to pay more for the picture, Fra Filippo pleads with 'tears in my eyes', for 'your house and a little corn and wine', which 'you could debit to my account'.

The earliest of the letters to Piero, written by Domenico Veneziano, is of exceptional interest for what it tells us about the ambitions of the new breed of painter. Domenico learnt that 'Cosimo has decided to have made a painted altarpiece, and he wants a magnificent work'. The project in question was almost certainly the new high altar for San Marco, where Cosimo was conducting a radical campaign of modernisation. The painter sees his obvious rivals as Fra Angelico and Filippo Lippi, but believes that they are already too busy, whereas Domenico himself is ready to 'produce something wonderful'. In his own words he 'has a desire . . . to do some famous work, and specially for you'. He accordingly asks Piero, to whom he is obviously known already, to intercede with Cosimo to ensure that he should at least be granted a portion of the task. We may imagine that such jostling for position when a major commission was in the offing was not uncommon, and that artists sought to activate whatever line of influence was available, but it is rare to find the manoeuvres so well documented, and it is new to find such an overt claim to establish a 'name' in surviving correspondence. In the event, the commission went to Fra Angelico (fig. 35), which is hardly surprising given his prominent position in the Observant Dominicans, the order which Cosimo had installed in San Marco.

Even the relatively small selection of documents that have been cited in this chapter give some idea of the variety of potential proceedings and situations which lay behind agreements to produce a work of art. The general tenor of the written records of patrons' dealings with artists is that of the commanders and the commanded, with, if necessary, the commanders having recourse to the full force of the law. This impression is likely to be broadly accurate for all artists in the fifteenth century, although there are a few scattered signs that the exceptionally ambitious, most notably Mantegna, were becoming people who needed to be handled somewhat differently from mere servants, court functionaries or tradesmen. To some extent, this chapter's concentration on contractual arrangements and related matters is bound to paint a picture of the subordinate position of artists, because of the very nature of this kind of documentation. However, the contractual relationship, whether underwritten by legal instrument or of an more informal kind, does provide the essential framework within which all artists expected to pursue their careers.

The limits of this kind of documentation are clear. We are rarely told as much as we might like about the determination of subject matter, since contractual agreements were primarily concerned to provide adequate legal formulas for the dominant purposes of establishing a price, delivery date and quality control. Alternative mechanisms for generating content will be examined in chapter V. And we learn virtually nothing about what we would call questions of style. The shortage of any but the most general references to fine colours, beautiful ornament and worthy artistry is not surprising for a variety of reasons that will become clear in later chapters, but lack of overt reference cannot be taken to

34.   Benozzo Gozzoli, *Altar Wall of the Medici Chapel* (with copy of the altarpiece by Filippo Lippi), Florence, Palazzo Medici-Riccardi

35.   Fra Angelico, *San Marco Altarpiece (Madonna and Child with Saints Lawrence, John the Evangelist, Mark, Dominic, Francis, Peter Martyr, Cosmas and Damian)*, Florence, San Marco

mean that the more elusive aspects of a work's visual quality were not of great concern to the patron in selecting the artist or responding to the result. We also, of course, find virtually no direct reference in such documentation to questions of urgent moment to the artist-theorists, such as perspective or indeed the successful imitation of nature. We need to turn to other kinds of record to encounter such matters.

III

Ideas

The Ordering of Artistry

T HE RENAISSANCE WITNESSED the birth of an independent theory of the visual arts – or, rather its rebirth, if we take into account the lost treatises from classical antiquity, such as the famed *Canon* by Polykleitos, the Greek sculptor whose treatise dealt with the mathematical proportions of the human body. Although knowledge of the existence of the ancient treatises provided Italian theorists with an important sanction for their act of writing about the visual arts, the disappearance of the Greek and Roman texts, with the exception of Vitruvius's Latin book on architecture, meant that they could not provide the direct foundations for Renaissance writings. And, in any case, it is doubtful if the ancient authors fully anticipated Leonardo and his successors in providing a comprehensive theoretical justification for the visual arts in terms of their being founded upon a supreme form of knowledge about nature and ultimately upon the rationale of divine design in the universe.

Even to begin to talk in such terms seems already to be entering a very different world from that of the contracts which featured so prominently in the previous chapter. The apparent contrast between the artist as tradesman and artist as intellectual is certainly there, and resulted in various tensions between the business of making artefacts and higher aspirations of art, as Leonardo's testimony openly acknowledged at the time. However, we cannot simply set the theoretical text and the contract beside each other as polar opposites without asking about the respective functions of each in the complex social and mental landscapes inhabited by the most ambitious Renaissance artists and by those with whom they were involved. When we realise that the first of the free-standing texts on painting as an intellectual discipline, the little book by Leon Battista Alberti, was written in 1435 by a university-educated scholar (not a workshop painter) and humbly dedicated to a Gonzaga prince in Mantua in the hope of patronage, and that Gianfrancesco Gonzaga would have automatically expected humanists as well as artists to be subservient to his demands, we may begin to wonder if we are underrating the ability of contemporary participants to embrace stances which we take to be incompatible. As with the legal documents, we need to ask about the nature of the various theoretical texts, identifying their intended and actual roles within contemporary contexts. Why were they written, for whom, and with what effect ?

Renaissance writing about the visual arts did not of course arise in a literary vacuum. Although none of the specialist ancient treatises survived, a number of known Greek and Roman texts had dealt with aspects of the theory and practice of art without being specifically about art as such. The section in Pliny's *Natural History* devoted to the history of art, which has already featured prominently in setting up the theme of the present book, provided the richest quarry for Renaissance scholars.[88] Alberti's *On Painting* cites Pliny, explicitly or implicitly, far more extensively than any other author. There were, however, strict limits to what Pliny could teach the Renaissance. He was not writing in a specialist manner about the visual arts. Indeed, they only feature near the end of his encyclopaedic book of universal knowledge, within the section devoted to metals and stones. And his thumbnail sketches of the contributions made by individual masters within the context of his breathless survey hardly provide an adequate vehicle for a sophisticated exposition of the intellectual and aesthetic basis of art. Those remarks he did make in passing do little to suggest that he would have been capable of doing so if the opportunity had arisen. There were, however, two pre-eminent points that Renaissance writers did glean from Pliny. They found evidence that the major artists were figures of some fame and status, and they learnt that the imitation of nature in eye-catching illusions of reality was ranked as a supreme achievement. This achievement is nowhere more clearly signalled than in Pliny's story of the rivalry between Zeuxis and Parrhasius. Zeuxis proudly showed his rival a painting of grapes executed with such skill that birds were attracted to the illusory promise of the juicy fruits.[89] He was then confronted with a painting by Parrhasius covered by a curtain, but, on trying to draw back the curtain to see the image, found that the curtain was painted. Parrhasius had triumphed by fooling a man rather than dumb animals. In case we should think that such *trompe l'oeil* foolery is a low aspiration, we should note that Leonardo extolled the power of painting to achieve such 'conformity with the imitated object' that we may see 'dogs barking and trying to bite painted dogs and . . . swallows fly and perch on iron bars which have been painted as if they are projecting in front of the windows of buildings'.[90]

On the other hand, there was a persistent Platonic undercurrent to the effect that literal imitation of natural appearance was a lowly activity, not only because it was servile but also because the raw reality of natural effects as discerned through the senses was itself imperfect. Plato had argued in book X of his *Republic* that the 'idea' of an object (the conception of the archetypal form as grasped by the higher faculties of the mind) was but imperfectly realised in the material form of that object, and that its depiction as seen from a particular viewpoint, say at an angle, was yet a step further removed from the true idea. Fortunately Plato had earlier in the *Republic* provided some passing succour for the artist when he acknowledged that while some painters were tied to sensory impressions, others might aspire to reveal what is 'truly beautiful' in order to produce something that corresponds to 'what Homer described as divine and godlike when encountered among mankind'. And there was a legend that Plato himself had practised painting. In a less compromising manner, Renaissance theorists could also look to the Roman authors, Cicero and Seneca, who openly acknowledged that the best artists could gain access to the 'ideas' of a more or less Platonic kind in conceiving their beautiful images. The reconciliation of the

80

ideal with the direct imitation of nature was to become a major task for Renaissance theorists, particularly in the sixteenth century.

Much of the ancient writing which addressed the visual arts was overtly literary in tone – either because it was using art as the subject of a literary exercise (without necessarily intending to say anything about art as art) or because the visual was being used as an analogy to make a point relevant to another field, such as poetry. Perhaps the most conspicuous and highly regarded of the former was the account of Apelles's *Calumny* by Lucian, the Roman author of the second century AD. Lucian's short tract, which we encountered in the first chapter, was devoted to the subject of calumny in ethical terms, not to the art of painting, but it provided the Renaissance with fundamental evidence about the nature of Greek art. For Alberti and Leonardo, Apelles's lost picture became the supreme example of an *invenzione* – that is to say a poetic conception of the kind of subject matter that could beneficially affect a spectator. Other comparable descriptions of actual or imagined works of art from antiquity were available in the Renaissance. The *Imagines* by Philostratus, written in the third century, provided a series of comparable exemplars of story-telling pictorial inventions, describing no less than sixty-five paintings in the loggia of a Neapolitan building. The kind of word-painting or *ekphrasis* involved in the evocation of the visual images represented an important and acknowledged skill for ancient authors and their Renaissance successors.

From a Renaissance standpoint, it was Horace's *The Art of Poetry (Ars poetica)* that set the tone for the ancient use of paintings or sculpture as sources for analogies when discussing the literary arts. In the introduction to his treatise, when discussing poetic licence, Horace decried extreme incongruities in fashioning bizarre forms of hybrid animals and humans, but conceded that 'the right to take liberties of almost any kind has always been enjoyed by painters and poets alike'.[91] The idea that painters and poets were equal in daring and liberty was much quoted in the Middle Ages and Renaissance, although not always with approval if the speaker was wishing to promote sobriety in image-making. Horace's phrase *ut pictura poesis* ('as painting, so poetry') was to become one of the standard *topoi* for theorists who wished to claim imaginative powers for painting equal to those of the poet. Even if the phrase did not achieve canonical status in the period which concerns us, it does serve to encapsulate one of the major aspirations which theorists and intellectually ambitious artists set for the visual arts. A comparable point of reference, cited by Leonardo amongst others, was Simonides's dictum, quoted by Plutarch, that 'painting is dumb poetry, and poetry is speaking painting'.[92]

Since words are the vehicle for writing about visual matters, it was perhaps inevitable, given both antique precedent and convenience of expression, that Renaissance art theory should very often fit into established literary moulds. This fitting not only involved an emphasis upon the literary qualities of narrative painting, but it also involved the adapting of the relatively highly developed theories of poetics and rhetoric to the visual arts. The adopting of *invenzione* as a foundation of art is a case in point, since it gained much of its status in Renaissance eyes from its praise by Cicero as the first part of rhetoric. On a more comprehensive scale, the whole cast of Alberti's treatise *On Painting* is reminiscent of pedagogic books on verbal skills, especially Quintilian's

Institutio oratoria and Cicero's *The Making of an Orator (De oratore)*, standard Roman points of reference for Renaissance stylists of the written and spoken word. The complete text of Quintilian's book had been rediscovered with much excitement by the humanist Poggio Bracciolini at St Gall in 1415. Such literary models inevitably resulted in a skewing of attention within written texts in favour of the more literary aspects of the visual arts and the treatment of those facets of the visual appearance of paintings that could best be handled by adapting criteria from literary criticism. In writing a specialist literature about art, Renaissance authors were attempting to say something new without an established basis for saying something old. In such circumstances, there were limits on what could be said about what. Not only were the Renaissance treatises particular kinds of literary product on their own account, operating within a constrained set of functions, but they were also limited by the available verbal resources. Many conspicuous characteristics of Renaissance art simply lay outside their potential scope. Just because something was not (or could not be) discussed, does not mean that it was unimportant to patrons, artists or viewers.

The medieval legacy in Renaissance writing on art is less easy to handle than the ancient precedents. This difficulty arises partly from the fragmentary nature of the medieval discussions, but more seriously from the hidden nature of that legacy. The hiding is both a result of natural continuities, in which some of the baggage of assumptions from medieval thought passed unexceptionably and unnoticed into Renaissance frameworks, and a consequence of overt strategies on the part of the Renaissance authors, who often preferred to parade their knowledge of antiquity (however imperfect) over what they had inherited from their immediate background. However, when we realise that the dominant function of most large-scale art in the Renaissance was to provide subjects for Christian devotion, we may reasonably expect to find powerful continuities in the forms and functions of art between the Middle Ages and the Renaissance. Indeed, the main medieval discussion of the religious functions of imagery and symbolism in the context of the fabric and rituals of the Church, the *Rationale divinorum officiorum*, written by the late thirteenth-century bishop Durandus, retained a high level of validity throughout the Renaissance.[93] The fact that there is no Renaissance equivalent of Durandus's text, until the need for the redefinition which was occasioned by the Reformation, does not mean that the views he expressed became obsolete. Rather, it is reasonable to claim that they were so much part of the fabric of assumption that they did not need restating in the form of a specially designed book. It is significant that in 1459 his treatise became the first book by a non-saintly or 'non-inspired' author to be printed. This is not to say that some of the forms and functions of Renaissance art did not pose a challenge to the kind of framework of divine enlightenment outlined by Durandus. Fra Girolamo Savonarola, for one, preaching in Florence in the later years of the quattrocento, felt the need to rail against the new kinds of secularism in both ecclesiastical and domestic art which fell outside his increasingly strict definitions of what was proper. But Savonarola's arguments about the functions and efficacy of art resided conceptually within the sets of assumptions shared by the artists and patrons. Even an artist like Botticelli, some of whose secular works stood decisively outside Savonarola's canons of acceptability, would have viewed the essential power of images (for good or for evil) within a similar conceptual framework to the Domenican preacher.

Perhaps the most striking point when we look for continuities between image-making in the Middle Ages and Renaissance, is the fact that the existence of the majority of the images illustrated in this book (and in any general book on Renaissance art) finds its justification in the second of the councils held at Nicea as long ago as AD 787. This council defined the threefold validity of religious representations – a very necessary justification in the face of biblical injunctions against 'graven images'. Sacred images were sanctioned to instruct us in the faith, serving most notably as 'books for the unlettered' (a much repeated formulation); they acted as reminders of the mystery of the incarnation and of the saints' holiness, since visual images impress themselves more vividly on the memory than words; and they were designed to move the observer to a state of devotion, a devotion directed to the subject through the image. The subordination of art to devotion, and the subordinate function of the artistry involved in its production, became less pronounced during the Renaissance, and a number of prominent clerics not unreasonably expressed the sentiment that artists were increasingly 'cultivating art at the expense of devotion'; but no Renaissance theorist would have deemed it thinkable to advocate the goal of 'art for art's sake' in the nineteenth-century manner. All high-level practitioners and theorists saw themselves as serving a higher truth, even if the perceptions of the nature of that truth and the means of revealing it might differ substantially. However paganised the definition of the transcendental goal became, the divine function of the designs which the artists brought into being – whether drawn from their head or copied from nature – ultimately remained unassailable as the highest goal for art in its most elevated forms.

In addition to the definition of the theological purposes of art and the basis of imagery, medieval writing also included some practice-oriented literature devoted to the business of making art. The finest of the treatises is *On Divers Arts* (*De diversis artibus*), written by a Benedictine author of the twelfth century, usually known as 'Theophilus' from a seventeenth-century inscription on one of the surviving manuscripts.[94] The three books of 'Theophilus's' treatise are devoted to painting, glass and metalwork. Each is prefaced by a justification for the practice of the respective arts, not in terms of the theory of art but on the grounds that the artisan's mastery of skill in producing glorious works in praise of God is one of the best acts that humans can perform following the Fall of Adam and Eve and our consequent need for redemption. The bulk of the treatise is devoted to technical instructions on the production of sumptuous images worthy of God's house, and stands as an implicit answer to the periodic attacks of those theologians, such as the iconoclastic Bernard of Clairvaux, who used the biblical injunctions to question the lavishness of ecclesiastical fashions. What we do not find in 'Theophilus' or any other author in the Middle Ages is any independent assertion of the intellectual rules and status of the visual arts as standing amongst the most highly regarded disciplines of the human mind. The manual arts, those involving carving, modelling, grinding pigments, priming panels and so on, were not liberal arts by definition. Lucian, author of the famous *Calumny*, had already told us in his 'Dream' (*Somnium*) that he had been trained to carve stone but warned aspiring sculptors that even the greatest master, like Pheidias, will always be ranked as a 'mechanic, a man who has naught but his hands'. Lucian's essay on his youthful dream recounts how the figure of 'Sculpture' had appeared as a masculine, unkempt woman, soiled by a 'heavy layer of marble dust', while 'Education' had assumed the guise of a fair, well-attired lady. In the ensuing battle of words, 'Education' won hands down, in the most literal sense, and the young man abandoned the trade of carving for the profession of letters. The artisanal nature of the visual arts was essentially confirmed in the Middle Ages; Durandus, for example, associated painters with 'mechanics and handicraftsmen'.

Variously ordered and categorised in the Middle Ages, the liberal arts were generally seen as comprising the trivium – logic, rhetoric and grammar (or poetry) – and the quadrivium – arithmetic, geometry, astronomy and music. There might, in some of the variant schemes, be the possibility for one of the mechanical arts to participate in the qualities of one of more of the liberal arts, but the craft elements involved in the production of visual images prevented painting and sculpture from being accorded the free-standing status of liberal arts in their own right. In the highly influential book *On the Education of the Gentleman* (*De nobilium puerorum educatione libellus gravissimus*) written by Pier Paolo Vergerio in the early quattrocento great emphasis was placed upon history, philosophy and letters as the key liberal arts, but he excludes even the genteel art of drawing from the list of desirable pursuits for the educated man. Late in the fifteenth century Leonardo was still complaining that 'you have placed painting amongst the mechanical arts . . . With justifiable complaints painting laments that it has been excluded from the number of the liberal arts.'[95] What Leonardo and the other theorists of Renaissance art were trying to accomplish was not only the demonstration of the equality of the visual arts with literary endeavours (or even, in Leonardo's eyes, the superiority of the visual media over the written) but also their possession of a *scientia* of their own; that is to say a body of rational understanding which gave access to fundamental truths. The 'science' of painting elucidated a set of causes or laws on the basis of which artistic effects could be generated according to rational procedures. Such questions were matters of more than academic interest. Status was integrally involved, and status affected working conditions, remuneration and what we would call artistic freedom.

We do, however, need to exercise some caution in framing generalisations about the intentions of Renaissance theorists, particularly in the fifteenth century. There was no recognised genre of art theory, no established school of art theorists, and no recognised or standard forms of book about the visual arts. The five writers who provide the focus for the central part of this chapter each embarked upon highly individualistic enterprises which resulted in quite different types of book, with considerable variations in their intended and actual audiences. Indeed, for such a new and experimental genre of writing, the audiences envisaged by the authors may not have been at all clearly defined in their own minds, and the actual readership remains highly problematic in all but one case.

Cennino Cennini, the first of our authors (in the order that is adopted in the following discussion), seems on the face of it to be writing a recipe book in the manner of 'Theophilus', but what he actually provides makes greater claims for the intellectuality of art than is generally recognised, and may not have been intended to serve literally as a workshop manual. The second, Alberti, was writing a humanist treatise in Latin with clear didactic intent for the educated classes, but he also provided an Italian version which seems to have enjoyed some measure of life in the circles of ambitious artists. Piero della Francesca, our third theorist, writes on technical matters of practical and abstract mathematics, making demands on the reader which few aspiring artists would have been capable of sustaining and which few patrons would have regarded as important for what they wanted from art. Ghiberti, the fourth author, seems at first to be providing a new kind of Plinian history in the vernacular, encompassing classical antiquity and his own more immediate predecessors, but he then provides a novel kind of autobiography, followed by an exposition of the optics of vision culled largely from medieval texts, with unfinished notes on human proportion. It is difficult to define whom Ghiberti saw as his readership, and it is evident that he did not gain a significant one. Our final author of the quattrocento quintet, Leonardo da Vinci, never seems to have settled on what kind of treatise he was intending to write. The surviving material in his manuscripts ranges from windy humanist debates about the status of painting with respect to other arts, especially music and poetry, to obsessively detailed prescriptions for minutely observed effects of light in shade in the leaves of trees. At times he seems to be indulging in courtly debate, and at others to be leading a tyro by the hand; sometimes he appears to be satisfying his own anxieties about the worth of his calling, while on other occasions he records research at the highest level into questions of seeing and representing. Only two of the treatises, Alberti's *On Painting* and Piero's *De prospectiva pingendi* (*On the Perspective of Painting*) seem to have been copied in sufficient numbers to be regarded as having been 'published', as far as that term is applicable before the era of printed books. The first to find its way into actual print was Alberti's, published in its Latin version in Basel in 1540. The next, an abridged compilation of Leonardo's writings, had to wait until 1651. Such a picture hardly suggests that the quattrocento theorists had provided authoritative and widely-read texts which publishers were rushing to print. All in all, we are dealing with an odd and heterogeneous genre, which has retrospectively assumed a prominence which their contemporary diffusion hardly warrants. We should not mistake the interest and utility of the texts for modern historians with their impact in their own age, either within or outside the world of the visual arts.

The book by Cennino Cennini, his *Book of the Art* (*Libro dell'arte*), probably written around 1400, looks at first sight relatively straightforward to characterise.[96] As befits a professional practitioner of a 'mechanical art', the bulk of his book is concerned with technical instructions on drawing and painting, with considerable attention to the materials and manual procedures needed to make a finely crafted product. In these respects, he is providing a kind of 'Theophilus' for the modern painter. But, read more critically, we can discern that the modern painter as characterised by Cennino is rather different from 'Theophilus's' monkish craftsman. For a start, Cennino tells us who he is, and of his artistic lineage. The book is composed by 'Cennino of Colle [in the Val d'Elsa, near Siena] in the reverence of God' and of various saints, 'and in the reverence of Giotto, of Taddeo [Gaddi, Giotto's pupil] and of Agnolo [Gaddi, son of Taddeo], Ceninno's master'.[97] His self-proclamation as an artistic great grandson of Giotto was an important declaration in literary terms, since the great Giotto had become the point of reference for any fourteenth-century author who wished to say something intelligent about painting. From the time of Boccaccio, Giotto had been regarded as the reviver of the 'dead' art of painting, and as the supreme imitator of nature. Boccaccio specifically says that Giotto triumphed over the kind of art that was better suited 'to delight the eyes of the ignorant than to give satisfaction to the intellect of those who know about painting', thus aligning the painter with those who sought higher values.

Although the first section of Cennino's book opens like that of 'Theophilus' with the Creation and the Fall, which explains the need for human toil, he carefully differentiates between the 'many utilitarian skills [*molte arte bisognevoli*]' that the 'royally endowed' humans were subsequently able to pursue.[98] The highest pursuits were those that pertained to 'theory' (*scienzia*). Painting is special in that it combines *scienzia* with skill of hand, and requires the exercise of imagination (*fantasia*) 'in order to discover things not seen, hiding themselves under the shadow of natural objects, and to shape them with the hand, presenting to plain sight what does not actually exist'. The notion of things hidden under the 'shadow' of natural objects is an odd one. It is almost reminiscent of the Platonic characterisation of seen reality as the shadowy image of the true ideas, but more probably reflects the Christian idea of 'seeing through a glass darkly'. Durandus had explained that 'the professors of the liberal arts, and of all other arts, seek how they may clothe, support and adorn with causes and hidden reasons those things which be set forth nakedly and without ornament'.[99] Whatever the intended reference in Cennino's text, the drift of his meaning is clear. On behalf of the painter, he is claiming the exercise of *fantasia*, the faculty of imagination which had played such a conspicuous role in Dante's struggles to envisage the supreme truth.

That Cennino was thinking in such ambitious terms is confirmed by the very next passage, in which he claims that painting 'deserves to be enthroned next to *scienzia* and to be crowned with poetry'. Normally, of course, it was poetry who could aspire to be crowned in the person of the poet, as in the famous laureation of Petrarch. Cennino justifies himself by claiming that the one (the only?) *scienzia* of the poet is the Horatian liberty 'to compose and bind together, or not, as he pleases, according to his inclination. In the same way, the painter is given freedom to compose a figure, standing, seated, half-man, half-horse, as he pleases, according to his *fantasia*.' Whether Cennino had access to the passage in Horace from which this idea derives, or whether, as is more likely, he gleaned his ideas from a compilation such as that by Durandus, he is genuinely striving towards a doctrine of *ut pictura poesis*. This triumphant assertion is followed by a confession of his own position as 'an unimportant practising member of the profession of painting', and by an expanded outline of his artistic lineage, adding most significantly that 'Giotto changed the profession from Greek [i.e. Byzantine] back into Latin, and took it into the modern era', echoing the praise of humanist authors.[100] The little package of concepts in this introductory section makes knowing references to advanced ideas in classicising literary circles. It testifies, if not to the author's wide reading, at least to his keeping open an alert ear in the environments in which he moved, most especially that of the humanist court at Padua, where he was in the service of the ruling Carrara family. The only firm reference we have to Cennino's career was when he was described in 1398 as '*familiaris magnifici domini paduani*' in the household of Francesco Novello da Carrara.[101] Giotto himself had been named as a 'familiar' (*familiaris*) at the Neapolitan court in 1330, and, although the artist-familiar was still very much a servant of the court, such an appointment represented a considerable professional achievement. Cennino married a Paduan, and his brother, Matteo, was a musician who played the *trombetta* at the court.

Although the main body of the book is dedicated to how-to-do-it instructions for the aspiring draftsman and painter of murals, panels etc., there are other glimpses of the ambitious *scienzia* of the introduction scattered at various points throughout the subsequent text. *Fantasia* features again when he discusses how the pupil may learn a good style and eventually acquire his own individual manner. He recommends that the apprentice should 'endeavour to copy and draw after as few masters as possible', otherwise he will become 'confused and capricious through volatile enthusiasms'. If you work steadily to copy a master who 'has the greatest reputation . . . it will be against nature if you do not gain some grasp of his style and spirit'. If this seems like a recipe for servile derivation, Cennino tells us that 'if nature has granted you any *fantasia* at all . . . you will eventually acquire a style individual to yourself, and it cannot help being good'.[102] The pedagogic procedure of copying was of course the standard one, but Cennino's recognition that the ultimate forging of an individual style was a desirable goal again reflects an out-of-the-ordinary set of ambitions.

The immediately succeeding section is worth quoting in full, because it establishes the visual goal of the artist in terms of what was regarded as the key achievement of the Giotto revolution:

> Mind you, the most perfect guide you can have, the best helm, exists in the triumphant gateway of copying from nature [*rittrare di naturale*]. And this outdoes all other models; and always rely on this with a stout heart, especially as you begin to gain some judgement in draftsmanship. Do not fail, as you go on, to draw something every day, for no matter how little it is it will be worthwhile, and will do a world of good.[103]

Even through the mixed metaphors, which betray Cennino's insecure literary skills, there is no missing the two principles upon which the past and coming revolutions were to be founded: the imitation of nature; and the discipline of *disegno*, which he associates firmly with the intellect. Throughout his 'recipes' the most important of the ends in view is the rational achieving of naturalistic effects – whether he is dealing with the system of graded bowls of pigment for progressively lighter flesh-colour for the modelling of faces, which he credits to Giotto, or how to depict a bloody wound. His much quoted recommendation that the way to 'acquire a good style for mountains' is to copy the arrangement of light and shade on 'some large stones, rugged and not cleaned up' has been seen as an example of his essentially medieval procedures, whereas it is (if we forget that Alberti is on the horizon) a clever way of bringing the complex patterns of chiaroscuro on geological objects in the scope of copying in the studio, so that the principles of rendering relief (the *rilievo* upon which Leonardo set such store) might be mastered.[104]

The section before his brief injunction on rendering mountains had dealt

36. Giotto, *Christ before Pilate*, Padua, Capella Scrovegni

with the depiction of architecture, which had provided the key to Giotto's construction of a spatial stage for his actors and which was to be at the centre of the coming revolution in perspective. Having reminded us to employ a comparable system of 'lights and darks' to that we have learnt for figures, he tells us to

> put in the buildings by this uniform system: that the mouldings which you make at the top of the building should slant downward from the edge next to the roof; the moulding in the middle of the building, halfway up the face, must be quite level and even; the moulding at the base of the building must slant upward, in the opposite sense to the upper moulding which slants downward.[105]

Once we set the awkwardness of the verbal description beside one of Giotto's paintings (fig. 36), the system becomes clear. Above and below the central horizontal, which remains invariable regardless of its orientation in space, the upper and lower margins of the walls are inclined consistently to provide a sense of converging perspective – without specific convergence to a single, central

88

'vanishing-point', in the later manner. A sense of systematic procedures is at the heart of Cennino's endeavour. He even tries to make a kind of Aristotelian ordering of colours, claiming, in general conformity with the tradition deriving from Aristotle's *On Sense and Sensible Objects*, that 'there are seven natural colours, or rather four which are actually mineral in character – namely black, red, [mineral] yellow and green – and three natural colours which need to be developed artificially, lime white, the blues (ultramarine and azurite) and [artificial] yellow'.[106] Again, this is not to suggest that Cennino directly studied the classical source – and his seven colours are not quite the same as Aristotle's – but rather to show that he was alert to its transmission over the ages through the Aristotelian tradition in one of its many varieties of philosophical or vulgar forms.

For whom was Cennino writing? The answer seems obvious. As he says himself, his book is designed 'to minister to all those who wish to enter the profession', and its consistent address to '*ti*' gives it the air of an intimate instruction for a young person. But was it really intended to be a workshop manual in the most literal sense, that is to say widely available in workshops as a set of instructions? The very limited number of manuscripts (no more than two having survived from the fifteenth and sixteenth centuries) suggests that it did not gain wide diffusion in Italian *botteghe*, if that was indeed its main purpose. If we take into account Cennino's career a rather different answer might suggest itself.

At the Carrara court in Padua he would have encountered the last phase of the foremost regimes for the patronage of humanist studies. The great Petrarch had himself been in and near Padua in the later years of his life, and his presence would have been a living memory when Cennino was there. Although the tastes of the younger Francesco were different to the literary inclinations of his father, Petrarch's protector, and the great humanist library had been seized by the invading Milanese in 1388, Cennino's patron undertook a substantial programme of cultural renewal in Padua after the Carrara regained control in 1490, concentrating particularly on practical wisdom. Cennino's keenness to exempt Paduan women from the charge that young ladies (like those in Tuscany) have a dangerous fancy for 'beautifying themselves with certain waters' might indicate that he was writing in a Paduan context, and his vocabulary includes Paduan words.[107] For the literary humanist at courts like Padua, the writing of tracts dedicated to a powerful patron (whether a hoped-for patron or an actual one) was one of the major ways to secure their position in terms of status and income. Amongst the literary genres were the production of pedagogic texts on a variety of subjects, taking as models ancient texts like Cicero's on oratory and the Roman treatise *On the Education of Children* which was falsely attributed to Petrarch. Vergerio's *On the Education of the Gentleman* was actually composed in Padua under Francesco Novello at the time when Cennino is likely to have been writing his book. In this context it is possible to think that the ostensible readership is the notional apprentice, but that the immediate motive for the writing of the text and the production of the manuscript (as a literally presentable object) was the impressing of a patron. An enlightened patron might be expected to welcome the establishing of his domain as a recognised centre for pedagogic excellence and a flourishing school of artists.

Direct evidence of the patronage of Cennino's first or prime manuscript is lacking, but the later production of 'instructional books' for artists fit the pattern I am proposing. Piero della Francesca's book on perspective is, for example, doggedly addressed to a young aspirant (as '*ti* or *tu*'), but we know that a manuscript (almost certainly the *best*) was presented to Federigo da Montefeltro, Duke of Urbino, for his prestigious library of ancient and modern learning. Whether or not Cennino's book was actually produced during his stay at the Paduan court is largely beside the point; what matters to our understanding of the emphasis upon *scienzia* in his book is what *type* of activity we think treatise-writing to have been. We have to remember that we are dealing with the era of the manuscript, a relatively exclusive product, not with a cheap printed book that could remain in an artist's studio becoming dog-eared and paint-stained. I think that he was trying to impress someone other than a twelve-year-old apprentice.

If we may at least suspect Cennino of authorial and social ambitions unusual in a mere artisan, we can confidently identify Alberti wholly with the highest literary aspirations. An illegitimate son in an exiled Florentine family, he was educated in letters and law at Padua and Bologna. Denied direct access to family money, he established his position largely through literary endeavours and his service in various secretarial capacities to the papal court. He wrote in both Latin and the vernacular on a huge range of subjects – including the life of the mind, the family, civic responsibility, practical mathematics, codes, horses, engineering, architecture and sculpture, as well as composing lively satires, tales and fables. He also became esteemed in the later part of his career for the unrivalled way in which he could exploit his extensive antiquarian knowledge to design buildings in the latest manner for such ambitious patrons as the Rucellai in Florence and the Gonzaga in Mantua. His ten-part treatise on architecture, *On the Art of Building* (*De re aedificatoria*), written in or before 1452 in emulation of Vitruvius's *Ten Books of Architecture*, preceded his book *On Painting* into print by over fifty years. *On Painting*, composed in 1435 after he had 'returned' to the Florence of his ancestors, was therefore just one smallish item in a large production.[108] In a sense, painting is used as one of many illustrations of the theme central to Alberti – the pursuit of *virtù* (high worth) in the face of the vagaries of *fortuna*. This was to be achieved by the cultivation of such activities as ensure that the individual comes into possession of the kinds of knowledge and skills which sustain enduring achievements. The necessary knowledge was framed in terms of the underlying order of nature, in Neo-Stoic terms.

His philosophy was perfectly summed up by the notion of man as 'the measure of all things':

> The Stoics taught that man was by nature constituted the observer and manager of things. Chrysippus thought that everything on earth was born only to serve man, while man was meant to preserve the friendship and society of man. Protagoras, another ancient philosopher, seems to some interpreters to have said essentially the same thing, when he declared that man is the mean and measure of all things.[109]

If this should seem too pagan and human-centred a formulation, Alberti was always keen to remind his readers that what man was to 'observe' and 'manage' was the order of God's creation. Although Alberti's central theme is properly termed philosophical, he was not inclined to prize abstract knowledge in the purely philosophical sense, but rather to look to the realisation of the comprehended order in concrete activities – though, equally, he did not recommend wholesale immersion in the stormy inconstancies of the practical life of politics and the urban struggle. Read in the context of Alberti's literary production – as it should be but rarely is – *On Painting* looks like a rather different kind of treatise than it appears if it is considered solely within the genre of 'art theory'. We know, in retrospect, that Alberti was virtually founding the genre, and he himself expressed some pride in being 'the first to write about this most subtle art', expressing the hope that his successors will perfect his principles. But I suspect that he would be disconcerted to find that his reputation as an author now largely rides on his authorship of *On Painting*.

On Painting perfectly succeeds in that most extraordinary and paradoxical of Renaissance achievements, the creation of a work that is deeply eclectic, paying repeated homage to the ancient authorities through quotation and paraphrase, and is yet strikingly original. None of his aesthetic criteria are novel, and the ordering of his treatise is based upon stock formulae for didactic treatises on verbal matters (especially rhetoric). But no-one had attempted to do specifically for painting what he was accomplishing, and in doing so he provided a wealth of material which had never previously been written down in the context of art theory. The air of novelty and excitement that emerges even from the measured language reflects his encounter with the latest deeds of the pioneering Florentine artists of the early Renaissance. As he recorded in the dedication to Brunelleschi of the Italian version of his text, produced a year later in 1436,

> I believed . . . that Nature, mistress of things, had grown old and weary, and was no longer producing intellects any more than giants on a vast and wonderful scale. . . But after I came back here to this most beautiful of cities from the long exile in which we Albertis have grown old, I recognised in many, but above all in you Filippo, and in our great friend the sculptor Donatello, and in others, Nencio [Ghiberti], Luca [della Robbia] and Masaccio, a talent [*ingegno*] for every laudable enterprise in no way inferior to any of the ancients who gained fame in these arts.[110]

No clearer demonstration of the *virtù* of the pioneers could be found than in Filippo Brunelleschi's dome of Florence Cathedral, 'towering above the skies, vast enough to cover the entire Tuscan population in its shadows', and under which Alberti was later to set his dialogue *On the Retreat from Hardship* (otherwise known as *On the Tranquillity of the Mind*).[111]

In keeping with good didactic principles, Alberti begins the first of the three books in *On Painting*, with a step-by-step exposition of first principles. Since he is dealing with visual matters, he begins with the fundamental geometrical components in the grammar of seen things – the point, the line, the surface and the solid body. He stresses that he is dealing with the 'coarse' geometry of material forms, not with the pure abstractions of the geometer. Such an attachment to the material manifestation of order is consistent with his proclivities. Material things are made visible through light, and the process by which we see such light is itself highly ordered. The rays from a surface enter our

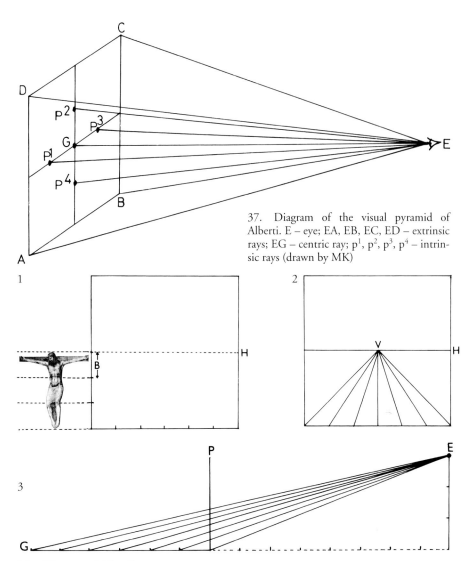

37. Diagram of the visual pyramid of Alberti. E – eye; EA, EB, EC, ED – extrinsic rays; EG – centric ray; p^1, p^2, p^3, p^4 – intrinsic rays (drawn by MK)

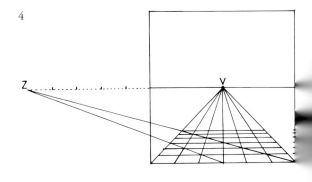

38. Diagram of Alberti's perspective construction 1. B – one *braccio* module (one-third of the height of a man). The base of the picture is divided into *braccia*, The height of the man at the front plane of the picture gives the level of the horizon, H. 2. The *braccio* divisions are joined to the perspective focus, V, to give the orthogonals. 3. lateral elevation, lines are drawn from *braccio* divisions behind the picture plane P to the eye at E. The points of intersections on P are noted. 4. The levels of the points of intersection are marked at the side of the picture plane, and locate the horizontal divisions of the tiles. Z is the 'distance' point, though Alberti only mentions using one diagonal to check construction (drawn by MK)

eye in the configuration of a cone or pyramid (fig. 37). The concept of the visual pyramid was drawn from medieval optical science, the *perspectiva* on which a number of Islamic and Christian authors had written, including John Pecham, whose treatise had become the standard textbook. Alberti's characterisation of the 'centric' (perpendicular or axial) ray in the cluster as 'leader and prince of rays' refers to its role as the prime certifier of clear sight and measurer of distance in the science of *perspectiva*. None of this is very original in itself, nor is it very sophisticated optically. What is novel, however, is his definition of the picture as the intersection of this pyramid, so that the optical array presented by the objects is recorded in due proportion on the flat picture plane. The geometry of the proportional transcription relies upon the simple theorem of similar triangles, a mathematical commonplace known to anyone educated in even the most rudimentary skills of estimating and surveying, but the conceptual step is immense. The imitation of nature is now demonstrably a matter of optical rule. The way the painter makes a picture in accordance with this rule is expounded through what we would now call a 'vanishing-point' construction (fig. 38), though the geometrical proof of why the intersection of the pyramid results in the pictorial construction is nowhere given by Alberti.

How we regard the historical significance of what Alberti is achieving in the first book of *On Painting* depends upon how we interpret the evidence relating to the actual invention of pictorial perspective, which should almost certainly be credited to Filippo Brunelleschi. We can be reasonably certain, on the basis of the biography of the great architect written (probably) by Antonio Manetti, that Brunelleschi achieved the perspectival rendering of three-dimensional forms in two demonstration paintings of the Florentine Baptistery and the Palazzo Vecchio (figs. 39-40).[112] Manetti describes the paintings, which are now lost, but tells us nothing about the technical procedures adopted by Brunelleschi. Since historians abhor such an explanatory vacuum at the heart of a crucial episode, speculation has rushed in to fill the void. He has been seen alternatively as founding his techniques upon medieval optical science or upon Ptolemeic methods of cartographic projection, as using mirrors or scientific instruments

39. Diagrammatic reconstruction of Brunelleschi's perspective demonstration of the Florentine Baptistery (drawn by MK)

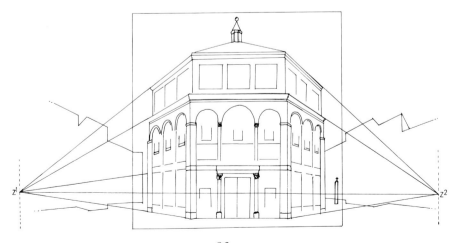

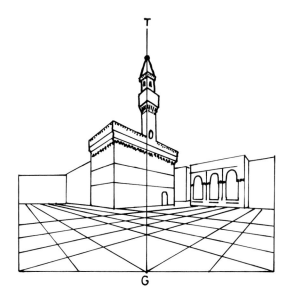

40. Diagrammatic reconstruction of Brunelleschi's perspective demonstration of the Palazzo de' Signori, Florence. GT – vertical through axis of sight. Note: the diagonal pavement lines denote the orientation but not the position of the pavement pattern (drawn by MK)

(such as an astrolabe), as undertaking projections from ground plans and elevations, and as adapting methods of surveying. The problem is that all these methods will theoretically deliver the same results, and there is no secure way of working back from Manetti's description to the method that was actually used. The best way of weighing the alternatives is to apply two criteria. The first is to look at what skills and inclinations Brunelleschi is known to have possessed. The second is to choose the explanation which involves the least redundancy. When combined, these criteria stand some chance of satisfying my overarching criterion for a historical explanation, namely that it should exhibit a 'whiff of reality'; that is to say it should make sense in terms of a real person operating with credible motives in real circumstances and in a manner which is generally consistent with the time and place in question. Without being able to argue through the various cases here, I can summarise my conclusions by saying that it seems most credible to me that he used his skills in practical mensuration (as in surveying buildings) to solve a pictorial problem in a way which combined respect for the proportional integrity of buildings with representational devices of the type pioneered by Giotto. I believe that no skills more complex than those of elementary surveying were required. The brilliance lay in seeing how to do something that painters had been trying to accomplish since the era of Giotto.

If this interpretation is right, or along the right lines, Brunelleschi's method was that of the practical operative, who saw abstract operations (in this case, geometrical projection) in terms of the instrumental procedures involved in their material demonstration. In this light, Alberti's achievement was to supersede Brunelleschi's dependence on actual buildings and empirical operations and to extract their underlying rationale in terms of the general case of an archetypal construction. The sculptor Donatello, in his bronze relief of the *Feast of Herod* (fig. 12), and Masaccio, in his *Trinity* (fig. 41) had already translated Brunelleschi's procedures into methods which could be used synthetically to construct imagined spaces, but Alberti's neat codification of the

41. Masaccio, *Trinity*, Florence, S. Maria Novella

construction in terms of the underlying geometry was specifically to give painting, as a discipline, a rootedness in the underlying order of things no less strong than that of other arts which claimed liberal status. As he says, his first book, 'which is entirely mathematical, shows how this noble and beautiful art arises from the roots within Nature herself'.[113] It thus meets his Neo-Stoic demands for excellence.

We should remind ourselves, however, that the exposition of the construction of the spatial armature occupies only one of the three books in *On Painting*. Perspective was the means not the end. Book II shows what is necessary to translate the linear rudiments of the optical geometry into a picture. The first of three necessary moves is 'circumscription', that is to say the delineation of the outlines of objects and their proportional distribution on the spatial armature. The achieving of a beautiful and eloquent arrangement of the parts is the province of the second procedure, 'composition', which builds progressively from 'surfaces', 'members' and 'bodies' in much the same way that the good author systematically composes his discourse from the components of language.[114] The aim of 'composition' is to achieve a decorous exposition of the significant subject, the *historia*. Alberti's examples of suitably affecting pieces of narrative art include an ancient relief of the dead Meleager – dead to his very fingertips – and the mosaic by Giotto of Christ and St Peter walking on the waters which was in old St Peter's in Rome.[115] A sense of tangible reality is then given to the composition by the third component, the 'reception of light', which results in the modelling of objects in light and shade and their harmonious colouring – avoiding extremes, as always, and maintaining decorum.

Having set out a demanding agenda for the achieving of systematic and communicative naturalism within a framework of order and restrained delectation, the third book, as Alberti admits, mops up those points that did not fall naturally in the first two sections. These points are concerned above all with the requirements placed on the person of the painter as someone who, as a 'good man', aspires to *virtù*.[116] The virtuous artist will be learned in the liberal arts, not least for the 'invention' of suitable subjects for the *historia*. The 'invention [*inventio*]' will give a literary kind of pleasure in its own right – just as 'the description [*descriptio*] that Lucian gives of Calumny painted by Apelles, excites our admiration when we read it'.[117] He (and Alberti tacitly assumes the artist is a 'he') will study nature diligently for its principles, above all for its beauty, always working in an orderly and systematic fashion to cultivate what gifts he has been granted. Although these gifts may dispose the artist to particular excellence in one branch of painting, say portraiture, a more rounded set of achievements is desirable. Finally, the painter should not fear exposing the products of his brush in the public forum, and the story of Apelles *post tabulam latens* is used to justify listening to the judgement of 'everybody'.[118] However, aware that indiscriminate attention to the ignorant and the wise alike was hardly desirable, he adds that the painter should ultimately 'follow the advice of the more expert'.

The overall effect of *On Painting* is of the demonstration of the nobility of painting through an exposition of the pedagogic principles which its highest practitioners must master, rather than an actual exercise in practical pedagogy for the young artist. Even the sections on perspective and circumscription, which have something of the air of how-to-do-it instructions, do not tell the young practitioner how to proceed in a range of practical circumstances. He is not saying that all perspectival pictures should somehow look like the completed construction in our fig. 38, but rather he is outlining those aspects of the construction that are invariant – the convergence of the orthogonals, the proportional diminution of equal horizontal intervals, the continuity of the diagonals through foreshortened squares, and the proportionality of the bodies (most especially human bodies) to their relative positions on the floor plan. The establishing of the position of the viewer relative to the picture, the nature of the space to be depicted and all the other pictorial decisions remain to be taken in relation to the subject and setting of the picture. The remaining sections of the treatise provide even less in the way of direct instruction for the tyro. The emphasis is consistently upon exhortations that will illustrate the status of painting with respect to nature and the goals of artistic excellence in telling a story which are akin to those of the ancient authors.

Once we begin to understand the character of the book, its dedication to Gianfrancesco Gonzaga of Mantua seems a logical move on Alberti's part. Mantua was the site of the famed humanist school, La Giocosa, run by Vittorino da Feltre (the subject of one of Pisanello's medals). The little book *On Painting* was potentially well fitted to find its place on the curriculum of the generation of young aristocrats which included such notable future patrons as Federigo da Montefeltro and Ludovico Gonzaga, together with a number of the sons of the leading humanist scholars. It would have helped to counteract the continued exclusion of the visual arts by Vergerio and the traditionalist authors of school curricula. Piero della Francesca and Mantegna might have had good reason to feel grateful to Alberti for their patrons' enlightened tastes. The production of the Italian version seems like a piece of friendly opportunism on Alberti's part, and we may well believe him when he tells Brunelleschi specifically that he 'did it into Tuscan for you'. The survival of the Latin version in some twenty manuscripts, compared to three in Italian, tells us much about contemporary perceptions of the audience to whom *On Painting* was addressed.

In fact, the patron of Piero della Francesca, Federigo da Montefeltro, in whose library *De prospectiva pingendi* was to be deposited, deserved the very praise which Alberti had directed to the Marquis of Mantua, who 'in glory of arms and the skill of letters' was said to 'excel by far all other princes'.[119] Piero's book, dedicated in a remorselessly specialised way to perspective constructions, also appears at first sight to lend itself to simple characterisation.[120] But on closer analysis, it is a puzzling production. Piero was not a trained humanist author in the manner of Alberti, but it is likely that he had a better education than most artists, probably acquiring the kind of knowledge that was taught in the so-called abacus schools. This training included practical mathematics, and Piero's first book, perhaps written as early as 1450, was a *Trattato del abaco* (a 'treatise on practical mathematics') in this tradition. His book on the perspective of painting was finished before the death of the Duke of Urbino in 1474, and his *Libellus de quinque corporibus regularibus* (on the 'five regular solids') was presented for the library after Guidobaldo da Montefeltro's succession.[121] *De prospectiva pingendi* is in one sense an almost unrelievedly mathematical treatise, with few literary grace-notes and very little introductory material to ease the

42. Piero della Francesca, *Perspectival Construction of an Octagonal Figure*, Parma, Galleria Palatina

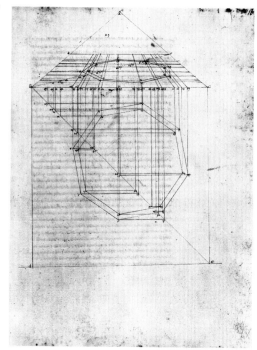

43. Piero della Francesca, *Perspectival Projection of a Head on to an Intersecting Plane*, Parma, Galleria Palatina

44. Piero della Francesca, *Completed Perspectival Construction of a Tilted Head*, Parma, Galleria Palatina

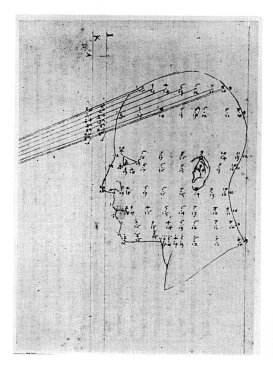

student's entry into the technical material. Piero begins with a brief definition of the three parts of painting, *disegno* (draftsmanship), *commensuratio* (measurement or calibration), and *colorare* (the application of colours under the influence of light and shade).[122] Only intending to treat *commensuratio*, he sets out the five necessary parameters:

> The first is sight, that is the eye; the second is the form of the seen thing; the third is the distance between the eye and the seen thing; the fourth is the lines which depart from the extremities of the thing and come to the eye; the fifth is the intersection [*termine*] which is between the eye and the seen thing, and on which is intended to locate the things.[123]

The remainder of the first book builds systematically from a definition of figures in a Euclidean manner, to the construction of a foreshortened ground plane on which plans of any configuration can be projected (fig. 42). The second book deals with the erection of solids on the foreshortened plane, retaining the due proportions of heights at various depths. The final section outlines an alternative method, the full-scale projection of designated points in the plans and elevations of an object onto an intersection at a given distance from the object and the eye. This method can cope systematically even with complex organic forms, such as a human head (figs. 43-4).

Since the treatise concentrates on perspective and is heavily indebted to Euclidean geometry as applied to simple optical rules, it may seem reasonable to align it with Book I and part of Book II of *On Painting*. However, the treatises by Alberti and Piero are quite different in their address. Alberti presents the basic elements of the perspective construction in terms of one universal exemplar. Since he does not tell the artist how to tackle all the varieties of perspectival construction that might be required in practice, he avoids long-winded passages of technical instruction. By contrast, most of Piero's text is laboriously concerned with the geometrical drafting of various constructions which differ only in the shape and complexity of the object but not in their basic method. He almost literally takes the reader by the hand as the constructions are pedantically laid out, point-by-point and line-by-line.

Does this condensed, geometrical character mean that we should recognise *De prospectiva pingendi* as a work of pure geometry, in the manner of Piero's book on the five regular solids? Is it a kind of painter's Euclid, who is heavily cited by Piero? The answer is definitely no, because Piero is almost exclusively concerned with the bread-and-butter operation of the constructions, and very little with axioms, general cases and proofs. He only provides one actual 'proof' (fig. 45), and even this has been problematic for later readers, not least because of problems in the labelling of the diagram in the surviving manuscripts, which have tended to obscure the basic correctness of Piero's demonstration.[124] How different his tone is from Euclid's can be judged from his first account of how to achieve the full plane projection of a geometrical plan, in which he recommends his reader to trace the rays using a 'thread of the finest silk' or a 'hair from the tail of a horse'. Nor is it possible to align Piero's treatise with the tradition of optical science, from which Alberti had drawn inspiration, since it states few optical principles and pays virtually no attention to the operation of light rays with respect to the eye. The overall tone of *De prospectiva pingendi* is

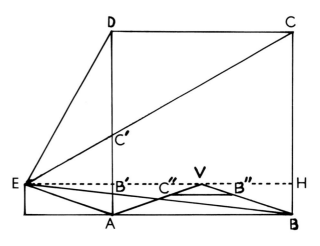

45. Based on Piero della Francesca's, *'Proof of the Perspective Construction*. ABCD – square. E – viewer; EH – horizon (not so labelled by Piero); V – focus of orthogonals from A and B; BE and CE are drawn, and points B′ and C′ noted. C′B′ is transferred (at the level of B′) to give C″B″.

actually closer to the practical geometry of the abacus books than to a work of pure mathematics or philosophical optics. It is a sort of geometrical 'cook-book' for the dedicated beginner. In the sixteenth century, Daniele Barbaro was to claim that Piero had written for 'idiots' – by which Daniele meant that Piero's readers were assumed to need multiple examples rather than being able to take the principles of the general case and apply them to any given problem.[125]

Given the tone of *De prospectiva pingendi*, it is possible to infer the kinds of explicit or implicit assumptions Piero made about its readership. He was assuming that the reader required practical instruction in perspectival construction on the basis of little existing knowledge; that he or she possessed the necessary motivation to work through a series of long-winded exercises; that the *'tu'* who is addressed is a young artist fired with the ambition to emulate Piero's level of exactitude; that the person undertaking the exercises was familiar with accurate drawing in fine lines with a straight edge and basic geometrical instruments; and that the reader was familiar with the rudiments of abacus-book operations. Above all, Piero's notional student required a notable combination of patience and high level of spatial visualisation if the procedures were not to collapse. Although a number of the assumptions are not unreasonable in themselves, taken collectively they set a series of requirements which few apprentice artists were likely to meet. Once again, it seems that we are dealing with a piece of 'demonstration pedagogy' – or perhaps Piero simply possessed little judgement of what ordinary mortals were likely to want and to accomplish.

Like Alberti's treatise, Piero's manuscript is known in Latin and Italian versions, but in this case it was originally written in Italian and translated into Latin by Matteo dal Borgo. The relatively modest tally of surviving manuscripts – four Latin and two Italian – suggests that it was more likely to be found in the context of a humanist library than in the hands of an apprentice painter. Its exceedingly indigestible quality seems to bode ill for its achieving a wide readership. However, its two main methods actually became the standard alternatives in the mainstream perspectival textbooks that were to be published in succeeding centuries. This impact is not because Piero's original text was widely read, but because it was known to a small number of theorists who wrote the standard texts. The full-scale projection method was broadcast in both German and Latin in Dürer's books on measurement, while large sections of the key methods were taken over in Daniele Barbaro's *La pratica della perspettiva* (1569), in spite of Daniele's rudeness about Piero's apparent audience. This story serves to remind us that the weight of the eventual impact of a text might not be directly proportional to the numbers of original readers.

Even this claim for posthumous impact cannot really be made for the fourth of the texts I am considering, the *Commentaries* (*Commentarii*) by Lorenzo Ghiberti, the famed sculptor of the Baptistery doors in Florence and the dominant figure in the decoration of the Guild Hall of Or San Michele.[126] It survives in only one manuscript and never seems to have been brought to the point where it could be considered as a coherently publishable book. In fact, Ghiberti himself may never have intended it to be judged in this light. It may well owe its origins more to the tradition of the *zibaldoni* – collections of wisdom and moral encouragement which were compiled within a family context as exhortatory memorials for the younger generations. The problem with aligning the *Commentaries* precisely with this tradition is that there was no established pattern for a *zibaldone*, and the first two of Ghiberti's three 'books' would represent an unusually joined-up and historically sequential set of 'commonplaces'. In favour of their identification as family memoirs are their production late in Lorenzo's life, as a kind of *summa*, and the family tradition he established through his sculptor son, Vittorio, and his engineer grandson, Buonaccorso, who was to compile his own *Zibaldone*, probably building upon material assembled by Lorenzo. What cannot be doubted is the ambition of Ghiberti's enterprise, which attempts to do far more than Alberti had attempted and yields nothing to Alberti in the intellectual claims it makes for art.

The first of the commentaries parades a Plinian history of ancient art in the context of a framework of claims about the requirements for a learned artist drawn largely from the stipulations for the architect in the *Ten Books* by Vitruvius, who had served the Emperor Augustus. Paraphrasing Vitruvius, Ghiberti insists that 'innate talent [*ingegno*] without discipline, or discipline without innate talent, cannot make a perfect maker of artefacts [*artefice*]'.[127] The key discipline went beyond mere diligence and extended to the systematic study of a range of liberal and related arts: grammar, geometry, philosophy, medicine, astrology, perspective, history, anatomy, theory of design, and arithmetic. He insists that 'sculpture and painting comprise a science, adorned with many disciplines and various branches of learning; it is the greatest invention of all of them; it is made with a certain level of meditation, during which it is composed according to rational considerations'.[128] At the root of the science of art lay optics, as he made clear at the start of the autobiographical section in the second commentary: 'in order always to understated first principles, I have striven to investigate in what manner nature functions in itself, and how I may be able to appraise nature, how the incorporeal images of objects come to the eye, and how the visual power operates, and how visual sensations arise, and by what means the theory of the arts of sculpture may be formulated'.[129] The word he used for the 'images' which come to the eye, *specie* ('species'), is a technical term from medieval optics and consciously signals his awareness of the most advanced science.

The second commentary, which retails the history of modern art from the innovations of Giotto – 'the inventor and discoverer of much learning that had been buried some six hundred years' – to his own career, is not ostensibly about theory, but the terms in which he praises the successive masters serve to underline his intellectual requirements. Amongst those who followed Giotto's example, Stefano did works 'with great learning'; Taddeo Gaddi 'was of marvellous talent [*ingegno*]' and was 'a very learned master'; Maso was 'a man of the greatest talent; and Bonamico 'had his art from nature'.[130] Of the Sienese masters with whom Ghiberti felt a special affinity, Ambrogio Lorenzetti stood out as 'a most expert master, a man of great talent [*ingegno*], most notable draftsman [*disegnatore*] and fully conversant with the theory [*teorica*] of art. One of Ambrogio's works, a lost narrative fresco of a Franciscan monk in Saracen lands, is subject to an especially extended *descriptio*, culminating in some vivid word-painting of a great storm which stays the execution of the friar and his companions:

> . . . We see the men and women folding their clothing over their heads, with hail thick on the shields, it really seems that the hail is striking the shields with the astonishing winds. We see trees bending to the ground, and some splitting, and everybody seems to be running off; we see the executioner falling under his horse which kills him. . . .[131]

Not surprisingly, Ghiberti's autobiography, which provides the immodest historical climax of the second commentary, stresses his dedication to learning and letters – inculcated by his worthy parents – which has led him to 'love the writing of commentaries'. And when he reaches the climactic work of his own career, his second set of Baptistery doors (fig. 46), heavy significance is loaded into the introduction to his *descriptio* of the narrative reliefs:

> I was commissioned to do the other door . . . of San Giovanni. In it I was given permission to carry it out in the way I thought would turn out most perfectly, and most richly and most elaborately. I began this work in square panels, two and a half feet in size. These stories, filled with figures, were stories of the Old Testament, in which I tried every way to be faithful in seeking to imitate nature, as far as was possible for me, with all the outlines I could produce and with fine compositions rich with many figures. In some stories I put a hundred figures, in some more and in some less. I carried out this work with the greatest diligence and the greatest love. There were ten scenes, all with buildings in proportion as the eye gauges them, and so true that when one stands away from them they seem in three dimensions. They have very little relief, and on the floors one sees the nearer figures apparently bigger and those farther off apparently smaller, as reality demonstrates. And I followed through the whole work with those measurements.[132]

The passage is replete with instructive intent: he was given *personal* control over the *invenzione* of the doors, although we know that no less an author than Leonardo Bruni had endeavoured to impose his own programme; he was using the latest form of square, 'pictorial' panels for his reliefs, rather than the older

46. Lorenzo Ghiberti, *The 'Porta del Paradiso' (East Doors)*, Florence, Baptistery

quadrilobe frames of his first door; he was aiming for perfection and richness in his telling of the significant stories, in keeping with the highest ideals of oratory; he applied unstinting efforts and devotion to the doors; he was insistent on following nature; and he followed the proportional demands of optical truth through the exercise of what Piero was to call *commensuratio*.[133]

It was perhaps natural that the third of his books should be largely dedicated to *perspectiva*, but, rather surprisingly, he does not provide a direct guide to the operation of pictorial perspective. Rather, he devised an elaborate and substantial collage of translated texts from the leading authorities on optical science: Alhazen, the Islamic philosopher whose theories laid the foundation for European optics; Roger Bacon and John Pecham, the thirteenth-century Franciscans; and, to a lesser extent, the Polish follower of Alhazen, Witelo.[134] He also drew upon Vitruvius for an account of perspectival scene-painting in Italy, and to praise ancient philosophers for 'having written on the things of nature'. He follows the standard sequence of the optical texts, which he splices together with some skill, beginning with light itself, and progressing through the structure and functioning of the eyes, to direct vision, reflection and refraction. What is apparently puzzling about the anthology is that Ghiberti nowhere attempts to show how it translates into procedures which the artist can follow. Many of the passages which he excerpts deal elaborately with the complexities and delusions of vision, in such a way that we might well be persuaded that the painter's simple science was but a very poor and schematic reflection of the visual process. If we view the *Commentaries* as a *zibaldone*, the parade of optical learning – as the kind of underpinning knowledge he would hope his heirs to acquire – makes greater sense, but the gap between knowledge and its application remains obvious.

In a broad sense, we may say that his demonstration of the complex science involved in understanding how we see provides a generic justification for Ghiberti to take the most sophisticated care in controlling the visual effects in his reliefs. More specifically, it would be reasonable to think that the doctrine of the weakening of the effects of the 'species' in the eye with the greater remoteness of the seen object provides the rationale for the progressive lowering of his relief in the distance. There is some support for this idea in the most substantial of Ghiberti's relatively few interpolations of his own observations in the optical section. This insertion occurs following a section from Alhazen in which the Islamic philosopher is discussing the perception of details under artificial illumination. Ghiberti records that he has been able to view 'in temperate light objects sculpted with the greatest perfection and made with the greatest skill and diligence'.[135] The examples of infinitely fine modelling that he gives are masterpieces of ancient art: a statue of *Hermaphrodite*, made with 'marvellous *ingegno*' and 'in which there were many sweet subtleties which present nothing to our sight unless they are disclosed by the touch of our hand'; a statue he saw in Padua, which similarly revealed to the touch subtleties that could not be discerned in 'either strong or temperate light'; a figure excavated and reburied in Siena which was believed to be by Lysippus, the Greek sculptor, which Ghiberti knew through a drawing by Ambrogio Lorenzetti; and a translucent chalcedony owned by the humanist and antiquarian collector Niccolò Niccoli which could 'not be comprehended well under a strong light'

47.   Lorenzo Ghiberti, *Story of Jacob and Esau from the 'Porta del Paradiso'*, Florence, Baptistery

but only when set against the light. The section then ingeniously resumes with Alhazen's discussion of the necessity of looking at smooth bodies decorated with finely sculpted designs under oblique illumination from a 'temperate' light.

If we translate the underlying idea that very low relief is barely discernible even under ideal illumination into Ghiberti's own practice of relief sculpture (fig. 47), we might argue that the nearest figures, fully rounded, give off punchy 'species', making a forceful impact on our sight, while the low-relief figures in the background are the source of weak and indefinite 'species', which ape the weaker impression made by far off objects. But this is to write words into Ghiberti's mouth, and potentially to invent a fourth commentary for him. Such an invention might be fun, but it would push the historical endeavour further in the direction of fiction than is customary, even in art history.

Ghiberti's anthology has not generally been regarded with much favour by most art historians, and the single manuscript known to us contains many errors, but the intellectual control needed to weave the texts together is not inconsiderable. The sharpest break occurs near the end, when he suddenly uses the preface to Vitruvius's eighth book to introduce aspects of the science of man,

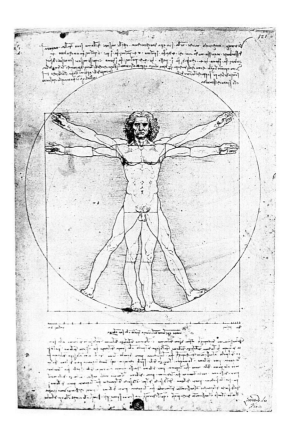

48. Leonardo da Vinci,
*'Vitruvian Man' (Human
Figure Inscribed in a Square
and a Circle)*, Venice,
Galleria della Accademia

subsequently quoting untranslated Latin passages from the Islamic authors, Avicenna and Averroes, on the forms and functions of parts of the body. He then reverts to an Italian paraphrase of the preface and opening section of Vitruvius's book III, where the great artists of antiquity, including Myron, Polykleitos, Pheidias and Lysippus, are used to introduce the topic of proportion or *symmetria*, including the famous observation that the extremities of a man with outstretched arms and leg will touch a circle centred on the navel (fig. 48). Ghiberti's own observations on the proportional measures of the body are next interspersed with appropriate passages from Vitruvius, together with the somewhat inappropriate section on ancient scene painting, before the text ends abruptly in the middle of the continuation of Ghiberti's personal analysis of human proportions. Whether Ghiberti himself stopped here, or whether the break is peculiar to the one surviving manuscript is unclear.

Whatever criticisms we may make of Ghiberti's literary efforts, the overall effect of the *Commentaries* is impressive, particularly for someone trained primarily as an artist. Ghiberti's career shows every sign of social and intellectual ambition. He had manoeuvred himself into positions of authority at the cathedral and Or San Michele, and came to mix in the highest intellectual circles in Florence. He was in close contact with the most avant-garde group of humanists, which included Niccolò Niccoli, astringent classicist and owner of the chalcedony. He joined them in seeking out and exchanging treasured manuscripts of ancient texts. In reading the *Commentaries* we need to bear this elite context in mind. Ghiberti's compilation as a whole seems not to have been primarily intended for broadcast through presentation to a patron or for circulation in the workshops. Rather, it tends to assume the guise of a treasury of knowledge, containing the intellectual 'secrets' which he wished to bequeath to those worthy of receiving it. His 'secrets' do not just reside in the highly technical procedures of bronze casting, gilding and so on, which would be passed down in the workshop, but also in a profound sense of the intellectual artist in the grand span of history and of the arcane wonders of visual science. We would probably be wrong to impute a single, unitary motive to Ghiberti in the undertaking of this compilation over a likely span of some years, but the main thrust of his endeavour does seem distinctly more personal and internally various than those of Cennino, Alberti and Piero.

Leonardo's writings are both publicly and privately oriented. There is no doubt that he saw his views, often of a polemic nature, as being broadcast on the widest possible stage, for the good of his beloved art. However, in practice, they largely remained within the essentially private medium of his voluminous and apparently disordered notebooks, and many of them correspond to thoughts in progress. There is a document known as the *Treatise on Painting* (*Trattato della pittura*) by Leonardo, which was circulated in various manuscript versions before its appearance in print in 1651, but this was a posthumous compilation from Leonardo's scattered notes by Francesco Melzi, an unusually well-educated pupil who had inherited his master's literary legacy.[136] Leonardo was a great planner of discourses on all manner of topics, and his notebooks contain lists of thematic divisions and subdivisions for the treatments of such sciences as 'On Water', 'On the Flight of Birds', 'On the Human Body', 'On Transformation' (a branch of geometry), and 'On the Elements of Machines'. The contents were generally laid out in the sectional manner of Aristotelian treatises of the later Middle Ages and early Renaissance. When we find him making cross-references to a section in his own 'book', we cannot have any confidence that there was actually a completed treatise on that subject. It is easy to be rude about the failure of Leonardo to complete projects, but faced with the enormous burden of universal knowledge he attempted to shoulder, both on his own behalf and on behalf of each of his projects, the wonder is that he completed anything at all. He repeatedly stressed that the painter must be 'universal', much as Ghiberti and Alberti had done, and he took the injunction literally. It is difficult to know what he intended to include in his *Treatise on Painting* – or, rather, it is difficult to know what he intended to exclude, since there was virtually no branch of knowledge that might not underpin the painter's portrayal of the natural and artificial worlds. For example, he wrote extensively on anatomy, an unquestionably relevant science – but how much could feasibly be included in a book on painting? A number of Leonardo's notes are specifically headed 'On Painting', and he did at various points give thought to aspects of the organisation of his intended treatise, including the setting down of an extensive list of headings for optical topics under the general title, '*della pittura*', in the large compilation in Milan known as the Codice atlantico.[137] But no definitive scheme survives, and it is unlikely that one was ever produced. If it was, he would likely have changed his mind in the fullness of time.

How then are we to handle Leonardo's 'art theory'? My starting point here, in keeping with the approach I am emphasising throughout this book, is to take into account the nature of what has come down to us – bearing in mind that the form in which his legacy has survived may bear little resemblance to its original nature. We talk of Leonardo's 'notebooks' or 'manuscripts', but such terms are convenient pieces of shorthand rather than adequate descriptions. What we possess, in various repositories throughout the world, is a wide variety of types of material. There are separate pages of drawings, sometimes later bound into volumes, which may have been subsequently dismembered (and even rebound again). These pages may themselves always have been separate or they might once have been gathered together and possibly bound by Leonardo. There are surviving notebooks, actually bound by Leonardo, but only a detailed study of the content and the physical composition of the books will help us to decide if Leonardo filled them as pre-bound 'notebooks' or whether they were assembled after the notes and drawings were made. The notebooks range from tiny 'pocket-books', packed with minuscule writing and multitudinous sketches, to books composed of larger sheets which contain quite polished diagrams and organised texts. Some appear to have served as portable jotters, while others, particularly those dealing with machines, appear to have been working towards publishable treatises (fig. 49). Sometimes a manuscript has been compiled from bunches of pages from other dismembered manuscripts. The compilations bound by later owners not surprisingly contain material originating from various dates throughout Leonardo's almost forty-year career as a filler of sheets of paper. Even the notebooks compiled by Leonardo himself generally contain material which is heterogeneous in content and sometimes varied in date. We also face the problem that some of Leonardo's legacy only survives in other people's transcriptions, as is the case with three-quarters of the material in Melzi's transcribed *Trattato*. And, of course, we have to take into account that if such a substantial proportion of the writing on art is lost, there is likely to have been at least as great an attrition of his writings on other subjects. Faced with such problems, the historian might well share Leonardo's own despair: 'This will be a collection without order drawn from many pages which I have copied here, hoping to put them in order in their places, according to the subjects with which they will deal, and I believe that before I am at the end of this, I will have to repeat the same thing many times.'[138]

How are we, faced with even more difficulties than Leonardo himself in coming to terms with his writings, to 'put them in order'. The answer is that there is no one method which will produce *the* right order. Which of the potential orders we choose depends upon the demands we make on the material. By a careful study of the content and codicology of some of the manuscripts, we can reconstruct the sequence in which Leonardo moved from one topic to another, and how his thoughts progressed within a single topic. We can show that there was 'a method in his madness', but it is not a method which leads naturally on to a single, definite mode of presentation. The detailed study of each manuscript (either as surviving or as reconstructed from dispersed elements), with commentary and facsimile, is best suited to revealing Leonardo's own sequences of thought. But he himself was aiming at presentation by topic, not according to the archaeology of his own procedures. We can group his notes

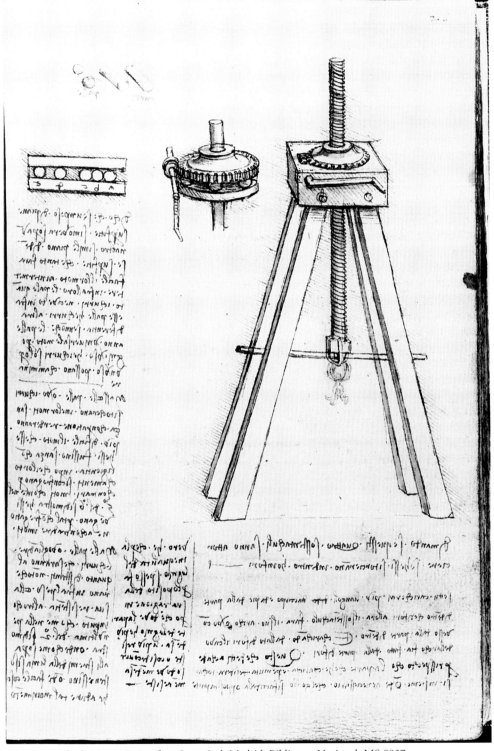

49.   Leonardo da Vinci, *Design for a Screw Jack*, Madrid, Biblioteca Nacional, MS 8937

by subject, in the kinds of anthologies which have been made (most notably by Richter and MacCurdy) and which have served successive generations of Leonardisti very effectively. But the subject-divisions cannot be definitively established in line with Leonardo's intentions, which were never rigidly codified, and such divisions do violence to the unity and fluidity of Leonardo's thought across what we regard as separate subjects. Transcription by manuscript or division by subject both also share the problem that they are likely to mingle material from very different dates in Leonardo's career. It is not surprising that a mind as inventive and receptive as Leonardo's should have evolved substantially in its attitudes throughout his career. One of the main tasks for the historian of Leonardo is to reconstruct the development of his views on particular topics, watching the impact of his reading, his contacts, his experiences and his investigations, and to gain an overall sense of whether the evolution of the mind that encompassed such diversity can be seen characterised in terms of some kind of mental unity. There are also other possible orders for the handling of the material, such as the grouping together of all his statements that refer implicitly or explicitly to the social status of artists in general and Leonardo in particular – the kinds of order that bear virtually no resemblance to any divisions recognised by Leonardo and differ radically from the established techniques for the editing of his writings. Clearly, different types of publications are required to bring all these different kinds of ordering strategy to bear upon such diffuse material.

In the context of the present chapter, I am obviously faced with an impossible task in giving even the truncated kind of overview that I have provided of the more unitary works by our four other theorists. Given my present emphasis upon thinking about what is being said to whom, I propose to think about content and address within the main topics covered by those of his surviving writings that can be reasonably identified as belonging to a fairly comprehensive treatise on painting. For convenience, I am taking the topics in more-or-less the order that I devised for an anthology of *Leonardo on Painting*, which used quite radical editing to splice Leonardo's views together into a more or less systematic whole.

In terms of public polemic, directed at an audience of influential people, not least the denizens of the courts, the most conspicuous of his themes is the supreme status of painting, which is not only promoted in Albertian terms as a liberal art but is accorded superintendency over virtually every form of visual knowledge. And visual knowledge is supreme, since, as Aristotle had insisted, the eye serves the chief of the senses. Painting is

> the sole imitator of all the manifest works of nature . . . [and] a subtle invention which with philosophical and subtle speculation considers all manner of forms: sea, land, trees, animals, grasses, flowers, all of which are enveloped in light and shade. Truly this is science, the legitimate daughter of nature, because painting is born of that nature; but to be more correct, we should say granddaughter of nature, because all visible things have been brought forth by nature and it is among these that painting is born. Therefore we may justly speak of it as the granddaughter of nature and as the kin of God.[139]

To achieve such universal and elevated imitation, the offices of the eye need to be systematically observed:

> Painting embraces all the ten functions of the eye; that is to say, darkness, light, body and colour, shape and location, distance and closeness, motion and rest. My little work will comprise an interweaving of these functions, reminding the painter of the rules and methods by which he may imitate with his art all these things – the works by which nature adorns the world.[140]

The visual functions or 'intentions' correspond in type to those that the medieval Aristotelians had identified as the fundamental properties of the world as presented to our sight.

The visual sovereignty of painting is used as the basis for his obsessive denigration of poetry, the descriptive powers of which are characterised as sequential, fragmentary, transitory, parasitic and wearisome. Painting affects the spectator more vividly by apparently presenting the 'real' thing to our sight, whether it is the lover looking at a portrait of his beloved, the worshipper kneeling in front of a devotional image, the city dweller admiring cool landscapes in times of oppressive heat, or a dog looking loyally at the depiction of its master. Anything the poet claims to be able to achieve through the invention of imaginative subject matter, the painter can accomplish with his *fantasia*, envisaging and depicting such terrifying visions as a Dantesque inferno, and composing 'a story which signifies great things . . . as when Apelles painted the *Calumny*'.[141] Painting's vividly instantaneous presentation of proportional harmonies, which lies outside the poet's potential, is rivalled by music (an art whose claims to 'scientific' excellence Leonardo takes very seriously), but even music is sequential and, when all is said and done, enters our receptive soul via a less noble sense. Even the visual art which seems to be the sister of painting – the art of sculpture – comes in for a beating from painting's self-appointed advocate. Not only is sculpture a sweaty, manual business, unsuited to a gentleman (as Lucian had argued), but it also entails a lesser mastery of visual 'science'. It borrows light from nature to model its forms; is deficient in representing colours, textures, transparencies and atmospheres; and generally requires a lesser range of illusory artifice.

These arguments for the superiority of painting, in what has become known as Leonardo's *paragone*, rely upon a number of rhetorical strategies which at their best rely upon exaggeration and at worst upon misrepresentation of the opposing case.[142] Their tone can best be understood in the context of a relatively formalised debate – either a real debate like the one in which Leonardo is recorded as participating in the Sforza Court at Milan in 1498, or the kind of written dialogues which the Renaissance had adopted in emulation of ancient models. The air of real debate is reflected in his determination to address the main types of poetic genre practised at court: the great narrative, the imaginative invention, the philosophical exploration, the eulogy, the love poem, the pastoral and the burlesque. On one occasion he places the arguments in the mouth of a known person, King Matthias of Hungary, a renowned humanist patron of the arts who is recorded as having commissioned a Madonna from Leonardo.[143] What we should not assume, as is often done, is that Leonardo was contributing to a well-established genre of courtly debate, even less that there was a kind of intellectual sport known as the *paragone* (a term which was only applied to the opening section of Melzi's compilation in 1817). Competitions were of course well known in the arts. There was a long tradition of poetic contests, and the status of poetry as a vehicle for truth or lies was an established matter of vigorous dispute. In the visual arts the humanists could point to the sportive rivalries recorded by Pliny, to say nothing of actual contests, like that which resulted in Ghiberti being awarded the commission for his first set of Baptistery doors. And anyone concerned with Horatian ideas of artistic licence could hardly avoid the cross-referencing between the attributes of painting and poetry. However, the set-piece air of Leonardo's verbal pitting of painting against poetry, music and sculpture is not found in earlier written debates about the status of various arts, and may have been his invention. If so, it was an influential invention, taken up in written form on a widespread basis, beginning with Castiglione's famous book *The Courtier* (*Il cortegiano*).

When we turn to Leonardo's thoughts on the optical techniques needed to realise painting as the supreme constructor of natural effects, we encounter a more heterogeneous body of material. Many of the passages correspond to thoughts in process, while many of the diagrams consist of the kinds of visual 'experiment' through which Leonardo characteristically researched his ideas. There are some developed and redrafted statements on perspective, most notably its basic definition: 'perspective is a rational demonstration by which experience confirms that all things will send their semblances to the eye by pyramidal lines. . .'.[144] And his insistence upon obedience to the general principles of atmospheric perspective is unequivocally apparent. But we encounter the overwhelming problem that Leonardo's ideas on vision, above all his views on the properties and behaviour of the eye, underwent radical changes over a twenty-five year span. He began from a standpoint identical to Alberti's, believing that the visual pyramid and the painter's construction stood in an unproblematic relation to each other and to the workings of the eye. As he became more closely acquainted with medieval optics – once quoting a translated passage from Pecham's *Perspectiva communis* (on 'standard optics')- so he came to realise that the visual pyramid was not a physical reality.[145] If, as was necessary, perception occurred at a surface rather than at an indivisible point, considerable problems arose for the definite vision of things, since different rays from one point on an object could pass through the pupil to impinge upon different parts of the receptive power. We now know that this problem is overcome by the focusing properties of the lens, but for Leonardo it did much to explain the range of uncertainties and delusions of vision which increasingly fascinated him. Many of the visual puzzles on which he wrote, such as curvilinear perspective (which he appears to have dismissed as a workable option), 'natural', 'artificial' and 'compound' perspective, binocular vision, the apparent diameters of rounded objects at different distances, effects of contrasts of colour and tone, errors in judging size and distance, the seeing of rapid motion, and the action of the pupil, probably never resulted in definitive solutions. But, taken collectively, they did predispose Leonardo to avoid simple, dogmatic linear perspective in his later paintings.

This is not to say that Leonardo despairingly abandoned himself to visual subjectivity. Rather, the effects which were subjective to the viewer could be rationally understood and codified. The problem was that such codification set ever-increasing demands upon the scrutiny of visual effects in action, and ultimately lead to the exhaustion of his or anyone's ability to accomplish all the large-scale and minute observations required in all given circumstances. We need only read his discussions of the proportioned effects of atmospheres of graded densities as we look through them at various angles, or his pretty scrutiny of light and shade in the leaves of trees to appreciate the extraordinary character of the task he set painting and at the same time to become aware of its ultimately unrealisable nature.

His demands for the painter's anatomical knowledge were no less stringent. To master the kind of decorum required for an Albertian *historia*, the painter needed to understand the machinery of the bodies of the old and the young, the strong and the weak, the skinny and the corpulent, the complacent and the active, the sad and the happy, the male and the female, the evil and the good, and so on. The necessary mastery required both the internal investigation of the functioning of the body (including the nature and performance of the brain which dictates expression and motion), and a programme of people-watching, in which their actions in situations of debate, conflict, labour, listening, rest etc. were observed and recorded in small and larger notebooks carried for the purpose (fig. 50). And, underlying the particularities of physiognomy and stature were the universals of proportion, not only the ideal scheme proposed by Vitruvius (fig. 48), but also the internally consistent proportions of differently constituted bodies, whether stocky or attenuated. As with his discussion of optics, the drawings and notes on anatomy and proportions range from relatively resolved compositions, as in the page containing the *Vitruvian Man*, to informal records of research in progress. Given this variety, it is impossible to infer a uniform purpose or clearly defined audience. Some of the anatomical investigations, particularly those devoted to the muscles and skeleton, were potentially positioned to make a notable contribution to anatomical science at the highest level, while other records are overtly directed at the young painter.

Indeed, there are sections in Leonardo's writings on art where he is clearly speaking to a young painter, encouraging the pupil to cultivate good habits in personal and professional practice, and regaling him with a characteristically heavy set of demands with respect to the imitation of nature. Some of the advice is concerned with seeing and representing, while other sections deal with more practical matters, such as the set up of lighting in a studio or courtyard to achieve effects of grace in the modelling of flesh. There are also impulsive descriptions of how to envisage some particularly dramatic scenes, such as battles and the deluge. These can be recognised as Leonardo's personal version of *ekphrases*, and can clearly be aligned with the kind of account that Ghiberti gave of the storm in Lorenzetti's lost mural. A brief sample is all that is possible here:

> . . . Oh, how many you might have seen covering their ears with the hands in abhorrence of the uproar caused throughout the gloomy air by the raging, rain-soaked winds, the thunder of the heavens and the fury of the fiery bolts. For others the mere closing of their eyes was not enough. By placing their hands one over the other they more effectively covered them in order not to see the pitiless slaughter of the human race by the wrath of God. Oh, how

50.   Leonardo da Vinci, *Studies of Figures in Digging, Pulling etc.*, Windsor, Royal Library, no. 12644v

51.   Leonardo da Vinci, *Study of a Deluge*, Windsor, Royal Library, no. 12380

much weeping and wailing! Oh how many terrified beings hurled themselves from the rocks! Huge branches of great oaks could be seen weighed down with men borne through the air by the fury of the impetuous winds. . . [146]

Ostensibly intended as an instruction on how to represent the subject, we may sense that the *descriptio* has assumed a life of its own, which has come to transcend its original purpose. How it might have eventually been set within a publishable literary vehicle is unclear, just as the function of the related *Deluge Drawings* (see fig. 51) cannot be defined with any certainty. The drawings do not appear to be preparatory studies in any straightforward sense. They could have been intended as illustrations for the *Treatise on Painting*, but the series as a whole seems to have an impetus which goes beyond such an illustrative function. And in what Renaissance medium could they have been adequately reproduced?

Even with a text that an author has placed before the world in published form, we should be wary of defining his or her intentions in too unitary and stable a fashion, though it is often reasonable to speak in general terms of an intended audience. In the case of Leonardo's surviving literary legacy, each part needs to be looked at in its own right, and, even then, is likely to resist neat codification.

If, as I have been requiring in relation to each of our five texts, the historian understands what kind of thing it is, the question still remains as to what use it may be put. The obvious answer is that the treatises illuminate practice, but even this solution poses a major problem, because we do not necessarily know whether we are dealing with a body of theory which dictated practice, or with a literary by-product of practice which is primarily aimed at making a point to those who might be receptive to the advancing social and intellectual claims of the artists. In the light of what has been said about the texts, it should be apparent that there is no simple answer to this question. The most straight-forward relation to practice is presented by Cennino's technical prescriptions, which both describe proven methods and are intended to guide the future making of pictures. His accounts have been brought into fruitful relationship with the data emerging from the technical examination of trecento paintings. However, we have seen that Alberti's perspective construction, for all its air of step-by-step instruction, is generic in character rather than providing a direct prescription for any specific act of picture-making. Ghiberti provides no instructions at all, and Leonardo's extraordinarily detailed analyses of optical effects rarely extend to ways that the requisite effects might be achieved in paint. Indeed, it is difficult to see how many of his observations could have been incorporated into pictorial practice, either on the technical grounds of what Renaissance media could actually achieve, or in the light of what was considered visually decorous in the kinds of picture Leonardo would have been expected to paint. Piero was certainly providing detailed and relatively comprehensive instruction on how to achieve specific acts of foreshortening. Although we may doubt the practicality of going through such long-winded procedures for every significantly foreshortened form in a painting, detailed scrutiny of even small details in large wall-paintings confirms that he did pre-plan the delineation of each element with meticulous care. Even where the detail was so high above the spectator as to be barely discernible, Piero transferred pre-arranged constructions via pricked cartoons. Clearly, getting something right was a matter of ethical imperative for Piero, regardless of the practicalities of viewing – much as his text took no cognisance of what it was reasonable to expect of less obsessive practitioners than himself.

The texts considered in this chapter can stand within a potentially large number of histories which are very different from the stories of how pictures assumed their visual appearance. We have seen plenty of evidence which could be considered within the social history of art, both in terms of the writers' own careers and more generally in the positioning of ambitious artists in their societies. We have examined them from angles which suggest that they might, for instance, play a role in the history of education, helping us to chart the rise of the educationally ambitious artisan. We have examined material which illuminates the provision of an overtly theoretical or 'scientific' base for the practical wisdom of the workshops, a theme which is to play a conspicuous role in the histories of what is conventionally known as the Scientific Revolution of the sixteenth and seventeenth centuries. We could set them within the history of their own genre, that is to say in the history of writing about art, which came to assume a character of its own and which at various stages throughout history became notably detached from the making of art in practical contexts.

The aspects of the texts relating to perception and representation (most especially perspective) have also been used in the most ambitious fashion to posit huge cognitive shifts, not only in the relationship between the spectator and the works of art, and in the birth of the idea that the history of art is a history of vision, but also in terms of a whole new way of seeing and conceptualising the world. However, it seems to me that all the great overarching theories both exaggerate the breaks between, say, the Giottesque manner and the invention of Brunelleschian perspective, and even more seriously they automatically conflate a mode of representation with a mode of seeing – in a disastrous manner. In their most extreme forms, the claims for a new mode of vision (corresponding to perspectival order in pictures) would lead to the natural corollary that inhabitants of the Byzantine world kept bumping into chairs, since they had no systematic way of 'seeing' the precise measure of space between one object and another. The present book is not the right vehicle for the exploration of such 'big' problems – although some of the issues will be broached in the final chapter – but the tenor of my present endeavour is consciously resistant to the removal of the business of art from the mechanisms for the pursuit of the business as a concrete human activity. The big theories, in the form in which they invariably appear, almost always violate the principle of functional understanding which I have been advocating, and indulge in the kind of grand intellectualising that spuriously abstracts our understanding from any 'whiff of reality'.

There clearly were radical and far-reaching moves being made in a range of arts and sciences in the Renaissance which permitted human beings to operate on their world with different kinds of powers, and gave them the means to record their achievements in newly effective vehicles of visual communication, but we should not mistake the tool with the definition of the task. The formulas in the texts we have been studying, like the visual techniques themselves, were tools – albeit complex and often ambiguously conceived tools – designed to perform more-or-less clearly envisaged functions for particular people in particular places at particular times.

IV   EVALUATIONS

THE CONTRAST BETWEEN the scales of value implicit in the kinds of contractual subordination we examined in chapter II and the inflationary intellectual claims of the theorists in chapter III raises obvious questions about potential conflicts of attitude and expectation between patrons and artists. If the theorists and the ambitious artists for whom they spoke enjoyed any measure of success in boosting the status of art and artists, can this be discerned in the valuation of their products? Or were prices and financial valuations insulated from any increase in the intellectual worth accorded to the practice of the visual arts? Or, at the end of the day, did the rhetoric of art's advocates fall on unrelievedly stony ground?

In thinking about the value placed on something, it is worth reminding ourselves that 'value' is a more complex concept than might be apparent at first sight. If we limit our sense of the value of an item to its financial worth at a particular moment, the idea of value is perhaps not too complicated – although the value of a Renaissance work of art could be identified either with the cost of its acquisition or with the kind of valuation (a notional resale price) it would be accorded in an inventory. In the case of works by living or recent masters the resale price would almost always be less than its original cost. But if we think about value in the more subjective terms of the value that an individual or a group of people place upon that item, we enter rather different territory. A contemporary example will help to define the kinds of complex and often intangible variables involved.

Let us imagine that a couple who were moderately well-off twenty years ago occasionally bought paintings at a local auction, for prices well below their combined monthly income, which seemed to represent a really serious sum of money for a painting. They have since stopped buying because their disposable income has not increased and the prices are higher. The persons in question own a car, the new price of which was four times their monthly income (though its value, like a painting by a modern master in the Renaissance, dropped immediately on its purchase). Do we literally assume that the car is more than four times more esteemed than any of the paintings in the eye of the owners? I think this is unlikely to be the case. How much is sensibly paid for a particular item is judged in relation to a general sense of reasonable expenditure in relation to needs and desires, and these needs and desires are determined by complex mixtures of rational priorities, unquestioned habits, established patterns of relative value, the behaviour of social comparators, and individual proclivities. The apportioning of budgets in households where the income is high enough to involve a range of expenditure on 'necessities' and 'luxuries' is most unlikely to be determined by a formula for the precise matching of financial value with other value systems.

Let us now suppose their house suffers a disastrous fire, and the owners have only time to rescue a few items. I suspect that driving the car out of the garage would not spring to most people's minds as their first priority. Providing the children are safe (although children have *no* obvious financial value), the owners are unlikely to decide what to rescue on a quick mental survey of those items which were most costly. There is a good chance that the paintings might feature well up the list of items to be saved, since they are 'irreplaceable' according to accepted notions of art and creativity – whereas a car is not. Items of so-called 'sentimental value' are likely to be assigned a high priority, such as family 'heirlooms'. Certainly it is not uncommon for someone whose house has been burgled to be more upset by the loss of personal items that acted as bearers of associations and sentimental meanings than by the theft of objects of greater financial value. In less extreme circumstances, it is not hard to imagine a situation in which particular items might temporarily assume an enhanced value. Suppose, for example, that our relatively modest collectors are to be visited by someone who is known to 'appreciate art' and has asked to look at the paintings. Their acquisitions now perform an enhanced role. Their frames are given a quick dust and their hanging is straightened, whereas normally they hang on the walls relatively unnoticed.

Oscar Wilde provided a wittily succinct way of defining the two poles of the value systems based on financial and other criteria, when he described his materialistic contemporaries as 'people who know the price of everything and the value of nothing' – an aphorism that has been used within the art world to categorise the attitudes of dealers. The poles are of course exaggerated for the purposes of humour. In this chapter we will see a complex interpenetrating of such differently founded value systems. I intend first to look at one kind of evidence for the remuneration of artists in the quattrocento, and then at the role of cost from the patron's standpoint. The valuation and evaluation of art will subsequently be studied through the examples of a Medici inventory, taking us into the birth of the practice of art dealing in its modern sense. Entering through the more personal account of patronage in Giovanni Rucellai's *Zibaldone*, we will move towards more subjective values, and be able to witness some other early effects of the artists' push for status. Finally, the very selective explosion of rewards for a few 'super-artists' will be studied in a few sixteenth-century instances.

Arriving at an accurate idea of what constituted a 'standard' payment for particular kinds of artistic production is difficult. There is a surprising variation in the prices patrons were prepared to pay and artists were willing to accept for apparently similar work under comparable circumstances. It is possible to propose some mean prices for types of painting and sculpture, but the erratic nature of the surviving agreements means that a precise average of all documented prices will not be all that helpful. The main evidence for payment occurs in contracts and in the ensuing records of the progress and completion of the commission – with or without disputes and processes of evaluation. Looking at, say, the stipulated payments for altarpieces, there are striking variations. Filippo Lippi was promised payment of as little as 40 florins in 1437 for his *Barbadori Altarpiece*, which turned out to be one of the most innovatory works of its time, while Fra Angelico had contracted to receive the handsome sum of 190 florins to paint an altarpiece for the Linen Guild in 1433, for which Ghiberti provided the marble frame.[147] Although Fra Angelico was to paint an area nearly half as large again as Filippino, and there is more extensive use of gilding in the Linnaiuoli tabernacle, the difference remains considerable. When we find that Piero della Francesca was to be paid a massive 320 florins in 1454 for an altarpiece in S. Agostino in his home town of Borgo S. Sepolchro, we are faced with an even greater discrepancy, not least because we would not instinctively expect remuneration in a smallish provincial centre to equal or exceed that in Florence.[148] Some artists did seem to be capable of commanding consistently high remuneration. Fra Angelico, rather in contradiction to what we might expect of a pious Dominican monk labouring humbly for the glory of God, was not only well rewarded for the Linnaiuoli altarpiece, but he was later paid 200 ducats a year by Pope Nicholas V as a retainer for working in the winter months, while at the same time being employed at a comparable rate (with expenses for materials and living) on the frescoes for the Cappella Nuova in Orvieto Cathedral.[149]

However, the prices paid to the same artist could fluctuate considerably. Neri di Bicci's *Riccordanze*, which provide the most complete record for any practice, indicate he might receive fees in the range of 40 to 14 florins for altarpieces of much the same relatively modest size and involving similar tasks.[150] Cima da Conegliano, working out of Venice, received 67 ducats for the altarpiece of the *Madonna, Child and Saints* in his home town of Conegliano in 1492, while the relatively modest town of Portoguaro paid the far from modest sum of 132 ducats for *The Incredulity of St Thomas* in 1497.[151] A survey of Venetian altarpieces between 1450 and 1530 reveals fluctuations between 17 and 450 ducats, differences which are not always explicable in terms of scale, materials or artist's reputation.[152] The outstanding price for a painting in the north of Italy was the 500 ducats paid to Lorenzo Lotto by the military commander, Alessandro Colleoni, for a large altarpiece in the church of SS. Stefano e Domenico in Bergamo (fig. 52).[153] The contract of 15 May 1513 stipulates that Lotto was to produce a 'magnificent and singular altarpiece or ancona with all the art and talent [*arte ingenioque*] that is humanly possible'. Why this price should have been so out of line is unclear; the mean price in the Veneto and surrounding territories appears to have been 80-100 ducats.

We should also remember that part of the payment might be made in the less quantifiable form of living costs or in the provision of marketable commodities, as we noted in chapter II in the cases of Albertinelli and Mino da Fiesole, or even by the transfer of property, as happened with Leonardo's commission for S. Donato a Scopeto. Occasionally, the commissioners undertook to house the artist for the duration of the contract – or, exceptionally, to provide a house in perpetuity. Such payments, which did not involve hard cash, may well have been financially attractive to both parties.

120

52. Lorenzo Lotto, *Bergamo Altarpiece (Madonna and Child with Sts Alexander, Barbara, Roch, Dominic, Mark, Catherine, Stephen, Augustine, John the Baptist and Sebastian)*, Bergamo, S. Bartolommeo

A range of factors account for discrepancies in levels and manners of payment, some of which are those which operate in any free-market economy. Although there is no evidence of anything like systematic competitive tendering for commissions, preliminary soundings about the prices to be asked by various masters may have preceded the more formal discussions. In 1474, the agent for the Duke of Milan obtained quotes in the range of 100 to 200 ducats for the painting of the vault in the chapel of the Castello, and finally recommended that a team of artists who had reduced their price from 175 to 150 offered the best all-in deal.[154] The need of an artist for work at a particular time could well act as a depressing factor on the level of payment he was willing to accept. An artist might also have been willing to accept lesser remuneration when particular incentives were involved. It may have seemed desirable to work at an especially competitive price for a prestigious patron or to supply a work in a highly desirable location. A painter might well have been willing to offer his services at cut price to his native town. Filippino Lippi, who had agreed to undertake the *Adoration of the Magi* in 1497 for the distinctly high price of 300 florins (a commission on which Leonardo had defaulted), was willing to supply an altarpiece for the Palazzo Pubblico in Prato 'for a reduced sum totalling thirty *fiorini larghi* in gold', on account of his feelings for the 'land in which he was educated' and his love for 'the men of the land of Prato'.[155] On the other hand, Piero della Francesca provided no such favours for S. Agostino in his home town. Perhaps a civic commission brought out more patriotic sentiments than an ecclesiastical or private contract.

The decisive determinant of price was, of course, what moneys were made available to meet the costs. The general tendency of commissioners was, naturally, to obtain something at the best possible price, but quality was a continual concern, and few patrons, particularly corporate bodies, were prepared to risk being supplied with something which did not match up to the standards of their rivals and comparators. The group dynamics of such decisions were complex and variable. One of the best documented of the kind of discussions that were involved in determining the sums to be allocated concerns the altarpiece planned by the Compagnia della SS. Trinità in Pistoia in 1455 (fig. 53), as recorded in a discursive minute by the chamberlain, the priest Piero di Ser Landi.[156] Although one member advocated that they should plan for 'a modest thing of little cost', another evoked the Compagnia's honourable history and the prestigious location of the work to propose the expenditure of between 150 to 200 florins, a high sum that was accepted by a narrow majority of '20 black beans to 17 white'. We will have occasion in chapter V to see how the chamberlain himself intervened over the content of the altarpiece that was subsequently commissioned from Pesellino.

In special circumstances, where expenses unavoidably proved to be greater than expected, or where the artist was successful in appealing for higher remuneration, the original payments might have to be increased. However, the sums established by corporate patrons were relatively immune from adjustment. When the Guild of the Cambio was seeking a statue of *St Matthew* (fig. 14) from Ghiberti in 1418, they were unsurprisingly concerned that the figure should be at least as grand as the *St John the Baptist* (fig. 54), earlier undertaken for the Calimala's niche on Or San Michele, but specifically debarred the sculptor from

53.   Pesellino (Francesco di Stefano), *Trinity with Sts Mamas, James the Greater, Zeno and Jerome*, finished by Filippo Lippi, London, National Gallery

citing the sum he had received for 'his salary, remuneration and work' on that or any other figure in settling his fees.[157] A more informal agreement with a private patron would tend to leave itself open to more subsequent haggling. A particularly baleful example occurs in a letter of 1457 written to Giovanni de' Medici by Filippo Lippi, whom we encountered in chapter II making a whining plea to Piero, Giovanni's elder brother. In the patron's absence, Filippo had been referring to Bartolommeo Martelli about the costs involved in a painting which involved some extensive gilding, but without success.[158] Of the 30 florins

55.   Filippo Lippi, *Sketch of a Triptych*, Florence, Archivio di Stato, VI. 258

necessary to meet the costs, the painter says that he had only received 14, and is no longer able to proceed. After a mix of assertions and grovelling, the letter, which includes a now much faded sketch (fig. 55) concludes:

> If the expenditure is not so much, I will go along with what it is. And so that you can be well informed I send you the drawing, how it is made in wood, the height and the breadth, and for the love of you I don't want to take more than a hundred florins from you for the labour; I renounce any more. I beg you to answer, for I am dying here and would like to leave, and if it was presumptuous to have written to you, pardon me, and I will always do, more sometimes and less sometimes, what pleases your reverence.

Fra Filippo, the disreputable monk, was known for his ability to stretch his patrons' patience, and it is easy to sense why. One hundred florins, over and above the expenses, was a high figure.

How can we match the sums a painter might expect to receive for his work with the standard of living? The most complete and extensively analysed data comes from the building industry, for which plentiful accounts survive. It has been estimated that a working man would have needed about 36 *lire* annually for food (given a diet extremely meagre by today's standards), with a further 20 for rent and 20 for clothing.[159] Against this total of around 76 *lire* can be set an income of 130 *lire* or so for an unskilled worker, which meant that two adults would be on the margin of decency. It was reported in 1480 that a five-person family could hope to live reasonably in Florence for 70 florins a year (about 400 *lire*). The income for masons ranged from about 175 *lire* to the 100 florins that

54.   Lorenzo Ghiberti, *St John the Baptist,* Florence, Or San Michele

125

Brunelleschi was to receive in 1426 as joint *capomaestro* for the cathedral dome, which is still less than the salary of senior civic officials, who might have expected to earn about 150 florins or more. Ghiberti, his busy partner, was awarded 3 florins a month, on condition that he spent at least one hour on site each working day.

One of the problems in making such comparisons is the changing exchange rate between the *lire* and the gold florins, which gradually increased from 3½: 1 in 1350 to 7:1 in 1500. In 1480, the 70 florins for a comfortable life was equivalent to about 400 *lire*. Those who received remuneration in florins (or equivalent gold coins issued elsewhere) were insulated against the devaluation of the silver coinage which the lesser workers received, and since prices remained relatively stable, their purchasing power improved, as did the value of their banked assets. Painters' fees were customarily set in gold coinage, even if the actual payment was made in silver coinage (*denari*), and they therefore fell on the favourable side of the equation. Filippo's aspiration to receive a clear 100 florins for his work on Giovanni's painting suggests that he was looking for a really rather good income, but the reality was that most reasonably successful artists in an urban environment around 1450 could probably expect to live at a level towards the top of that of most skilled workers, but not equal to that of a lawyer or higher civil servant. The Tuscan *catasto* returns in 1427 for Florence, Pisa, Pistoia and Arezzo place artists near the middle of the league table, with an average wealth (including all assets and credits) of just under 350 florins, compared to lawyers at 1,080 florins. Probably the best paid positions available to artists were as superintendents of major building projects or as officials permanently in charge of the architectural fabric of a city or state. A particularly high salary was accorded to the now little-known Giovanni da Siena, who declined to return to his native city in 1428 because he was receiving '300 ducats per year and board for eight persons' at the court of Ferrara, and had been accorded the status of an 'inventor and engineer' rather than a man who practises a 'manual skill'.[160]

The cost of a work of art could vary greatly in a manner that was independent of the net remuneration to the artist. The biggest variations were occasioned by the differing materials in which a work was to be executed. In Venice, where there had been a long-standing tradition of using splendid and costly stones, the large altar and tomb slab which executors ordered for the long-deceased Madonna Verde della Scala in SS. Giovanni e Paolo cost over 421 ducats. Guigliemo de' Grigi, who contracted to make the architectural components in the altarpiece in 1523, was to be paid 145 ducats, and the sculptor of the statue of the Magdalene received a fee of 40 ducats, payments which were less in total than what went on the acquisition of the fine marble, alabaster, porphyry and serpentine.[161]

Our modern tendency to assess the aesthetic merits of a work rather than the quality of its materials can cause us to overlook values that patrons took very seriously. Looking at the sculptural figures undertaken for the guilds who were filling their niches on Or San Michele, following the governmental decree of 1406 commanding them to do so, we might make an easy equation between figures of similar size and high artistic worth, such as the *St Mark* (fig. 56) by Donatello and the *St Matthew* (fig. 14) by Ghiberti. But the fact is that the stone

56.
Donatello, *St Mark*, Florence, Or San Michele

statue by Donatello is unlikely to have cost the Linnaiuoli more than 100 florins, the highest evaluation for one of the equivalent prophets for the cathedral, while the bronze *St Matthew* set back the Cambio in excess of 1,000 florins. Why did the shrewd bankers on the board of the Cambio, including Cosimo de' Medici, apparently spend over the odds? It was a matter of public esteem. Bronze was a far more prestigious medium than stone: the casting of a full-scale statue in bronze was recognised as a modern triumph; bronze was a medium which evoked particular associations with classical antiquity; the rival guild of the Calimala had already demonstrated their magnificence in commissioning a bronze *St John* from Ghiberti; and the sheer fact of the cost of bronze meant that it was exclusive to those powerful few who had the

57.   Michelozzo, *Tabernacle of the Madonna*, Florence, SS. Annunziata

wherewithal to pay for it. The gilded statue of *St Louis* (fig. 16) later made by
Donatello for the Parte Guelfa's niche was literally meant to outshine even the
bronzes commissioned by the Calimala and Cambio. It cost 449 florins without
the expensive gilding and the making of the splendid tabernacle.[162] When the
Mercanzia later commissioned two bronze statues, the *Christ and St Thomas* (fig.
15), for the niche from which the *St Louis* had been ousted, they were

committing themselves to the conspicuous expenditure of large sums, as befitted their important role in the regulation of merchant life in Florence. Late in the day, after the group had been completed, the Mercanzia still owed 400 florins on the bronze, and the overall cost must have been considerably in excess of the 957 *fiorini* 545 *lire* which is recorded in the incomplete accounts.[163] Given the cost of materials, it is not surprising that when Donatello's bronze equestrian memorial to Erasmo da Narni in Padua, the so-called *Gattamelata*, was subject to its final evaluation in 1453, it was estimated at 1,650 ducats.[164]

The brandishing of such conspicuous expenditure was not the sole prerogative of proud corporate bodies. Piero de' Medici, whom we already encountered as a patron in chapter II, was not inclined to hide the munificence of his benefactions. When he paid for a spectacular architectural tabernacle built by Michelozzo in 1467-8 to house a revered image of the Madonna in SS. Annunziata (fig. 57), the cost was not just evident in the lavishness of the materials but, in case anyone should miss the point, an inscription records that 'it cost four thousand florins for the marble alone'. A Medicean property, a house on the Borgo S. Lorenzo, bringing an annual rent of 50 florins, was assigned to the Calimala on the understanding that they ensured the continuance of devotions to the image, including oil for thirty silver lamps, the purchase of candles and a yearly procession on the feast day of the Annunciation.[165]

A nice sense of how a contemporary eye viewed this glorious ensemble can be gained from the *Theotokon* ('Mother of God') written in 1455 by Fra Domenico Corella, a prominent Dominican based at S. Maria Novella. As part of his guide to the visual glories of Florentine churches he visits the Annunziata, recording that 'in this temple resides a worthy image, of marvellous power, renowned for many miracles', which has attracted a large number of wax votive figures placed by the great and good, including representations of 'powerful lords' and 'fierce leaders . . . on enormous horses'.[166] His Latin verses laud Piero's new tabernacle:

But though this famous image of God's mother
Was celebrated by an enormous populace,
Still the structure of that ancient chapel seemed
For Her neither suitable nor sufficient.
Noting this, Piero, undoubted heir of Cosimo,
His country's splendour, guardian of his house,
Wishing to place her in a worthy setting,
Made this work, worthy for a Virgin.
For, well composed throughout of snowy marble,
It surpasses other dwellings in cost and skill.
A single space is located inside the four new columns.
The whole is roofed above by a flat vault
Which antique sculpture drawn by a modern tool
Adorns, and covers with gilded foliage too.
Where many lilies shimmer on green stalks,
Ripe fruit grows red, the sign of the house of the Medici.
Held by an Angel's hand, glitters high the crown,
Which the holy Mary wears on her sublime forehead.

129

The pious Virgin's altar, night and day,
Shine with many lamps, replacing gleaming heaven.

The tone of delight is not so very different from that of 'Theophilus', over three hundred years earlier: 'a human eye cannot decide on which work it should first fix its attention; if it looks at the ceiling panels, they bloom like tapestries; if it surveys the walls, the likeness of paradise is there; if it gazes at the abundance of light from the windows, it marvels at the inestimable beauty of the glass and the variety of this most precious workmanship'.[167] The great difference, though, is the overt crediting of the patron as the author of the work in Piero's case. The glory of God, via the 'Mother of God', is still the definitive end, but the human agent for the promotion of that devotion is now little inclined to retreat behind a veil of humility.

Fra Domenico also singles out for special praise the silver chest in the small oratory adjoining the shrine, which contains precious votive offerings of great value, and which was adorned by 'Iohannes, angelic painter', who is said to be

No less in name than Giotto or Cimabue,
Whose fame was bright in the Tuscan cities,
As the poet Dante sings in his sweet voice.
He flourished in his many virtues, also,
Gentle in his talent [*ingenio*], devout in his religion.
So, above all other painters, to him deservedly
Was given the grace of rendering the Virgin.
As shown by the beautiful form of the divine Annunciate,
Often described by his hands.

The angelic Iohannes is the painter who was baptised as Guido di Piero and had taken the name 'Fra Giovanni of the brothers of San Domenico at Fiesole' when he entered the Dominican order at some point in his twenties. Fra Domenico was right to allude to the frequency with which Fra Angelico (as he came to be called in succeeding centuries) painted the Annunciation. It features on the panels for the doors of the silver chest in the church which is, after all, named after the 'Most Holy Annunciation'; it is the subject of a number of his altarpieces; and it appears more than once in the frescoes in the adjacent Dominican priory of San Marco. Comparing four of his Annunciations gives a good sense of how different visual evocations of 'value' – ranging from the richness praised by Fra Domenico to a studied abstinence – are not so much expressions of their creator's style or artistic taste as spiritual orations attuned to their functions.

The silver chest *Annunciation* (fig. 58), one of a rich set of small panels, is both brilliant and solemn. The event is placed in a courtyard of considerable refinement, and the angel is adorned with rainbow wings and gilded dalmatic. His outstretched hand, signalling the divine origins of the child, is pointedly silhouetted against the *hortus conclusus*, the 'enclosed garden' of the 'Song of Songs', which was symbolic of Mary's inviolate nature. The scrolls at top and bottom juxtapose Isaiah's prophecy of the Virgin birth of Emmanuel, and Luke's New Testament proclamation of the conception of the son called Jesus. The emphasis upon Christ is appropriate at the start of a narrative cycle of

ECCE VIRGO CONCIPIET 7 PARIET FILIVM 7 VOCABIT NOMEN EIVS EMANVL. YSA.VI.C

ECCE CONCIPIES IN VTERO 7 PARIES FILIVM 7 VOCABIS NOMEN EI̯ IHESVM. LVCE . I . C .

58.   Fra Angelico, *Annunciation*, Florence, San Marco, Museo (formerly on the Silver Chest)

59.   Fra Angelico, *Annunciation*, Madrid, Prado

Christ's life which is intended to speak a message of redemption. Something of the same visual quality of decorous richness is apparent on a much larger scale in the splendid altarpiece provided for his 'home' church, S. Domenico at Fiesole, and now in the Prado (fig. 59). Adorned with much delicate gilding, and with the verdant meadows of the Garden of Eden, from which Adam and Eve are expelled, the altarpiece portrays the Virgin (the 'new Eve') as at once humble and as the glorious subject of our devotion at the moment of Christ's incarnation.

When we turn to the frescoed *Annunciation* (fig. 60) in the third of the twenty cells for the brothers on the first floor of the dormitory at San Marco, the visual language dispenses with all but the minimum of decoration. Only the raised haloes and pretty wings of the angel retain some degree of restrained

60.   Fra Angelico, *Annunciation*, Florence, Monastery of San Marco, Cell 3

61.   Fra Angelico, *Annunciation*, Florence, Monastery of San Marco, Upper Corridor

richness. Gone is the Virgin's cloth of honour, her *lapis lazuli* mantle and starry vault. The image is no longer intended for public devotion as an adjunct to the ritual of the mass, but is for solitary monkish contemplation, for the kind of sustained and profound meditation which the Dominican 'witness' on the left, St Peter Martyr, practises in exemplary manner through the exercise of prayer. The richness is no longer that of materials and saturated colours in contrasted profusion but of an inner light which is evoked by the pearly glow of the illuminated surfaces. Between the poles of simplicity and sumptuousness stands the *Annunciation* (fig. 61) at the top of the stairs which lead to the corridors connecting the cells. As we ascend towards this vision of the Annunciate Virgin, set in a strongly delineated loggia beside the *hortus conclusus*, the inscription on the platform of the loggia regales us (or rather regaled the monks) with the instruction that 'When you come before the image of the inviolate Virgin take care that you do not neglect to say an Ave'. Thus the angel's biblical greeting – '*Ave, gratia plena, dominus tecum*' ('Greetings, most favoured one! The Lord is with you') – becomes identified with our 'Hail Mary' as we make our journey from one zone of the monastery to another. As befits its more ceremonial function, there is more ornament than in the cell fresco, including a row of three elegant Corinthian capitals, set against the five Ionic, seemingly to denote Mary's 'feminine' grace according to the bodily decorum associated with the classical orders.

There is no reason to think that the varied levels of richness in the four images simply reflect the available sums of money. Medicean finance was driving the enterprise at San Marco no less than at SS. Annunziata and S. Domenico at Fiesole. The levels of ornament and colouristic display represent the visual equivalent of decorum in rhetoric; that is to say it obeys the rule of appropriateness in the matching of style to function. Actual value as conveyed by materials and metaphoric value as carried by style allow Fra Angelico to speak in the right voice in each setting – and in a manner sympathetic to each patron.

The sums of money that Cosimo and Piero de' Medici put into such projects was considerable. Cosimo's grandson, Lorenzo il Magnifico, looking back on his family's expenditure over a period from 1434 to 1471 (commencing with the return of Cosimo after a brief exile and ending seven years after his death), notes the 'incredible sum' of '663,755 florins spent on buildings, charities and taxes, not counting other expenses'.[168] For example, Cosimo had spent 180,000 florins on building projects at S. Lorenzo and the Badia at Fiesole. Although Lorenzo had good reason to regret that such sums were now lost to him, at a time when the Medici banking empire was showing signs of strain, his *memoriale* informs his sons that 'it gave great lustre to the state and this money seems to have been well spent and I am very satisfied'. The fabric of buildings comprised the greatest expense for a large-scale patron. In the biography of Cosimo by Vespasiano da Bisticci (whose manuscript emporium benefited from Cosimo's patronage) we are told that the 'Pater Patriae' set aside some 10,000 florins for the rebuilding of San Marco as a form of grand penance suggested by Pope Eugenius IV to expiate a financial sin and more generally to mitigate the accusations of usury to which any banker is subject.[169] The alliance between Cosimo and the ambitious Dominican Observants, who had taken over San Marco in 1436, was a shrewd move, resulting in the most modern monastery of its time, equipped with the important library of ancient and modern letters

62. Michelozzo, Library, San Marco, Florence

135

which Niccolò Niccoli had left to Cosimo in 1437 (fig. 62). Fra Angelico was himself a far from humble cog in this machinery, as a senior figure in the local Dominican hierarchy. His pictorial decorations, which use modernised forms of pictorial rhetoric in the service of redefined devotion, were an integral part of Cosimo's programme of reform.

In 1438 Cosimo and Lorenzo had, for a sum of 500 florins, acquired rights to the main chapel in the church, and they decided that the old high altar of San Marco should be dispatched to S. Domenico at Cortona in favour of a more fitting work. It was probably in connection with this project that Domenico Veneziano had written in 1438 to Piero, Cosimo's son (as we saw in chapter II), but in the event it was Fra Angelico who unsurprisingly received the commission for the altarpiece, which was installed in 1440 (fig. 35). Compared to the old centre-piece by Lorenzo de Niccolò, which was an elaborately pinnacled polyptych of the *Coronation of the Virgin*, the new focus for devotions was both striking for the novelty of its unified space and notable for the prominence of the Medicean saints, Cosmas and Damian. It is Cosimo's name-saint who enjoins us with entreated glance and eloquent gesture to worship the Virgin and her Son, ruler of the world. The predella panels, which originally ran along the base of the structure, tell the stories of the two saints, including their healing roles as *medici*, in vividly narrated *historie* of an Albertian kind. The altarpiece is unlikely to have cost more than 150 florins (the price of Gentile da Fabriano's splendid altarpiece for Palla Strozzi), and would have made but a tiny dent in the tens of thousands of florins spent on San Marco as a whole, but its importance as providing a Medicean presence as the central focus for devotions in the church is clearly of the first order and cannot be judged in proportion to the immediate financial outlay. And for the artist, as Domenico Veneziano's letter to Piero testifies, when he was soliciting the commission, the prestige of such a flag-ship project made it far more desirable than another project promising similar financial rewards.

In addition to the direct documentation of expenditure on Medicean projects, we are fortunate to possess detailed information from domestic inventories about their extensive possessions of artefacts. One of the most informative of the documents records the contents of the Palazzo on the Via Largha (fig. 63), the 'palace of Cosimo', on the death of Lorenzo in 1492, but, as the heading makes clear, we are not looking at the original document: 'This book of inventories is copied from another inventory, which was made at the death of magnifico Lorenzo de' Medici, copied by me, the prelate Simone di Stagio dalle Pozze, today, 23 december 1512, as commissioned by Lorenzo di Piero de' Medici.'[170]

The reason for the original stock-taking after Lorenzo's death is obvious. The transcription of a twenty-year-old inventory is less so. In the autumn of 1512 the Medici had been reinstated in Florence, with Spanish assistance, following their expulsion by the Republican factions in 1494. Much of their property had been sequestered in 1494 by the reformed Republican government, and the younger Lorenzo di Piero, grandson of il Magnifico, was beginning to seek some kind of restitution or redress. The survival of the inventory in only a transcript is unfortunate in a number of respects, not least in judging its authorship. Knowing who (or what type of person) compiled an inventory is of obvious importance to how we read it. The content of the entries and rather uneven valuations do not suggest the employment of a notary or other outside

63.   Michelozzo (and others), Palazzo Medici-Riccardi, Florence

professional, but rather of someone resident within the household who was intimately acquainted with the possessions within the palace but was not of great learning. A suitable candidate is Francesco d'Agostino Cegia, the faithful steward and supporter of Piero di Lorenzo, who worked assiduously in Florence after the expulsion to realise the value of some of the more saleable items, especially the jewellery. Cegia's '*libretto sagreto*', composed in a style entirely consistent with the inventory, secretly records the clandestine transactions he undertook on behalf of the Medici between 1494 and 1496.[171] For his trouble, the unfortunate Cegia was decapitated by the Republican regime on 16 December 1497.

Generally, art historians have used the information in the inventory to establish the presence of surviving works, hoping to learn of their authorship and subject matter, and less frequently to establish their setting and value. There has accordingly been a tendency to quote entries on art selectively extracted from the inventories. By contrast, I think it will be illuminating – and more in keeping with the purpose of the document – to undertake a survey of how the inventory handles the range of material under its purview. To accomplish this end, I will be looking primarily at two rooms listed as Lorenzo's, and at the study or *schrittoio*. Other sections of the inventory will provide useful comparative material.

The inventory of the 'palace located at the corner of the via Largha, in the quarter of S. Lorenzo, called the palace of Cosimo' (fig. 63), begins with the entrance and the ground floor rooms, some of which are used for storing wine and other provisions. On the sixth folio of the inventory, we come to the 'large ground-floor room, called the chamber of Lorenzo', which was probably in the far right corner, overlooking the garden.[172] The first item is a huge *spalliera*,

64.　Paolo Uccello, *Battle of San Romano*, London, National Gallery

three-and-a-quarter *braccia* high and twenty-three *braccia* long (i.e. about 1.9 x 13.4 metres), made from cypress wood and decorated with walnut *intarsie*, in which is set a cupboard (*armadio*), 3¼ *braccia* high, with seven shelves and two doors, and a chest (*chassa*) of fifteen *braccia* along the base, all valued in total at 30 florins. We immediately encounter some typical problems in reading an inventory. The term *spalliera* generally denoted panelling at back or 'shoulder' level, but its usage might vary in particular circumstances across a wide range, including the upright back of a chest, cupboard, sideboard, bed, couch or bench, a free-standing panel or tapestry arranged as part of a decorative ensemble, and other decorative hangings of cloth or leather. In this case, the *spalliera* seems to have consisted of built-in panelling running along one of the long walls of the room (about 10 metres) and extending along at least part of one of the shorter walls. The *chassa*, at under 9 metres, would not have filled the long wall, but would have left room for a door. The term *c(h)assa* is itself one of a series of words (and their derivatives) used in the Renaissance to denote what we would call chests, including *cassone, arc(h)a, goffano* (*coffano*), *scrigno* and *forziero* (the most common term in fifteenth-century Florence), depending upon size, function, regional usage, date and the idiosyncrasies of the inventorist. Turning to even the best modern dictionaries does not necessarily tell us precisely what the inventorists were looking at. Sometimes the 'chests' were free-standing items, but they were not infrequently integral parts of the structures of other items of larger furniture, or, as here, built into the woodwork which lined the walls.

　　The next item does little to clarify the precise arrangement. It lists six gold-framed pictures above the *spalliera* and a *lettuccio*, occupying 42 *braccia* in total (i.e. about 24.5 metres), which would have taken up the equivalent of one long and two short walls of the room. The paintings were 'three of the Rout of San

65. Antonio Pollaiuolo, *Hercules and Antaeus* (small version), Florence, Uffizi

Romano and one of a battle of dragons and lions and one of the story of Paris, from the hand of Pagholo Uccello and one from the hand of Francesco di Pessello, in which there is a hunt'. They are collectively valued at 300 florins (i.e. an average of 50 each). Of these, only the three Uccello battle scenes now survive (fig. 64), and they seem to have been adapted in shape by the artist himself to fit their setting – which suggests that they were originally begun for the older Medici palace (i.e. before 1444) or for another location. Then follow seven candlesticks 'around the room', at 160 florins, and a group of other pictures: 'a large *tondo* [a round painting] with surrounding frame worked in gold, in which is painted Our Lady and Our Lord and the Magi who come to make offerings, from the hand of fra Giovanni [Fra Angelico]' at 100 florins; a painting of the 'head of St Sebastian and other figures and arms and *palle* [Medici emblems] in a tabernacle by the hand of Squarcione', worth 10 florins; a panel of St Jerome with six other little paintings at 10 florins; a framed panel of the 'head of the Duke of Urbino [Federigo da Montefeltro]', and one of the 'head of Duke Galeazzo [Sforza of Milan], from the hand of Piero del Pollaiuolo', both valued at 10 florins.

The valuation of the Fra Angelico *Adoration* (fig. 66) is the highest of any picture in the inventory. It matches the 'tapestry cloth to hang on the wall, 20 *braccia* long and 6 *braccia* high, on which is a hunt of the duke of Burgundy'

66.   Fra Angelico (and Filippo Lippi), *Adoration of the Kings*, Washington, National Gallery

stored in a *cassone* in the chamber of the Sala Grande, and surpasses the three large canvases of the *Labours of Hercules* (fig. 65) by Antonio Pollaiuolo in the Sala Grande itself, which were estimated at only 20 florins each.[173] As in other rooms, the pictures in Lorenzo's *chamera terrena* are a miscellany. The triumphant Florentine battle, won under the command of Niccolò da Tolentino, who was a crucial ally of Cosimo, and portraits of important players in the diplomatic game are oriented towards political affairs, in a way that would make an impression on important visitors. Although the room contained both an ordinary bed (a *lettiera*) and a day-bed (a *lettuccio*), guests of status might be admitted to such an apparently private chamber. The fine *tondo* (fig. 66), now generally recognised as having been finished by Filippo Lippi, may well have held important family associations, since its round format alluded to a birth plate (*desco da parto*) and such pictures were typically commissioned to celebrate the arrival of a baby, perhaps Lorenzo himself in 1449 or his brother, Giuliano, in 1453. The story of Paris, probably his judgement of the beauty contest between Aphrodite, Athena and Hera, and Pesello's hunt confirm that there was nothing like a programme or even an *ad hoc* homogeneity in the decorative ensemble.

67. *King Solomon Reclining on a Lettuccio*, from the *Malermi Bible*, Venice, c.1493

The bed, in poplar with walnut decorations, is valued at only 4 florins (perhaps an error in transcription?), less than its coverings and its two sets of hangings: a canopy (*padiglione*) in linen at 10 florins; and a set made from 'six pieces of red say [wool or silk], embroidered with gyrons and falcons' which was accorded a value of 60 florins.[174] The *lettuccio* is a more splendid structure than the bed – with cupboards (*armadi*) and 'caskets' (*chasette*) – measuring over 9 *braccia* long (well over 5 metres) and valued at 45 florins (fig. 67). One of the cupboards is given over to arms and armour, including 'three daggers in the bolognese manner and an iron mace worked with damascening' (16 florins), and 'two cuirasses and a doublet of lamé in the milanese style, all beautiful' (50 florins). The other contained various candlesticks and vessels, a number of which were damascened, including '*quattro chandellieri dommaschini da torchi* [in the Turkish manner]'. Having listed the contents of the compartments in the *lettuccio*, the inventorist returned to the cupboards of seven shelves in the *spalliera*, which were largely occupied by eating and drinking utensils and other vessels. A group of items, including nineteen plates and two vases and two *vasetti minori* 'in porcelain and in various colours' was valued at 150 florins. It is unclear whether these and other porcelain items were genuine Chinese porcelain or early imitations, but the highish values suggests that they were the real thing. Other pieces of furniture, such as a *ciscranna* (a seat comprising a chest with a *spalliera*) and chairs and a table, were modestly valued at a few florins each. The list finishes with 'a spit for pigs and a hatchet'.

Smaller lateral chambers serviced the main room, containing such items as 'a foot basin, of brass, and a warming pan' in the *stufa* (bath chamber), no doubt of particular value in winter, when the heavier bed hangings would also come into their own.[175] A 'pair of chests [*forzerreti*] which make a bed' in the 'room above the *stufa*' may have served a personal groom who slept in an adjacent room or been pressed into temporary service as needed, while a '*saletta terrena degli staffieri allato alla camera di Lorenzo*' (small ground floor hall of the household staff beside the room of Lorenzo) was equipped with a communual table over 4 metres long.[176] The domestic quarters of the palace were organised in suites of rooms, with a *camera* and *anticamera* as the minimum set. Piero, Lorenzo's son, seems to have been assigned a suite comprising a study (containing a diamond pendant worth 3,000 florins), and antechamber with a room above, a chamber, and an armoury (*munitione*) which contained large quantities of joust armour.[177] A large quantity of more functional arms was stored in a large armoury in the upper part of the palace, with such items as 'forty-four crossbows', valued at 106 florins.[178]

The fourteenth folio of the inventory, compiled when the inventorists were moving through the rooms on the first floor, lists the contents of another '*chamera grande di Lorenzo*', which contains far less in the way of decorations.[179] The most notable are a marble relief of the *Ascension* (probably the *Ascension of Christ and the Giving of the Keys to St Peter* in the Victoria and Albert Museum, London) at 15 florins, and a 'Flemish cloth [*panno di Fiandra*] of 5½ *braccia* long and 4 *braccia* high, in which are depicted arches, landscapes and figures' at 25 florins. Above the doors were busts of Lorenzo's father, Piero, and his mother, Lucrezia Tornabuoni. There were also some small-scale mementoes and curiosities, including 'a gilded copper lily of the *palio* of St John' (a tournament prize), an ostrich egg and 'a mirrored ball with a chord of silk'. The greater part of the listing involves very large quantities of clothing in two *forzieri* and a *chassone*. The list of the contents of the first *forziero*, for instance, begins with nine *luchi* (long tunics) of values ranging from 60 to 10 florins, depending upon the materials (and perhaps also on condition), while there were no less than twenty-two *robette* (short robes) in the second, the most expensive of which is '*una robetta di dom.[asc]o chermisi foderata di zibellini* (a robe of scarlet damask lined with sable), estimated at 30 florins. A greater selection of figurative decorations were to be found in the antechamber (*antichamera*) of this room, including Donatello reliefs, religious paintings by Fra Angelico, Pesello and Filippo Lippi, and depictions of Rome, Italy and the 'universe'.[180] This room also had its own *lettiera* and *lettuccio*, together with a large *cassapancha* (couch) of ten *braccia* (almost 6 metres) with a *spalliera* of pine and *pettorali* (sides?) in walnut *intarsia* at a modest 5 florins.

There were of course other inhabitants of the palace than Lorenzo and his immediate family. A room is listed as the '*chamera di Bertoldo over de' chamerieri* [manservants]' was apparently assigned to Bertoldo, the sculptor, who seems to have been on intimate and familiar terms with Lorenzo, beyond those of a conventional *familiaris* of the household.[181] Bertoldo's room seems to have contained Brunelleschi's two perspectival demonstrations of the *Baptistery* and the *Palazzo dei Signori*, though the latter is surprisingly listed as 'a canvas' (*panno*). There was also a room for a priest, 'on the terrace' on the first floor, which was furnished in a far from austere manner, with such items as an intarsiated bed, two *cassapanche*, a substantial *lettuccio*, a gilded *forziero*, a *chassetta* of three *braccia* containing a set of steps (*una schala*), and various chairs.[182] The paintings included religious subjects and a 'picture of wood, in which is painted the image [*impromta*] of Madonna Lucretia [Tornabuoni]',

142

Lorenzo's mother. Most of the items were deemed to be of modest value, but a 'small picture, in which are painted 6 half-figures' is unexpectedly valued at 60 florins, though no author's name is given. The overall impression of the inventory is of a residence plentifully furnished with quality items, to serve a variety of public and private functions, but falling far short of the large-scale abundance of a princely castle in which was housed a large court.

At the end of the inventory there are listings of various other property holdings, with estimates of the revenue that should accrue.[183] In the area of Careggi, where the Medici owned a country villa (in which Cosimo had installed the philosopher, Marsilio Ficino), they held several farms. Typical is 'the farm with a worker's house, of 100 *staiora*, located in the quarter of S. Piero at Charaeggi and in the place called il Fondello, along the hedge, worked by Salvestro Romanello and now Piero Perini, which yields 98 *staia* of wheat, 39 *staia* of corn, 19 barrels of wine, 7 barrels of oil and 192 *libre* of fruit and sundries (*vantaggi*). (A *staiora* = ca. 525 square metres; a *staio* = 24.36 litres; a *barile* of wine = 45.5 litres; a *barile* of oil = 33.4 litres; and a *libra* = 339.5 grams.) The revenue is estimated at 40 florins, but no capital value is given. By comparison, town properties in Pisa were given such values. 'A shop with a house above, located on the Lungharno opposite the piazza de' Chavoli', which brings in 40 florins, is estimated to be worth 700 florins.

Although the compilation of such lists and figures may seem remote from the appreciation of art, and might not make for the most exciting read, they do introduce an air of reality into the understanding of values and priorities. The advantage of gaining some sense of how sections of the inventory function, even in the necessarily summary form given here, is that the character of the document emerges more clearly and a general sense of relative financial worth begins to emerge. The paintings and relief sculptures are not in the main valued very highly, but the assigning of notional prices to works by modern masters was probably a somewhat arbitrary business, because there was no established market in the fifteenth century for the collecting of 'second-hand' works of art. By contrast, there was a developed market for second-hand clothes, especially those of fine quality. Without a mechanism for trading paintings, it is doubtful if the 'price' of 100 florins for Fra Angelico's *Adoration of the Magi* (fig. 66) could have been readily realised in hard cash. Its gilded frame might have been worth a fair sum on its own, but the large Pollaiuolo paintings of *Hercules* (fig. 65) only rated a value of 20 florins, including their gold frames. The one field of collecting in which there was genuinely a market for existing 'works of art' witnessed some astonishing valuations and prices paid. This field involved the acquisition of prized 'antiques' which had survived from Greece and Rome, and which were now being avidly traded and excavated in increasing numbers.

In the 1492 inventory, ancient artefacts were valued on a quite different scale to the other possessions. Particularly prized were small-scale objects, such as cameos and cups and flasks in semi-precious stones, such as jasper, crystal, agate and sardonyx. They were mainly held in a smallish room or study known as the '*schrittoio*', which seems to have been established by Lorenzo's father as a literary and visual treasure-chest in which he could study his rarest and most delectable possessions.[184] The sculptor-architect Filarete wrote in his treatise on the imaginary city of Sforzinda that Piero 'il Gottoso' (smitten with gout and arthritis) liked to be 'carried to his studio', where he 'would look at his books as if they were solid pieces of gold' and 'take out some of the effigies and images of all the Emperors and Worthies of the past, some made of gold, some of silver, some of bronze, of precious stones or of marble and other materials, which are wonderful to behold. Their worth is such that they give the greatest pleasure and enjoyment to the eye.'[185] Of these treasures, the first to be listed in the inventory, 'a large flask [*rinfreschatoio*] of jasper with two handles finished with silver gilt, weighing 13½ *libre*', sets the tone, with a value of 2,000 florins.[186] Even the cheapest cameos, at 50 florins, were worth more than most of the pictures. The top value, an astonishing 10,000 florins, was assigned to 'a dish [*schodella*] of sardonyx and chalcedony and agate, in which there are several figures and on the outside a head of Medusa, weighing 2 *libre* and 6 *oncie*', now known as the '*Tazza Farnese*' (fig. 2).[187] It had entered Lorenzo's possession in 1471, purchased from Pope Sixtus IV della Rovere. To our eyes, the *Tazza* is an unusually fine example of Hellenistic gem carving, but we would hardly accord it the supreme place in the items housed in the palace or even recognise it as a truly major piece of classical art. But for collectors in the early Renaissance, such items were the most revered and delectable products of the supreme ancient masters, and for the richest enthusiasts cost was of little account.

Filarete reports of Piero that 'when it is a matter of acquiring worthy or strange objects, he does not look at the price'. One of the more curious of the 'strange objects', a 'unicorn horn 3½ *braccia* long' (a narwhal tusk), was handsomely valued at 6,000 florins.[188] There were stocks of expensive jewels, confections of precious materials, images in mosaic and illuminated manuscripts. An '*anchonetto* [small tabernacle] of gold with 10 places for various relics, with a sapphire at its centre' warranted a value of 300 *florins*. The painted images were small scale, including a little *Deposition* by Giotto, at 10 florins, and the *St Jerome* by Jan van Eyck (fig. 68), described as containing 'a little cupboard [*armarietto*] with a number of books in perspective . . . coloured in oil, in a case' and valued quite highly at 30 florins.[189] A series of maps, including *mappamundi*, images of the Holy Land, Rome and the castle at Milan provided vicarious travel and implicit mastery of the rare and exotic – further exemplified by the elephant's tusk (no value recorded).[190]

Of the items in the *schrittoio*, the ancient works most conspicuously warranted valuations out of proportion to their material value. Financial value reflected demand. In the climate of high prices for antiques and necessarily limited supply, it is not surprising to find that a few alert individuals saw the possibility of exploiting the new market. No one was shrewder than Giovanni Ciampolini, a Roman merchant, antiquarian collector, and one of the earliest 'dealers'. From the first in his negotiations with il Magnifico, via Medicean agents in Rome, he used all the tricks, praising 'his own objects . . . to the sky' and selling them only after elaborate displays of reluctance.[191] Nofri Tornabuoni of the Medici Bank in Rome reported in 1489 that 'Ciampolini . . . is demanding an insane sum' for an antique head in his possession. Ciampolini gained a notable reputation for having a special nose for the discovery of newly excavated antiques, and established himself as the master of connoisseurship (a necessary skill when faced by the inevitable forgeries of such pricey objects). A letter written by Luigi Barberini, who was also acting on Lorenzo's behalf in

68. Jan van Eyck, *St Jerome*, Detroit, Institute of Art

Rome, perfectly captures the febrile atmosphere in which new antiquities were sought. Ciampolini, Luigi reported,

> was informed that in a monastery were found some beautiful objects. . .; we would have had them, but the rumour reached the ears of Cardinal Giuliano della Rovere [the future Julius II and owner of the *Apollo Belvedere*], who went there and commanded that nothing be given to anyone, nor any more excavation done, because what had been discovered he wanted, and thus he would conduct the excavation himself. Nonetheless, by our instigation Giovanni Ciampolini with a companion, who was the middleman and who informed him about these objects, managed in such a way with his skills that excavation was done during the night'.

Sweetened by a loan from Lorenzo of 100 ducats, Ciampolini secured a

145

marble group of *Three Fauns* from the dig for his Florentine patron, but only after the price had apparently escalated from about 30 to 50 ducats, backed up with the threat that he could sell it elsewhere for 100. Ciampolini was an avid collector on his own behalf, and his dealing activities were probably subordinate to his own acquisitive instincts, but when he did decide to sell (for financial or other reasons), all the recognisable instincts of the professional art dealer were precociously in place.

The foundations for Ciampolini's enterprise had been established in the fourteenth century, when the vogue for ancient revivals had spread from literature to the evocative remains of ancient monuments and artefacts, which became favoured collectibles for those who prided themselves on access to true taste *all' antica*. The tone for the fifteenth century seems to have been set by Niccolò Niccoli, who can genuinely be described as a collector in the modern sense. A prickly arbiter of taste and unyielding advocate of ancient values, Niccoli spent more than his modest fortune on the amassing of a major collection of manuscripts, which were bequeathed via Cosimo to the 'public' library at San Marco, and a much praised collection of objects, with a special emphasis upon antiquities. Vespasiano described Niccoli as demonstrating 'wide judgement, not only in letters, but also in painting and sculpture, and he had in his house a number of medals, in bronze, silver and gold; also many antique figures in copper and heads in marble. . . and a vast number of vessels'.[192]

The story of one of his most prized possessions, a chalcedony (later identified as *Diomedes and the Palladium*, and now lost), will give the flavour of the kinds of work he admired and whose appreciation he actively promoted. He first saw the gem hanging as a pendant from the neck of a child on a Florentine street. We may suspect that the child's father was delighted with Niccoli's offer of 5 florins. While in Niccoli's possession, it was described by Ghiberti as 'more perfect than anything I have ever seen' and was 'praised to the heights by all those of discernment [*ingegni*]'.[193] As we saw in chapter III, Ghiberti described how its subtlety of modelling could only be revealed by carefully contrived illumination. (Ghiberti was himself a collector, and his collection was valued at 1,500 florins on his death in 1455.) The qualities of the chalcedony were such that it was deemed to have come from the hand of Polykleitos himself. It subsequently passed to Ludovico Trevisan, Patriarch of Aquilea, and was in the hands of the Venetian Pietro Barbo (later Pope Paul II) by 1457, when it was valued in an inventory of his extensive collection at 80 ducats.[194] When Pope Sixtus IV sold his predecessor's treasures in 1471, Lorenzo keenly acquired it, together with other items, including the *Tazza Farnese*. Lorenzo literally left his mark on the history of the chalcedony; the side of the altar on which the figure sits was proudly carved with 'LAV.R.MED' in reverse. It was used very directly as the model for one of the large marble *tondi* above the arcade in the courtyard of the palace on the Via Largha (fig. 69), and was to remain in Michelangelo's memory in 1508 when he came to design the *ignudi* on the Sistine ceiling. The 1492 inventory describes it as 'a chalcedony with a figure half sitting on an altar with a foot underneath and the left leg extended, an arm behind with a knife in the hand, a drapery over the shoulder and outstretched arm and in the hand an armed figure in gold, engraved transparent without a backing'.[195] It was valued at 500 florins.

69.   Medallion based upon a Ancient Gem, Florence, Palazzo Medici-Riccardi

The steady rise in the cost of the chalcedony, from Niccoli's 5 florins, is a consequence of conditions favourable to the establishing of a buoyant market. Even if there was a lively demand for paintings by the best modern masters, there was little problem of supply. A Pollaiuolo destroyed or given away could be replaced with its equivalent for a relatively modest outlay. The demand for ancient art was Italy-wide, and rapidly became international. Having a base in Rome helped, particularly when rapid moves were needed to lay claim to the latest of the excavated marvels. The great Venetian collection of the Grimani was assembled by Cardinal Domenico during his lavish residence at Rome. But Lorenzo, as we have seem, operated effectively by proxy, as did Isabella d'Este in Mantua. Although Isabella was only in Rome for two shortish periods, her network of agents and correspondents in Italy and Greece acted with notable efficiency in securing acquisitions of antiques to meet her self-confessedly 'insatiable desire'. The ill and aged Mantegna, though her favourite artist, was heavily pressured in 1506 to lower the price of his 'dear ancient' bust of *Faustina* when his poor financial position forced him to seek cash.[196] At least Mantegna managed to hold out for his asking price of 100 ducats in the face of Isabella's attempts to establish a lower valuation. She sought the best advice when

147

70. Antico
(Pier Jacopo
Alari-Bonacolsi),
Venus Felix,
Vienna,
Kunsthistorisches
Museum

collecting by proxy, and on one occasion asked Leonardo da Vinci to evaluate ancient vases formerly in the Medici collection.[197] Particularly drawn, as Piero de' Medici had been, to rare and curious items (including a 'unicorn's' horn), she specialised in gems and vases in semi-precious stone, which she housed in her *grotta*, a small inner chamber, which privileged guests were allowed to enter after inspecting her *studiolo*, with its paintings by Mantegna and others. A very showy, presentation version of the inventory of her possessions, drawn up in 1542, three years after her death, lists 1,620 items, including 72 vessels, 46 engraved gems, and large numbers of coins and medals.[198]

A perfect example of the kind of delectable objects favoured by Isabella and the Mantuan court is the overtly precious bronze statuette of *Venus Felix* by Antico in Vienna (fig. 70), adorned with silvered eyes, fire-gilt hair and drapery, and with a limewood base inset with gilded Roman coins. Antico (the apposite nickname of Pier Jacopo Alari Bonacolsi) had been involved in Isabella's attempt to reduce Mantegna's price for the *Faustina* and came to act as one of her trusted advisors. As an artist, he became renowned for his small-scale variants of famous ancient sculptures. Isabella obtained her first cast from him – a *spinario* – in 1501, and was a regular patron thereafter. In 1519 Antico offered to recast for Isabella some much admired bronzes which had originally been made twenty years earlier for Cardinal Ludovico Gonzaga, who had been deemed to be an alternative purchaser of the *Faustina*, because 'he delights in such things, and is a spender'.[199] It is not known precisely for whom the Vienna *Venus* was made, but its aesthetic, material and antiquarian qualities perfectly express the courtly tastes of the self-conscious connoisseurs of *all' antica* beauty, amongst whom no one stood second to Isabella.

When a group of objects acquires a value directly related to perceptions of their relative quality, connoisseurship becomes a valuable skill in its own right. The problems are encapsulated in a letter of 1430(?) from the great antiquarian Poggio Bracciolini to Niccolò Niccoli, in which he reports that his agent is seeking antiques in Chios: 'he tells me that he has in my name three marble heads, by Polykleitos and Praxiteles, of Juno, Minerva and Bacchus, which he greatly praises. I cannot confirm the names of the sculptors; Greeks as you know are talkative, and perhaps he faked the names to sell them higher'.[200] Having 'an eye' for the real thing became important in such circumstances. Filarete's compelling picture of Piero il Gottoso in his *schrittoio* conveys an idea of the kinds of visual refinement to which the leading connoisseurs aspired:

> He takes pleasure first from one thing and then from another. In one he praises the dignity of this image because it was done by the hand of man; and then in another that was more skilfully done, he states that it seems to have been done by nature rather than man. When we see something made by the hand of Pheidias or Praxiteles, we say that it does not seem made by their hand; it appears to have come from heaven rather than to have been made by man.[201]

There are also growing indications in the fifteenth century that the recognition and discerning of supreme skill in the 'hands' of great masters was beginning to be applied to the collecting of works by artists in a more general sense, even if the law of supply and demand did not immediately push up prices for contemporary masterpieces. When Niccolò Niccoli and Lorenzo de' Medici (Cosimo's brother) visited Poggio Bracciolini's Tuscan residence, attracted by the opportunity to view Poggio's collection of ancient works, the conversation as reported by Poggio ranged from the admiration of antiques to more general questions of the nobility of art and artists.[202] 'Lorenzo' in the dialogue jokingly accuses Poggio of buying into a noble lineage 'since images of his ancestors were lacking'. 'Niccoli', in his austere fashion opines that 'wisdom and virtue alone raise men to the praise of nobility'. 'Lorenzo' responds by noting that collecting 'is hungered and sought after by outstanding talents [*ingeniis*], for it is well known that the most learned men have devoted much labour and study to the buying of statues and paintings'. He is prepared to extend the concept of nobility more generally to 'sculptors and painters, whom their art makes famous and distinguished, and rich too . . . and widely known for their great achievements'. However, some caution is in order before we take 'Lorenzo's' comments at face value. Poggio's text is a literary work, full of irony and wit, and 'Lorenzo' is making clever play on the concept of nobility, extending it to anyone who has done something outstanding and famous – including notorious thieves. The safest use of such a passage is to say that the opinions are not literally to be ascribed to the participants, but that they are at least conceivable stances in the intellectual currency of the day.

A less ambiguous witness to a sense of pride and nobility in owning works by the best-regarded masters is found in the *Zibaldone* by Giovanni Rucellai, the banker and merchant who in 1451 ranked for tax purposes as the third richest man in Florence, and whose son married into the family of the richest, the Medici.[203] Giovanni's *Zibaldone* is a miscellaneous assembly of wisdom, edifying history and patriarchal *memoriali* intended for his heirs, published in 1960 in a selected and reordered form. Amongst moral and spiritual exhortations, are accounts of the good civic life, exemplified by Florence and her leading citizens, not least Giovanni himself. Of most interest in our present context is his proud list of the buildings and works of art in which he has invested. He documents his most conspicuous act of patronage, Alberti's great temple-front at S. Maria Novella, and records the complete remodelling of the Rucellai precinct, with its innovatory palace facade to an Albertian design, a grand family loggia, and Alberti's learned reworking of S. Pancrazio to house a 'sepulchre in the form of the sepulchre at Jerusalem'.[204] He expresses particular satisfaction with the rural delights of his out-of-town villa, 'Lo Specchio', at Quarachi, which gives 'great pleasure to the eye and respite to the body'.[205]

Rucellai's self-consciously discerning taste in modern art is clearly a source of pride:

Memorandum that we have in our house many items of sculpture, painting, intarsia and inlays from the hand of the best masters who have existed over a goodly period, not only in Florence but also in Italy, and the names of which are these, i.e.
    master Domenico of Venice, painter;
    friar Filippo of the order . . . painter;
    Giuliano da Maiano, woodworker, master of intarsia and inlays;

Antonio di Jacopo del Pollaiuolo, master of disegno;
Maso Finigherra, goldsmith, master of disegno;
Andrea del Verochio, sculptor and painter;
Vittorio di Lorenzo Bartolucci [Ghiberti's son], sculptor [intagliatore];
Andreino dal Chastagno, called 'of the hanged men', painter;
Paolo Uccello, painter;
    Disiderio da Settignano / Giovanni di Bertino / masters of carving [di
       scharpello].[206]

For a patron writing around 1470, this is indeed a good list, containing a fair proportion of the practitioners who are most highly ranked, then as now. Its emphasis is quite different from an inventorist's. The name of the master for the inventorist is not of prime concern in its own right; it is one descriptor in a set of data to effect identification and valuation. The 1492 inventorist did not know, for example, the author of the altarpiece in the chapel in the Medici Palace (actually Filippo Lippi). For Rucellai's particular purposes, he broadcasts his values to his heirs through the names of the masters, including, of course, Fra Filippo (whose less than honorable affiliation to the Carmelites he could not recall).

Other sections in the *Zibaldone* confirm Giovanni's recognition of the pre-eminent visual culture of Florence. In his account of the leading citizens of Florence, Brunelleschi is accorded fourth mention, after Palla Strozzi, Cosimo de' Medici and Leonardo Bruni (humanist author and chancellor). The short eulogy of the great architect encapsulates how Giovanni's generation were coming to define their cultural position:

Filippo di ser Brunellescho, of whom it is said that, since the time that the Romans ruled the world, there has never been a man so singular in architecture, eminent in geometry and perfect master of sculpture; in similar things he has the greatest intellect [*ingiengnio*] and imagination [*fantasia*]; the Roman manner of ancient building was rediscovered by him.[207]

More generally, he notes that he is living at a place and time when architecture, sculpture and all the arts were thriving, including '*intarsie* and inlays in such skilful perspective that no brush could render it better'.[208] The painters and draftsmen in the succession of Giotto and Cimabue were demonstrating the proper command of 'art, measure and order'.[209] When he visited Rome and itemised the impressive features of St Peter's, he not only noted such wonders as sixteen columns from Jerusalem but also picked out for special mention the mosaic of the 'ship of the Apostles, a very fine thing, which is said [rightly] to be from the hand of Giotto'.[210]

Not the least spectacular of Giovanni Rucellai's own acts of patronage, in terms of visual splendour and cost, was the *festa* for the wedding of his son, Bernardo, to Nannina, daughter of Piero di Cosimo de' Medici in 1466.[211] A huge apparatus of platforms, canopies (to keep off the sun and costing 300 *lire*), hangings, tapestries, *spalliere*, heraldic devices, tables and sideboards occupied the area of the piazza and loggia in front of the palace – the urban space that Giovanni had expensively moulded to suit his aspirations. Nothing was stinted, whether costumes, music or comestibles for the 670 diners. The 260 capons,

500 ducklings, 236 pullets, 470 pigeons, were all faithfully listed in the *Zibaldone*, at a cost of 1,500 *lire*, while the next item records the expense of the 'fifes and trombones' at 20 *fiorini larghi* or 120 *lire*. The eating was spread over three days. Near the end of the lengthy list are 'four calves for to be eaten by the peasants', presumably workers from his country estates. In good banker's fashion, he totals up the whole cost, which comes to 6,638 *lire* (i.e. over 1,100 florins). Nannina's dowry was provided by Piero at 2,500 florins, of which 2,000 was deposited in the Monte (the dowry bank), and 500 invested in gifts to the bride, which were estimated to be actually worth 1,200 florins. The first item listed is 'one pair of *forzieri* with *spalliere*, very rich'. As well as lavish clothes, the gifts included 'one little book of Our Lady illuminated with decorations in gold'.

Looking back in 1473, at the age of seventy, Giovanni takes contented stock of his account with the world. His great outgoings are summarised: 60,000 florins to the *commune*; 10,000 for five daughters' dowries, and unspecified sums on his architectural projects, with 1,000 ducats on gold brocade hangings in S. Pancrazio alone.[212] He has devoted fifty years of his life to the pleasures of earning money and spending it, and has latterly come to the opinion that spending is of 'greater delight than earning'. Overall, his expenditure has given him 'the greatest contentment and the greatest delight, because it redounds in part to the honour of God and to the honour of the city and to the memory of me'.

There is evidence that Giovanni's developed pride in the Florentine visual heritage was not isolated in Florentine aristocratic circles in the later fifteenth century. The 1492 inventorist generally takes care to record the names of works by the pioneers, Giotto, Masaccio, Donatello and Fra Angelico, who were already being defined as standing in a great succession, and two of whom, Donatello and Fra Angelico, were especially identified with the Medici. The low valuations of their works does not mean that they were not valued in other senses. The lack of a developed market does not imply a lack of regard, as is shown by a notable acquisition by the younger Piero de' Medici, Lorenzo il Magnifico's generally maligned son. The account of Piero's acquisition is found in the *registro giornaliero* (daily register) of S. Benedetto, a monastery outside Florence:

> Piero di Lorenzo di Piero di Cosimo di Giovanni di Bicci de' Medici learnt that we had in our possession a little panel, painted by the hand of Cimabue, painted on both sides: on one side was a Deposition from the Cross, with the Maries and other saints, on the other side was Christ who places one hand on the shoulder of Our Lady and the other on St John the Evangelist's. And he sent a request to buy it, whereupon Niccholo di Lionardo, prior, gave it to him personally on November 20, 1490, in the presence of don Paolo Coppini and brother Panutio, and Ghalieno the embroiderer [who was later to serve on the committee for placing Michelangelo's David]. And he showed much gratitude in having it, and plentifully offered to do all he could do for us, no less than his ancestors.[213]

It was in this same year that a plaque was installed in the cathedral, eulogising Giotto as painter and architect of the bell-tower. The inscription was composed by the great poet, Angelo Poliziano:

That person am I, by whom extinct painting was revived,
With my hand that was as sure as its was accomplished.
What my art lacked, Nature lacked too:
No-one was privileged to paint more or better.
Do you admire the gracious tower sounding to sacred chimes?
According to my model it reaches up to the stars.
But since I am Giotto, why recite such deeds?
That name alone sustains a long song of praise.[214]

When Lorenzo was unsuccessful in persuading the city of Spoleto to repatriate the remains of Fra Filippo Lippi, tiresome in death as in life, he ensured the construction of a fine tomb in Spoleto Cathedral to the design of Filippino, the dead painter's son. Cristoforo Landino had already stressed Florentine artistic pre-eminence in his commentary to Dante's *Divine Comedy*, presented to the Florentine government in 1481, in which he glossed the poet's lines on how Giotto's esteem had triumphed over Cimabue's. He provided succinct assessments of leading modern artists, most notably Masaccio, Fra Filippo, Castagno and Fra Angelico.[215] In the 1490s when Antonio Manetti added supplementary lives to his vernacular translation of Filippo Villani's trecento account of notable Florentines, he included no less than eight artists in his role call of 'fourteen notable men from 1400 onwards'.[216] They were all from the 'pioneering' years: Brunelleschi, Donatello, Ghiberti, Masaccio, Fra Angelico, Fra Filippo, Uccello and Luca della Robbia. Set in such a context, the young Michelangelo's purposeful turning in the early 1490s to the study of the past masters, Giotto, Masaccio and Donatello, is a fashionable act of Florentine traditionalism.

As mastery became a more prominently acknowledged value, so we find increasing claims that the true value of art and artists resides in something quite separate from the worth of the materials used, to which the inventorists' values were still strongly tied. Alberti had already criticised those 'who make excessive use of gold, because they think it lends a certain majesty to painting'.[217] Imitation of the effects of gold through the painter's skill is more worthy. This is not to say that rich adornments were necessarily to be despised, 'for a perfect and finished painting is worthy to be ornamented even with precious stones'. Filarete credits Piero de' Medici as recognising 'the noble mastery of ancient angelic spirits who with their sublime intellects have made such ordinary things as bronze, marble and such materials acquire such great price'.[218] Skill transforms semi-precious stones, like Piero's cameos, so that they become 'worth more than gold'. Later in the century Leonardo was scathing about 'a certain breed of painter who, having studied little, must spend their working lives in thrall to the beauty of gold and azure'. There probably always had been a sense that the best masters could command the best prices specifically for their skill, over and above material costs and the stock rate for the job, but voices to this effect began to be recorded more forcefully in formal contexts. Not surprisingly artists themselves were the most insistent.

We have already noted that Francesco del Cossa, who was one of the team of painters undertaking murals in *La Schifanoia* for Borso d'Este at Ferrara (fig. 20), wrote directly to his lord in 1470 complaining about his remuneration.[219]

Cossa's letter reveals that the group had already submitted a petition without success, and he is now trying to separate his case from theirs, since 'I am Francesco del Cossa, who have made by myself the three wall sections towards the antechamber . . . [and] have begun to have a little of a name'. His somewhat rambling letter, with its ritual obeisances, does not testify to great skills of advocacy, but his main points do emerge: he has devoted sustained study to his art and deserves more than 'the most miserable assistant in Ferrara'; he has used as good gold and colours as the other painters, so that his extra skill should be additionally rewarded; he has 'done almost the whole work in fresco, which is good and advantageous work, and this is recognised by all masters of the art'; and if his master does not want to create a precedent by paying him more than the others, he can fall back upon 'appraisals [*extime*]'. In short, Cossa deserves more than the standard rate of 'ten *bolognini* [i.e. ⅒ ducat] to the foot', at which rate he claims that he will be 40 or 50 ducats down on the transaction. The letter is annotated in Latin with the Borso's laconic response: 'let him be content with the set fee, for it was set for those assigned to the individual fields'. If Cossa's claims should be taken as portraying him as an isolated genius labouring to produce unaided masterpieces for a pittance, the evidence of his frescoes shows clear evidence of team-work and corner-cutting, not least when the same equestrian image of Borso d'Este is replicated throughout the scenes in a relatively mechanical manner.

In spite of Cossa's problems, court employment promised better and more secure financial prospects than the urban market-place. Of the Republican city-states, only Venice seems to have put goodly salaries in the reach of painters, either through an appointment as official 'painter to the state', for which Michele Giambono was offered 300 ducats a year in 1439, or through income-bearing sinecures, such as those obtained by the Bellinis and Titian.[220] Generally, courts offered the best bet. In 1449 Sigismondo Malatesta wrote from Rimini to Giovanni de' Medici seeking a good master to decorate his chapel and promising to award the painter with 'an annual salary, as high as he wishes'.[221] Whether the reality matched the promise is not known. Amongst the painters working in the first half of the century, Pisanello seems to have gained the highest salaried income.[222] The annual stipend of 400 ducats he was granted in 1449 by King Alfonso V in Naples compared favourably with that of humanist *stipendiati*, but he appears not to have enjoyed his prosperity for long, since there is no record of him as an active artist after 1450, and he died in 1455. In the later fifteenth century Mantegna was the artist who had come closest to living in a 'princely' manner, with a substantial and fashionable dwelling designed by himself (fig. 111, below). His promised starting salary of 15 ducats a month with provisions and housing provided a fair base-line, above which he could look to attract appropriate rewards for specific projects.[223] His property holdings and titles gave him the substance and status of a gentleman. However, as his forced sale of his beloved *Faustina* testifies, his income did not wholly match his aspirations, and by the end of his life he had overreached himself financially.

Even if the great majority of fifteenth-century artists were unsuccessful in establishing themselves as a 'super-artists', with levels of remuneration which stood decisively outside the norm, the upgrading of the artist's profession, which had found increasing literary expression, was to bear greater financial fruit in the next, albeit in a very selective manner. Mantegna's later successor in Mantua, Giulio Romano, seems to have experienced few difficulties in becoming a citizen of enduring substance. The new breed of 'super-artists', Michelangelo and Raphael in Rome, and Titian in Venice put together sources of income which moved them to a far higher position on the economic scale than any of their fifteenth-century predecessors.

Early in his career, however, Michelangelo was working very much within the established patterns. His appointment in 1501 to carve the giant *David* carried a monthly salary of 6 florins for two years (i.e. 148 florins in all) plus expenses, with an option to receive a higher sum at the end.[224] On 24 April 1503 he contracted with the Consoli of the Arte della Lana to make twelve Apostles for the duomo at only two florins a month for twelve years, but in this case the salary was underpinned by the gift of a house on land that the Guild had specially purchased: 'the aforesaid Consoli and Opera are obliged to erect a house for the habitation of the said Michelangelo . . . according to the model made or to be made by Simone del Pollaiuolo [*il Cronaca*] . . . up to a total of six hundred florins'. Michelangelo throughout his career seems to have been interested in deals which brought him property, since buildings and land represented tangible assets with income-earning potential. In the event, the contract for the Apostles was annulled when Michelangelo left for Rome, and the consuls ordered the house to be finished and leased.

Later, in 1512, the 2,000 ducats that Michelangelo held in a Roman bank, shortly after receiving the final payment for the Sistine ceiling, were dispatched to Florence for deposit in the Hospital of S. Maria Nuova (where Leonardo also banked), with instructions that his agent should seek to invest it in a property.[225] It seems that he had received a total of 3,000 ducats for the ceiling, which compares favourably with the 1,000 ducats that Pinturicchio was promised in 1502 for the vault and wall decorations in the Piccolomini Library in Siena Cathedral, of which 300 was assigned in advance as expenses.[226] Pinturicchio's contract specified that he should use the newly fashionable motif of *grotteschi* in the ancient manner, and that he should undertake the cartoons and at least the painting of the heads with his own hand. The 2,000 ducats which Filippino Lippi was reputed to have received for the Caraffa Chapel in Rome, after his services had been provided by Lorenzo il Magnifico as a diplomatic 'gift', seems more nearly to be approaching the inflated prices of the next century.[227] We have already noticed Filippino's report in 1498, that Cardinal Caraffa had awarded him 250 florins for his 'mastery alone' when he was making marble adornments for the altar. Andrea del Verrocchio, towards the climax of his work on the *Christ and St Thomas* in 1483 had already been paid 306 florins for his '*magistero*', and was promised a further 494 florins on completion, though the full payments were never forthcoming.[228] The idea of specific payment for 'mastery', as a separately quantifiable sum, may have been a growing fashion in the late fifteenth century.

A major factor in the inflation of a few artists' salaries was the increasing taste amongst a few grand patrons for projects on a huge scale. Raphael's career in Rome between 1508 and his death in 1520 bears witness to a series of appointments to sinecures, handsome salaries and good remuneration for specific projects, all of which were designed to bind him to the papal court and to help realise the pope's ambitions. We do not have a complete record of his income, but we know, for example, that his position as architect at St Peter's brought in an immediate 1,500 ducats in 1514, committing him for five years, and in 1520 he was receiving a standing payment of 300 ducats a year, in the form of a retainer.[229] It was in 1514 that he wrote to an uncle in Urbino,

> I find myself at present with possessions in Rome worth three thousand ducats, and fifty gold scudi in income, because his Holiness of Our Lord has provided me with three hundred gold ducats to attend to the building of St Peter's, which I shall not lack for as long as I live. And I am paid for what I do at whatever price I myself fix, and I have begun to paint another stanza for his Holiness, which will amount to two thousand gold ducats.[230]

The idea that Raphael was given a blank cheque is unlikely to have been literally true, but if we take it that he proposed fees to which Pope Leo X assented, we can still think that something like a normal *pacta* (albeit an unusually generous one) was in operation between artist and patron. In addition to specific payments for the series of rooms frescoed in the papal apartments, Raphael received fees for his work on a series of other projects, including the very expensive tapestries for the Sistine Chapel, the *loggie* of the Vatican, the *stufetta* of Cardinal Bibiena, and a series of free-standing paintings, such as the great diplomatic gifts of the *St Michael* and the *Holy Family* to Francis I. This is to say nothing of his 'outside' work, which, as in the case of the decorations for Agostini Chigi's Roman villa, could be substantial undertakings in their own right. Some idea of how prices were becoming inflated in this climate of large-scale activity and patronal competition can be gained from Leonardo Sellaio's report to Michelangelo in 1520, that a value of 1,000 ducats had been placed on Sebastiano del Piombo's *Resurrection of Lazarus*, commissioned by Cardinal Giuliano de' Medici in conjunction with the 'rival' altarpiece from Raphael of the *Transfiguration* (fig. 71).[231] This estimate was formulated in relation to Sebastiano's own bill for 850 ducats, a subsequent dispute involving Michelangelo, Sebastiano's mentor, and an act of arbitration, in which the Sienese architect and painter Baldassare Peruzzi played a key role.[232]

Records of Raphael's acquisition of land and properties, by gift and purchase, show him rapidly becoming a citizen of substance. His purchase in 1517 of a Palazzo in the Borgo of St Peter's which had been designed by Bramante for the Caprini family, at a price of 'three thousand ducats *da camera*', was a spectacular affirmation of his status and financial position.[233] The house contained five shops at ground-floor level, for which he would have received rent. He also invested in a vineyard, and received the concession of a 'perpetual lease' on a substantial plot of land (about 266 × 40 m.) under the jurisdiction of St Peter's.[234] At one point it seemed that he had identified a likely wife with a promised dowry of 3,000 gold *scudi*, though the plans did not come to fruition.[235] The 'Michelangelo sect' in Rome, centred on Sebastiano, scathingly referred to the increasingly grand Raphael as the 'prince of the synagogue'. Marcantonio Michiel, the diarist, reported that on his early death in 1520, Raphael also possessed 3,000 ducats of properties at Urbino, and was worth overall some 16,000 ducats.[236]

71.   Raphael, *Transfiguration*, Rome, Vatican, Pinacoteca

We can chart the rise in Michelangelo's salaried income though a series of letters and legal agreements. In 1524 Pope Clement VII was seeking to bind Michelangelo to his service through the award of an annual salary.[237] Perhaps reluctant to commit himself too completely, when the Julius Tomb was still hanging around his neck as an increasingly heavy burden, Michelangelo proposed to the worthy Fattucci, who was acting for him in Rome, that a salary of 15 ducats a month would be appropriate.[238] Fattucci, like any good agent with a client who seemed to undervalue his own services, acted to secure a larger sum, and the banker, Jacopo Salviati, determined on behalf of the pope that the artist should receive 50 ducats a month plus expenses (including the rent for a house near S. Lorenzo in Florence).[239] Some of the benefits of that portion of Michelangelo's income that he invested in property can be gained from his Florentine *catasto* return in 1535, where he lists ten properties, of which one was inherited, one was for his personal use (in the Via Ghibellina) and eight were investments.[240] Typical is the 'plot of arable land comprising 8 *staiore* in the parish of S. Stefano-in-Pane, a property called Stradello, bought by me on 20 June 1512'. All together, the Florentine holdings brought in over 216 florins a year. A year later when he was appointed by Paul III as the pope's supreme architect, painter and sculptor, he was promised the grand salary of 1,200 *scudi*, of which 600 was to come from the revenues of the Ferry on the Po above Piacenza.[241]

This source of income, liquid assets in the literal sense, was not essentially different in type from the concession that Leonardo had been granted by Louis XII to water from the canal of S. Cristoforo in Milan, rights which he bequeathed to his servant, Battista de Vilanis, who also inherited half of the master's Milanese vineyard.[242] However, there is no indication in Leonardo's will in 1519 that he had accumulated assets on Michelangelo's scale, although he and his household did receive very substantial salaries from King Francis I during 1517 and 1518. 'Lyenard de Vince, Italian painter' was awarded 2,000 *écus soleil* over the course of the two years, and his ammanuensis, Francesco Melzi, 'Italian, gentleman', was granted 800, while Salaì, Leonardo's 'servant' (whom we will shortly meet more intimately), was paid 100.[243] For the last three years of his life, Leonardo was housed in noble style in the fine manor house of Clos Lucé, near the royal chateau at Amboise (fig. 72). The French king, avid to buy into the Italian manner, was a conspicuous spender on artists' remuneration. Rosso Fiorentino's salary in 1539 for one year was equivalent to Leonardo's, at 1,000 gold *écus*, and shows that Francis remained keen to attract Italian masters by paying salaries that were high by international standards.[244]

Michelangelo's income from such a geographically remote asset as the Po Ferry proved erratic, and by 1550 he reckoned that there was an accumulated shortfall of 2,000 *scudi*, not least because the pope had lost control over the region in 1547.[245] In response, the pope granted him the office of Civil Notary in the Chancellery at Rimini, another income-bearing sinecure in the papal domain.[246] The way in which cocktails of quite considerable riches could be mixed for a few leading artists from various concessions, sinecures and formal duties is reflected in the documentation of Giulio Romano's service in the Mantuan court from 1525. The young and already prosperous Giulio was appointed to a series of prestigious positions and granted land and property by

72.   Manor House of Clos Lucé, Amboise

Federigo Gonzaga, certified by various instruments and decrees which give fulsome praise to the artist's 'noble talent [*ingenium*]' and, almost inevitably, dub him as the new Apelles serving the new Alexander.[247] In 1527-8 he was granted rights to a state sawmill in perpetuity as a steady source of income.[248] Although some of the direct payments intended for Giulio seem to have been embezzled by a court treasurer, he obtained enough remuneration to live in some style in a palace of his own design on a site he purchased for 1,000 ducats in 1538.[249] Vasari reported that Giulio was worth 1,000 ducats a year by the time of his death in 1546.[250]

There is, as we have seen, no necessarily direct correlation between what an artist is paid and the book value assigned to products of his hand, but the rise of the 'super-artist' did establish conditions in which there was a substantial demand by leading patrons for works from a small group of internationally recognised artists. An early indication of the rise of a market for contemporary masters is Isabella's d'Este's dispatch of an agent in Venice to see if anything could be acquired from the studio of the recently deceased Giorgione in 1510.[251] She was particularly interested in a '*nocte*' (a night scene?) which was reputed to be '*molto bella et singulare*', but asks Taddeo Albani and others 'who have judgement and [understanding of] design' to see if a '*mercato*' can be struck on any desirable item. Taddeo replied that two 'nights' were owned by the Contarini and the Becharo families, the latter of which was better, but that 'neither one nor the other is for sale at any price, because they had them made to satisfy their own pleasure'. The concept of the 'priceless' painting is beginning to emerge. Once again, the Renaissance could look to ancient precedent: Pliny told how Zeuxis gave his works away because (to quote Alberti's version) 'he did not believe that any price could be found to recompense the man who, in representing and painting living things, behaved like a god among mortals'.[252]

159

Shortly after the deaths of the famed Raphael and Leonardo, there are indications that their paintings became highly collectable, and that values began to rise quite steeply. In Leonardo's case, the most striking evidence occurs in the valuation of paintings in the estate of Salaì in 1525. The rascally Salaì (Giovanni Jacopo di Capproti di Oppreno) had joined the master as a ten-year-old in 1490, rapidly gaining a reputation for petty pilfering and other misdemeanours. As an adult he seems to have become something of a 'front man' for Leonardo, and by fair means or foul he accumulated a surprising level of wealth for someone who was still termed a 'servant' in Leonardo's will.[253] Salaì had received the other half of Leonardo's Milanese 'garden' (a vineyard given by Ludovico Sforza), where he had already built a house. He was of sufficient moment to have attracted a wife with a 1,700 *lire* dowry. When he unexpectedly met with 'violent death' in January 1524, his sisters made a division of his property according to values recorded in a notarial document of 21 April 1525, which has survived in two versions.[254] One version, for the most part written by the same hand throughout, with various corrections and annotations, appears to have been the initial record, which then provided the basis for a second version, which begins in a different hand. The start of the formal list of the late artist's possessions, probably in the same hand as the first version, begins on a folio headed '*copia*' and dated '1525 on the first of April in Milan'. Strictly speaking the two documents do not appear to be an *extensa* and an *imbreviatura*, but rather a roughish and fair copy containing the same information.

The first listed item comprises two diamonds, estimated at 50 *scudi* (also listed as 252 *lire*, 10 *soldi*). Amongst the subsequent items we find a chalcedony listed at 500 *scudi*, various pieces of fine clothing and a list of people by whom he was owed money, in sums ranging from 800 to 30 *lire*. His house on its half of the vineyard is valued at 1,100 *lire*. Most notable are the values assigned to a list of paintings (transcribed from the neater copy):

One painting [*quadro*] called a Leda	sc. 200. l. 1,010
One painting of St Anne	sc. 100. l. 505
One painting of a woman portrayed	
One painting called la Honda C°(?)	sc. 100. l. 505
One painting with a St John large	sc. 80. l. 404
One painting with a St Jerome large	sc. 40. l. 202
One painting with a half nude	sc. 25. l.126 s.5
One painting with a St Jerome half nude	sc. 25. l.126 s.5
One painting with a St John little young	sc. 25. l.126 s. 5
One Christ in the form of a God the Father	sc. 25. l.126. s. 5
One Madonna with a son in her arms	sc. 22. l.101
One Christ at the column not finished	sc. 5. l. 25

Not the least of the apparent problems with the list is the absence of any author's name. However, if we remember that the purpose of the notary's list is to permit valuations for a fair *divisio*, rather than to communicate information to someone who is interested in paintings as such, the missing name is of no functional consequence. The parties knew which painting had been assigned what value, and they would not have needed to be told about their authorship. The high prices for the leading items, recorded in all their notarial sobriety, leave little

73.   Leonardo da Vinci and Studio, *Madonna of the Yarnwinder*, Drumlanrig, Collection of the Duke of Buccleuch

doubt that they were by Leonardo, and that Salaì had characteristically managed to come into possession of the best of the paintings in the master's hands after (or even before) Leonardo's death, including the *Mona Lisa* (called 'la Joconda' in an annotation on the rougher version) and the *Virgin, Child and St Anne* in the Louvre. The *Leda*, the much-admired painting which subsequently entered the French Royal Collections, where it cannot be traced after 1694, was at 200 *scudi* well beyond any value we have seen for a second-hand modern painting, and was worth as much as Salaì's house. Perhaps the value of 100 for the *Mona*

161

Lisa (fig. 4) is even more remarkable, since the 'face' value of portraits generally resided in the significance of the sitter for the owner, but Leonardo's image of Lisa del Giocondo (who was not famous in her own right) seems to have transcended this normal limitation and became admired on more universal grounds as a great painting of an archetypally 'beloved' lady by the rarest of masters.

The pictures of lesser value in the Salaì list appear to have been smaller-scale items, mainly devotional pictures for domestic settings, such as the 'Madonna with a son in her arms', which may have been one of the prime versions of the *Madonna of the Yarnwinder* (fig. 73) or a work of comparably modest dimensions (i.e. about 50 × 36 cm.). Such items appear to have been produced within the workshop as 'Leonardos' in a general if not in a wholly autograph sense. Leonardo specifically recommended that painters should 'keep aside some good work, saying, this is worth a good price, this is medium-priced and this is run-of-the-mill, thus showing they have works in all price ranges'. We do not perhaps think of Leonardo as someone who ran a *bottega* in which customers could find 'off-the-peg' items, but it is likely that the '25-*scudo*' picture was of precisely this type, and that Salaì himself would have participated in the production of some of them. The *Leda* on the other hand was clearly a work for a major collector, and was probably acquired with other items from Salaì's estate by King Francis's agents after 1525, when he was avidly importing works from Italy.

From the 1520s onwards, as we move beyond the main chronological boundaries of this study, an increasingly significant gap appears to have opened between the jobbing painters who continued to rely upon the normal kinds of business arrangements and those artists who could command special terms of employment. A nice incident which indicates the way that things were going for a few privileged artists is provided by the strange case of the Titian *Annunciation*, which was ostensibly given away to a patron who had not ordered it – emulating the precedent of Zeuxis. The story will provide a suitably grand incident on which to end a chapter where the first cited payment was the modest 40 florins promised to Filippo Lippi for his *Barbadori Altarpiece*. In 1536 Titian, already famed in Europe and honoured by Emperor Charles V as a Knight of the Golden Spur and Count Palatine, completed a large altarpiece of the *Annunciation* (now destroyed) for the nuns of S. Maria degli Angeli on the Venetian island of Murano.[255] The nuns baulked at Titian's high price of 500 ducats, which was five times what he had received for the *St Peter Martyr Altarpiece* and matched the wholly exceptional fee for Lotto's *Colleoni Altarpiece* in Bergamo. He seems to have been encouraged by his friend, Pietro Aretino, to send the picture as a gift to the Empress Isabella, Charles's wife. Always with a shrewd eye on the cultivation of diplomatic advantages which would bring enduring benefits, Aretino presumably judged that the picture would do Titian more good in imperial hands than isolated on Murano. Aretino's own career as a man of affairs, and as an author specialising in satire and published letters to the famous, had been built on the cultivation of powerful national and international connections. The ploy worked, perhaps better than either man can have anticipated. Charles sent Titian 2,000 *scudi*. In his subsequent letter to the painter, Aretino congratulates Titian on his wisdom in sending 'the image of the

Queen of Heaven to the empress on earth', and composes a rapturous *ekphrasis* of the light, colour and divine narrative of the *Annunciation*.[256] Titian and Aretino are locked into a system of mutual interests in which the accruing of international reputation is the means to lasting fame and earthly wealth. Aretino widely broadcasts the supremacy of the 'divine Titian', just as Vasari was to laud the 'divine Michelangelo'. The actions of Titian and Aretino show that we are entering a world in which the perception of the status of a supreme artist and expectations of financial rewards were being radically transformed, with concomitant changes in what the artist and his supporters regarded as acceptable behaviour.

V

MEANINGS

I N THE TYPES of sources we have encountered so far, the motive that may be regarded as the prime reason for the making of works of art has been explicit only occasionally, and often only implicit in the most general sense. This motive resided in the wish to make something that *meant* something to somebody – or, in almost all cases, meant various things to various people in various positions of interest and degrees of involvement. And if we are speaking about the reception of the work, the numbers of people for whom it bore (or may have been intended to bear) meaning might be very large indeed.

I am here using 'meaning' in a broad sense. At this preliminary stage, an effective if inverted way to gain some kind of grip on this broad usage is to look at the puzzlement of so many spectators faced with an archetypal product of modernism – say an example of minimalism by the American painter, Barnett Newman (fig. 74) – in which the old criteria of meaning have broken down. There is, in my experience, one question likely to be asked above all others by spectators who find such works difficult, obscure, unintelligible and even infuriating – not least in this case because it bears no obvious relationship to its title, *Eve*. The question is, 'What does it mean?'

This is by no means an easy question to answer, because the properties which defined potential meaning in more conventional works of art are, given the questioner's frame of reference, locked into an indissoluble union with the recognisability of objects through levels of resemblance with known things. Pliny's cobbler, for instance, experienced no difficulty in recognising that Apelles was trying to depict a sandal, even if the painter had rendered its details incorrectly. By contrast, the potential definitions of meaning which are available for the painting by Newman all depend upon criteria which reside within the world of 'Art', whether these criteria deal with the formal properties of abstract works or with the armatures of commercial, institutional and critical support which underpinned the rise and success of the art of Newman and his associates in the Abstract Expressionist and Minimalist movements in America. From the formalist point of view the explanations would centre upon such factors as the notion of the autonomous picture, which refers only to itself and its own reality, rather than evoking the reality of other objects through illusion, yet paradoxically capable of being accorded elliptical titles such as 'Eve'. The more institutionally oriented explanations would need to address the argument that

164

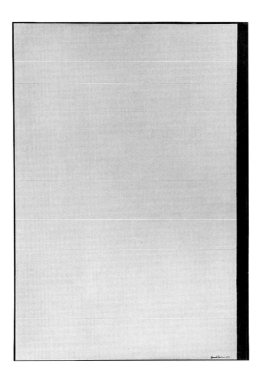

74. Barnett Newman, *Eve*, London, Tate Gallery

this kind of art was seen by those responsible for pushing American cultural policy into a place of world leadership as truly American, twentieth-century and progressive. I do not wish to engage here with current debates about the validity of specific interpretations of the success of the American avant-garde, but rather to suggest the kinds of explanations that could begin to answer the question, 'what does it mean?' – and to locate the potential explanations in relation to the cobbler's expectations about what meaning could be with respect to a painting. Although we have witnessed strenuous efforts on the part of Renaissance patrons, who were connoisseur-collectors and art theorists, to detach themselves from the outlook of the cobbler – in terms of both speculating and making – the Renaissance concept of meaning resided within the same framework of imitation and recognition that the cobbler took for granted, rather than within the concept of 'Art' as a separately definable cultural activity in its later sense.

The dominant sense of meaning in the pre-Modern periods was linked to the 're-presentation' of what was taken to be a shared visual experience, though in the Renaissance the pleasure to be taken from imitation alone was not generally taken as a self-sufficient rationale for a work of art. Whereas, for example, a twentieth-century viewer looking at a cloud study by Constable (fig. 75) – looking at it in the wake of Impressionism – might regard the satisfaction to be gained from a compelling evocation of the nebulous beauty of such very British clouds as a sufficient end, a Renaissance spectator would have expected such a fragment of reality to be embedded in a more overt framework of allusion. The sight of a brilliantly painted sky in the Transfigurations by Giovanni Bellini and Raphael (fig. 71) would have been a potential source of delight for a Renaissance

75.　John Constable, *Study of Clouds*, London, Victoria and Albert Museum

spectator, and could well have moved a critic versed in humanist writing to raptures of *ekphrastic* praise, but a cloud would not on its own be sufficient to justify the making of the picture – *unless* it carried a deeper symbolic message or allusory meaning, such as the cloud which impregnated Io (Jupiter in one of his copulatory disguises).

Even if the Renaissance spectator did not understand the allusions being conveyed, there was a general expectation that intelligible allusions would be present. When neither Vasari nor anyone to whom he spoke could make head nor tail of the *fantasia* of clothed and unclothed figures painted by Giorgione on the facade of the 'German Warehouse' on the Grand Canal which served German merchants as a business centre and repository in Venice, he did not conclude that they meant nothing.[257] And, in any event, the human forms were at least recognisable as such. What Vasari was seeking was the appropriate key – the kind of textual key that explained the hidden significance or symbolic meaning of recognisable objects, either singly or in combination. The ways in which we might, almost five hundred years later, hope to find keys to meaning in Renaissance artefacts will be one of the more prominent themes in this chapter. But it is not the whole substance of what I want to accomplish, since the unravelling of narrative, allegory and symbol through textual keys – what is

166

called iconographical study – only elucidates one of the varieties of meaning in the broad context of meaning as a whole. Alongside such directly intended content, we also need to be alert to a plurality of other ways in which works could be meaningful in a Renaissance framework of making and viewing. These ways range from other forms of entirely intentional meaning, such as the artist's demonstration of learned skill in perspective or the patron's brandishing of conspicuous expenditure, to the implicit and often automatic expression of social and political values relating to, say, the position of women or the aristocratic imposition of order. How we demonstrate the validity of interpretations based on what we discern as implicit values – using hindsight to impute inadvertent motives – is fraught with problems, unless we are unconcerned with the dangers of using Renaissance works in a cavalier fashion to illuminate our own concerns or demonstrate the legitimacy of our own stances.

SACRED STORIES

I think it will be helpful to define more systematically the ways in which meaning may enter works and be drawn out of them, There are, I think, three general ways in which meaning was embodied in a Renaissance artefact. The first is by explicit intention, as in the devising of an allegory or the portrayal of someone as befits their status; the second is by providing an image which is knowingly a field for interpretation, as when a painter provides a devotional image of the Madonna and Child which could serve in a variety of potential dialogues between the spectator and adored figures; and the third is by the tacit embedding of attitudes, such as the greater acceptability of portraying agedness in men than in women. And, whether the artist likes it or not, the work of art never ceases to provide various degrees of interpretative scope for spectators who will read into it what they will. In drawing out potential meanings there are two main strategies: firstly, using contemporary written evidence to define contemporary intentions and modes of viewing (to define what has been called the 'period eye'); and secondly, availing ourselves of viewing positions disengaged in time and place to establish ways of looking which are distinct from those that could be articulated in the period itself. The disengaged modes will be examined in a more sustained way in the final chapter, but in as much as no modern interpreter can hope to avoid all the perils of dislocation, even in the act of defining the relevance of sources from the period itself, we cannot insulate the one strategy entirely from the other. A concrete example will serve to clarify how this rather dry and artificial enumeration of categories can help to identify interpretative approaches through which we can make the meanings live again for the modern viewer.

   The example I have chosen, almost inevitably, is one of the *causes célèbres* of Renaissance iconography, in this case the *Baptism of Christ* (fig. 76) by Piero della Francesca. My intention here is not to undertake a full (or necessarily fair) review of the many historically ingenious interpretations of the picture in its whole and its parts, nor to propose a definite solution which sweeps away all the previous hypotheses, but rather to gain some sense of what kind of explanation

76. Piero della Francesca, *Baptism of Christ*, London, National Gallery

77. Matteo di Giovanni and studio, *Sts Peter and Paul, Stephen, Mary Magdalene, Arcano, Anthony Abbot, Catherine and Egidio, with the Annunciation, Stories from the Life of St John the Baptist, and the Fathers of the Church.* (Altarpiece formerly housing Piero's *Baptism*), Borgo San Sepolchro, Museo Civico

does what kind of job and of the relative statuses of different types of strategy. In keeping with what has gone before, I intend to begin with a minimal functionalist explanation, remaining as far as possible within the parameters of the kinds of motives which can be derived from the generating documents which have survived for works of this kind.

In the case of the *Baptism*, we do not have a contractual document or other form of primary source which tells us about the circumstances of the work's production, so that we have to assume it was brought into being by a procedure analogous to those which can be documented for comparable objects. We do, however, know something of the painting's original function and patronage. Unsurprisingly for a panel painting of this size, it was a component in an altarpiece, though, more unexpectedly for a painting which is so up-to-date in its deep space and architectural figure style, it was not part of a modern Renaissance structure but was a stylistically alien component in a highly traditional polyptych, the other panels of which are attributed to Matteo di Giovanni (fig. 77). The shield on the left of the predella box is that of the Graziani, one of the two leading families in Borgo San Sepolchro, Piero's home town, while the right is inscribed OP[ER]A, probably indicating that the body responsible for the fabric of the building contributed to its cost. But what building? The frame with its subsidiary panels was previously in the cathedral in

Borgo San Sepolchro, but the whole altarpiece was documented in the church of S. Giovanni d'Afra in 1649. However, it was not in S. Giovanni in 1583. Various suggestions have been put forward for its original location, the most plausible of which is that it was intended for an altar near the font in the Badia (which became the cathedral in 1520) dedicated to St John by Diosa, widow of Giovanni dei Mazzetti in 1406. If this is the case, it is necessary to suppose that a member of the Graziani had later taken over the rights to the altar and commissioned a new altarpiece. The scenario of the transfer of the altar to other patrons and the later removal of the altarpiece to other locations conforms to what typically happened when donations lapsed and a church was remodelled.

The minimal interpretation assumes a model of the following fictional kind. The widow's gift had not resulted in the commissioning of an altarpiece, and by 1450 the Opera of the cathedral took the matter in hand and obtained the promise of finance from one of the Graziani, say Giovanni di Bartolomeo, prior of the lay Fraternity of S. Bartolomeo. The subject – the climatic event in John's preparing the way for the Lord – was chosen because of the dedication of the altar (coincidentally or not coincidentally the name of the later Graziani patron). The painter, as would be expected by a patron employing a competent master, was acquainted with the standard format for the Baptism. Thus Piero shows the essential figures of Christ and John the Baptist, with the equally essential river Jordan. The source was the Bible, though we need not necessarily assume that the painter needed to refer directly to the Bible in order to paint the picture. Giotto was said to 'know the stories', and the same would be expected of Piero. Angels were not required by the Bible, but they had become more-or-less standard adjuncts of the scene, both because they decorously carried Christ's discarded garments and because their presence underscored the spiritual nature of the event for the spectator. The dove of the Holy Spirit and the fan of gold rays descending from on high (now less conspicuous through the loss of gilding) do not correspond to the biblical account in a literal sense, but had become the visual sign of the infusion of the Holy Spirit into Christ, accompanied by the declaration of God, ringing down from heaven: 'This is my beloved Son, in whom I am well pleased'. It is likely that the lost lunette above the main panel depicted God the Father.

This account provides the miminum necessary brief to explain the composition of the scene. But, on its own, this brief will not make an adequate picture, unless the protagonists were set artificially and iconically against a neutral ground, such as a gilded surface employed by Niccolò di Pietro Gerini (fig. 78), with a minimal reference to slopes and trees beside the river. Once the artist embraces wider pictorial ambitions in the setting of the scene, something more is required. A river is set in a landscape, and typically nourishes trees and other plants. Rivers tend to be in valleys. Towns are frequently built on the banks of rivers. And hills appropriately surround valleys and serve to introduce some visual 'relief' into the background. The event could be set in an otherwise unpeopled landscape, as in Giovanni Bellini's later *Baptism* for Vicenza (fig. 30), but the presence of other figures adds human interest and sets off the prime event in scale and theme. The man undressing, his reluctant shirt clinging damply to his body, signals that others are to be baptised, and conforms to a number of other depictions, including that by Masolino in Castiglione d'

78. Niccoló di Pietro Gerini, *Baptism of Christ with Saints Peter and Paul,* London, National Gallery

Olona, while the figures who are conspicuously not in a state of actual or potential undress provide a neat foil in a not uncommon manner and can be justified as belonging to one of the groups of potential bystanders who reject the Baptism or more specifically as the Pharisees and Sadduces whom John denounced as 'vipers'.

Is any more required – before we go into raptures about Piero's monumentally calm figures, 'blond tonality' and spacious landscape? I think we should not automatically assume that anything more is necessary – whether or

171

not the raptures are on our personal agenda. Such a stricture may seem disappointing for an aspiring iconographer who has been brought up on heavy theological exegesis of religious art, using learned quotations from the Church Fathers and other sources of spiritual moment. It may be tempting to delve into the indices of the *Patrologia latina* – the great compendium of the writing of the early Latin fathers of the church undertaken by the Abbé Jacques-Paul Migne – looking, for instance, at the fathers' exegeses of *arbor* in biblical texts to determine the significance of the conspicuous tree. The *Patrologia latina*, published in Migne's impressive establishment between 1844 and 1890, occupies 217 volumes of text with 4 volumes of Indices. The *Patrologia greca*, with texts in Greek and Latin runs to a further 161 volumes. The 'Index of Memorable Pronouncements' in the *Patrologia latina*, for example, reveals references to *arbor* in the writings of St Cyprian, St Peter Chrysologus and St Gregory. A host of other references could be traced by following the indices to biblical motifs. References to the baptism itself cover six pages in the indices. A more recent source of reference, the *Iconclass* of H. van der Waal, contains three pages of references to trees, with cross-references to forest, grove, names of trees, tree of knowledge, tree of life and tree trunk. Which should we select? Should we be thinking generically about the 'Tree of Life' which God decreed should be protected by an angel with a flaming sword? Or the tree which was to provide the wood for Christ's cross? The answer is that there is no way of proceeding with confidence, since there is no source in the Renaissance which specifically prescribes this manner of interpretation. I cannot prove the approach is wrong, but as a system of interpretation it remains a model, the validity of which cannot be satisfactorily anchored in direct testimony from the period.

However, returning to the context in which the image was generated, we may suggest an interpretation for the tree that has some kind of non-arbitrary anchor. The town in the middle distance has been reasonably identified as Borgo San Sepolchro itself, though the resemblance is not topographically precise. The origin of the town's name, referring to Christ's Holy Sepulchre, was explained in a legend. Two pilgrims had returned from the Holy Sepulchre in Jerusalem with relics, and, while they were resting in the Valle di Nocea, their treasured relics were miraculously transported high into one of the walnut trees after which the valley was named. The consequence was that the relics could not be carried to another place. On this site the pilgrims duly built an oratory, around which the town grew. The pilgrims, Arcano and Egidio, were later canonised, and feature as saintly pilgrims at the base of the flanking pilasters of Matteo's frame. The large foreground tree in Piero's central image is demonstrably a walnut, carefully differentiated from the other trees in the picture. The textual anchoring of the tree to the legend is not as secure as if it relied on primary documentation, but the unusual choice of the walnut tree, in conjunction with the town resembling San Sepolchro and the presence of the two relevant saints, generally meets the criterion of specific matching. It also meets the criterion of plausibility with respect to the accessibility of the legend to the patron and to the artist as natives of the town.

Remaining with the theme of trees for the moment, there is another feature that catches our eye as being curious. Behind Christ are a series of tree stumps, which are neither stock elements in Baptisms nor commonly expected features in a valley. Perhaps they are spatial markers added by Piero to step out the recession into depth, or perhaps he wanted something more interesting than grass. Maybe they were the trees cut down to build the city or plant crops. Sustaining such reductionist or common-sense explanations becomes more difficult when we read in the Bible that John warned the multitudes that 'now also the axe is laid unto the root of the trees; therefore every tree which bringeth forth not good fruit is hewn down and cast into the fire'.[258] This seems instinctively to sound like the 'right' allusion, but is it any better than looking in the forests of the *Patrologia latina* for theologically meaningful trees? In that I cannot demonstrate any Renaissance exegesis of a picture which directly sanctions it, there are no better reasons for believing it. However, it may be that the kind of literature which talked directly about pictures in the Renaissance simply did not deal with this issue, since it was not something that was written about within the genres of 'art writing', and was taken for granted. Just because we cannot show that a particular kind of bridge was built does not mean that nobody crossed the river. But, equally, we should not build bridges irresponsibly and opportunistically, wherever we might personally find it convenient. The only answer is, I think, to operate with intuition and common sense, not just commonsense in our terms but in terms of what we can learn of the mental habits of patrons, artists and viewers. The relative accessibility of a text, however transmitted, is clearly important in establishing levels of plausibility on a common-sense basis. An important element in the intuitive component is the judging of when a textual match is sufficiently compelling that it provides an explanation for a feature in the painting, which seems to demand more than casual attention. Judging that demand is based upon such superficially contradictory criteria as the recurrent nature of a feature in paintings of a particular subject, or, as in this case, the conspicuous unexpectedness of the motif in a particular work.

An example of a recurrent feature is the 'enclosed garden', which we have already seen in Fra Angelico's Annunciations (figs. 58-61) – to which we could add Annunciations by Domenico Veneziano and Botticelli, as well as by other masters across Europe. In each instance, the artist need not necessarily have consulted the Bible or the exegetical literature which explains that the *hortus conclusus* of the *Song of Songs* was emblematic of Mary's inviolate nature.[259] A full citing of all the relevant theological texts would not be irrelevant, in the sense that the garden is a site for interpretation, but neither would it be necessary if we are concentrating on the resources immediately available to the artist and entering directly into the making of a particular work. On the other hand, the inclusion of an exceptional feature, such as Piero's truncated trees, supposes some unusual move or moves during the genesis of a particular work. Whether these moves involved the patron, a notional 'programmer' (say the prior of the Camoldite monastery) or the artist himself is an intractable problem in the case of Piero's *Baptism*. We will return to this issue more generally later in the chapter, when we look at examples in which responsibility for the genesis of content is more clearly located.

Perhaps the most contentious of the 'conspicuously unexpected' features of the *Baptism* that seem to demand explanation is the very odd characterisation of the water of the river in the section of the bed nearest the spectator. Most of the tranquil river reflects the inverted forms of the figures and landscape, disposed with a real sense of how the equality of the angles of incidence and reflection reveal such features as the distant trees silhouetted above the convex contours of the hills. However, the nearer zone reveals only a brownish smudge of pebbles and sand. Something odd is happening here. If we accept that the strange effect is not simply the result of damage to the paint surface, it is difficult to avoid trying to explain it. We may imagine our unsophisticated spectator, puzzled by Newman's abstractness, being equally worried by what appears to be a mistake in such an otherwise meticulously made picture. What does it mean?

It had been argued that the apparently dry section of river bed refers to an ancient legend of the stopping of the very flow of the Jordan at the moment of the momentous event. However, the thin ribbons of impasted paint around Christ's ankles denote unequivocally that he is standing in water. (The failure of earlier observers of the 'dry bed' to notice this feature reminds us that hard and repeated visual scrutiny of a picture in the original is a high desideratum if we want to say anything reliable about it.) Although considerable ingenuity has been exercised in arguing that, while the water is present, Piero has made it 'look' as if the bed is dry, any answer which attempts to have it both ways should be distrusted. The main problem with the dry bed explanation was, even before it became suspect on detailed grounds, that it might not have been looking for explanation in the right kind of place. I should like to suggest an alternative strategy which, if not necessarily right, does show that other models for the way that this feature entered the painting may attain a good degree of plausibility. Taking my key from Piero's known concern with the construction of a rational analysis of the behaviour of light and its representation, I should like to suggest that he can be seen to exploit a special compound of observation, explanation and representation.

A series of investigators in the succession of Ptolemy had undertaken sustained investigation of the passage of light through transparent media, and a number of medieval philosophers had expressed interest in the way that some media could both reflect light and allow it to pass through. The English Franciscan Roger Bacon observed in the thirteenth century, that 'There are certain bodies of moderate density, such as water, in which reflection and refraction occur simultaneously. For by refraction we see fish and stones in it, and by reflection we see the sun and moon, as experience teaches.'[260]

The philosophers explained what happens to light as it passes from a rare to a denser medium by mechanical analogy. For example, if a sword strikes downwards on to a plank of wood, the more nearly perpendicular the impact, the more forceful it will be and the more likely it is to penetrate deeply, whereas a glancing blow tends to deflect off the surface. It would be logical to use this analogy to explain why we see through water when we look down at a steep angle, but tend to see reflections at shallower angles. However, none of the classical or medieval authors seem to have taken precisely this step.

Putting the various factors together, a working hypothesis suggests itself. Piero's own observations of nature revealed the general principles governing whether we see through water or see reflections from its surface, and that he rationalised them in terms of a critical angle. At angles closer to the perpendicular than the critical angle we would see through the surface, while at

79.   Water with reflections

angles further from the perpendicular the light would reflect off the surface. In reality (fig. 79), the transition between seeing through and seeing reflections is gradual rather than abrupt, but there is a nice sense of deductive logic to what I am proposing as 'Piero's law'. In its qualitative nature such a law is entirely consistent with the approach of much medieval optics.

But are there other adequate explanatory models within the optical field itself? As Leonardo had observed, the reflection of a "shadowy" body in water will make the pebbles on the bed of a stream more apparent, an effect he attributes to the augmentation of the shadowed modelling of the pebbles, while the uniform light in the areas unaffected by the dark reflection will effectively bleach out the modelling of the individual objects (fig. 80).[261] A dark reflection of this

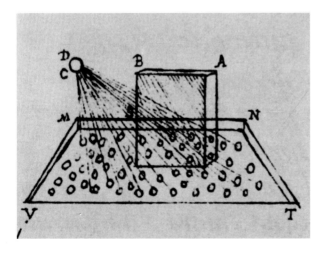

80.   Leonardo da Vinci (after), *Study of Pebbles seen under Water in Illumination and Shade*, Rome, Vatican, Codex Urbinas Latinus 1270 (the 'Trattato della Pittura') fol. 139r.

kind can indeed produce a sharp edge between the transparent and reflective portions (fig. 81), but this is not what Piero shows happening, since there is no dark object that can be reflected at this point in the river. On the other hand, it is not possible to produce this sharp transition between transparency and reflection by shadows cast down onto the water, as if it were shaded by the tree. I suppose it is possible to argue that the strange effect is a result of the action of the gilded stream of divine light, which could behave in whichever way it wanted. However, a strong burst of natural illumination would serve to lighten the river's bed, and it would hardly be appropriate to characterise divine light as producing a duller effect than its earthly counterpart. I prefer to adduce what I am calling 'Piero's law', which is necessarily a hypothetical model but does at least have roots in Piero's known interests and knowledge.

This necessarily summary discussion of the minimum interpretation, and of the big tree, the stumps and the visible river bed does not come anywhere near to exhausting the possible interpretations of the picture on iconographical or optical grounds. For instance, much ink has been spilt over the angels, with their differentiated gestures, glances, costumes and head-dresses. All the explanations, ranging from a reference to the wedding feast at Cana (celebrated on 6 January, the same day as the Baptism and the Adoration of the Kings), to an elucidation

81. Water with reflections and shadow

of the hierarchy of angels, are learnedly opportunistic and without adequately demonstrable anchors in the documented reality of the making and reading of pictures in the Renaissance. Such interpretations may be entertained as hypotheses, and instinctively ranked according to degrees of remoteness from the known circumstances, but they cannot be regarded other than as hypotheses unsusceptible to conclusive demonstration. This is not to say they are wrong; there simply is no clear way of knowing if they are right, either in detail or general type.

Above all, what we should not forget, as we weave elaborate webs of exegesis around the details of the picture, is that it is first and foremost an image for the veneration of St John, who was responsible for the institution of the first sacrament, the Baptism. When the bishop paid one of his periodic pastoral visits of inspection to S. Giovanni d'Afra in 1629, the altarpiece was described as 'an icon [*iconem*] painted on panel with images [*imaginibus*] of St John the Baptist and other saints, with an ornament [*ornamento*] of gilded wood' – which precisely corresponds to the purpose for which the image was generated. It was not a story-telling narrative of Christ's Baptism but an 'image' for devotions to St John as *the* Baptist. The situation is much the same as when an Annunciation appears as an altarpiece. Mary's angel registers her identity and nominates her as the *Annunziata*. She is the focus of devotion through the significance of the Annunciation, just as John is the focus for Piero. The central placing of Christ, a matter of almost invariable decorum, should not lead us to misidentify the prime function of the image. All other interpretative strategies, should flow from this starting point.

One of the problems in extrapolating general interpretative principles for religious art from the scrutiny of a richly rewarding example is that it cannot be taken as typical, as will become apparent when we look at further case studies in religious and secular art during the course of this chapter. When we do have documentation of the way that content entered paintings of an apparently similar type, we find a surprising variety of strategies. Opportunism and improvisation in particular circumstances was often the order of the day. A particularly nice instance is provided by the altarpiece of the *Trinity and Saints* (fig. 53) painted by Pesellino for Pistoia. We noted in chapter IV that the chamberlain of the Compagnia della Trinità wrote an unusually chatty minute of a meeting held on 10 September 1455. Having settled on the price of 150-200 florins, the attention of the Compagnia turned to the 'chief figures in the altarpiece'.[262] They decided that there should be two pairs of flanking saints:

> For one it was determined that it should be St James the greater, because he is protector of the region, and the other should be St Zeno, who is likewise the protector of all the priesthood in Pistoia, and the third should be St Jerome, and because the fourth was lacking, I, priest Piero di Ser Landi, humbly begged the Compagnia, seeing that I was devoted to the glorious saint messer Saint Mamas the martyr, that if they were willing that such a figure should be painted there, I would wish to make a great celebration each year for the said Compagnia and to leave in perpetuity for the said celebration six minas of grain.

Without this minute, we would be hard pressed to identify Piero's beloved St

Mamas, a shepherd martyr of the seventh century, and even more taxed to explain his inclusion. It would be wrong to take the chamberlain's opportunistic insertion of his favoured saint as a precise model for other commissions, but his minute does provide a valuable insight into the kind of discussions and thought processes which went into decisions about the altarpiece of a corporate body. Decisions by individuals were naturally different in their dynamics, but dedication of altars and devotion to particular saints (including name saints) provided the basic determinant of personalised content in the great majority of cases.

On the other hand, there were undoubtedly instances where a great deal of coherent advanced planning was involved in such a way that complex and profound theological meanings were built into the image. We would be safest to assume that this was the case when we know something of the protagonists involved in the commission and can frame some sort of reasonably precise idea about the viewing skills of the spectators. Such conditions are fulfilled by the images provided by Fra Angelico for the monastery of San Marco in Florence. We have already noted the allegiance between Cosimo de' Medici and the newly installed Observant Dominicans, which accounts for the spiritual, financial and political impulses behind the highly ambitious programme of building and decoration. The dominant figures amongst the reformed Dominicans were both Florentines, Cardinal Dominici, first great leader of the Observants, and Fra Antonino, who was to become Archbishop of Florence in 1446. The two houses over which they held most sway were S. Domenico at Fiesole and San Marco in Florence, where Fra Angelico exercised his vocation. As we have seen, he was far from being a cloistered monk immersed in a world of naive piety. He was a conspicuous figure in his order, assuming positions of responsibility, and a much travelled artist who attracted substantial remuneration from papal and other sources – even if that remuneration technically belonged to the order and not to the artist. It is with these factors in mind that we can begin to search for meaning in his frescoes.

One important aspect of the context for meaning has already been encountered, namely the way in which the placing of the *Annunciation* at the top of the stairs leading to the monks' quarters (fig. 61) gave it a role distinct from the equivalent subject when portrayed by the same painter as a splendid altarpiece (fig. 59) or within a monk's simple cell (fig. 60). Our progress around the cloister and into the interior spaces is punctuated by images which are, to use a modern term, 'site specific'; that is to say they perform carefully attuned roles in relation to the nature of the space as we make the transition from one zone of the monastery to another. Thus as we move to enter a door into the church, a watchful St Peter Martyr enjoins us with finger on lip to observe the required silence, while the fresco on the adjoining wall brings us face to face with St Dominic confronting the spiritual and physical reality of Christ's sacrifice (fig. 82). This image, in the important and conspicuous field at the end of the northern arcade, was originally the dominant painting in the cloister. It can be described as a *Crucifixion*, but it might more properly be entitled *St Dominic Meditating on the Crucifix*, because it depicts the spiritual transport through which the anguished Saint obtains communion with the still living Christ. It is not a biblical narrative as such, but rather sets a contemplative ideal for the

82. Fra Angelico, *St Dominic with the Crucified Christ and a Dominican Saint*, Florence, Monastery of San Marco, Cloister

monks. By contrast the frescoes in the monks' cells are narratives, in as much as they portray events from the life of Christ with story-telling clarity of the highest order (fig. 83). But even here, the images stop far short of being imaginative *reportage* of what it might have been like to be present at the event. The lack of naturalistic elaboration is not the result of artistic limitations on Fra Angelico's part, since he had many more naturalistic devices at his command than he used in the monks' frescoes. Rather he has concentrated on the essential nature of the event for its specific significance in this context. The monks of the reformed order, shut silently in their austere yet harmoniously proportioned cells, were expected to pass long hours in spiritual exercises, amongst which the most effective was the mental envisaging of the central realities of Christ's life. The image became a form of purified memory, in which the story lived again out of its original time and space as an event of eternal and vivid verity. Thus it is that in the image of *Annunciation* (fig. 60) the praying observer, *St Peter Martyr*, envisages the miraculous conception in his inner eye, as the monk is exhorted to do on his own account.

We describe figures like St Peter as praying, which is indeed the case, but our modern sieve is too coarse to catch the potential nuances in the act of praying, which was not a single, undifferentiated activity in the context of Dominican observance in the fifteenth century. A Dominican compilation, the *De modo orandi*, outlined the varied modes of prayer adopted by St Domenico, with a carefully orchestrated range of bodily and manual gestures, and became an exemplary text for the Observants.[263] The hands, for instance, could be held across the chest, thrown wide open or placed together, as here, in a gesture which

83. Fra Angelico, *Transfiguration*, Florence, Monastery of San Marco, Cell 6

specifically signifies a meditative mode. We do not need to see the actions of Fra Angelico's praying Dominicans as literal illustrations of the literary source. Rather the source in this case alerts us to the greater internal refinement in the category of 'praying', and gives an insight into the kind of sensibility with which the painter was entering into dialogue, in the context of an attuned audience.

Fra Angelico represents the strong case for the religious iconographer. For the great majority of painters and paintings we possess no such advantages. Even with a famous artist like Botticelli, whose paintings lead us to expect a high level of intellectual sophistication and a developed knowledge of subject matter, we have no free-standing evidence of his literacy or learning. In fact what we know of his background as the last of four surviving children of a tanner whose family rose to modest prosperity suggests that the young Alessandro would have received no more than a decent basic education in literacy and numeracy. He was first apprenticed to a goldsmith, the profession of his second eldest bother (who became a specialist in gold leaf for painters), and subsequently to Filippo Lippi. This is hardly the obvious training for a 'philosophical' painter. However, his religious paintings and his mythologies (which we will encounter again in this chapter), demonstrably embody sophisticated content in such a way as to raise the obvious question of responsibility for the invention of the subject matter. An informative example is the fresco of *St Augustine* (fig. 85) which he originally provided for the screen in the church of the Ognissanti, flanking the door into the choir, as a companion piece to Ghirlandaio's *St Jerome* (fig. 84) which is dated 1480. The fresco was moved when the screen was demolished in the sixteenth century, as part of the campaign of theological and liturgical reforms, and was detached from the wall following the disastrous floods of 1966. Now on display in the refectory, as a work of art, it has been severely dislocated from its original functional context.

Even a cursory inspection reveals that it is not simply an image of one of the early Church Fathers sitting in appropriately scholarly manner in a bookish study. The saint is staring raptly at a burst of light from the upper left, characterised as linear rays (originally with more prominent gilding) which pass in front of an armillary sphere. He was writing on a sheet of paper before his attention was distracted. These clues, and the proximity of St Jerome allow us, at least provisionally, to recognise what is happening as an event described in an apocryphal letter from 'St Augustine' to St Cyril, which probably originated in the late thirteenth century.[264] The letter tells how Augustine was writing to Jerome enquiring about the joy of the blessed in heaven, when he saw a burst of 'indescribable light', smelt an 'ineffable . . . fragrance', and heard the disembodied voice of Jerome, who had just died in Jerusalem, telling him that it was futile to strive for a complete understanding of the ultimate mysteries of heaven while shackled with the limitations of our earthly comprehension. The message is one of the strictly finite limits of human intellect before the final revelation.

Yet, so far we have ignored two unexpected lines of more or less legible text in the middle of the writing-like scribbles on the left-hand page of the geometrical text. These lines have been subject to various readings. The two most recent alternatives are: '*Dove sa'martino 'è'chashcato e dove andato a fuor dela porta al prato* [Where's St Martin – He's fallen down. Where's he gone to? – He's outside the Prato Gate]'; and '*Dove Sant agostino a d[eo] sp[er]ato e dove andato a fuor dela porta al prato* [Where's St Augustine placed hope in God and where he went outside the gate to the meadow]'. The second of these readings appears more immediately promising because it recalls the key moment in Augustine's *Confessions*, when he underwent his decisive conversion from a

84. Domenico Ghirlandaio, *St Jerome*, Florence, Ognissanti

85.   Alessandro Botticelli, *St Augustine*, Florence, Ognissanti

Ciceronian and Platonising philosopher to an evangelical Christian. He tells how, in a state of mental turmoil while discussing the Scriptures with a companion, they went into his small garden.[265] Sitting alone in distress under a fig tree, he heard a childish voice repeatedly incanting, 'take and read'. Returning to the bench where his companion was sitting, he opened his book at the section in Paul's Epistle to the Romans which reads, 'Not in rioting and drunkenness, not in chambering and wantonness, not in strife and envying, but put on the Lord Jesus Christ, and make no provision for the flesh to fulfill the lust thereof'. Henceforth, Augustine devoted himself to Christian devotion. Could the event actually be the prelude to the conversion, or the moment when he heard the voice, or his reading of the Bible, rather than the incident described in the letter? There are a number of pointers which favour the letter rather than the *Confessions*: the implicit narrative in the fresco does not correspond at all closely to that of the *Confessions*, since the painted vision is occurring indoors; Augustine is obviously witnessing a wonderful light as described in the letter; he is a mature bishop rather than a youthful Ciceronian; the time on the clock, equivalent to our modern 8 o'clock in the evening, is consistent with the sunset hour of the writing of the letter; and he is clearly writing on a single sheet of paper, not reading a book. Not least, the use of the letter serves to make a neat link with the adjacent St Jerome.

This failure of the text of the painted narrative to fit with the event of conversion, suggests that the other, more generally accepted reading, would be worth a second look. The reference appears to be to the church of S. Martino fuori la Porta al prato, which no longer exists and may have been demolished in whole or in part by 1480. That is to say, the translation should read, 'Where's S. Martino. It's fallen down. Where's it gone to? Its outside the Porta al Prato'. But by whom would such a reference be included and for what purpose? The inconspicuous lines of text do not fit the normal mode of inscriptions in paintings, and it is unclear who might have been expected to read them. They are extraordinarily informal, and have something of the air of a jokey rhyme. To explain them, we need to begin inventing fictional scenarios, which are not susceptible to any kind of of demonstration. In such circumstances, we should not be afraid to admit that we lack an adequate interpretative model for such a strange insertion.

The strangely fugitive inscription is not the only element in the painting which raises questions about the appropriate model for the interpretation of meaning. The intellectual paraphernalia with which the saint's study has been equipped – the armillary sphere, representing in schematic form the system of the cosmos in its Ptolemaic configuration, the book with marginal illustrations of geometry, and the weight-driven clock with visible foliot wheel at the top – present an unusually coherent set of tools for cosmological exegesis and specu-lation, embodying as they do the components of mathematics and time as the foundations of astronomy. When we recall the letter's stern injunction that the saint should set aside futile speculation on matters which lie outside the human mind, we may wonder if a carefully planned message about the limits of earth-bound reason is being signalled. Are the cosmological tools being disparaged? Or has the narrative simply been adopted as a convenient visionary link with the pre-existing St Jerome – without profounder implications? Or are the items in the study approved references to the saint's philosophical achievements? Augustine was, after all, one of the most important philosophers of his time.

Our knowledge of Botticelli, beyond what we may suspect from his paintings, provides no evidence of which of the explanations are correct, or even if we are looking in the right area. There is some evidence in the patronage of the fresco that might key our interpretation into the most learned circles in Florence around 1480. The shield with its diagonal band of wasps (*vespe*) is that of the Vespucci family, near neighbours of the painter. The renown of the family was to be ensured by the great explorer of the new world, Amerigo, whose uncle, Fra Giorgio Antonio Vespucci, was a Platonising philosopher and devout Christian in the circle of Marsilio Ficino. Fra Giorgio acted as tutor to Lorenzo di Pierfrancesco de' Medici. In his will of 1499, after he had entered the Dominican order under the compelling influence of Savonarola, he decreed that Botticelli should be commissioned to decorate the family's chapel with scenes from the life of St Paul and St Denis the Areopagite. St Denis, an exceptional and erudite choice, was an Athenian convert whose writings are strongly Neoplatonic in tone.

Even if we begin to view Botticelli's fresco within this climate of Neoplatonic theology, we still do not have clear guidance as to how far and how deep we should go in juxtaposing texts and ideas with the image, unless we are simply using the image as a gateway into questions of intellectual reason and transcendent revelation in Medicean circles, without addressing the more pedantically specific question as to how meaning actually entered this particular image in the circumstances of its making. And even if we stop long before we begin to weave a dense web of theological texts, the fugitive inscription and the choice of the letter still require explanation in terms of the reason and mechanism for their choice. Do we see the artist as the learned devisor of the content, aware of the letter and the *Confessions*, or do we need to posit some kind of external 'programmer' – someone like Fra Giorgio Antonio Vespucci? The will of 1499 presupposes that the painter had access to the stories of the St Denis's conversion, baptism and martyrdom, which were certainly not stock subjects in any painter's repertoire. It is likely that Botticelli would have been provided with guidance on the narratives, but would this have gone any further than telling him the basic outlines of the events? The only definite answer to this question lies in knowledge which is unlikely to be yielded by written documents, since we would require inside knowledge of the kind of personal interchanges between painters and clients which lie outside the formal procedures recorded in writing. There is no formula to which we can resort to frame answers to questions of this kind, since the ways of proceeding are likely to have varied widely according to personalities and circumstances. We need to balance what we know about the artist, the patron, other parties involved, the nature of the subject, the intended audience and function of the work, and a variety of other pertinent circumstances to formulate a credible model in each case, bearing in mind comparable instances where the whole or part of the process may be better documented. On balance, I think it is likely that Botticelli was given enough basic information by Fra Giorgio to achieve the desired end of linking the two saints in their appropriately equipped scholars' studies, without requiring elaborate skill in theological exegesis from either the painter or most of the likely spectators. What Fra Giorgio and his circle were capable of seeing *into* the picture could well have been a very different and far more erudite matter.

There is at least some evidence to suggest that leading artists had access to a basic range of vernacular texts on such regularly required subjects as the lives of the saints. Records of what artists possessed in the way of reading materials is scarce, but we do possess the 1498 inventory of the studio and household possessions of the deceased Tuscan sculptor, Benedetto da Maiano, whose works would not necessarily lead us to expect an especially high level of erudition.[266] In the 'writing rooms' of Benedetto and Giuliano, his brother, who was a renowned master of *intarsia*, there were twenty-eight books, the majority of which are religious texts of popular devotions and stories of well-known saints, with a vernacular Bible and two anthologies of biblical texts. Items such as 'a book of the saints [perhaps the *Golden Legend*], large and beautiful, in leather covers, in the common tongue' would have been of obvious utility in Benedetto's practice, as well as serving his own devotions. A small group of ancient texts, including a 'life of Alexander', suggests that one or both of the brothers had some access to Latin, unusually for artists, while a group of literary compositions, such as a Dante, a book of *novelle* and a chivalric poem, indicates some literary interests.

It is difficult to know how far the Maiano brothers' basic library was typical of artists, but it is interesting that some of their texts were also amongst those owned by Leonardo da Vinci, including the popular *Flowers of Virtue*. Leonardo's booklists, in the Codice atlantico in the 1490s and in the second Madrid Codex probably from 1504, cannot at first sight be taken as typical of artists' holdings, given the wide range of books on natural philosophy, mathematics and other technical subjects, but with respect to texts of Christian stories his holdings in the vernacular are perhaps not out of line with what a major master might have been expected to possess or to have access to.[267] He owned a Bible, a book of sermons (un-named), Augustine's *Sermons* and *City of God*, the works of S. Bernardino, a book of the passion of Christ, a text on St Margaret, the *Dreams of Daniel*, and a *Life of St Ambrose*. This clearly falls far short of being a reference collection for Christian iconography, but it does show the scope of the kinds of text to which artists undertaking major commissions might be expected to have recourse as the foundation of their ability to portray the sacred stories.

THE INVENZIONE

The thrust of art theory in the Renaissance provided artists with encouragement to claim competence in *invenzione*; that is to say in the devising of content in a way to rival the powers of the orator or poet. Leonardo specifically claimed the painter could equal the poet in the invention of telling subjects, like Apelles's *Calumny*, and that the subject as painted would surpass any poem in visual impact. Ghiberti, whose acquired learning enabled him to participate in the humanist habit of swapping prized manuscripts of ancient texts, was not constrained by the elaborate *invenzione*, which no less an authority than Leonardo Bruni, the humanist chancellor, provided for his second set of

Baptistery doors (figs. 46-7). Bruni submitted to the Guild of Cloth Merchants a scheme for twenty scenes and eight prophets, indicating that he 'would like to get together with whomever has to design it to make him pick out everything significant that the stories carry'.[268] This scheme, which envisaged a lay-out of the traditional kind, was overridden in favour of a new distribution of ten square reliefs in the new pictorial manner, the choice of which we may reasonably credit to Ghiberti himself. This is not to say that Ghiberti was given *carte blanche* to do whatever he wanted, and we may imagine that the Opera expected to see models of the reliefs as they were designed, just as he provided a drawing of the intended appearance of *St Stephen* for the Arte della Lana before providing the statue for their niche on Or San Michele. However, the overall change and the detailed *invenzioni*, particularly the tricky distribution of various narratives within the same fields, may be seen as Ghiberti's own elegant solutions. What he does share with Bruni is a concern that the telling of the stories conform with the principles of rhetorical communication and good manners upon which humanists insisted. Bruni set specific standards for the visual rhetoric when he insisted that the reliefs should be *illustri*, *significanti* and *gentile*, with a full *varietà de disegno*. Ghiberti tells us that he asserted his own '*licenza*' to do whatever he considered would 'turn out most perfect, most ornate and most rich', treating each of the '*effetti*' (incidents) in the '*istorie*' (narratives) with all the inventiveness, compositional skill and ornamentation that Bruni would require in a literary work made according to Ciceronian criteria.

Instances of externally devised programmes are rare from the quattrocento. Another exceptional example is the *invenzione* that Guarino Guarini, translator of Lucian's *Calumny*, provided in 1447 for a series of painted Muses in the *studio* that Leonello d' Este was creating at Belfiore.[269] Having outlined the meaning of the Muses as 'seekers' who 'have contrived various activities and arts,' Guarino then tells of their names and attributes, so that each might be characterised in a recognisable manner. For example, Urania, the Muse of Astrology, should 'hold an astrolabe and gaze at the starry heaven above her'. Where such an exceptional subject was involved, we may imagine that someone competent, like Guarino, was expected to provide more or less detailed instructions to the artist. We have already encountered a comparable case in chapter II, when Isabella d' Este was taking elaborate steps to ensure that Perugino in Florence provided something appropriate for her *studiolo* in Mantua (fig. 29).[270] She sent detailed instructions and a drawing of her own 'poetic invention' as elaborated by the humanist Paride Ceresara, and even a piece of string to indicate the height of the largest figures in Mantegna's adjacent painting. When she learnt that Perugino was departing from the authorised scheme, she gave her emissary stern instructions to ensure that he did not 'pervert the whole sentiment of the fable'.

During the course of the middle and later years of the sixteenth century, the era of Vasari and the later Mannerists, a taste grew for elaborately learned schemes of decoration. As literary men began to take increasing pride in their association with the visual arts, the written *invenzione* seems to have become a more formalised exercise, and is more likely to have been recorded for posterity. We cannot be certain that the scarcity of surviving *invenzione* in the earlier period necessarily reflects their rarity in practice, but the impression conveyed by contracts and related evidence is that content was generally a matter for verbal interchange between the artist and patron (or the patron's nominee) rather than for written instruction. Even where the verbal instructions were quite precise, they inevitably fell far short of telling the painter what every aspect of the picture should look like, and a patron employing a reputable master would expect elegant and appropriate inventions in the main or subsidiary parts of the composition. The great majority of religious commissions and a high proportion of subjects for domestic settings concerned time-honoured or familiar subjects, and the painter would be expected to be visually literate in the way to tell the stories or characterise the figures. When something exceptional was planned, the burden of responsibility is likely to have shifted away from the artist, but not necessarily in all cases.

Probably the most startling evidence of an artist apparently being given his head is found in Michelangelo's letter of 1523 to Fattucci, which we have already encountered when we discussed agreements between patrons and artists. Michelangelo specifically relates that when he proposed an alternative scheme for the Sistine ceiling (fig. 19) the pope 'gave him a new commission that I should make what I wished'.[271] What we cannot do is to take this assertion at face value. The letter was, as we have seen, devoted to the establishing of the extent of Michelangelo's undertakings on behalf of Julius, emphasising the way in which he had provided value for money over and above the strict requirements, in such a way as to provide Fattucci with arguments which he could use on the artist's behalf in attempting to settle his tangled dealings with the della Rovere heirs of Julius. He was not entering into a realistic account of how the content of the ceiling was devised, but rather underlining the high level of responsibility that he was accorded and the extra work that was entailed. There is no case for thinking that Julius literally said, 'do whatever you want', and then waited to see what he got. Their entering into a 'pact' is most unlikely not to have been preceded by an exchange of views about what was most fitting in this most important of papal chapels. In fact, Michelangelo's letter does give some glimpse into the terms of reference within which such an interchange took place.

Michelangelo's original agreement involved the depiction of twelve Apostles in the 'lunettes' – almost certainly the spandrels where the prophets and sibyls are now located, with additional compartments filled with decorations 'in the usual manner'. The painter told the pope that 'it would turn out to be a poor thing [cosa povera]'. When the pope demanded why, Michelangelo responded that it was 'because they [the apostles] were themselves poor'. Considered on its own, this hardly seems to provide an adequate answer to the successor of St Peter, let alone to supply adequate justification for the pope to give the painter his head. Clearly we are dealing with a compressed and laconic account of a conversation which involved the kind of verbal sparring at which painter and pontiff were adept. Further hints of the framework are provided by Vasari and Condivi, who both relate that one of the key issues between the artist and his patron was the question of 'richness'. Vasari tells that when the pope requested the adornment of the figures with gold, Michelangelo argued that 'in those days they did not wear gold . . . they were holy men, who despised wealth'.[272] Condivi also says that Michelangelo justified his failure to adorn the ceiling with *lapis lazuli* and gold on the basis that the original protagonists were poor men and women.[273] We should not take either of these accounts as verbatim transcriptions of actual conversations, but they do suggest that the locus of debate centred around the concepts of richness (*richezza*) and poverty (*povertà*), in which an ironic interplay was made between the poverty of the ancient protagonists, the literal richness of the pope's proposed adornments and the alternative richness of Michelangelo's multi-figured narratives and supporting witnesses. Michelangelo's 'non-poverty' was not of the literal kind – of the kind that might be expected with expensively decorated compartments 'in the usual manner' – but in rhetorical effect through the *invenzione* of telling narratives and complex *effetti* in the Ghibertian manner. What Michelangelo's letter apparently refers to, in typically laconic and allusive manner, is the way that he was capable of engaging the pope in knowing humanist debate about different kinds of richness and poverty, and that it was these and other signs of Michelangelo's intellectual command that led the pope to agree to the kind of scheme that Michelangelo was proposing. But there is no case for thinking that Michelangelo had not been required to make a proposal or that the pope or his plenipotentiary did not require subsequent and continuing evidence of what was about to transpire on the vault of his chapel.

The surviving drawings for the earliest schemes of the vault bear out Michelangelo's account of the original scheme. A drawing in the British Museum (fig. 86) shows a seated figure in a niche-like throne, with a conventional series of decorative compartments of varied sizes and shapes occupying the main area of the vault. What close examination of this drawing shows is that he has roughly laid in the line of the cornice and contours of the lunettes in blank stylus incision. However, the pen lines are improvised with little reference to the established proportions, and the resulting architectural articulation would have been difficult to reconcile with the realities of the actual vault. What appears to be a subsequent scheme is recorded on a sheet in Detroit (fig. 87). In this instance, the figurative content is largely suppressed so that the architectonic structure can be studied in its own right. The stylus underdrawing is now more precise and elaborate, and the drawn lines depart from the underlying armature in a less cavalier fashion. The design as a whole exhibits greater structural coherence, with a simplified arrangement of compartments, which resembles the final solution of alternating large and small fields in the vault itself, although the way the planned cornice would have related to the actual architecture remains problematic.

The two drawings, rare survivals of what was probably an extensive series of sketches of early thoughts, show that there were greater elements of continuity between the original and final conceptions than Michelangelo's account might suggest. What we can watch, albeit in fragmentary form, is the fluidity with which the designs evolved as Michelangelo thought 'out loud' on paper. The basic scheme of large seated figures in the spandrels, anchored to the key structural members of the vault, of a series of large and small fields, with some accessory characters, is present from the first. Both drawings indicate that Michelangelo was thinking of using angels in one of their customary roles in decoration, that is to say supporting or carrying other elements. We can see the herm-angels in the first design metamorphosed into free-standing angels

86.   Michelangelo, *Study for the Sistine Ceiling*, London, British Museum

87.   Michelangelo, *Study for the Sistine Ceiling*, Detroit, Institute of Art

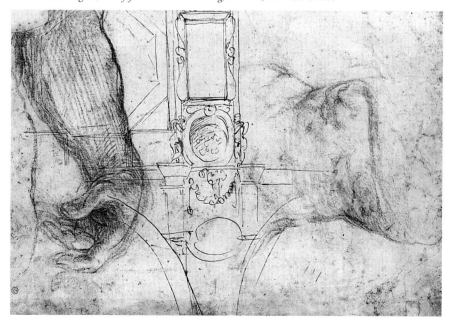

holding oval frames in the second, and finally into the grand *ignudi* flanking the narratives and supporting medallions. There is no reason to think that they shed their angelic personae during the process. Smaller genii have taken over the job of aiding the seers in their secret prognostications, while paired 'marble' infants adorn the sides of their thrones . The bronze nudes in the awkward triangular spaces above the spandrels may present greater problems, but only if we make them do so. In the great majority of the decorative borders around religious narratives, whether frescoes or manuscript illuminations, there are space-filling figures, which do not have specific meanings but visually complement the scenes. Thus Michelangelo's bronze nudes evoke the air of a distant, heroic age; they are pregnant with the kinds of struggle for release which he saw as inherent in the human condition, without necessarily being specifically identifiable. A figure can be decorative, without specific identity, and yet not be devoid of meaning in the broader sense.

What the designs suggest, as do other sets of drawings for complex ensembles, is that there was at no point anything that could be described as a fixed 'programme' during the creative process, and that the final solution to the content of the ceiling emerges organically at a late stage in the evolving series of designs. Form and meaning evolve in reciprocal dialogue, through ratiocination, fantasy and serendipity, and not all the invented components carry the same degree of significant content. The uneven burdens of meaning (and types of meaning) carried or not carried by parts of the same scheme of decoration bother modern iconographers more than it would have troubled contemporary artists and viewers.

Of all Renaissance artists Michelangelo provides the richest evidence about the fluidity and allusiveness with which meaning entered into and might be extracted from works of art. Although Michelangelo's poetic imagination cannot be taken as strictly representative of Renaissance artists as a group, and his written output seems to take us into a wholly atypical dimension, the way that his imagination works in the reciprocal evolution of content and form seems to me to differ mainly in degree from that of other inventive artists, albeit to a marked degree compared with the great majority of his contemporaries and predecessors. One of the nicest instances in which Michelangelo provides an allusive reading of one of his own creations is the text appended to one of his studies for architectural details in the Medici Chapel (fig. 88), on which he was working between 1519 and 1534. Even the architectural details are subject to the play of the draftsman's *fantasia* as he transforms one of them into a humorous profile. Michelangelo envisages the time of day to be speaking:

> Day and Night [fig. 89] are speaking and say 'we with our swift course brought Duke Giuliano to his death, and it is entirely just that he takes revenge on us as he does, and the revenge is this: that we have killed him; he thus dead has taken the light from us and with his closed eyes has fixed ours so that they no longer shine above the earth. What would he have done with us then, were he still to live.[274]

This nice conceit is not literally the programme by which we should interpret the figures, since it is in the nature of a poetic improvisation, but it does reveal key aspects of Michelangelo's habits of mind when dealing with such matters as

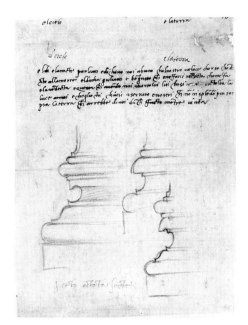

88. Michelangelo, *Study for Column Bases for the Medici Chapel*, Florence, Casa Buonarotti

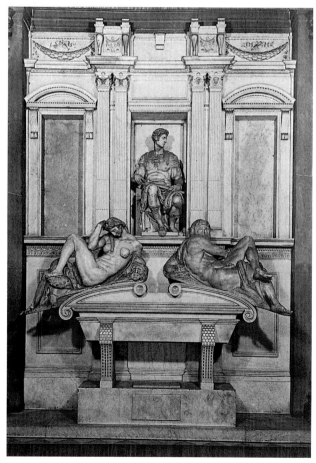

89. Michelangelo, *Lorenzo de' Medici with Night and Day*, Florence, S. Lorenzo, New Sacristy

192

90.   Michelangelo, Window in the drum of the dome, Florence, S. Lorenzo, New Sacristy

mortality, time, vision and light. The whole quality of the musing, here as in other of Michelangelo's literary works, is deeply imbued with a Dantesque use of sightlessness as an expression of profound deprivation, either in the face of the final reality of death or by confrontation with the blinding majesty of the ultimate truth. Once attuned to these proclivities, one of the key motifs in the chapel can be seen (literally) as the contrast between the light from above, directed down into the space by carefully stepped window embrasures (fig. 90) and the poignantly mute sightlessness of the figures, as they stare at us, at each other, and into vacant space without seeing. None of the pupils are drilled, and as the Medici dukes turn to the visitor who has entered a few steps into the chapel from the original door from the church, so we enter a silent and pale world of eyes whose lights have been eternally extinguished. Such motifs clearly do not explain the iconography of the whole work, but they do indicate the species of meaning that entered the work and which Michelangelo sanctions as valid interpretations. The poetic allusiveness and fluidity of both intention and reception are clearly embedded in the work as an essential part of its constitution.

One factor we need to respect when we bring even texts and images by the same person into juxtaposition is that both function within their own conventions and frameworks of interpretation. When we bring, say, Michelangelo's poetry and late Crucifixion drawings together, we need to remember that the poetry functions as *poetry*, just as a depicted Crucifixion is articulated in relation to a visual *type*. Respected in Roman intellectual circles as a '*gran Dantista*', as an authority on the *Divine Comedy* in all its poetic and philosophical complexities, Michelangelo was saturated in the Florentine poetic traditions which descended from Dante and Petrarch. Although his poetic voice has a highly idiosyncratic tone – we might almost say 'rough-hewn' by analogy to sculpture, or 'licentious' by analogy to the set rules which applied to architectural composition in the 'ancient manner' – he self-consciously uses many of the literary devices pioneered by the Tuscan authors, including irony and paradox in a way that should caution against too literal a reading of every poem as direct statements of Michelangelo's thoughts. He uses such conventional figures as freezing in fire and burning in ice, dead while alive and alive in death, pained by sweetness and sweetened by pain . . . with knowing virtuosity, in much the same way that he paraded obvious pleasure in his unrivalled facility for carving marble and in creating poses which deliberately demonstrated his mastery of *difficoltà* in the human figure. We also need to take into account, as with all the sources we are examining throughout this book, the nature of the address of the documents.

Were Michelangelo's poems private musings, exercises in talking to himself? A few may fall into this internalised category, but as early as 1518, before he had a poetic *oeuvre* of any real size, one of the madrigals had been set to music by Bartolommeo Tromboncino, and was therefore in the public domain, communicating to a far from personal audience.[275] In 1533, Michelangelo's banker, friend and literary correspondent, Luigo del Riccio, prepared and circulated fair copies of the *Rime* (*Poems*), at least two of which were also set to music. The most vivid testimony to the fact that his poetic activity was a matter of note and comment came in 1546, when Benedetto Varchi delivered a lecture to the Florentine Academy on the sonnet which begins, 'The best of artists never has a concept a single block of marble does not contain' – the poem which, as we will see, appears to give us the best leverage on Michelangelo's view of the conceptual process behind the creation of a statue.[276] Other of the poems are specifically addressed to named or known recipients, who would not only recognise them as personal communications from Michelangelo but also have the sophistication to recognise that communication by poem took place within certain conventions and literary modes of expression. There probably is no overarching answer to the question of how we read the poems in terms of Michelangelo's innermost thoughts, and we need to look at each example in terms of its manner, subject matter, address and reception. This being said, however, there is a strain running throughout the poetry, which becomes urgently apparent in the later writing, which transcends the conventional poetic voice, and which I find it impossible to read other than as the expression of feelings at the deepest level. Taking such decisions, however hard we work on our historical methods to control our readings, ultimately relies on personal intuition. Let me put some flesh on the bare bones of these generalisations by looking at examples of the types of poetic production with which he was involved.

A group of early sonnets and madrigals assume the tone of love songs, very much in the Petrarchian tradition, addressed to an ideal and (in this case) unknown lady. Many of the stock figures appear, praising the beloved's brow, cheeks, neck, breast, and, inevitably, her eyes, the prime weapons of love:

> A burning beam from my beloved's eyes,
> Come forth and flies: so brilliant is its light,
> Into my heart through mine, though shut, it breaks.[277]

Elsewhere, he shows that he was sufficiently aware of the nature of the conventions to burlesque their potential absurdity:

> . . . your mouth is just like a pocketful
> Of beans, it seems to me, and so is mine.
> Your eyebrows seemed dyed in a crucible
> And more than a Syrian bow they twine. . . .
> And when I look upon you and each breast,
> I think they're like two melons in a satchel. . .[278]

This burlesque character is certainly present (as is the 'Syrian bow') in the famous sonnet on the agonies of painting the Sistine Ceiling that he sent to Giovanni da Pistoia, himself a poet and writer of comedies:

> I've got myself a goitre from this strain. . .
> My belly's pushed by force beneath my chin.
>
> My beard toward Heaven, I feel the back of my brain
> Upon my neck, I grow the breast of a Harpy;
> My brush, above my face continually,
> Makes it a splendid floor dripping down. . .
>
> In front of me skin is being stretched
> While it folds up behind and forms a knot,
> And I am bending like a Syrian bow.[279]

Though there is a conventional element of humorous self-mockery in the poem, as there is in the grotesque self-portrait mannikin that accompanies it (fig. 91), there is adequate testimony to the extreme physical discomforts that he faced in painting the huge area of the curved vault and to his feeling that 'here I am living ill-content and not too well, faced with an enormous task, without anyone to manage for me and without money'. This is just one of repeated complaints about his state of health. We gain a clear sense, particularly in his later poems, of his feelings of bodily inadequacy and even of the repellent nature of the flesh in which his soul resided, and we may detect something of the same feeling emerging during the course of even the triumphant act of creation on the ceiling.

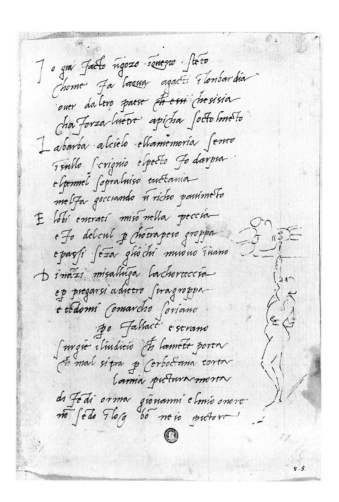

91. Michelangelo,
*Poem and Sketch of the
Painter at Work on the
Sistine Ceiling*, Florence,
Casa Buonarotti

Some poems were specifically created within the context of overtly literary activity. When Francesco Berni sent a poem in praise of Michelangelo to Sebastiano del Piombo, the sculptor's friend and one-time amanuensis, Michelangelo himself replied in *terza rima*, but through the lips of Sebastiano, making play upon 'Medicus', as the Medici pope, and 'dried meat ' (*carnesecca*), as Cardinal Carnessechi.[280] The same tone of poetic wit is nicely exemplified by the sonnet he sent to Giorgio Vasari on the publication of Vasari's *Lives* in 1550. After conventionally elegant praise of Vasari's own art – which hands back nature's beauty even lovelier – he seems to infer, to double-edged effect, that his admirer's writing is to be preferred to his painting:

> You now, however, with a worthier labour,
> Have settled down with learned hand to write,
> And steal her glory's one remaining part
> That you lacked, by giving life to others.[281]

If there was a certain barb in Michelangelo's praise, it was lost on Vasari, who proudly published the sonnet in the second edition in 1568.

During the 1530s and 1540s, when he was nearing his old age, or, as he felt, was already there, a large group of confessional poems express intense relationships with three special friends who become the focuses of deep love. Two are younger male friends, the Roman nobleman, Tommaso Cavalieri, and Cecchino de' Bracci, nephew of Luigi del Riccio, who died at the age of fifteen. The third is Vittoria Colonna, widowed Marchioness of Pescara, a woman of high literary accomplishments and devout spirituality. The central theme of the poems to the young men is the way that the transcendent grace of the youths' countenances and bodies (not least in contrast to Michelangelo's own ageing flesh) is both reflective of their beloved souls and resonant with the divine beauty that lies beyond earthly realisation. As he wrote to Tommaso:

I see within your beautiful face, my lord,
What in this life we hardly can attest:
Your soul already, still clothed in its flesh,
Repeatedly has risen with it to God. . .
All beauty that we see here must be likened
To the merciful Fountain whence we all derive,
More than anything else, by men with insight.[282]

The sense of ascent to the divine through the contemplation of beauty is made verbally manifest in the poems and visually manifest in one of the finished drawings he presented to Tommaso in 1532-3, the *Rape of Ganymede*. Known only through copies (fig. 92), it depicts the abduction of the beautiful youth by Zeus in the form of an eagle, one of the god's many rapacious disguises. Whether or not a specifically Neoplatonic explanation is in order, it is clear that

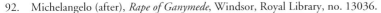

92.   Michelangelo (after), *Rape of Ganymede*, Windsor, Royal Library, no. 13036.

the glorious and acquiescent body of Ganymede is being transported heavenwards and into a spiritual realm where once carnal passions could now be endowed with divine beauty. Ganymede's transport may consciously mirror the loss Michelangelo felt on parting from Tommaso.

His direct, personal love of younger men was, as he admitted, different from that he felt for any woman:

> The love of which I speak reaches higher;
> Woman's too much unlike, no heart by rights
> Ought to grow hot for her, if wise and male.[283]

Whether or not such love was consummated through a physical relationship is not demonstrable through written sources, and seems to me to be of little significance for his art. However, the poems do reveal the charge he received from the beautiful male form, a charge that has a strong erotic component, and suggest that his creations, visual and verbal, do embody aspects of the sublimation of this impulse in terms of a philosophical and theological expression of the divine ideal.

This is not to say that he was incapable of deep relationships with women, or rather with one woman in particular, Vittoria Colonna. Her own religious convictions and personal example were deeply sustaining for Michelangelo, and, after some ten years of deep friendship, he was devastated by her death in 1547:

> But heaven has taken away from me the splendour
> Of the great fire that burned and nourished me;
> I am left to be a coal, covered and burning.[284]

Compared to the direct expressions of love in the poems to men, the majority of those written for Vittoria while alive work a triangular relationship between his artistic creations, the shaping influence of her soul and the ultimate contemplation of the divine. It was to Vittoria that he directed his most famous sonnet, in which he typically laments the shortcomings of his art in the face of the divinity embodied in her person:

> The best of artists never has a concept [concetto]
> A single block of marble does not contain
> Inside its husk, but to it may attain
> Only if the hand follows the intellect.
>
> The good I pledge myself, bad I reject,
> Hide O my lady, beautiful, proud, divine,
> Just thus in you, but now my life must end,
> Since my skill [arte] works against the wished effect.
>
> It is not love then, fortune, or your beauty,
> Or your hardness and scorn, in all my ill
> That are to blame, neither my luck nor fate,
>
> If at the same time both death and pity
> Are present in your heart, and my low talent [basso ingegno],
> Burning, can grasp nothing from it.[285]

This is the sonnet glossed by Benedetto Varchi, who used the Aristotelian notion of the form-generating soul to emphasise the centrality of the *concetto* to Michelangelo's vision: 'Art is nothing else than the form [*forma*], that is the model [*modello*] of the artificial thing, which is in the soul, that is, in the imagination [*fantasia*] of the artist, which form or model is the shaping principle or the artificial form in matter.'[286] Varchi then provides a raft of similes for this 'efficient cause' in the artist's mind: species, form, image, semblance, idea, example, exemplar, similitude, intention, concept, model, simulacrum and phantasm. The conceptualising emphasis in Michelangelo's own theory of art is nicely mirrored by Varchi's cumulative search for an all-embracing definition of the inner visionary power at the core of the artist's soul, a power which now provides the definition of art's highest purpose, in contrast to the nature-based imitation of Leonardo and his predecessors. There can be little doubt that Michelangelo's sense of the conceptual foundation of art is intimately related to the powers of visualisation ideally required of any sculptor who approaches a marble block and needs to 'see' the figure within. The difference in his case is of degree. His technique of carving, entering a block impulsively from a given angle, often diagonally (fig. 93), moving intuitively through the mass of marble to release the pre-envisioned forms, indicates a power of spatial visualisation which has never been surpassed. The philosophical conceit of the *concetto*, with its learned allusions, and the deepest instincts of his artistic vision are seamlessly conjoined. It is unique in the Renaissance to find 'theory' and practice so profoundly harmonised.

However, this sense of equilibrium was increasingly undermined by a sense that his personal powers of conceptual visualisation and physical execution were in actuality inadequate to realise the desired unity. Towards the end of his life, as he incessantly strained to reach out to the ultimate vision of Christ's grace and the reality of his sacrifice on the cross, so he became aware not only of the shortcomings of his personal art but also of the base quality of the physicality of art itself:

> . . . the passionate fantasy [*fantasia*], which made
> Of art a monarch for me and an idol,
> Was laden down with sin, now I know well,
> Like what all men against their will desired. . .

> There's no painting or sculpture that now quiets
> The soul that's pointed toward that holy Love
> That on the cross opened its arms to take us.[287]

The late *Crucifixion Drawings* (fig. 94) ache with the paradox of a visual medium striving to express a vision which can barely be discerned with the inner eye let alone be realised adequately in the material form of pigment on paper. The very indefiniteness of the drawings, the forms quivering on the edge of the seen and unseen, is not so much a result of failing visual or manual powers as an attempt to 'paint the unpaintable' – to display the visionary truth to our external eye without prescriptive imitation of material form. As far as this impossible goal

199

94. Michelangelo, *Drawing of the Crucifixion with the Virgin and St John*, Windsor, Royal Library

93. Michelangelo, *Slave for the Julius Tomb* (the *'Atlas'*), Florence, Galleria dell' Accademia

can be attained when material form is the only resource available to the visual artist, Michelangelo has succeeded. But not of course by his own lights.

This highly selective examination of Michelangelo's poetic creations has taken us into what may seem to be an atypical world of written 'sources', and it has certainly carried us beyond the main chronological limits of this book. It is true that there are no truly comparable writings by other Renaissance artists. Other artist-poets, such as Bronzino, nowhere operate on such a complex and profound level. However, the very closeness of the written source to the sculpted or painted creation – or the *apparent* closeness – does highlight what I have been emphasising as the key points in reading written evidence for meaning. We need to read the texts with a clear sense of their own existence as cultural products of specific kinds – working within established parameters of expression in the period, speaking in a specific voice to a particular audience, and requiring sensitive interpretation in their own right. The document is not the automatically stable given which anchors the ambiguities of the artefact. However, this is not to say that only arbitrary conclusions can be drawn. With attention to genre and context, the document can be seen to say something meaningful and decipherable. Even if an allusive poem is an unusually unstable document, it can still deliver a particular kind of understandable meaning, both in itself and in relation to visual material.

SEEN IN ITS SETTING

The personal nature of Michelangelo's poems, like any direct testimony written by an artist, plays overwhelmingly to the notion of the artist as a personal creator, as the author of his own emotional world, to which we are granted privileged access. If we believe that 'Art' is above all about personal expression, in a post-Romantic manner, clearly such sources will assume the highest importance. Where they are lacking, the emotional substratum will necessarily be inferred from the works themselves. However, all Michelangelo's painted and sculpted works, like those of his predecessors, were made in a context of patronage which required something more (or even something other) than the expression of the author's personal feelings. Indeed, in the case of overtly public works, like the great marble *David* (fig. 95), the primary 'job' of the sculpture for the commissioners and the viewers was not that it should be 'a Michelangelo' in our sense but that it should embody a non-personal meaning in terms of its ostensible subject – the youthful slayer of Goliath – and in relation to any theological and allegorical resonances which the subject was meant to carry in the particular circumstances of its commissioning and display. The *David* is in fact a good case study for the juxtaposition of sources which can be used to posit contrasting priorities in determining what the statue is really 'about'.

The personal, 'Romantic' and even post-Freudian dimension is signalled, however, laconically, in an annotation on a drawing for a David (probably to be executed in bronze), which reads: 'David with his sling; I with my bow, Michelangelo' (fig. 96). The implied self-identification, assuming the 'bow' to be the sculptor's bow-drill, has lead the making of the statue to be seen as 'a search for identity' on the artist's behalf. But everything we know about the

95. Michelangelo, *David*, Florence, Galleria dell' Academia

202

97. Donatello,
David (marble),
Florence, Bargello

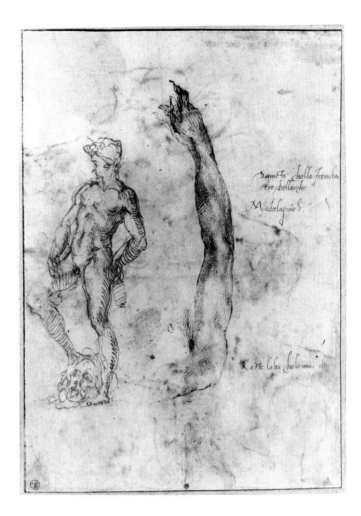

96.
Michelangelo,
*Studies for a Statue
of David*, Paris,
Louvre, Cabinet
des Dessins

work's genesis and display speaks of a series of functions in sharp contrast to any psychological internalising of meaning. The huge marble block had been obtained by the Opera of the cathedral for the sculpting of one of the gigantic prophets planned for the buttresses. According to a document of 1501, it had been 'badly blocked out' by an earlier sculptor in 1466, and subsequently abandoned. In this sad state, the splendid block had lain dormant in the Opera's workshop for thirty-five years.[288] Having undertaken a search for a sculptor who could resurrect it, the Consuls of the Arte della Lana and the Opera decided in favour of Michelangelo, who apparently promised to find a figure within the confines of the damaged block and without additional marble being added. He was to be paid 6 *fiorini larghi* a month for two years, 'and the Opera is to assist him with shelter and accommodation, and men [as helpers] from the said Opera and wood and everything he should need'. Michelangelo's first act, in September 1501, was the striking of a 'node' or 'knot' (*nodum*) from the chest of the figure, perhaps the kind of knot of drapery that had featured on Donatello's earlier clothed *David* (fig. 97). When it was finished, an expert

204

committee was set up on 25 January 1504 to determine its location, which apparently was no longer intended to be one of the high buttresses on the Duomo. The committee comprised a group of 'competent masters, citizens and architects', including Leonardo, Botticelli, Filippino Lippi, Piero di Cosimo, Perugino and Giuliano da Sangallo. Some favoured one placement, some another. The preferred locations ranged from a site in front of the cathedral to more 'civic' sites outside the Palazzo della Signoria and within the adjacent Loggia de' Lanzi (favoured by the majority, including Leonardo, Giuliano and Piero). The Herald of the Palace, who introduced the debate, argued that the *David* should replace Donatello's *Judith and Holofernes* in front of the palace, on the grounds that 'the *Judith* is a sign of death, and is not fitting, as we have the cross and lily for our emblems, and it is not fitting for the woman to kill the man, and above all, this statue was erected under an evil star, as things have gone continually from bad to worse since then: even Pisa has been lost'. The final choice, ignoring the majority view, was that it should be placed on a pedestal to the left of the main door of the palace.

Embodied in these records, explicitly and implicitly, are a series of motives for the making of the statue and some strong clues about how it was seen as acting in a public forum. It will be worth summarising the main points, because they will provide the essential foundation and control for further interpretative strategies.

Firstly, the statue had its origins in a commission for a religious subject, the prophet David, and the portrayal of the prophet in an intelligible and appropriate manner is the *sine qua non* of the project. We know that the cathedral was not 'simply' a religious building but embodied a series of civic values. Its construction had absorbed a large proportion of state revenues, and the sculptural programme for which the Wool Guild was directly responsible, was a matter of civic concern. The earliest of the 'Renaissance' decorations, the sculpture around the Porta della Mandorla, contained a series of images of the ancient hero, Hercules, as sanctioned by the tradition of 'Hercules Florentinus', in which the hero's courage had become a humanist emblem of the Republic's own desired level of valour in the face of external threats, especially from the Visconti tyranny of Milan. The *David* itself belonged to a programme of *giganti* for the cathedral, involving Brunelleschi and Donatello, which overtly carried resonances of heroism in the ancient manner.

The second factor is that the commission became detached at some point from the aspiration to complete the set of *giganti* for locations high up on the cathedral. We cannot document the stage at which the consuls of the Arte della Lana decided that the *David* was not necessarily destined for one of the buttresses. The original programme had long since lapsed, with only one statue definitely in place, Donatello's colossal *Joshua*, made from terracotta and painted white. The resuscitation of the grand block was not, therefore, necessarily motivated by the purpose for which it had first been obtained. The possibility that the figure might not even be located at the cathedral might seem surprising, but the fluidity with which the religious domains of the church and the secular territories of the state and guilds merged in a Renaissance city, nowhere more so than in Florence, explains how a cathedral commission could make the transition into a civic arena. Donatello's earlier marble *David* (fig. 97), either made initially for the cathedral or at least entirely appropriate for an ecclesiastical setting, was installed in the Sala dell' Orologio of the Palazzo dei Signori against a wall decorated with Florentine lilies. It was also accorded a patriotic inscription: 'to those who bravely fight for the fatherland, the gods will lend aid even against the most terrible foes'.

The third point is that the statue's appropriate placement was a matter of very direct concern to the government, and that the discussions centred on sites charged with considerable political significance. The Herald's comments on the failure of Donatello's *Judith and Holofernes* to exercise a beneficial talismanic influence on Florentine affairs may hardly be of the highest sophistication, but they may be taken as representative of a mode of public interpretation which can be documented when the *David* was later joined by other major sculptures in the Piazza della Signoria. The concern of the committee also indicates that the work itself was a source of pride, that it was a great figure deserving a prestigious and (as some advocated) secure location. A huge naked youth, an athlete poised for resolute action, could hardly have been seen in official circles other than as an accomplishment to rival the ancients and to declare Florence as the true heir to the heroic legacy of classical Rome.

The three facets of meaning that can be drawn out of the documentation – the literal portrayal of David as the slayer of Goliath, his role as a holy allegory of civic resolution, and his standing as a more general emblem of Florence's self-image – provide the basis for our minimum brief. How much further do we need to go? In terms of conventional iconography I would not be inclined to go significantly further. The kind of suggestion that sees David's impressive right hand as a reference to his characterisation as *manu fortis*, metaphorically as the strong hand of God, is ingenious but does not seem to be strictly necessary. However, Michelangelo's poetry does suggest that the visual power of the *David* feeds upon the sculptor's conscious recourse to his *alta fantasia*, equivalent to the 'lofty imagination', which lent Dante's poetry a verbal power beyond that of the standard rhymester. The role of *fantasia* will feature in the next chapter, when we look at the annexing of poetic values in the visual arts. The way that the sources, albeit the exceptional testimony of Michelangelo's poems, now allow us to talk of painting and sculpture in terms previously reserved for literature shows how far the framework of interpretation was changing in the period itself. The conceptual framework within which Michelangelo generated meaning brought to the fore elements of a personal vision that could not have been overtly acknowledged in the work of his predecessors.

The *David* was of course making its effect in the context of a long tradition of public statues in Renaissance Florence, often commissioned by public bodies for public locations. In all the locations, the civic – in the secular sense – and the religious were conjoined in various kinds of equilibrium. The sculptures on the exterior of Or San Michele, to which Ghiberti, Donatello and Verrocchio had made such outstanding contributions, were commissioned for an overtly 'political' location, in which each guild strove to express its status in the context of one of Florence's most prestigious buildings, located on the prime highway between the cathedral and the Piazza della Signoria. We should remember, however, that the Guild Hall was also a site of major religious devotion, housing a revered image of the Virgin, set in a splendid tabernacle by Orcagna, and that the guilds themselves took devotions to their patron saints very seriously. Given such a tradition, public statuary in Florence ought to provide established parameters for the mode of communication of the *David*, parameters which should be accessible to the historian. But matters are much less straightforward than we might hope. If we turn to the direct evidence of the intentions of the commissioners and makers, and of the reactions of the viewers, we will arrive at a far more constrained account than existing interpretations lead us to expect. The surviving documents relating to the commissioning of the statues for Or San Michele spell out at least some of the intentions of the guilds. The contractual record of the Money-Changers' Guild (Arte del Cambio), which set in train the events leading to the making of Ghiberti's *St Matthew* (fig. 14), is typical in tone:

> the said Lorenzo di Bartoluccio promises and agrees by a solemn undertaking with the said consuls and four Guildsmen to do the said figure of St Matthew in fine bronze at least as large as the present figure of St John the Baptist of the Guild of Merchants [actually for the Cloth Merchants], or larger if it seems better, at Lorenzo's discretion . . . The said Lorenzo furthermore promises the said consuls, members and operai that he wishes to have for his salary and remuneration for the said work whatever shall be decided by them. And he promises not to claim to his own benefit the same sum he had as salary from the Guild of Merchants.[289]

The sense that the guild's statue should be bigger (or at least not smaller), and in no way inferior to those of other guilds (but not more expensive) is clear, not least in the decision to fund a bronze statue in contrast to the much cheaper marble. This document provides the basis for our minimum brief. St Matthew, who was a money-changer before he accepted Christ's calling, was the saint of the guild. They wanted the best, in the most prestigious medium, and they chose a master whose reputation in bronze sculpture was second to none. Ghiberti knew what images of the Evangelist were meant to look like, and provided a version in the most up-to-date Renaissance style, full of echoes of ancient statues of orators. Is any more needed to explain the meaning of the figure? If we restrict ourselves to contemporary documents, this is the beginning and end of the story. However, we may feel intuitively that something more is involved. If we are telling the story in terms of the successions of styles and parade of master artists, we will inevitably be drawn into comparisons with Donatello's statues for Or San Michele and become involved in the definitions of individual artistic personalities. If we are seeking to insert the programme of decoration at Or San Michele into a civic context, to which it certainly belongs in a generic sense, we will need to confront the extent to which the mores of Republican Florence in the early fifteenth century – which can be defined through a rich series of writings, above all those of Leonardo Bruni – are somehow embedded in the statues as the result of conscious intention or unconscious expression. Some of the figures lend themselves to the political interpretation better than others. Donatello's *St George* (fig. 98), made for the Armorers' Guild, has inevitably become the focus of attention, seeming to embody the civic resolution which the Florentines proudly proclaimed in the face of threats from tyrannical Milan. The saint's four-square resolution,

98. Donatello, *St George*, Florence, Bargello (formerly Or San Michele)

youthful valour and frown of human resolve have been hailed as the perfect expression of the 'civic humanism', which Florentine statesmen developed in the war of rhetorical words with Milan. Yet the statue was for the Armorers', and St George was a knight, not a robed prophet, and he was famed for his act of valour in slaying the dragon to free the captive princess. Is this not reason enough for Donatello's characterisation?

When we turn to another of Donatello's statues for Or San Michele, the *St Louis* (fig. 16), the civic interpretation becomes harder to sustain in its most obvious mode, in spite of the fact that the commissioning institution was the Parte Guelpha, not a 'trade' guild but a political grouping embedded in the power structures of Renaissance Florence. The *St Louis*, undertaken in the visually splendid medium of fire-gilt bronze, so as literally to outshine the guilds' statues, certainly fulfils the demands of magnificence, but it is difficult to see the pious air of the youthful saint, swamped by his ecclesiastical robes, as expressive of Florence's civic resolution and armed defiance of tyrannies. Indeed, it is far easier to see the contrast between the meek, angelic expression of the saint's face and his incongruously voluminous robes as an expression of his reluctance, as the former heir to the throne of Naples who had become a humble Franciscan,

209

to accept grand office as the Bishop of Toulouse. To arrive at such a meaning, Donatello would only have needed to have known the popular story of the saint, who resigned his unwelcome office after a few months and died shortly thereafter, at the early age of twenty-three.

On the other hand, Donatello's earlier *David*, as we have already seen, was displayed in a republican setting and with a patriotic inscription. In that David, the biblical slayer of Goliath, was in general terms an obvious and potent symbol of military valour against the odds, and could more specifically serve as an exemplar for the Republic of Florence at times of threat, any image of David with the head of Goliath would have done equally as well. Or would it? Is there something in the form and expression of Donatello's statue that is consciously or unconsciously 'in tune with the times'? Does it, by some form of intention or osmosis, speak of the deepest-held Florentine aspirations at the time of its making? The elegant youth with bland, classicising countenance, does not perhaps stand most obviously for stern civic resolve, but the triumph of the beautiful representative of God's chosen people, standing victorious over the gory head of the defeated Philistine, might be seen as aligning itself with Florence's aspiration to be seen as the new cradle of civilisation, in emulation of ancient Rome and Athens. Some idea of how what we regard as a far from assertive male image could be accorded civic values is provided by the bronze *David* (fig. 99), which was recorded as standing on a pedestal at the centre of the courtyard of the Medici Palace in 1469. While in the palace its base bore an inscription: 'the victor is whoever defends the fatherland. All powerful God crushed the angry enemy. Behold, a boy overcame a great tyrant. Conquer O citizens.'[290] The point is that David was a boy – or at least a youth – who should have stood no chance against his gigantic adversary, but his God-given *virtù* ensured his victory. He had specifically rejected the armour that Saul had given him, and had gone unprotected (or 'naked') into battle. The more beautiful and pubescent the youth, the more the contrast between the vulnerable victor and the mighty foe would have been pronounced. We may feel in our post-Freudian age that more than simple narrative is involved in Donatello's characterisation, but the fundamental justification for the parameters of the portrayal are established by what was deemed appropriate for the subject and the setting. Psychoanalysis of Donatello through his works seems to me not be the job of the historian, not least because it cannot be made to adhere to any of the records that have survived.

Whether or not Donatello actively envisaged patriotic meaning in his early marble *David* at the time of its making, or embedded such a meaning through more unconscious means, it was clearly seen as capable of acting effectively in such a context. It is not difficult to envisage that a sculptor as responsive to communicative context as Donatello was affected in the way he regarded the potential of his later creations – that the conceptual field within which his statues were invented was, at the very least, affected by the way his earlier work had been able to assume a communicative role in a political context. Does this mean that all the subsequent works express political values? In the generic sense in which a statue like the *St Louis* is designed to impress, on behalf of an organisation which saw itself as the guardian of Florentine virtues, it does make a political statement. We may also say that the classicising features of the statues,

99.   Donatello, *David* (bronze), Florence, Bargello

even in the face of *St Louis* and the *all'antica* angels on his crook, speak generically of the annexing of Roman ideals by the rulers of Florence. But these generic senses are so general that they cease to give us much interpretative leverage once they are acknowledged as the background conditions for the programmes of exterior sculptural adornment of Florentine buildings. And, each of the background conditions might apply equally well to comparable schemes in other cities. For example, the great set of figures by Giovanni Pisano for the facade of Siena Cathedral are hardly less generally expressive of moral resolve than Donatello's prophets for the Campanile. We may be tempted to seek a specifically republican mode in the Or San Michele figures, and it is possible, for example, to juxtapose a patriotic text by Bruni with the *St George* to considerable suggestive effect, but the *St Louis* would require either a different text or a very different way of adhering the same text to the image, and the *St Matthew* would require another, the *St John* another, and so on. Ultimately the effect is rather arbitrary, however ingeniously we interweave image and text. I suspect that the generic conditions, our minimum brief and the individualistic self-assertion of the artists as the makers of famed objects provide a framework within which all the subtle richness of the figures can be embraced. The subcompartments within this framework would then contain the more specific aspects of meaning – overt civic courage in the case of the *Davids*, and youthful if beleaguered piety for *St Louis*, and so on. However, this is hardly novel. And it is in the nature of the academic industry of interpretation that something new needs to be said – preferably a new *kind* of thing needs to be said – so that even an inherently satisfying and historically rooted mode of interpretation has to be overthrown. But we should not automatically surrender something that works in relation to the documentation in a desperate desire to say something new.

If it is difficult to make a text of civic humanism adhere in a non-hypothetical way to the statues at Or San Michele, how much more difficult it will be to attach specific political or governmental values as embedded in a painting in a private chapel, like Masaccio's *Tribute Money* (fig. 100). However, it has been claimed that the story of the miraculous finding of the tribute to Caesar, which had been demanded by the tax collector, was depicted as a kind of validation of the Florentine property tax, the *catasto*, which had been introduced in 1427. This interpretation has seeped insidiously into the framework of received wisdom on the Brancacci Chapel. When the characterisation of Masaccio's style – Romanising, grand, austere, rhetorical, restrained, anti-luxurious – is thrown into the equation, we have a superficially attractive case for recognising a specifically 'Republican art'. But when we realise that the subject is depicted as just one fresco in an extensive cycle of St Peter's life, we may wonder whether this particular field was intended to carry such a burden of meaning. The attention it has received is due to its being the only large field surviving entirely by Masaccio's own hand. Looked at in contemporary terms, a cycle of St Peter might be seen as representing adherence to the papal cause, or more properly as the name saint of Pietro di Piuvichese Brancacci, who had founded the chapel in the 1360s. The stylistic argument also collapses readily in the face of even mild scrutiny. Felice Brancacci, the head of the family and owner of the chapel when Masaccio was at work, was the son-in-law of Filippo Strozzi, whose great ecclesiastic commission, Gentile da Fabriano's *Adoration of the Magi*, cannot by

100.　Masaccio, *Tribute Money*, Florence, Capella Brancacci

any stretch of the imagination be seen as breathing an air of Republican *gravitas*. If there is a reason for the choice of the 'austere' Masaccio, it is more likely to lie in the satisfaction he had provided when painting an altarpiece for S. Maria del Carmine in Pisa, the sister church of the Carmelite order within whose precincts Masaccio was now working.

We should bear in mind that the works in Renaissance cities acquired meaning in very definite relation to the nature of the space they inhabited. The modern tourist visiting the city, and the modern historian using photographs as a tool of research are far less sensitive than a fifteenth-century inhabitant of the city to the civic, religious and private functions, values, associations and meanings adhering to particular locations. The interpretative stances of the same Renaissance spectator in, say, the Brancacci Chapel and standing in front of the Palazzo dei Signori would be clearly differentiated in such a way that differently attuned expectations and interpretative mechanisms would come into play. The sieve through which we look at 'a Donatello' as a product of 'the Florentine Renaissance' in the period of 'the Republic' tends to be much too coarse, and to encourage us to carry an interpretation which may be valid for one type of work in one type of location into other areas where it would have had little contemporary relevance.

A religious work in a civic setting, such as an altarpiece in the government palace, would carry the same meaning in relation to the core of religious observance as an altarpiece in a church, and even perform comparable liturgical functions when required to do so, but it would also be expected to sustain a series of specific resonances in its particular space. Thus the altarpiece which was commissioned for the great new Council Hall in Florence, built after the expulsion of the Medici in 1494, left unfinished by Fra Bartolommeo (fig. 101), gave St Anne a central position, since she was especially identified with the Republic. It was on St Anne's day, 26 July, in 1343 that the Duke of Athens was expelled after a brief tyrannical rule. The other figures represented a who's who of Florence's divine patrons, including St John the Baptist and St Reparata, and, of particular importance in the context of the hall's planned decorations, St

213

101. Fra Bartolommeo, *St Anne Altarpiece (Madonna and Child with Sts Anne, John the Baptist, and other Saints)*, Florence, San Marco, Museo

Victor and Sts Peter and Paul, on whose feast days were celebrated the battles of Anghiari and Cascina, which Leonardo and Michelangelo were commissioned to paint on adjoining wall spaces. The planned ensemble was intended to be completed by a statue of Christ as Saviour, for which Andrea Sansovino signed a contract in 1502. In such a context, the political implications of the religious subjects were clear, straightforward and relatively general, with none of the layered allusions which are necessary to impute political meaning to Masaccio's *Tribute Money.*

Much the same directness and transparency is apparent in the decorations of civic and institutional buildings in Venice, the City that probably contained more religious subjects on a large scale in such settings than anywhere else in Italy. The particular structure of society in Venice resulted in a plethora of decorative schemes which directly spoke of how religious narratives, devotional observance and civic ritual were fused in Renaissance cities. The most spectacular suite of decorations were those in the Doge's Palace itself, the very seat of government. The Sala del Maggior Consiglio, the vast hall which housed the key assembly of some 2,000 Venetian patricians drawn from 150 noble families, had long been adorned by a huge fresco of the *Coronation of the Virgin* made in the 1360s by Guariento in homage to Mary as the patron saint of Venice. The image on the end wall became so much a symbol of the spiritual heart of the Republic that it continued to be restored even when it must have seemed archaic in manner. Only with the disastrous fire of 1577 did the old fresco finally perish, to be replaced with Tintoretto's dramatically energetic canvas of the court of Heaven, the so-called 'Paradiso'. The paintings on the other walls illustrated episodes from the twelfth-century story of the vital support provided by the Doge of Venice to Pope Alexander III in his struggles against the Holy Roman Emperor, Frederick Barbarossa, which resulted in the doge being accorded a status alongside that of the pope and emperor. Gentile da Fabriano and Pisanello were amongst the painters who were called upon to undertake the protracted execution of the cycle of narratives which spoke so loudly of Venice's perception of her own status as symbolised by the doge, her titular head of state. Then in 1474, Gentile Bellini began the process of substituting canvases for the deteriorating frescoes, a long-term project to which Giovanni Bellini, Titian, Tintoretto and Veronese eventually contributed.[291] The loss of this second cycle in the great fire greatly impoverishes our knowledge of Venetian history painting and of civic decoration more generally.

Not the least characteristic of the Venetian institutions were the two hundred or more Scuole, the confraternities of laypersons which played such a conspicuous role in the city's public life. In Chapter II we saw Gentile and Giovanni Bellini agreeing to provide paintings for the Scuola di San Marco to replace ones by their father that had been burned. Vital matters of prestige were involved, just as they were for the Florentine guilds, and the rival Scuole clearly wished to secure the services of the best masters. One Scuola in particular pioneered direct civic imagery in a highly innovative way. The Scuola di San Giovanni Evangelista, one of the six powerful Scuole Grandi, commissioned a team of painters to provide a great series of canvases for its headquarters. The narratives in the cycle concern miracles performed by a revered relic guarded by the Scuola in its Albergo, a fragment of the True Cross. The miracles are

102.   Vittore Carpaccio, *Miracle of the True Cross at the Rialto*, Venice, Galleria dell' Accademia

portrayed as happening deep within the very fabric of the city, and none is more remarkable than the almost square picture that Carpaccio provided (fig. 102). He has shown an incident of 1494 in which a demonically possessed man was cured when the Patriarch of Grado raised the relic above his head. The procession in honour of the Cross can be seen wending its way across the old Rialto Bridge, while the miracle takes place on the balcony of the Patriarch's Palace. The presence of obvious portraits in the foreground emhasises the status of the members of the Scuola within the context of the rituals of the city and its unique architectural fabric. Carpaccio's picture should not be taken as a 'documentary' in our sense, but it is a document of civic and religious pride which vividly exploits a recognised location peopled with recognisable individuals participating in an event which was a 'real' miracle occurring in their very own time and in their very own city.

When we turn to secular subjects in non-republican settings, the political references are generally apparent at a straightforward level, even when the

216

103. Andrea Mantegna, *Oculus and Fictive Decoration*, Mantua, Castello di San Giorgio, Camera degli Sposi, Ceiling

subjects do not portray the rulers, their acts or their immediate ancestors. Thus, whatever the immediate reason for the genesis of Mantegna's great series of nine canvases depicting the *Triumph of Caesar* (fig. 25), and wherever they were to be located in the Palazzo Ducale in Mantua, their appeal to the Gonzaga Marquises was clear in a general sense – Caesar was, after all, famed as a Roman ruler of immense military prowess – and we know that they were proudly displayed to prestigious visitors. The rhetoric surrounding the notion of the ruler in Renaissance Italy was saturated in Roman imagery, and there can hardly have been a despot who was not at some time accorded the title of one of the 'Caesars' in a humanist panegyric. Thus it was that the ceiling of the *Camera degli Sposi*, undertaken earlier for the same Gonzaga court (figs 24 and 103), was boldly adorned with medallic busts of the first eight Ceasars, painted in fictive marble relief against mosaic backgrounds and around the witty central oculus. The general motive for the annexing of Roman ruler imagery is reasonably clear. But from this unexceptional point, the questions arise as to how far and how specifically we should push the aligning of the Mantegna *Triumph* and the decorations of the *Camera degli Sposi* with more specific contemporary circumstances and events.

Even where the subject directly represents, as in the *Camera*, the ruler and his family, the issue of the degree of restraint we should impose on our interpretation is no less important than in more apparently allusive conjunctions of antique subjects and contemporary meaning. Mantegna's decorations in the *Camera picta* (as it was called) will serve as a convenient and visually spectacular case study. On the face of it, the main focus of the content of the decorations on the walls below the vault could hardly be more obvious, and was recognised as such by important visitors. The two walls with figurative decorations depict Ludovico Gonzaga, his wife, Barbara of Brandenberg and their family – *al naturale* as the Milanese ambassadors noted in 1470 . On the north wall the marchese and marchesa sit in the company of his family and courtiers (fig. 24), including a favourite dog and court dwarf. A beakish secretary speaks quietly into the marquis's ear, perhaps about the contents of the letter his master holds, while a visitor or visitors apparently assemble at the steps on the right. The air is predominantly domestic, but the action of the secretary and attendant persons reminds us that the family man was very much also the man of affairs.

The west wall shows Ludovico and his sons and grandsons outdoors, with other figures, horses and boar hounds. Two of Ludovico's sons are portrayed as members of the church: Francesco, conspicuous in his cardinal's robes, and his youngest brother, Ludovico, who had been appointed a papal protonotary at the age of nine. Federigo, who was to succeed Ludovico, is on the right, and his elder son, Gianfrancesco, whom we have encountered as the later supplicant in the *Madonna della Vittoria*, stands between Cardinal Francesco and the marquis. Above the door, active *putti* support a tablet which tells us (in elegant Latin letters) that 'For the most illustrious Lodovico, second Marquis of Mantua, a prince most excellent and of a faith most unbroken, and for the illustrious Barbara, his spouse, glory beyond the compare of women, their Andrea Mantegna completed this poor work to do them honour in the year 1474'. Ludovico and Barbara are thus the prime subjects, as dynastic heads, but there are also portraits of people who were not immediate members of family and court in Mantua itself. Fortunately, letters between the marquis and his ambassador to the Duke of Milan in 1475 inform us of the names of two of the inserted dignitaries and the kind of circumstance that lead to their inclusion (even if their identity with specific figures is now somewhat uncertain).[292] The ambassador reports Duke Galeazzo's dismay that 'your lordship, in a memorial to the two paltriest men in the world, has had His Imperial Majesty [Frederick III] and the aforementioned King [Christian I of Denmark] portrayed in your chamber' and omitted the duke himself. Since Ludovico owed his title to the Emperor, and Christian was the husband of Barbara's sister, their inclusion is understandable, but the Duke's pique at being excluded from what was 'unanimously' said to the 'the most beautiful chamber in the world' gives some idea of the prestige involved. The Marquis rather disingenuously instructed his ambassador to explain that since Galeazzo had not liked a previous portrait undertaken by Mantegna, he thought it wise not 'to do something he [the

Duke] would not like'. Mantegna, the marquis explains, 'is a good master on other things, but in portraits he could have more grace'.

What has been said so far indicates that the visitor to the room in the palace was faced with what is essentially a group portrait of the Gonzagas and their court, with a few favoured allies, portrayed with a kind of naturalness which was unprecedented. However, the very naturalness with which some of the figures relate to each other gives some grounds for suspecting that something specific is happening – that we are looking at a *historia* rather than a series of integrated portraits. The most elaborate reading suggests that the two walls should be understood together as telling a key story in the fortunes of the family. What we are watching on the West wall, it is suggested, is a meeting in 1462 at Bossolo, when Ludovico first greeted Francesco as a new cardinal. The fireplace wall, according to this line of argument, portrays the arrival of the news in Mantua. There are a number of immediate problems with this interpretation. The most obvious difficulty is that the meeting was an event of some moment but hardly seems sufficiently significant to warrant its choice as the signal story in such a remarkable decoration. There is also a substantial problem in the envisaging of a unified, tightly conceived narrative programme embracing two separate walls which do not seem to have been decorated in a single, continuous campaign. However, the most fundamental difficulty is that we are dealing with such an innovatory work in type and setting that we do not really have a secure sense of what *type* of interpretative strategy is appropriate – whether the painting is a group portrait type of thing or a narrative type of thing.

There is one essential recourse to which we have not turned, and that is to think (very much in tune with the last few pages) about the context. The *Camera degli Sposi*, the 'Room of the Spouses' (or 'Wedding Room') is presently misnamed. The room is on the first floor in one of the corner towers of the old Castello di San Giorgio, the interior of which was remodelled as part of the expanding palace complex. It was approached by a wide curving ramp suitable for horses. It is known to have contained a bed, but it was not quite a bedroom in our sense, since it also functioned for the conduct of court business and the reception of privileged guests. Understanding the kind of audience (in the literal sense of an audience chamber) for the decorations does not solve the question of meaning, but it does slant the probability in the direction of the paintings' having a generic function in establishing the composite image the Gonzaga wished to cultivate – as political players of European significance, as deeply integrated with the Roman Church, as a dynastic family in which father, wife, sons, daughters and courtiers of both sexes all played their assigned roles, as aristocratic rulers of a sympathetic kind, as managers of local affairs, as cultivators of courtly pursuits, as worthy successors to the great Roman rulers, and as partisans of the new culture *all'antica* – rather than telling a personal story to be deciphered by the few in the know.

This problem of knowing which type of interpretation is appropriate for novel types of picture besets a number of the rising kinds of secular genre in Renaissance interiors. In the very first chapter we reviewed some of the possibilities for a Botticelli mythology, the *'Minerva' and the Centaur*. The possibilities are, if anything, even more legion for Botticelli's *Primavera* (fig. 3). Having used as my first case study in this chapter one of the biggest *cause célèbres* of religious iconography, Piero's *Baptism*, it is probably appropriate that the final one should concern what is one of the most extensively discussed iconographical puzzles in Renaissance secular painting. Whole monographs have been devoted specifically to its content, to say nothing of a host of scholarly articles. To do justice to such literature is clearly impossible in this context, but it will be possible, as in other cases, to set out some criteria for what may be the least insecure of the kinds of strategy we might adopt.

An astonishingly large number of explanatory 'sources' have been adduced for the *Primavera*, covering not just a wide range of authors but also many different kinds of text which rely upon a wide variety of types of proposed relationship with the content of the picture. The sources fall into two main categories, modern and ancient. Amongst the modern sources, considerable attention has been paid to a letter from the Neoplatonic philosopher, Marsilio Ficino, moralising correspondent of the young Lorenzo di Pierfrancesco de' Medici. We have already encountered this Lorenzo in chapter I as the owner of Botticelli's '*Pallas' and the Centaur* (fig. 10). Other contemporary written sources posited for the content have included the vernacular genres of rustic song, love poetry and festivals. Of the ancient sources, Apuleius's *Golden Ass* has been claimed to do the kind of interpretative job that is required of the 'prime source', that is to say providing the core text for the appearance of the picture, more-or-less in its whole and in at least some of its parts. In his account of the Judgement of Paris, Apuleius describes a dumbshow in which Venus lasciviously parades her beauty.[293] Other ancient texts which have been taken to have some kind of explanatory value have included Seneca's account of the Graces, and Ovid's narrative of the metamorphosis of Chloris into Flora. Most of the proposed sources, like those relating to festivals, are not claimed to be the main generating text, but each may perform one of a variety of functions, ranging from being generally suggestive to providing precise explanations for component parts of the picture. To varying degrees many of the proposed sources can be made to work with the picture and may produce apparently attractive insights. But they cannot all be 'right' – at least in the sense that we normally mean when we say that we have the right source or sources for a picture. None of them produces such a precise fit to the whole and the parts that it is entirely compelling. Is there any way to make a choice? Or do we have to make a choice at all? Or should we simply continue looking for the obvious key which has so far eluded us?

It will come as no surprise, in the light of the emphasis I have placed on identifying the functional field within which a historical artefact was designed to operate, that I intend to begin by asking if we have any concrete idea of why the picture was made, for whom, for what location and with which spectators in mind. My starting point is the same 1499 inventory of the town palace of Lorenzo and Giovanni which we used in chapter I for the *Pallas*.[294] The *Primavera* is plausibly if not definitively identified with 'a painting on wood attached above the *lettuccio*, in which is painted nine figures of women with men' in the 'ground floor room which is beside the room of Lorenzo'. Since the painting, according to the best estimate of dating on stylistic grounds was painted no later than the early 1480s, the 1499 reference cannot be taken to confirm absolutely that one of Pierfrancesco's sons was its intended recipient. However, we should be very cautious in detaching it from Lorenzo and from the brothers' palace just because we want to construct a meaning that fits uncomfortably with the documentation. Once this connection is accepted as the best starting point, the letter of Ficino to the young 'Lorenzino' assumes a special status, since it speaks of Venus to the most likely patron. The letter, cast in terms of a kind of literary horoscope, involves a level of rapture normally reserved for religious subjects. Venus, the star on which Lorenzino's 'Luna' should finally fix her gaze, is described as 'Humanitas':

> Humanitas herself is a nymph of excellent comeliness born of heaven and more than other beloved of God all highest. Her soul and mind are Love and Charity, her eyes Dignity and magnanimity, the hands Liberality and Magnificence, the feet Comeliness and Modesty. The whole then is Temperance and Honesty, Charm and Splendour. Oh, what exquisite beauty! How beautiful to behold. My dear Lorenzo, a nymph of such nobility has been wholly given into your power. If you were to unite with her in wedlock and claim her as yours, she would make all your years sweet and make you the father of fine children.[295]

Between them, the inventory and the letter do not provide the explanation for the picture. The letter, for all its apparent relevance, does not provide a programme for the content of Botticelli's painting. Nor does it necessarily provide an explanation for what generated the image, though it might conceivably have been the trigger. But it does provide a good indication of the kind of mental framework within which the image was invented and could have been viewed.

Within this framework, we can think more concretely about how the picture might have been conceived. A vital step, obviously, is the identification of the figures, a process which is based upon matching Botticelli's characters with known images and written accounts. Without going through this process here, we can say that the figures have generally been recognised as Venus, in the centre, flanked on the left by the Three Graces and Mercury, and on the right by Flora, Chloris and Zephyr. Overhead, the blind Cupid prepares to fire his arrow, apparently in the direction of the elegant neck of the central Grace. Given the fact that we do not have a single source which embraces all the major aspects of the picture, we may reasonably try to assemble it from various accounts, positing some kind of invented programme that brought the accounts together. The problem is that we do not have too few potentially relevant texts but that we are embarrassed by too many. Accounts of Venus, and the qualities over which she held sway, are legion, as are those of Cupid. Mercury, as another major ancient deity associated with a planet, was widely discussed by many different authors. There are a number of exegeses and images of the Three Graces which seem to be equally germane but not consistent with each other. Each iconographer who discovers another new text which can apparently be brought to bear on the image understandably tends to claim that he or she has found *the* source. One component for which there seems to be a satisfying written source is the group on the right. In Ovid's *Fasti* we read:

A Grecian nymph was I, Chloris by name -
Change but some letters, it becomes the same

As Flora, mark you – and among the Good
Within the Happy Fields was my abode.
How fair I was it scarce beseems to tell:
But to a god I seemed desirable.
For as I roamed abroad one April day
The West Wind saw me, and, though I said nay,
Took me by force . . . [now]
Eternal spring is mine, trees ever green
Earth clothed in herbage, azure skies serene;
And as my bridal gift and marriage dower
He gave me governance of every flower.[296]

We cannot assume that this account of the transformation of Chloris into Flora is *the* source, but it is at least probable, and may provide an indication that the picture was compiled by someone who was sufficiently well versed in such ancient literature to devise the *invenzione* of the ensemble in a fluent manner. Choosing between the plural texts for the other figures, is a matter of balancing the neatness of the fit with the availability of each source. Thus, for example, Seneca's account of the three Graces, Aglaia, Euphrosyne and Thalia, 'ever returning upon themselves with linked hands', seems to match nicely.[297] However, alternative identifications are suggested by two medals originating in Lorenzo's circle. On the reverse of a medal of Giovanna Tornabuoni, the Graces are named as 'Chastity, Beauty and Love', while the medal of Pico della Mirandola calls them 'Beauty, Love and Voluptuousness'. Perhaps one of the contemporary sources is to be preferred, but it does not decisively eliminate the ancient account as a potential generator of content, since Humanists were adept at conflating meanings from different sources.

Even if we can follow such procedures in the interpretation of the components, we still do not have a clear sense of what kind of overall meaning is intended. Are we dealing, to take two extremes, with a high-flown form of painted philosophy or a delightful piece of secular invention which works a playful theme on mythological characters, with a particular emphasis on scantily dressed women? The function of the painting, as integral to a piece of furniture, leans towards the latter interpretation, while the Ficino letter takes us in the former direction. For all the apparent incompatibility of the modes of interpretation, they can both be sustained if we ask the corresponding documents – the inventory and the letter – to do different kinds of job. Thus we may regard the immediate genesis of the picture as the devising of a delightful ensemble on the theme of the spring months over which Venus and Mercury preside. We may even make the more specific proposal that the ensemble was devised as a gift to celebrate the politically motivated wedding in 1483 of Lorenzo with Semiramide Appiani, daughter of the Lord of Piombino, an important port city. We may imagine its assembly, much in the manner of a secular *Sacra conversazione*, with Venus and her attendant saints and angels, not as a narrative or mythology, but as an assemblage evoking the realm of the goddess – an orange grove in the Garden of the Hesperides – and symbolising the specific season which is uniquely conducive to the flowering of young love. Like a *Sacra conversazione*, in which we need not assume that the artist loaded or was asked to load all the theology of the Virgin into the altarpiece, we need not adduce the full panoply of texts about the ancient gods for the *Primavera* when we reconstruct how Botticelli generated his picture. According to this parallel, the Ficino letter and related Neoplatonic texts can be regarded as providing a vital underlying sanction for the commissioning of this *type* of picture and give an insight into the set of knowledge and attitudes through which some privileged viewers may have been able to endow it with high significance – without assuming that the Neoplatonic texts were somehow 'used' by the artist. If we are alert to the way that sources may do different kinds of job, we can also rescue other texts whose direct relevance to the genesis of the picture cannot be demonstrated. If we accept that we may gain insight into potential viewings, generic and specific, from a wide range of texts on the ancient gods, we can bring them to the picture without trying to give them an intentional or causal role. But if we do this, we need to acknowledge that it is a relatively weak procedure. At best it illuminates in a general way the contextual base for our understanding of possible contemporary viewings.

Nothing that has appeared so far does anything to help answer the question of the author of the *invenzione*. From direct evidence of the artist, patron and patron's circle, we should probably incline towards thinking that Botticelli was given the subject, at least in its outline. We have also formulated a loose rule that the more exceptional the subject, the more likely it is that we need to look beyond the resources available to the artist. But it would be imprudent to be dogmatic about the need for some elaborate programme of Neoplatonic theology. Even someone who wrote elaborate exegeses of Neoplatonic theology would not necessarily see the outlining of the subject matter of a decorative painting as a high philosophical exercise.

Before leaving the *Primavera*, and bringing the discussion to some kind of untidy conclusion, there is one further aspect of its visual qualities that might be embraced within the remit of meaning, namely the extent to which the style 'means' something. If we describe the painting as a refined, elegant, courtly ensemble of gracious figures, depicted in suavely linear manner – a standard kind of description which does seem reasonably appropriate – we will not simply be describing in a neutral way but using a series of words rich in implicit and explicit meaning. Is this style of graceful refinement inherently 'courtly', and is it especially attuned to the courtly ambitions of the Medici in the late fifteenth century, in contrast to the austerity of Masaccio in the heroic earlier years? We saw that this kind of equation was unsafe with respect to Masaccio and Gentile da Fabriano, and we have no greater reason to trust it now. Indeed the inventories of the Medici suggest the juxtaposition of objects of considerable flamboyance with works of pious sobriety. However, there is a way to rescue the obvious sense that the style adopted by Botticelli speaks of genteel delectation rather than muscular conflict. The way lies in the decorum of style appropriate to subject and function – a well-known principle of rhetoric. In this case there appear to be two intersecting decorums. The most obvious is the appropriateness of a manner of handling line and detail which is reminiscent of tapestries and *cassone* painting – in other words Botticelli speaks with a voice which would sound right for the kind of object he was producing for a cultivated secular environment. This decorum of graceful line also relates to his study of a class of ancient objects, particularly cameos and reliefs, like the *Tazza Farnese* (fig. 2), acclaimed by connoisseurs like Piero and Lorenzo de' Medici as the ultimate exemplars of refined design and craftsmanship. The second kind of decorum relates to the behaviour of the participants in the painting, whose controlled motions and gestures speak the contemporary language of gracious deportment. The Graces move with precisely that gliding restraint recommended in dance treatises for the well-bred woman. Both decorums become fully articulate within the terms of visual reference of the period itself, but there may also be a common core of more universal reference to how we read the bodily movements, across a wider range of cultural contexts than postmodern theory generally allows.

If a consistent picture of how meaning entered works of art has not emerged in this chapter, this impression is almost certainly an accurate reflection of the way that the issue resists easy generalisation. Where we can document the detailed circumstances under which subjects were conceived, we tend to find variety and opportunism rather than systematic consistency. With the more common subjects, say a small-scale *Madonna*, the minimum exchange between patron and artist would have sufficed. A large altarpiece would have required a more specific determination of tailor-made content in relation to such factors as the dedication of the altar and the church, the patron's devotional inclinations and other local impulses. The more exceptional and elaborate the subject, religious or secular, the more special mechanisms would have been needed to determine the content, and the more likely it would have been that the patron or the patron's agent would have taken the lead. But the abiding problem is that the kinds of documents that have survived do not relate to the specific mechanisms, since written 'programmes' were not obligatory components of the transactions. This problem means that we have to use a good deal of well-informed intuition and common sense in bringing texts to bear on pictures and sculptures.

A precise matching of written source and picture, particularly where the text can be directly associated with the persons or circumstances involved, or located close to them, may mean that we are genuinely dealing with a generative source, but such tidy matching is the exception rather than the rule. The broader accretion of texts around an image, in the learned manner that became fashionable in iconographical studies, does not so much deal with the way that meaning actually enters the specific work but with the weaving of contexts for possible readings and the provision of a general basis for the choice of a particular kind of subject. In building any model for how content is determined, we should bear in mind that for works with relatively complex subjects there was probably not a single definitive moment in which all the aspects of meaning were irreversibly established in advance of the making of the artefact. In many instances, the fully crystallised sets of meanings would not have emerged until the whole process of execution was either complete or so developed as to preclude variation. And even when the process was complete, the object could not precisely control the way its meaning was read. What was in the picture or piece of sculpture set clear parameters upon possible interpretations, but the meaning could not be definitely stabilised for all time. As the context of viewing has changed over the ages, often with the removal of the work from its original location, so the recovery of the original resonances has become progressively more problematic. However, all is not lost. Even if we, at our inevitable remove from the Renaissance, cannot hope to recover the precise resonances of the object in the eyes of those responsible for the work, the historian can still work systematically towards a reconstruction of the kinds of factors that were present in the transactions which brought such an artefact into being. On this basis we can build the most plausible model for how a specific object functioned to carry meaning in the circumstances of a particular commission. Again, my crucial test of plausibility is that any model should be credible in terms of real people doing real things in real circumstances. It is on this basis that history may retune our processes of seeing so that we may enter into a direct human dialogue with those who generated the images.

VI
'ART' AND THE 'ARTIST'

THE STATUS OF artists, their remuneration and way that their products were valued according to different criteria – and the progressively elevated status of at least a few notable individuals – have been apparent in a number of the sources which have already crossed our path. In particular we have heard the insider writers on art, the 'art theorists' as we now call them, making new claims about the intellectual qualities of their craft. This chapter is concerned to bring together a range of evidence about the ideas of 'art' and the 'artist' as expressed in the testimony of people who are directly or indirectly writing about these issues.

What needs to be said at the outset – and explains why I have placed 'art' and the 'artist' in inverted commas in the title of this chapter – is that our two terms were not current in the period in anything like the modern sense. *Ars* or *arte* corresponded more closely to the Greek *techne*, and meant 'craft' or 'technique' or 'skill'. There simply is no real equivalent of our 'Fine Art'. So why use the modern terms at all? I have two excuses. Firstly, they are concepts which have meaning for a modern reader in such a way that they provide a practical point of entry to the subsequent discussion. Secondly and more profoundly, we will be able to see in Renaissance writing clear signs of the foundations for the concepts which subsequently became enshrined in our institutions and literature of 'Art'.

In fact, throughout what follows we need to be more than usually alert to the problems of the meaning of Renaissance words in terms of their modern translations and connotations. We will, for example, encounter words that we translate – or may be tempted to translate – as 'genius', 'imagination' and 'fantasy', when the modern implications of the words may be wholly or largely foreign to the period itself. Awareness of this problem will be accompanied by our normal cautions about taking due care to understand what is being said in terms of the nature of the text, its function, its audience and its reading. We also need to be alert to what the texts cannot be expected to say within their functional and conceptual parameters and within the limitations of contemporary vocabulary.

The first topic in this chapter will concern attitudes towards art as a cerebral activity, and how it was ranked in relation to cognate pursuits, particularly the literary endeavours at the heart of the humanists' enterprises. The evidence will be drawn from two kinds of source: the insider writings of practitioners and theorists, of the kind we met in chapter III; and more general literary testimony about the attitudes of those who were on the side of the 'consumers', namely the patrons and interested observers who put pen to paper. Since it was exceptional to record opinions about art at this time, neither of these groups can be characterised as 'typical' observers – as far as a typical observer can ever be defined at any time in the history of art – but at least they stand at or close to the heart of the making of some of the most ambitious kinds of work in the Renaissance.

The second topic will be concerned with signs of the rise of the named artist as someone recognised as having special worth through merit, talent and achievement – what the Renaissance called *virtù* – and who was seen as having recognisable individuality, much as Dante, Petrarch and Boccaccio were regarded as distinct in their characters and products. Indeed, one of the key questions is the extent to which there was a conception that the works expressed the character of their author – the extent to which the special characteristics of the *virtù* of the particular person spoke to the viewer through his products. The main evidence here will be writings on individual artists, particularly those texts in which some kind of comparative evaluation is offered. Finally, as a way of bringing the various issues into concrete focus in the context of how artists actually pursued their careers, I will look in more detail at the cases of Leonardo and Mantegna, the prime examples of the rise of what may be called the 'super artist', the painter-intellectual who becomes increasingly detached from the general run of practitioners in terms of the construction of reputation.

The majority of the texts cited in this chapter, particularly in the earlier sections, will not primarily speak of economic and social issues – though important implications for these issues may lie behind the production of the texts and the underlying stances of the authors – but will be oriented towards intellectual definitions of art and artists within a certain kind of cultural debate. If an exposition of what the sources tell us might at first seem to be rather abstracted from concrete historical contexts, this is in itself an indicator that something significant was happening, since one of the signal trends in the writing on the visual arts will be the claiming of some kind of absolute validity for the highest forms of artistic production, a validity which plays towards artistic rather than functional values. Thus, whereas a contract is by its nature embedded in a very specific set of circumstances, the content of a theoretical treatise like Alberti's *On Painting* is consciously oriented towards the exposition of timeless truths. The fact that such truths should be advocated in influential forums by highly regarded authors was itself a powerful social lever for the promotion of the artists' status. The foundation of the Florentine Academia del Disegno in 1563, under the auspices of the Medicean Grand Duke and at the instigation of Giorgio Vasari, is a testimony to the efficacy of the campaign for a heightened status for what we now call the 'Fine Arts'.

The standard interpretative touchstone for the visual arts was the body of theory, commentary and biography which had already built up around the verbal arts of rhetoric, literature, and most especially of poetry. This is partly a matter of inevitability, since authors trained in literature and its theory would automatically carry a set of values from literary culture and would more or less automatically annex literary terminology when trying to establish a way of saying something about an art form which suffered from an underdeveloped critical vocabulary. But it is also a question of direct competition, since the contexts of patronage not infrequently threw the status and regard for humanist authors into sharp relief against the traditionally modest position of 'manual workers' in the visual arts. Certainly this is what the artists felt. Both the intellectual nature of this competition and the concordant social tensions are apparent in Leonardo da Vinci's so-called *paragone* (comparison of the arts). The other prime source for the way that Renaissance writers were able to characterise the visual arts were the discussions that had survived from classical antiquity, as we saw in chapter III. The chapters on artists in Pliny's *Natural History* provided the most obvious source, but more sophisticated vocabulary and attitudes could be gleaned from authors like Apollonius and Lucian, who were not primarily writing about the visual arts in their own right. In fact, many of the humanist sources which historians have used to analyse attitudes to art in the Renaissance are extracted from texts which are using the visual arts to make points in a wider context rather than consciously contributing to 'art theory'.

By the time that Alberti was writing there was already a substantial quantity of high level writing on poetry, not only surviving from classical antiquity but also within the late medieval and early Renaissance periods. Three star authors, Dante, Petrarch and Boccaccio – the *Tre Coronati* (the three crowned with the poet's laurel) – became the major focuses of attention. The huge theological, philosophical, historical and literary complexity of Dante's *Divine Comedy* not only set standards of intellectual ambition for subsequent authors of poetry but also occasioned an industry of interpretation. Dante himself had set the tone with the commentaries he provided for his *Vita Nuova* and *Convivio*. In the latter, he formulated a highly influential, four-level interpretative framework, embracing the literal, allegorical, moral and anagogical meanings.[298] The allegorical interpretation seeks the 'hidden truth' behind the literal 'story', while the moral concerns what the story teaches us. The anagogical mode draws attention to the parallels and implications with the exegesis of other 'stories' in such a way as to explicate meaning at the highest spiritual level. The many subsequent commentaries on Dante became major vehicles for the exploration of notions of poetic truth, and those few passages in which he referred to art or artists provided significant opportunities for literary people to comment on visual matters. However, there is no indication in any of the contemporary exegesis of Dante that we can safely extend his four-part interpretative scheme into the non-verbal realm; that is to say carrying it back into our exposition of the meanings of paintings and sculptures in the previous chapter.

Dante had additionally, with Petrarch and Boccaccio, become the focus for biographical writing, and the *Tre Coronati*, were subject to the earliest sustained attempts in the Renaissance to write what may be called literary biographies. There were ancient precedents, most notably Diodorus's *Lives of the Philosophers*, but more immediately available models were the lives of saints, particularly those of St Francis. At the start of the period with which we are concerned, Leonardo Bruni, humanist chancellor of Florence, whom we have encountered as attempting to intervene on the programme for the Baptistery doors, wrote important lives of Dante and Petrarch, and intended to write on Boccaccio. No visual artist was subject to such a treatment, until Ghiberti included a kind of autobiography in his *Commentaries*, although, as we will see, a reasonably substantial body of comment had built up around Giotto, as the exemplary artist in the fourteenth century.

My tactic in looking first at the extent to which art was recognised as an identifiable and worthwhile activity will centre upon a number of the key terms which assumed special value in discussions of the making of art, terms which were generally annexed from literary criticism. This tactic will not reveal the whole story, but in the context of our present endeavour to find out *how* to respect the nature of our sources, a concentration on words and their meaning will be appropriate, and the set of closely-linked terms I have chosen will act as a kind of barometer for significant changes in the intellectual climate. The first is *ingenium* (or *ingegno*), often translated as 'genius', but misleadingly, as we will see. The second is *inventio* (or *invenzione*), which is a prime activity in poetry and rhetoric, and came to assume special status in the figurative arts. The third term is not so much one single word, but embraces those words – *imaginativa, imaginazione, phantasia* and *fantasia* – which we generally translate as 'imagination'. The notion of *fantasia* came to assume particular importance, not least because of its association with Dante and its significance within late medieval theories of the working of cerebral processes, according to notions of faculty psychology.

Ingenium, or in its Italian form, *ingegno*, was an important concept for those ancient authors to whom the Renaissance humanists especially looked for guidance on the nature of creativity. Its meaning should not automatically be equated with what we call 'genius', which in its post-Romantic sense is a transcendent quality of mind which takes someone endowed with it into realms beyond those of ordinary mortals and stands apart from the operation of logical processes. Perhaps the best translation is 'inborn talent' or 'innate brilliance'. Cicero provided some key texts. In *The Making of an Orator*, he stressed that the Romans as a race were innately endowed with *ingenium* and *cogitatione*, but that these inherent qualities could only bear fruit with the steady acquisition of systematic knowledge, not least of rules.[299] For *ingenium* to be operative specifically in the creation of poetry, it should ally itself with the fires of inspiration: 'I have often heard it said, as they say Democritus and Plato have written, that no man can be a good poet who is not on fire and inspired by something like frenzy [*afflatu quasi furoris*]'. One passage in Cicero's *The Speech on Behalf of Archias the Poet* – quoted by Boccaccio amongst others – became a stock point of reference for Renaissance definitions of the poetic faculty: 'poetry depends solely on an inborn faculty, is aroused by a purely mental activity and is inspired by a divine spirit'.[300] At extreme levels, access to inspiration could verge on insanity. As Seneca had written, 'there has never been any great *ingenium* without some touch of madness'.[301] The idea that poetry at its highest level required a form of divine *afflatus* became something of a commonplace in Renaissance poetics. Where this quality of inspiration differed from modern notions of genius is that it never became detached from rational knowledge and the necessary rules through which a piece of literature or oration assume an appropriate form. Indeed, Leonardo Bruni in his *Lives of Dante and Petrarch* differentiated between those poets who depend upon the hidden forces of frenzy arising from their own *ingegno* and those who exploit knowledge, study, discipline, forethought, philosophy, theology, astrology, arithmetic, geometry, history and other worthy disciplines.[302] Not surprisingly, Dante is the supreme representative of the second and more approved type of poet, whose work avoids the sterility of pure fantasy.

Generally speaking, it was difficult to credit visual artists with the admired poetic faculties. Perhaps the greatest barrier lay in the lack of freedom in the determination of subject matter. An artist commissioned to paint an altarpiece of the Madonna and four named saints could hardly be aligned with the poet sitting down with a pen and a blank writing surface. The rule-based framework of naturalistic imitation also seemed to place limits on the liberty of the sculptor or painter to exercise free-ranging license, and the visually concrete nature of his media meant that the artist could not literally describe speech, sentiments, and the working of the mind. In Angelo Decembrio's *De politia literaria*, Leonello d'Este of Ferrara is made to say 'the *ingenium* of writers . . . is a divine thing and beyond the reach of painters' – who are condemned to work within more prosaic restraints.[303] It was rare for someone outside the group of 'insider' theorists to regard *ingenium* as a necessary attribute for the maker of artefacts. An exception was the Sienese humanist, Aeneas Silvius Picolomini, who became pope as Pius II. In a letter of 1452 he explained how antiquity showed that the arts flourish together at times of excellence, while in his own era he points to the simultaneous rise of painting under Giotto and literature under Petrarch.[304] The conjoined evidence is that 'the *ingenium* of painting and the *ingenium* of oratory aspire not to be vulgar but elevated and great'.

When Alberti came to consider the nature of the *ingenium* appropriate for the painter, he both accepted the rule-based constraints of an art based on the systematic imitation of natural appearance and the kind of Stoic reservations which Bruni expressed about the unbridled exercise of creative fervour.[305] Citing the famous recommendation in Seneca that the writer should derive inspiration from the study of diverse authors, just as the bee gathers nectar from various flowers, Alberti draws the moral that the painter should draw the principles of his art from the inherent rules of nature rather than relying 'upon one's own *ingenium* on setting about paintings as do most of the painters of the present day'.[306] Not only will artists who surrender wholly to the dictates of unfettered *ingenium* become negligent in the study of nature, they will also tend to leave their works unfinished after the initial transport of enthusiasm has worn off and will be prone to paint figures that are indecorously wild in gesture and motion. As a writer who advocated the Stoic *virtù* of moderation in all aspects of behaviour in civic society, Alberti characteristically avoided the extremes, emphasising that diligence, learning and moderation are needed if natural talent is to achieve worthy expression. He was certainly well aware of Vitruvius's formulation of the general rule for the harnessing of talent: 'neither *ingenium* without discipline, nor discipline without *ingenium*, can result in a perfect artist'.[307] Ghiberti translated just this passage in his *Commentaries*, while Francesco di Giorgio in his writings on architecture adapted it to give a more rule-based slant to the formula: '*ingegno* without doctrine [*dottrina*] or doctrine without *ingegno* cannot make a perfect artist'.[308] Elsewhere Francesco ingeniously works the key concept of *disegno* into the topos: 'just as we see many who have doctrine and do not have *ingegno* and many are endowed with *ingegno* and not with doctrine, so many have doctrine and *ingegno* but do not have *disegno*'.[309] Although he was specifically writing about architecture, Francesco was also a practising painter and sculptor. *Disegno*, in his formulation, was assuming its universal role as the foundation of all the visual arts. However, such general formulations about *ingenium* or *ingegno* were unusual even in insider writing, and the term was generally reserved to denote the attributes of an exceptional, named individual – with the implication that the general run of practitioners stood at a remove from the highest realms of innate talent and that it was not a general requirement for the routine making of artefacts.

The artist for whom the attribute of *ingenium* first became widely accepted was Giotto, not least because Petrarch and Boccaccio both praised his supreme 'talent'. Petrarch's formulation, widely echoed in later texts, is particularly nice, coupling *manus et ingenium* ('hand and talent') in a way that underscores the essentially cerebral and non-manual qualities of Giotto's *ingenium*.[310] By the time that Filippo Villani wrote his *De origine civitatis Florentiae et eisdem famosis civibus* ('On the Origin of the City of Florence and its Famous Citizens') in the early 1380s, Giotto had become the founder of a Florentine tradition and the master whose example should be followed above all others.[311] Such was his '*arte et ingenio*' that he should be regarded as superior to the famed masters of antiquity. Giotto became such an automatic point of reference when humanists wished to mention an artist of the modern era that we should not read too much into all the derivative citations, and they were certainly not aiming to imply that artists in general deserved an elevated status. With the exception of Giotto, it was easier for a humanist to praise the long-dead artists of antiquity, whom contemporaries could little hope to emulate. Thus the antiquarian, Poggio Bracciolini, felt entirely comfortable when looking at ancient sculpture to record that he was 'moved by the *ingenium* of such great artists' who can represent 'the very forces of nature . . . in marble'.[312] The ancient masters exhibit *ingenium* and *ars* when, in true Plinian manner, 'they render a mute and lifeless thing as if it breathed and spoke; often indeed they represent the emotions of the soul'. Similarly, as we will see when we look at the notion of the artist, Lorenzo Valla, has no difficulty in crediting *ingenium* to two of the greatest masters of ancient Greece, Pheidias and Praxiteles.[313] Again we are dealing more with the literary devices of antiquarian humanists than with profound statements about the practice of Renaissance art.

It was this tendency that Alberti nicely turned on its head in the letter of dedication of the Italian version of *On Painting* to Brunelleschi. He confessed that whereas he once believed that tired nature no longer produced *ingegni*, his return to Florence showed him that the talents possessed by Brunelleschi, Donatello, Ghiberti, Luca della Robbia and Masaccio were at least equal to those of the ancient masters.[314] The idea that it was appropriate to describe modern masters in such terms was taken up most conspicuously by Bartolommeo Fazio in his *De viris illustribus* ('On Illustrious Men'), written at the court of Naples in 1456, in which brief critical résumés were given of the qualities of the painters, Gentile da Fabriano, Jan van Eyck, and Pisanello, and the sculptors, Ghiberti and his son, Vittorio, and Donatello.[315] Gentile is credited with an 'ingenio adapted to every kind of painting', while Pisanello is accorded 'virtually a poet's ingenio for depicting the forms of things and expounding feelings'. Ghiberti and Donatello are respectively credited with ingenio combined with artifice, and with ingenio and arte (in the sense of skill). It is less surprising to find Ghiberti making a comparable move, not only when he associates Giotto's ingegno with doctrine, but also when he praises the Sienese painter Ambrogio Lorenzetti as 'a great ingegno, most noble draftsman and fully conversant with the theory of his art'.[316]

The supreme position achieved by Giotto in early humanist writing is matched in the fifteenth century by the reputation achieved by Filippo Brunelleschi, and it is probably no coincidence that the crowning achievements of both men's careers centred on the cathedral, the greatest expression of Florence's civic and religious values – Giotto's in the design of the Campanile and Brunelleschi's in the building of the great dome which, according to Alberti, seemed 'vast enough to cover the entire Tuscan population with its shadow'.[317] So notable was Brunelleschi's feat, no less in retrospect than in his own day, that he was accorded the extraordinary privilege of a memorial bust (based on a death mask) and a tablet with a laudatory inscription within the cathedral itself. The inscription was composed by Carlo Marsuppini, the distinguished humanist who was Chancellor of Florence:

> How valiant Filippo the architect was in the Daedelian art is documented both by the wonderful vault of this celebrated temple and the many machines invented by this *divino ingenio*. And on account of the excellent qualities of his soul and his singular virtues, his revered body was buried in this soil on 15 May 1446 by order of his gracious fatherland.[318]

Brunelleschi had begun his career as a goldsmith, and had painted the two panels in which perspective was first demonstrated, but it was as the maker of a structure that appeared miraculous in modern times and as a brilliant contriver of devices rather than as a figurative artist that he merited such supreme praise. We saw in chapter IV that Giovanni Rucellai, a major patron of Alberti's architecture, acknowledged Brunelleschi's *ingegno* and *fantasia* in building.[319] The builders of major structures tended to achieve levels of esteem substantially in advance of those of painters and sculptors in the *quattrocento*. It was only in the sixteenth century that we find any parallel for the esteem in which Brunelleschi was held, and then it is generally in connection with the great all-round artists – Leonardo, Raphael, Giulio Romano and Michelangelo – who practised as architects in addition to demonstrating high skill in other fields. Only Titian was widely recognised as having achieved such 'divine' status by being a painter alone.

During the course of earlier chapters I have deliberately flagged those instances when an artist has been credited with *ingenium* or *ingegno*, by inserting the term in its original language – as I have done with *fantasia* and its variants. Amongst the earlier instances of these were such diverse talents as the pious Fra Angelico and the courtly Pisanello. No painter before Mantegna was the subject of more attention from the humanist poets than Pisanello. The fashion was set

104. Pisanello, *Vision of St Eustace*, London, National Gallery

by Guarino Guarini of Verona, translator of Lucian's *Calumny*. Working at the court of Ferrara, where he taught Leonello d'Este, Guarino had ample opportunity to witness Pisanello's remarkable skills, and his poem was specifically occasioned by his receipt of the painter's gift of a painting of *St Jerome* (now lost).[320] In the very first line the artist's *ingenium* is prominently signalled, as an introduction to a rapturous *ekphrasis* of the multitudinous naturalistic and story-telling details characteristic of the painter's works on large and small scales (fig. 104). Later in the poem he speaks again of Pisanello's *ingenium*, dubbing it as *ingens* (mighty) and associating it with his 'artful fingers and learned colours'. Inevitably Pisanello is matched against a roll call of ancient artists, including Apelles, and it is they who are found wanting. Further poems in the same eulogistic and descriptive vein followed by Tito Vespasiano Strozzi, Basinio of Ferrara, Lionardo di Pietro Dati of Florence and Ulisse degli Aleotti (who was later to write a convoluted poem on Mantegna).[321] Strozzi even goes so far as to talk of Pisanello's 'divine *ingenium*'. One of the two poems by Ulisse is particularly interesting, since it relates to two portraits of Leonello d'Este by Pisanello and Jacopo Bellini which were produced in direct competition in

233

1441. The victory of Bellini, as adjudicated by Leonello's father, Niccolò III, gave Ulisse an opportunity to work a modern variation on Dante's pictorial example of the vagaries of *fortuna* – Giotto's surpassing of the once famed Cimabue. The second of Ulisse's poems advertises Jacopo as the teacher of the 'divine Apelles'. Jacopo Bellini himself seems to have been in no doubt that his status warranted such praise. In 1448 he inscribed his damaged and much-restored *Madonna and Child* in the Brera in Milan with the far from modest claim that 'Bellini produced these forms with his *ingenua*'.[322]

As the poems on Pisanello make clear, the visual quality in paintings that was likely to merit most praise from an author versed in Plinian criteria and the classical *ekphrasis* was the perfect and detailed imitation of nature such that objects seem to be in full relief. Paradoxically such high humanist praise worked to constrain the extent to which the painter or sculptor could be regarded as responsible for the kind of inventiveness – for the ability to generate a brilliant *invenzione* – which was so admired in an author or orator. The literary arts were also involved with issues of imitation and reality, but their freer choice of subject matter and more ready exploiting of imaginative fictions set the literary discussions within a different framework. The key problem was that the Renaissance painter or sculptor was not generally expected to be the person responsible for the genesis of the project to make a picture or even for the determination of its subject matter. A competent master would be expected to know enough about the 'stories' and the characterisations of the participants to portray the normal range of subjects without detailed instruction, but the basic decisions on content resided with those who ordered the work. The priority accorded to others for invention contrasted strongly with the situation in verbal pursuits. Cicero, from whom many Renaissance authors took their cue, regarded invention as the first part of rhetoric, and defined it as 'the devising of things true or probable'.[323] That Cicero's notion of invention could be applied to the visual arts is most vividly witnessed by Fazio, who in his 'On Illustrious Men', outlines a three-part scheme of *inventio, dispositio* (arrangement) and *expressio* (expression), which is adapted from Cicero's three first parts of rhetoric, *inventio, collocatio* (composition) and *elocutio* (mode of delivery).[324] Comparing the painter and the poets, Fazio comments that 'almost equal attention is given both to the invention and arrangement of their work'. Although Cicero's idea of inventing things which are 'true' reminds us that we should not think of inventiveness in terms of our later conception of the more anarchic aspects of artistic originality, to credit someone with powers of *invenzione* was a significant acknowledgement of intellectual capacity. When we find artists being so credited, something of significance is happening.

Alongside this usage of invention with respect to subject matter, there ran the notion of the 'inventor' in the more technological and scientific sense. It was in this latter mode that Vitruvius hailed Pythagoras and Archimedes as 'inventors'.[325] When Brunelleschi is credited as the inventor of perspective by his biographer Manetti, just as he was by Landino in his commentary on Dante, it was this more technical sense that was paramount.[326] Not surprisingly, *invenzione* of this kind features relatively regularly in the literature on Renaissance architecture and engineering, and became associated with the possession of exclusive skills and 'secrets'. Brunelleschi was reported as saying during the years 1427-30 that it is inadvisable 'to share your inventions with many'.[327] The true inventor should only 'share them with the few who understand and love the sciences. To describe too much of one's inventions is one and the same thing as to debase one's *ingenia*.' This more technical sense of invention is also being evoked when Ghiberti tells us that Giotto was 'the inventor or discoverer' of the 'doctrines of art which had lain buried for six hundred years'.[328] As well as discovering the doctrines, there was also a feeling that Giotto was unusually well-versed in matters of the content of paintings; he had such 'a full knowledge of the stories' that his works 'emulated poetry', as Villani testified.[329] This should not be taken to imply that he was given a free hand when determining what to paint in, say, the Scrovegni Chapel in Padua, but it does imply that he could be accorded a greater amount of responsibility to translate general instructions into specific form than most painters.

During the course of the fifteenth century, we are more likely to find painters or those who wrote about painting formulating claims that *invenzione* is a legitimate part of the artist's responsibility. Alberti, not surprisingly as someone with a humanist education, identifies *invenzione* with the devising of the subject matter for a painting, and accords it a high status: 'indeed, *inventio* is such that even by itself and without pictorial representation it can give pleasure'.[330] Almost inevitably the example he subsequently cites is Apelles's *Calumny* in Lucian's *ekphrasis*, which 'excites our admiration when we read it'. The extent to which he accords the inventive power specifically to the painter is, however, not wholly clear. He recommends that painters should seek out the company of 'literary men, who are full of information about many subjects and will be of great assistance in preparing the composition of a *historia*, and the great virtue of this consists primarily in its *inventio*'.

When Antonio Filarete expounds the form and adornment of his ideal city, he advocates that the artist should be well read – as he considered himself to be – so that he could devise '*belle inventioni*' as Apelles did in his *Calumny*.[331] Although it is a treatise specifically on architecture and architectural planning, Filarete's text, composed in Milan as a rather one-sided dialogue with a prince (identifiable as Francesco Sforza) and finally dedicated to Piero de' Medici, contains some revealing passages on the relative responsibilities of the patron and an intellectually ambitious artist for the invention of schemes of pictorial and sculptural decoration. Some of the images, such as one of a bull lead by a *putto* were conceived by the patron as complete *invenzioni*, while others, such as the elaborate allegory of *Reason and Will* (fig. 105) required a good deal of detailed elaboration by the draftsman.[332] He explains that Reason sits on a heart, holds scales and reins (each of which controls one of the senses), wears lead slippers and has three faces, to see the past, present and future. Will, who has wings on feet and shoulders, places her foot on a wheel, holds a tilted balance and grasps the world. Some inventions are claimed as Filarete's sole responsibility. For his novel *Houses of Virtue and Vice* he decided that he needed representations of their general nature, rather than separate depictions of the cardinal and theological virtues and the named vices in the standard manner.[333] He considered using the story of Hercules at the crossroads, in which the mighty hero is confronted by a choice between the seductive charms of a beautiful woman advocating the easy path of vice and a sterner maiden who invites him to pursue the stonier road of

105. Antonio Filarete, *Design for an Image of Reason and Will*, Florence, Biblioteca Nazionale, Codex Magliabechiano, II, 1, 140, fol. 69v

106. Antonio Filarete, *Design for a Statue of Virtue*, Florence, Biblioteca Nazionale, Codex Magliabechiano, II, 1, 140, fol. 143r

virtue, but found that it 'did not satisfy my mind'. He thus set himself to the devising of separate embodiments of Virtue (fig. 106) and Vice which were to be realised, somewhat improbably, as giant sculptures at the summits of their respective houses. Virtue, an armoured angel with a head like the sun, is poised on a diamond of rectitude, and holds trunks of laurel and date. At his feet is a fountain of honey and the mountains that must be conquered by the virtuous. Although we may sometimes doubt Filarete's common sense, he did himself work as a sculptor on projects with elaborate iconographies, most especially his bronze doors for St Peters in Rome, and the way he characterised his own ambitions as an 'inventor' of subjects clearly reflects the growing aspirations of ambitious artists to assume conceptual responsibilities which were previously regarded as the prerogative of patrons or their agents.

A nice indication of the tensions which could arise when a highly motivated and opinionated patron attempted to circumscribe the freedom of artists who had won considerable stature is provided by the correspondence of Isabella d'Este in the early years of the sixteenth century, as she strove to obtain paintings from leading masters for her *studiolo* in Mantua.[334] Since she was extending her trawl to painters working in other cities, she necessarily needed to rely on the kind of written instructions which are unlikely to have been necessary in the more normal circumstances on employing an artist based locally, as indeed was Mantegna, who provided two finished paintings for the *studiolo*. The poles of compliance and freedom, as we have already noticed in chapters II and IV, are vividly apparent in her attempts to negotiate appropriate subjects with Perugino, who was resident on Florence, and Giovanni Bellini in Venice. For the *Battle of Chastity and Lasciviousness* (fig. 29), Perugino was repeatedly pressed to obey the dictates of what she called her 'poetic *inventione*', which she also called a *fantasia* and *historia*. The iconographic details of her *inventione* were supplied by her court humanist, Paride da Ceresara, and were transmitted to the artist both in written form and in a small drawing. The less than happy results have already been noted. By contrast, her agent in Venice persuaded her that Giovanni Bellini needed to be given a looser reign if she was to succeed in obtaining a painting from him. In 1501 she requested 'some history [*historia*] or ancient fable, otherwise one of your own *inventione* in which is depicted something which represents a subject which is ancient and of fine significance'. The painter promised to supply a '*fantasia* of his own type'. Even so, four years later when she was characteristically persisting in her efforts, she neeeded to be reminded by Pietro Bembo, the Venetian poet, that Bellini 'does not like to be given many written details which cramp his style; his way of working, as he says, is always to wander at will in his pictures, so that they can give satisfaction to himself as well as the beholder'. One of her agents, however, expressed the opinion that 'in *invencione* [*sic*] no one can rival Mantegna, who is truly most excellent' .

The correspondence of Isabella, involving agents of high sophistication such as Pietro Bembo, indicates that terms like *inventione*, *fantasia*, *historia* and *fabula* (or *favola*) did not necessarily have clearly differentiated meanings when they were used to refer to subject matter, but each potentially carried its own special loadings or associations, which could be brought to the fore in different contexts. *Fantasia* carried the most complex body of associations. A well-read Renaissance humanist would be versed in its prestigious antique antecedents and its use in later poetics. Isabella herself would have been aware of a key passage in younger Philostratus's *Imagines*, a copy of which she cherished: 'the art of painting has a kinship with poetry . . . An element of *fantasia* is common to them both'.[335] A standard point of reference would also have been Quintilian's textbook on oratory, in which he notes that *fantasia*, a Greek term, corresponds to a 'vision' in Latin, and refers to the way in which things can be imagined by the mind in such a vivid manner that 'they seem to be before our eyes'.[336] Characteristically, Quintilian expresses reservations about allowing 'fantastication' too free a reign, but with discipline it can be turned to good account. It is this visionary form of *fantasia* that occupies such a central place in Dante's armoury as a poet of the highest intellectual and spiritual ambition. It is only at the very end of the *Divine Comedy* that the poet's *alta fantasia*, like any human faculty, finally proves inadequate in the face of the ultimate vision of the divine.[337]

Alongside the *fantasia* of poetics, the Renaissance inherited a conception of 'imagination' from medieval notions of the brain and its functions. The basic idea, on which there were many variations, was that the ventricles (cavities) of the brain housed the various faculties of the mind. The three main ventricles were commonly thought to contain, respectively: the *sensus communis* (where sensory impressions were gathered together), together with *fantasia* and *imaginativa* in the first; the rational faculties of thought and judgement in the second; and memory in the third. The division of labour between *fantasia* and *imaginativa* was variable, as was the terminology itself, but generally speaking *fantasia* was assigned the role of the free combination of sense impressions, while *imaginativa* worked with the rational faculties to produce dreams and other imaginative constructs. Although there was a relatively standard and unremarkable use of the verb *imaginare* to designate the process of imagining something – much as we might say, 'Let us imagine that. . .' – the Renaissance literature associated with the arts also used the terms for imagination in consciously loaded ways to allude to the poetic or philosophical traditions, and sometimes to both.

A precocious and somewhat unexpected use of *fantasia* occurs in Cennino Cennini's book. In the introductory section, already noticed in chapter III, he boldly declares that painting demands both '*fantasia* and manual operations . . . in order to discover unseen things, hiding under the shadow of nature, and to fix them with the hand, demonstrating what does not actually exist'.[338] Making clear reference to Horace's *The Art of Poetry*, he states that 'the painter is given freedom to compose a figure standing, sitting, half man, half horse as it pleases him, following his *fantasia*'. Later in the treatise, Cennino uses a derivative term in a manner which suggests that he was as alert to the dangers of *fantasia* as Horace. He tells the aspiring painter that if he follows one master today and another tomorrow, he will be 'bewildered through enthusiasm [*fantastichetto per amor*], since each style will traduce your mind [in turn]'.[339] However, if the painter assiduously studies one good master, *fantasia* can be turned to positive advantage, since it will assist the student in developing his own particular manner – assuming that 'nature has conceded you any *fantasia* at all'. As we have seen, Cennino can hardly be characterised as a learned author, and his quite sophisticated sense of the role of *fantasia* suggests that he was drawing on ideas that were already current in Padua, and perhaps also in Florence.

In view of what we have already seen about Filarete's 'fantastic' inventions, we will not be surprised to find that he is a keen advocate of the role of *fantasia*. It is the faculty of *fantasia* that is responsible for the formation of the initial idea, for the overall invention. In keeping with standard humanist attitudes, it does not stand alone but needs to be coupled with the rational faculties of thought. He regularly couples the verb *fantasticare* ('to fantasticate') with *pensare* ('to think').[340] In elaborating the image of *Reason and Will* (fig. 105) which his patron has conceived, he 'thought and fantasticated [*fantasticato*] on these fantasies [*fantasie*]'.[341] Exactly the same process of thought and fantastication results in his novel representations of Vice and Virtue when he sets his '*ingenio*' to work on the problem.[342] He is clear that one of the key roles for the artist is to 'investigate and search for new *fantasie* and new things'.[343] That the process was intimately associated with the highest faculties of the rational intellect is underscored by his telling how Archimedes was killed while 'designing and fantasticating circles and triangles'.[344] The ancient pedigree of Filarete's characterisation of the role of *fantasia* is given fictitious emphasis by the 'Golden Book' in Greek which he purports to have discovered and had translated.[345] The supposed ancient author, not unexpectedly, provides full precedent for Filarete's conception of *fantasia*. The 'Golden Book' not only recommends that the artist should be learned 'in letters' but also that he should be granted an unconditional stipend of 100 ducats to give him the necessary freedom to fantasticate at will.

The relatively concentrated citing of *fantasia* by Cennino and Filarete is not matched by any other theorist before Leonardo. In other kinds of writing there are some scattered references before Isabella's conspicuous use of the term in connection with the invention of content. We would not be justified, therefore, in assuming that there was a wholesale adoption of the term to indicate that the visual arts partook of Dante's kind of high inspiration. Indeed, whether with respect to *fantasia* or any other cluster of terms which denote imaginative freedom, there is only a slow seepage of the idea that a poetic form of inspiration was a prerequisite for good art. However, the instances in which such acknowledgement was made do reflect a growing tendency for writers on the visual arts to annex desired attributes from literary arenas and laid the groundwork for the kind of claims that were to be made in subsequent years, above all by Leonardo.

RECOGNISABLE ARTISTS

The Renaissance in the visual arts is, in terms of the written record, signalled most clearly by the numbers of individual artists about whom we have biographical information. The Renaissance invented the writing of artists' lives, the genre which still occupies the most conspicuous place in art publishing, particularly in the popular arena. Not the least remarkable aspect of this phenomenon was the advent of the artistic autobiography, the germ of which was sown in Ghiberti's *Commentaries* and which reached its culmination in the extraordinary and sometimes fantastic account of his own life written by the Florentine sculptor and goldsmith, Benvenuto Cellini. Some of the reasons for the sudden efflorescence of biographical writing and its continued consequences will be considered in the final chapter. For the moment we may note the rise of the individual artist, known by name and personality, as a conspicuous fact. My concern here is less to look at the various lives as such than to study the notion of artistic individuality upon which they were predicated.

There almost certainly had been a long-standing recognition that some painters were better at some things than other things, and that their skills had some distinctive quality to them, but probably with no more intention to credit them with high qualities of individual genius than would have been accorded to bakers who produced distinctive bread. Painters could gain reputations as suppliers of, say, small-scale Madonnas, or, in the case of Simone de' Crocefissi in *trecento* Bologna for the Crucifixes after which he was named. The recognition that there was something special and admirable about an artist's individual style required more than this sense of specialised skills.

Again, the limited but continually surprising Cennino takes the lead. We have already seen how he credited *fantasia* with the acquisition of a 'style individual to yourself'. The terms he actually uses are *maniera* ('manner') and *aria* ('air').[346] *Aria* is the more unexpected and sophisticated term. It had been used by Petrarch to refer to that 'certain shadow, which our painters call an air [*aerem*], most apparent in faces and eyes, that causes the resemblance which, upon our seeing of the son, recalls to our mind the memory of the father'.[347] This implies that 'air' was something that was recognised instinctively but alluded precise description and systematic analysis. Although he does not specifically refer to *aria*, something of the same underlying idea is present in the formulation that Matteo Palmieri uses in his treatise *On Civil Life* in 1438-9 when discussing modern versions of ancient texts.[348] He notes, by analogy, that a copy of a perfect figure by Giotto, however much it may duplicate its features, 'would nevertheless be different to the extent that it would be separately imagined [*imaginare*] by each person'.

If artists each exhibited their own *maniera* or *aria*, there arose the problem of how each style might be characterised – and it really was a problem, given the lack of an established system of art criticism. Many of the early attempts are rudimentary. Alamanno Rinuccini, in his short account of Florentine painters in the dedicatory letter to his translation of Philostratus's *Life of Apollonius of Tyana*, recognised the existence of equal excellencies, but could do not better than say that the paintings of Filippo Lippi are more rich (*ornatus*) than those of Fra Angelico.[349] Ghiberti, as a practising artist gives fine descriptions of individual works using a form of *ekphrasis*, but he has similar difficulty in characterising and differentiating the overall styles of the main masters. For example, amongst the Sienese masters whom he so admires, Ambrogio Lorenzetti is described as 'most noble in composition' and 'very expert in the theory of art' while Simone Martini and Lippo Memmi are termed 'appealing masters [*gentili maestri*]', which hardly takes us very far if we want to be able to recognise their works.[350] Bartolommeo Fazio does somewhat better, as might be expected from an author who made perceptive use of Pliny and was well versed in the discussion of types of oratory in Cicero in other ancient authors. Although Gentile is recognised for his universality – 'suited to all kinds of painting' – he is especially renowned for 'his decoration of buildings'. Pisanello, 'in the opinion of experts passed all others', in the 'painting of horses and other animals', while Donatello receives special praise for 'faces that live' (a phrase borrowed from Virgil's *Aeneid*).[351] However, even Fazio describes the painters' specialities – naming horses for courses – rather than really characterising their styles.

The most sophisticated attempt to evoke different styles in the fifteenth century occurs in Landino's preface to his great 1481 edition of Dante's *Divine Comedy*.[352] Masaccio is justly described as a 'supreme imitator of nature, with great and general modelling [*rilievo*], a fine composer, simple and without ornament, because he devoted himself solely to the imitation of truth and to the modelling of figures'. By contrast Filippo Lippi's paintings are 'gracious and rich [*ornatus*] and supremely ingenious [*artificioso*]'. Filippo is equally adept at imitating 'the true and the fictitious'. Fra Angelico is recognised for a style that is 'beautiful and devout and very rich with great facility'. Uccello and Pisanello both exhibit specialised talents, the former as a 'great master of animals and landscapes, skilful in foreshortening because he understood perspective well', while the latter is 'particularly adept at animals'. A particularly nice account is given of Castagno, who 'was a very great draughtsman with great modelling, enamoured of the difficult aspects of art and of foreshortening, very lively and vigorous, with very great facility in execution'.

That there was an increasing propensity to characterise different styles towards the end of the century is confirmed by a neatly succinct report to Ludovico Sforza in Milan by his agent in Florence, who was assisting in the duke's search for a suitable master. Four leading painters are assessed:

Sandro Botticelli, most excellent painter on panel and on walls: his works have a virile air [*aria virile*] and show the highest rationality and harmonious proportion. Filippino, son of the excellent Fra Filippo: pupil of the aforesaid, son of the most noted master of his time: his works have a most sweet air [*aria più dolce*]. I do not believe they show as much skill [*arte*]. Perugino, notable master: and particularly on walls: his works display an angelic air [*aria angelica*], and very sweet. Domenico Ghirlandaio, good master on panels and better on walls: his works have a good air [*aria buona*], and he is expeditious and handles a lot of work.[353]

If art is imitation of nature, as all Renaissance authors accepted, and different painters have different styles, as was increasingly recognised, the corollary would seem to be that one style must be better – i.e. be a more faithful imitation – than another. Indeed, the implication of absolute rules for imitation, by Alberti and Leonardo in particular, seems to lead inexorably to the rejection of individual style. Drawing upon Pliny, Alberti recognised that many of the ancient masters had won renown in particular branches of painting, such as Heraclides who was 'famous for painting ships', and he recognised that 'each one had a different ability', but cautions against being content to cultivate only those specialised gifts given to us by nature.[354] Universality was the most desirable goal, as Leonardo later stressed. However, like so many other factors in this earliest period of modern literature on the visual arts, seemingly inconsistent ideas co-exist without causing much difficulty. Thus we find the advocacy of naturalism standing alongside a recognition that the individual manner of one artist is not necessarily better than the different style of another master. There are clear signs that it became increasingly possible to recognise differences without necessarily having to say that one style is inherently better than another. Referring characteristically to ancient rather than living artists, Lorenzo Valla, for instance, imagines that he can delight equally in the works of Pheidias and Praxiteles because 'I understand the diversity of the *ingenium* of the two artists'.[355] Transferring the idea to modern artists, Alamanno Rinuccini in 1472 followed his brief assessment of Florentine painters – Cimabue, Giotto and Taddeo Gaddi, who are credited with *ingenium*, and Masaccio, Domenico Veneziano, Filippo Lippi and Fra Angelico – by declaring that 'they were all considered different among themselves in their variety, yet very alike in excellence and goodness'.[356]

If the painters exhibited individual styles of equal merit, and if these styles could be characterised, the next problem obviously concerns why the individuality arose. The most general and obvious answer – that God makes us distinct as individuals – does not take us very far in proposing a mechanism. The most accessible model lay in astrology, as was to be adopted in the sixteenth century by Vasari and even more extensively by Lomazzo. It had occurred to at least one fifteenth-century author. Giovanni Cavalcanti, in his *History of Florence*, wrote:

Just as are the stars in heaven, so are the human creatures. And thus each human power differs from the others to the extent that the influences of the natures of the stars differ; so a particular power was in Pippo di Ser Brunellesco that was not in Lorenzo di Bartoluccio [Ghiberti], and a

particular *fantasia* was in Gentile [da Fabriano] that was not in Giuliano d'
Arrigo [Pesello], according to the different *fantasia* and understandings that
men possess. . . and from the diversity of *ingegni* amongst men comes a
corresponding diversity of skills [*arti*].[357]

The notion that there was something inherent in each artist at the deepest
level found expression in the idea that 'every painter paints himself' – a tag that
seems to have gained popularity in late fifteenth-century Florence. Leonardo, as
we will see, glossed the idea in some detail, but it was already expressed with
some sophistication by Girolamo Savonarola, the reforming Dominican, whose
fiery preaching was to precipitate the fall of the Medici in 1494. In one of his
sermons on Ezekiel, he claimed that,

> Every painter paints himself. He does not paint himself as being a man,
> because he makes images of lions, horses, men and women that are not
> himself, but he paints himself as a painter, that is according to his concept
> [*concetto*]; and although the *fantasie* and figures that the painters paint will be
> diverse, they will all correspond to his concept. So too the philosophers,
> because they were proud, described God in swollen and haughty ways.[358]

This idea could be expressed literally in terms that each painter tended to
make all his figures look somewhat like himself, and more generally in that the
character of a particular artist's personality was mirrored in his works. Thus a
devout master, such as Fra Angelico, would paint serenely devout works, while
an irascible master like Castagno would exhibit a fiercer *aria* in his paintings. In
the hands of Leonardo, Vasari and other later authors, the identity of virtuous
artists with virtuous works – already implicit in Alberti's moralising injunctions
to avoid excess in all things – became a central plank in their requirements for
good art. Indeed, it is in Leonardo's writings that we find almost all the trends
we have seen *in nuce* in this chapter emerge in defined form.

LEONARDO AND THE SEARCH FOR STATUS

We have already seen in chapter III that Leonardo developed the very highest
claims for painting as 'the sole imitator of all the manifest works of nature . . .
[and] a subtle invention which with philosophical and subtle speculation
considers all manner of forms'.[359] In his specific challenge to the poet, in tones
which sometimes breathe an air of obsession, he asserted that his art trumped
all the main genres of writing: 'great fictions' such as the *Inferno*; significant
events in history, like battles; rapturous expressions of love; pleasant pastorals;
burlesques and satires; and all kinds of representations of admired persons,
divine and earthly. Whatever territory the poet claims to inhabit, the painter
will provide a more vivid and accessible picture of the mental and physical
scenery.

In his arguments he exploits all the kinds of key terms we have been using as
indicators of the development of ambitious attitudes towards the merits of the
visual arts. Characteristically he inverts the Horatian tradition, not so much
granting painters the licence accorded to poets but conceding that the poet may

be considered as 'free as the painter in *inventioni*'.[360] He agrees with Alberti that '*inventione* or composition of narrative [*storia*]' is the 'end of such *scientia*'.[361] When he looks at stains on walls into which he imaginatively projects new subjects, he is seeking 'various *inventione*'.[362] Human powers of invention occupy a central place in Leonardo's ideas, in all the fields we now know as art, science and technology. He sees inventiveness as taking the human potential for making things beyond the scope of those created by nature. The painter's works are 'more infinite than those made by nature' allowing him to invent an infinite number of things that 'nature never created'.[363] He writes that 'nature is concerned only with the production of elementary things but man from these elementary things produces an infinite number of compounds, although he has no power to create any elementary thing except another like himself, that is his children'.[364] This notion of invention is not that of the alchemists, who aspire to create gold and the 'philosopher's stone', but involves compounding and building upon the multitudinous items created by nature.

The essentially combinatory nature of invention corresponds to the powers traditionally accorded to *fantasia*, and it is no surprise to find that he regularly invokes this imaginative faculty when he wishes to praise painting. In the comparison with sculpture, he claims that 'painting is more beautiful, has more *fantasia* and greater variety'.[365] The painter's 'hands represent that which is found in his *fantasia*', and 'whatever exists in the universe through essence, presence or *imaginatione*, he has it first in his mind and then in his hands'.[366] The painter should learn 'to make the effects of nature through his *fantasia*', on the basis of his deep understanding of how nature works.[367] The notion of *fantasia* working to generate inventions on an essentially rational basis recalls Filarete's coupling of fantastication with thought. When he came to consider how the faculties of the brain are actually arranged, Leonardo specifically brought together the *sensus communis* and the imaginative and rational faculties in the central ventricle, assigning the first ventricle to the *imprensiva*, the receptor of impressions (fig. 107). This rearrangement gives a physiological basis for the way in which the analytical and imaginative potentialities of the mind work in close harness in the painter's remaking of nature. Increasingly in his later art theory, after 1500, rational re-creation and the exercise of judgement tend to take precedence over the more free-ranging qualities of poetic *fantasia*, but the essentially imaginative nature of the process of remaking remains constant throughout his writings.

It was the faculty of judgement – above all with respect to the rational re-creation of nature according to its laws – that prevented the mental remaking of nature from becoming a subjective and individually arbitrary business. Whereas Cennini's *fantasia* had provided the artist with access to an individual style, Leonardo's overriding demands for the ever more scrupulous observation and remaking of every natural cause and effect left no obvious room for individual style. His demand for an art of absolute truth means that the issue of individuality is largely blocked from his purview. The only sustained confrontation comes when he addresses the commonplace that 'every painter paints himself', and he leaves us in no doubt that such auto-mimesis is a vice not only in practice but also at the deepest level of theory. Noting that 'figures often resemble their masters', he warns that:

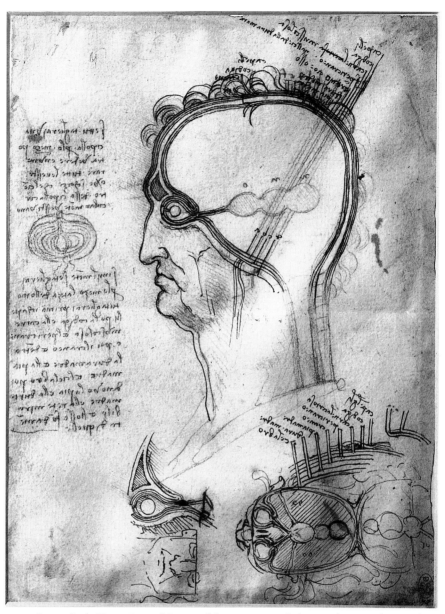

107.   Leonardo da Vinci, *Saggital Section of the Human Head Showing the Ventricles*, Windsor, Royal Library, no. 12603r

The painter should make his figure according to the rules for a body in nature, which is commonly known to be of praiseworthy proportions. In addition to this, he should have himself measured to see where his own person varies much or little from that termed praiseworthy. With this information he must studiously oppose falling into the same shortcomings in the figures he makes that are found in his own person. Be advised that you must fight your utmost against this vice, since it is a failing that was born together with

244

judgement, because the soul, the mistress of your body, naturally delights in works similar to that which she produced in composing her body. And from this it comes about that there is no woman so ugly that she does not find a lover, unless she is monstrous.[368]

He notes in detail that 'each peculiarity in a painting has its prototype in the painter's own peculiarity'. Not the least problem with failing to correct one's own idiosyncratic propensities is that the negligent painter cannot aspire to be universal. Painters prone to little motion, will naturally be best at portraits, while those who are brisk in manner will portray lively figures. The answer lies, as always in the systematic study of nature and, in true Renaissance manner, in the observation of decorum with regard to the kind of subject and the types of actors in a narrative.

The remaking of visual effects according to nature's own principles endows the painter in Leonardo's eyes with something approaching god-like powers. It is the faculty of invention that distinguishes humans from animals, in such a way that man 'shows himself to be a divine thing'.[369] He speculates that 'the divinity which is the science of painting transmutes itself into a resemblance of the divine mind in such a manner that it discourses with free power concerning the generation of the diverse essences of various plants, animals and so on'.[370] Painting is 'not only a science but also a divinity, the name of which should be duly revered and repeats all the works of God the most high'.[371] The painter 'is lord and god of all the things he wishes to generate'.[372] Such extreme claims for the god-like artist, the remaker of the visual world, master of the poet and paragon for the practitioners of all other arts and sciences, highlight what has been a recurrent tension in the kinds of source we have been examining throughout this book; that is to say the reality of the artist's daily existence as a contracted professional in contrast to the growing intellectual claims for art as a supreme form of visual knowledge and vehicle for the communication of meaning at the highest level.

How can the voice we hear in the *Treatise on Painting* be reconciled with the documents concerning Leonardo's actual career – the routine contractual agreements, the disputes, legal rulings, irritable letters from patrons to their secretaries, and humbling letters from Leonardo to patrons? To a large degree they cannot be reconciled, since the old realities and the new aspirations come into open conflict in Leonardo's pursuit of his career. Although he may have been at the court of Milan for as many as eighteen years, undertaking important works for Ludovico Sforza and his household, we have no evidence that he was literally a 'courtier', that is to say an immediate daily member of the duke's entourage. What evidence we have of contacts between Ludovico and his employee suggests that Leonardo communicated on significant issues by letter and that secretaries dealt directly with him on matters of business. More personal, verbal relationships are, of course, likely to be elusive for the historian, and the two men undoubtedly enjoyed some measure of personal contact, but we should not be misled by our modern-day estimatation of Leonardo's stature into thinking that Ludovico let his 'engineer and painter' forget his due place in the court hierarchy. Leonardo may claim that the painter was a god-like master of nature remade, but the duke, as a Renaissance prince struggling to cope with

245

chronic political instabilities, knew that the real life and death issues lay elsewhere than in the painter's craft. Ludovico, like the Gonzaga in Mantua, the d'Este in Ferrara, the Montefeltro in Urbino and the Aragonese in Naples, recognised that the patronage of notable artists, poets and musicians cast lustre on his regime, and that art might serve on occasion as a diplomatic lever, but pictures and fine words were expendable in the face of military realities.

Within such constraints, however, there is a good deal of evidence that Leonardo, like a few other notable court artists, was being recognised as someone of more than menial status. Like Pisanello before him, he and his works feature in the eulogies of courtly poets. Bernardo Bellincioni, his fellow Florentine with whom he collaborated on theatrical events, speaks of Leonardo, Giorgio Merula (the humanist), Caradosso (the medallist) and Gieronimo 'the master of artillery' as 'divine stars' in Ludovico's court.[373] Leonardo clearly established what today would be called 'an image'. Gaspare Visconti, an aristocratic Milanese poet whose book of sonnets Leonardo owned, wrote in mildly satirical vein about the painter's own propensity to auto-mimesis, in a way that indicates knowledge of Leonardo's own ideas:

> There is one nowadays who has so fixed
> In his conception the image of himself
> That when he wishes to paint someone else
> He often paints not the subject but himself.

And, in the last verse of the sonnet, Leonardo's temperamental idiosyncrasy is recognised, as it must have been at the court:

> It is true that he neglects important matters,
> That is to say his brain goes wandering
> Each time the moon wanes:
> Hence, when it comes to making a good poem
> And to make paintings which work well as a whole,
> He lacks fetters, restraints and chains.[374]

At least two of Leonardo's portraits of prominent ladies of the court were eulogised. In 1493 Bellincioni's poem in honour of the image of *Cecilia Gallerani* (fig. 108), the duke's teenage mistress, was posthumously published.[375] The poet seeks to soothe Nature's feelings of having been literally outfaced:

> Nature, with whom are you angry, whom do you envy?
> It is Vinci who has portrayed one of your stars!
> Cecilia, so very beautiful today, is the one
> Beside whose beautiful eyes the sun appears as a dark shadow.

> The honour is due to you [Nature], even though with his painting
> She seems as if she would listen and not chatter.
> Consider, to the extent that she will still be alive and beautiful,
> The more will be your glory in future ages.

> Give thanks then to Ludovico, or more
> To the *ingegno* and hand of Lionardo,
> Which permit you to participate in posterity.

108.   Leonardo da Vinci, *Cecilia Gallerani*, Cracow, Czartoryski Museum

Anyone who will see her thus, though it will be too late
To see her alive, will say: it is enough for us
To understand what is nature and what is art.

The portrait of another of the duke's mistresses, Lucrezia Crivelli, perhaps identifiable as the picture in the Louvre wrongly known as '*La Belle Ferronière*', was the subject of three Latin epigrams by an unknown poet, which work comparably conventional variations on the conjoined glories of nature, Ludovico and his beloved, as transmitted by Leonardo to posterity.[376] The sheet is preserved amongst Leonardo's papers, but it may be symptomatic of his lack of regard for such trifles that he used its reverse for his geometrical investigations.

The clay model for the mighty equestrian memorial to Ludovico's father attracted particular attention from writers, not only because of its size and artistic power but also because it invited direct comparison with revered works of antiquity, given the survival of the equestrian statues of Marcus Aurelius in Rome and the 'Regisole' (the so-called 'Sun King') at Pavia. Baldassare Taccone, another of the court poets with whom Leonardo collaborated as a theatrical designer, included a poem in its honour as part of his celebratory publication on the occasion of the wedding of Ludovico's niece, Bianca Maria to the Holy Roman Emperor, Maximilian in 1493. Leonardo, eulogised as a 'fine painter and fine geometrician', has demonstrated such rare *ingegno* in his 'great colossus', that neither Greece nor Rome ever saw anything larger, and none of the revered sculptors of antiquity – Pheidias, Myron, Scopas and Praxiteles – could ever have produced anything more beautiful.[377] Again emphasising size in its own right, no small matter given the ancients' well-attested admiration for colossal works, Luca Pacioli prints a line on the scale of 1:36 in the margin of his *De Divina Proportione* (*On Divine Proportion*) to give the reader a precise way of envisaging the immense proportions of Leonardo's 'earthen horse', which was to be at least three-times life-size.[378] Fame is literally the spur, and Leonardo's notebooks testify that he was no more immune from the conventional aspiration to leave his mark on posterity than the most ambitious literary and visual artists of the Renaissance.

Luca Pacioli, the mathematician and alumnus of Piero della Francesca, who joined Leonardo at Ludovico's court in 1496, provides some of our clearest evidence of the extent to which Leonardo's aspiration for himself and his calling were beginning to achieve some measure of recognition. In his *De viribus quantitatis*, he recorded with pleasure the circumstances which had lead to the painter producing the illustrations of regular and semi-regular geometrical bodies for his book *On Divine Proportion* (fig. 109).[379] Luca expresses delight with,

> the supreme and very graceful figures of all the Platonic solids and regular mathematical bodies and their derivatives, which it is not possible to imagine done better in the world in perspective design, even were Apelles, Myron, Polikleitus and the others to return amongst us; they are made and shaped by the ineffable left hand, most fitted for all the mathematical disciplines, of the prince today amongst mortals, that first amongst Florentines, our Lionardo da Vinci, in that happy time when we found ourselves together on the same payroll [*a medesimi stipendiati*] in the most marvellous city of Milan.

109. Leonardo da Vinci, *Truncated and Stellated Dodecahedron*, from Luca Pacioli, *De Divina Proportione*, Milan, Biblioteca Ambrosiana

110. Leonardo da Vinci (after), *Knot with ACADEMIA LEONARDI VI.CI*, Milan, Biblioteca Ambrosiana

Pacioli also gives concrete evidence that Leonardo's ideas on the arts and the status of painting were given at least one public airing. He testifies that the painter participated in a learned debate on 9 February 1498 in the Sforza castle.[380] Matching visual evidence of Leonardo's moves to bring his ideas and talents to public notice in the court is provided by the series of engraved knot designs labelled 'ACADEMIA LEONARDI VINCI', with variants (fig. 110), which do not necessarily provide testimony of the establishment of an actual academy for the visual arts but are best regarded as overt advertisements of his ambition to emulate the intellectual status of philosophers, as signalled in the Renaissance by the informal academy that Marsilio Ficino established under the Medici in Tuscany. But, the reality was that when Ludovico's regime came under heavy pressure Leonardo and Pacioli remained mere *stipendiati*. The bronze intended for the horse was used to make canon – probably of the conventional kind and not to Leonardo's design – and his regular salary fell into arrears. And on Ludovico's fall to the invading French armies in 1499, Leonardo and Luca were left to seek further employment in other cities.

The following years reveal a pattern of Leonardo's less than successful attempts to establish himself in the tough atmosphere of Republican Florence, and a series of court attachments, first to Cesare Borgia, largely in the capacity of a military engineer and map-maker, and subsequently to the French King Louis XII, now in charge of Milan. When Louis referred to Leonardo as 'our dear and good friend Leonardo da Vinci, our painter and engineer in ordinary', when he was insisting in 1507 that the Florentines release the painter from his obligations to paint the *Battle of Anghiari*, we gain a clear sense that the obtaining of Leonardo's services was an important prize, and a matter for high-level diplomacy, but we need to treat the phrase 'our dear and good friend' with some caution.[381] As we saw with Pisanello at the court of Naples, documents appointing artists as *familiares* to courts are effusive in a way that has more to do with elegant conventions than the actual relationship between artist and patron.

Paradoxically, it was within the conventionally stratified environments of large courts that artists seemed to have found the best opportunity to rise to high status rather than in the market-led environment of an urban centre like Florence, in which all makers of things needed to survive on the basis of remuneration for products. As Filarete had recognised, it was as a *stipendiato* of a court that the artist would most likely find time and space to research and 'fantasticare'. In the last three years of his career, Leonardo seems to have achieved something close to this position. Probably towards the end of 1516 Leonardo travelled to France to enter Francis I's service. As 'premier peinctre et ingenieur et architecte du Roy', Leonardo was housed in noble style in the manor house of Clos Lucé (fig. 72), adjacent to the royal castle at Amboise. He was expected to be active in his professional capacity, but he also served more generally as an ornament of the court and as something of a visitor attraction. On 10 October 1517, he was visited in his 'palace' (as he called it in his own note on 24 June 1518) by the Cardinal of Aragon and his entourage, where they admired the paintings and notebooks that Leonardo had taken with him to France.[382] The most vivid evidence that Leonardo had achieved much of his desired status comes in a report by the Florentine goldsmith and sculptor, Benvenuto Cellini, who followed Leonardo as one of Francis's artistic imports from Italy. Cellini tells us that

> King Francis, being enamoured to an extraordinary degree of Leonardo's great talents, took such pleasure in hearing him talk that he would only on a few days deprive himself of his company . . . I cannot resist repeating the words which I heard the King say about him, in the presence of the Cardinal of Ferrara and the Cardinal of Lorraine; he said that he did not believe that a man had ever been born who knew as much as Leonardo, not only in the spheres of painting, sculpture and architecture, but that he was also a very great philosopher.[383]

Cellini, like any ambitious sixteenth-century artist, had his reasons for bumping up Leonardo's status (and thus potentially his own), but even if we allow for a certain amount of gilding of the lily, we may reasonably conclude that the young apprentice in Verrocchio's workshop had travelled a long way.

MANTEGNA, 'GOD AMONGST PAINTERS'

The early career of Andrea Mantegna, the adopted son of Squarcione from whom he fought to gain legal separation, seems even less promising than Leonardo's for an aspiring artist-intellectual. At least Leonardo's father was a prominent notary. However, no painter was to establish a higher reputation than Mantegna in the fifteenth century and none was to be the subject of more admiring comments by writers of a humanist bent. Even before his arrival at the Gonzaga court in 1460, following three years of pressure from the marquis, Mantegna had been the subject of two laudatory poems. The first, an Italian composition by a certain Ulixes (probably Ulisse degli Aleotti who had composed two poems on Pisanello), makes its way through a horrible tangle of humanist allusions and unclear syntax :

When fortune and the well-disposed heavens
Released from its own nest into the salty waves
That divine spirit, in whom nature infused virtue
That conquers all others with the brush,
Of an angelic face under a veil,
That confounds every soul with stupor
And already crowned with those sacred fronds
That fear from Jove none of his arrows,
With industrious hand and *alto ingegno*
The image gathered in the conception
Formed into a painting proper, living and true.
Do not then hold me in disdain
If I wish by whatever affect
To make his image eternal on earth.[384]

The allusion to the salty waves appears to concern the legend of Venus's birth, while the motif of crowning with 'sacred fronds' apparently refers to the traditional laurel garland of the crowned poet. Whether the image painted by Mantegna was that of a nun – 'an angelic face under a veil' – as generally assumed, or depicted another veiled woman, divine or secular, is unclear in the absence of any surviving painting. That an elaborate tribute was intended is clearer than what Ulisse is actually trying to say.

The other poem, altogether more coherent in measured Latin, was written in 1458 by the Hungarian humanist, Janus Ponnonius, in praise of a double portrait of himself and his fellow scholar, Galeotti Marzio.[385] The eulogy involves a goodly selection of the stock humanist *topoi*: the inevitable comparison with Apelles; 'faces that live for centuries'; likenesses that 'want but a voice'; the total emulation of nature; and a well-deserved fame that 'spreads your name over all the world'. As 'god amongst painters', Mantegna surpasses the ancients in *ingenio* and *arte*. And, as to the portrait itself, 'a heap of Arabian incense is not of so great price'. Again the relevant painting appears to be lost, but it is good to know that at least one perceptive critic found Mantegna's style better adapted to portraiture than Ludovico Gonzaga thought. We have already quoted the Marquis's opinion, as expressed to the Duke of Milan, that 'Andrea is a good master in other things, but in portraits he could have more grace'.[386]

On moving to the Mantuan court, Mantegna established his credentials as a learned artist to such effect that he became a valued companion of humanist scholars. One of his closest friends was Felice Feliciano, who gave a revealing account of a play-acting expedition on and around Lake Garda in 1464 in company with Samuele da Tradate and Giovanni Antenoreo (perhaps Giovanni da Padova, the architect).[387] During their two days of travel they searched out

251

ancient remains, especially the kinds of inscriptions which were a strong mutual interest of Mantegna and the antiquarians. They recorded 'in the present note-books' such items as 'a most worthy memorial to Antonius Pius Germanicus' and 'a huge memorial to Marcus Aurelius'. Each participant assumed a Roman rank: Samuele was *imperator*; Mantegna and Giovanni were *consules* as *viri primarii*. Samuele was adorned with garlands of myrtle, periwinkle and ivy, and the boat was decorated with laurel and other 'noble leaves'. As the 'bright troop' went on their merry way, to musical accompaniment, they were acting out a historical *fantasia* in which past and present merged within the type of dream journey of which poets had written. In a characteristic fusion of ancient and modern, they ended the second day by rendering praises to the Blessed Virgin and her son, 'the most high thunderer', in gratitude for 'having illuminated our hearts to assemble together and opened our minds to seek and investigate such outstanding places, and caused us to see such worthy and different diverting things and antiquities'. The eccentric Feliciano also dedicated a sonnet to Mantegna and two collections of antique inscriptions, expressing the hope that 'you should become as learned as possible, and be a man of consummate knowledge in all worthy subjects'.[388]

In all, some fourteen relatively substantial humanist accounts of Mantegna or his works are known, including a prominent notice in Jacopo Sannazaro's much admired *Arcadia*, in which the prize for a shepherd's wrestling contest was a great wooden vessel on which Mantegna had painted a composition resembling Zeuxis's *Satyr Family*.[389] In our present context, not the least revealing of these accounts is that by Battista Fiera, who composed a dialogue on how the virtue of Justice might be represented – an *inventione* of the type that Filarete fantasticated.[390] Fiera tells how Momus, mischievous son of Night and Sleep, acting as the interlocutor, receives Mantegna's reports on his fact-finding journey around Rome to seek the opinions of philosophers on a suitable iconographical formula for Justice. The suggestions range erratically from a one-eyed figure holding scales, or adorned with many eyes, to Fiera's own idea that she should be covered by large ears. Discouragingly, a Carmelite theologian tells him that Justice could not be represented at all, since it resided only in God's supreme judgement on our death. In the face of such capriciousness, Mantegna portrays himself as a man of stoic resolution in his dedication to the making of perfect works, assuming the motto, *hic labor, hic lachrymae* ('this is my task, this my sorrow'). Fiera's picture is an overtly literary one, somewhat satirical in tone, and should not be taken as a literal report of the painter's views, but the framework within which it is cast – Mantegna's consultations with learned men and the display of his own philosophical virtue – would have only worked if it had some measure of credibility for its contemporary readers. A number of writers testify to Mantegna's ability to covey an image of virtue and courtesy, including Pietro Bembo, though there is enough independent documentation to suggest that the painter could be fiercely combative when slighted, and that his Gonzaga patrons knew that he required careful handling. In 1480 Federigo Gonzaga cautioned the Duchess of Milan that 'these excellent masters commonly have something fantastic about them [*hanno del fantasticho*]'.[391]

The most striking and sustained tribute to Andrea came from his fellow painter, Giovanni Santi of Urbino, Raphael's father, who seems to have harboured substantial if largely unrealised literary ambitions. In his *Rhyming Chronicle*, written in honour of Federigo da Montefeltro, Giovanni recorded that when the Duke was in Mantua he was much taken with Mantegna's surpassing artistry.[392]

> . . . He [Federigo] had admired with the greatest delight
> The marvellous painting and exalted art
> Of the *alto ingegno* of the noted Andrea Mantegna
> . . . Of all the parts of this art
> He possessed the full and clear body.
> More than any man in Italy or foreign part
>
> . . .
>
> One sees first of all he has in himself
> Great draftsmanship, which is the true foundation
> Of painting, then, second in him comes
> A glowing adornment of *inventione*
> Such that, if all *fantasia* were
> Dead and extinct, as I see and feel,
> They would be born again in him.
>   . . . He astonishes
> All who see and note his foreshortening,
> Which fools the eye and makes the art rejoice,
> Perspective, which brings in its train
> Arithmetic, also geometry,
> And great architecture turns to it.
> With the most *ingegno* possible in man
> He glows and shines, expressing great concepts
> So that I am left stupefied in my mind . . .

Giovanni does not fail to note the social implications of Mantegna's career, giving praise to the Gonzaga prince 'who advanced him to knightly rank because of his great painting'.

Such literary praise needs to be verified by the documented reality. We have already seen in chapter II that Mantegna was awarded a reasonably handsome monthly stipend of 15 ducats with provisions and the promise of other awards, though his sometimes testy correspondence indicates that regular payments were not always forthcoming. The additional rewards came to include grants of land of the kind that artists so valued, including a plot in Mantua near Alberti's church of S. Sebastiano, on which he built himself over a period of some years a fine palazzo, with a notable circular courtyard in an *all'antica* manner (fig. 111). The most substantial of the gifts consisted of some 120 acres granted to him by Marchese Francesco in 1492, perhaps directly in response to a typical petition from the artist for the payment of arrears on his salary. The decree granting the land, is prefaced by a notable piece of humanist puffery:

> For Hiero, king of Syracuse, the friendship of the great architect Archimedes was no mean illustration of his fame. Amid the great decisions of Alexander, he is above all glorious for not having wanted any other painter than Apelles, any other sculptor than Lysippus. Augustus derived glory and honour for

having shown so much favour to Vitruvius, the architect of Verona, whom he raised from a base condition by ennobling him. In these circumstances what rank could we accord to Andrea Mantegna, this man of consummate virtue, without dispute the most remarkable of all those who profess painting though the diversity of his talents [*ingenii*]? What rank should be accorded to him? We have thought long on this subject. For we know the benefits he has received from us and our ancestors, father and grandfather; we consider the remarkable works, so worthy of admiration, which he earlier painted in our chapel and in the room of our palace [figs. 24 and 103], and the Triumph of Caesar [fig. 25] which he is now painting with figures so full of life and animated that they give the impression not of a representation but of a living spectacle . . .[393]

In keeping with the tone of this encomium, Mantegna showed no less an eagerness for titles than for lucrative rewards. He was knighted by the Gonzaga, but seems to have been frustrated in his ambition to emulate his brother-in-law, Gentile Bellini, who had been made a count palatine by Emperor Frederick III in 1469. He was granted the right to the Gonzaga coat of arms, and adopted their high-flown motto, *Ab Olympo*, which adorned the doorways in the courtyard of his house and the grand funerary chapel he planned in Sant' Andrea. By the time of his death in 1506, after long years in the service of the Gonzaga, Mantegna had achieved a social and artistic rank in advance of that of any of his predecessors or contemporaries. But as a number of unhappy documents from his last years testify, his success did not insulate him from financial difficulties and personal problems with his health and his family. Perhaps he had overreached himself in his ambitions to set himself up as the prince of painters, living in the style of a minor noble. In any event, if posthumous fame is of any consolation to the dead, he may now be well satisfied with the way in which his efforts to cultivate renown have born fruit. Acclaimed by contemporaries as an *ingegno* endowed with high *fantasia*, and as a master of *inventione*, *prospettiva* and *arte*, he perfectly embodies the trends which we have been recording in this chapter – though we should perhaps end by cautioning ourselves that the kind of evidence we have been studying tends inevitably to illuminate those artists who were the exception rather than the rule.

111.   Courtyard of Andrea Mantegna's house, Mantua

VII   PRESENT PROSPECTS

THE PURPOSE OF this book has been to look at the evidence in contemporary
sources which may guide us in the viewing of Renaissance artefacts. We have
seen that the sources themselves are as much products of their culture as the
artefacts and similarly need to be interpreted within their functional contexts.
We have also maintained that what we define as a 'source' involves implicit or
explicit assumptions about what we think sheds evidence on the work's genesis
and more fundamentally about what we think are the essential attributes of a
'work of art'. Although these qualifications mean that we cannot simply take the
evidence as given in an unquestioned manner, a contemporary document clearly
has a status – a kind of authenticity – that any later source must necessarily lack.

Given such a status, there is a serious and logical case to be made for saying
that the proper and demonstrably valid job for the historian of art is to
concentrate upon the authentic relics in order to reconstruct the circumstances,
general and personal, that lead to a work coming into being – and for saying that
the ultimate power of art as 'art' is not susceptible to historical analysis, even if
it might be evoked by suggestive word-painting in the hands of a skilled writer.
In effect, this is to say, albeit in a relatively sophisticated way, that 'I know what
I like' – and that the history of images in its strictest historical sense involves
something else. In this sense, to talk of art history is to combine in a single name
two incommensurable kinds of mental activity, one aesthetic, personal and
elusive, and the other historical, objective and concrete. This nice divide, which
might conveniently circumscribe the task of the analytical researcher into the
documents and material survivals of art, is not, however, even sustainable in
terms of the contemporary sources at which we have been looking, and which
reflect in a multifaceted way a rich kaleidoscope of intersecting economic,
political, social, personal and artistic factors. The 'history' and the 'art' act as
reciprocating levers on all those involved, just as they do for the later art
historian, even if the conceptual frameworks for the functions of 'art' then and
now are very different. Thus, for example, even a contract of the most sober and
legalistic kind is underpinned by conceptions of the power of images and their
ability to convey meaning to all those involved in their generation and viewing.

Why, if the genuine documents of the period can be used to paint a richly
authentic though sometimes elusive picture, do we need to go outside the
framework of contemporary sources at all? Or, to put the question in a less

extreme form, are modes of interpretation which cannot be illustrated in Renaissance texts necessarily limited to the building of speculative models of what we may think art to have been in the period? Are we willing, in effect, to say retrospectively to protagonists in past cultures that we know more of what they were really doing than they did themselves? There are three main reasons, at which we have already hinted, why we need not feel constrained by the scope of contemporary sources.

The first, providing we assume that a reasonably representative group of sources has survived, is that the frameworks within which things were written down were limited to a set number of genres of literary production, and that each of these genres was itself limited in what it could say by its conventions and accepted terminology. There were, as we indicated when we looked at the generation of content, types of verbal transaction that were simply not recorded in writing. And we also need to allow for the likelihood that there were things of importance which could not be said because there was then no way of saying them.

The second is that the visual possesses an inherent potential to operate in fields where the verbal cannot go. The challenges this property poses to the verbal involve the signalling of those special realms of competence for the visual and arriving at verbal means of heightening the spectator's ability to operate in these realms. Much of the history of writing about art has engaged in a perpetual quest to narrow the gap between what the visual can do and what the verbal can suggest. Modern modes of writing have found new ways of bringing word and image closer together, without ever suggesting that the gap will ever completely close. Indeed, the gap may best be seen in qualitative rather than quantitative terms.

The third reason for moving beyond the primary sources involves what is called historical perspective. Historical perspective has some definite advantages, as well as manifest shortcomings. At its simplest, our temporal remove gives us a chance of seeing the wood for the trees in a way that no contemporary could. Part of the strength of our later perspective is that we can see more clearly where events were going, though this formulation carries the strong danger that we may fall into the trap of inevitability; that is to say seeing trends as inexorably leading to a particular end – and choosing to highlight those events which conform to the assumed trends. Thus we might be tempted to follow Vasari in defining the quattrocento as a kind of transitional age, necessarily leading to the triumph of the High Renaissance. I do not think it is right to talk of any artist and work of art as transitional in the sense that they belong purposefully to some kind of incomplete programme, and I am strongly resistant to the common formulation that such-and-such a work 'anticipates' a later one, whether by the same artist or by another. Each work belongs to its own context in the sense of the reality of its coming into existence at a particular moment. We may say that there were features which were drawn out and developed in later art, but this is as far as I would go.

If we accept, provisionally for the moment, that contemporary sources contain an incomplete expression of the making and viewing of artefacts in the period itself, and that we can usefully look back with historical hindsight, how might we amplify our modes of interpretation in a manner which is not arbitrarily tied to our present assumptions and values? I intend to work *towards* a way of answering this question – and this book has consistently been concerned with *ways* of answering rather than with prescribed answers – by looking at some of the widely diverse strategies adopted within the field of art history during its development as a historical discipline and within the modern industries which have grown up around art, including dealers, auctioneers, galleries, cultural tourism and specialist publishers. I will not be providing a historiographical review of writing on Renaissance Art, not even of the selected classics, like Pater, Burckhardt, Wölfflin, Venturi and Chastel. Rather I shall select a group of representative texts which show clearly the diverse ways in which our age has tried to fill in what seems to be missing from the kinds of sources we have encountered so far.

My strategy in selecting from this potentially enormous body of material is consciously personal, reflecting both the kind of notions to which I was first introduced, as I became conscious in the early 1960s as a student of science that there was such a thing as art history, and the kinds of approach of which I have subsequently become conscious as the subject has broadened its concerns. One advantage of this personal approach is that it enables the reader of this book to do in some measure what I have been saying we should do with the more authentic primary sources; that is to say aspiring to understand the text in terms of why it has come to assume its particular character. The selection does not aspire to be fully representative, nor do I intend it primarily to provide approved exemplars of art-historical writing – although some of the passages are exemplary of their kind. And I am well aware that any excerpted quotation taken outside its full context is bound to do violence to the author's arguments. However, I am confident that the texts give a good indication of the range of *types* of writing, from those most exclusively focused on the visual qualities of the objects to those which take imaginative leaps from artefact into the most ambitious realms of speculation about the nature of the human condition. I have also quoted from a range of sources not normally considered part of 'serious' art history, but which relate to the more popular aspects of the cultural business of 'Art'. I will explain in due course why such 'vulgar' sources have been used. Let me begin, for reasons both of personal chronology and of analytical solidity, with the approach which deals directly with analysis of the look of works of art.

Following inglorious efforts in natural sciences at Cambridge, and becoming engaged with art history under Michael Jaffé's tutelage, I became a postgraduate student in Renaissance studies at the Courtauld Institute of Art, mainly with John Shearman, where the emphasis was placed firmly on the stylistic assessment of sculpture, painting and the graphic arts to determine the visual power of the works, their attribution, their dating, their reconstruction (if necessary), and their place in the development of their author's career and of art in local and broader contexts. The key tool was a written analysis of style, nicely exemplified by the posthumously published lectures of Johannes Wilde, the Hungarian scholar who taught at the Institute between 1947 and 1958. Wilde is speaking about the final phase of Giovanni Bellini's career:

The most important fact concerning this last period of Bellini's career is that he evolved a real late style – a style which in a way was also up to date, that is to say was in step with the general development of Italian painting. This

258

applies to him alone of all the members of his generation. I shall try to illustrate this with a small selection of his late works.

The altarpiece of the *Baptism of Christ* in the Gothic Church of S. Corona at Vincenza [our fig. 30], was painted in the first years of the new century; it commemorates a pilgrimage to the Holy Land undertaken by one of the citizens of Vincenza. The central figure shows an attempt at classical *contrapposto* – it can profitably be compared with the somewhat timid nudes of Perugino, Bellini's contemporary in Central Italy, with their simple outlines. The action of S. John the Baptist has, like all the representations of movement by Bellini, something of that unreal duration which is known to us through slow-motion pictures. But these two figures, as well as the angels in the rich folds of their garments and the forms of the landscape, contribute to the building up of a very rich surface pattern, which was to become one of the main qualities of the new Venetian painting. Its elements are different colours of equal intensity, with no vacuum left between them. One cannot properly speak of zones of depth in this case; the landscape is not a measurable space in which the figures are placed, nor are the mountains pyramids and cones. Their flat forms are piled up, right to the line on which the semi-circle of the sky rests, forming a background full of colour, and yet its function is not entirely unlike the gold ground in Byzantine mosaics.[394]

Wilde is alert to questions of patronage, location and subject matter, yet the central function of art history is defined as the analysis of the visual qualities of the work within the developmental history of what we call 'Art'. This, for Wilde, is clearly what distinguishes art history as a teachable discipline from straight history, economic history, social history and so on. It is founded on the discipline of long and hard looking at as many works as possible in the original. There are clear signs of the impact of the kind of formalism which took its cue from modern abstraction and defined the act of picture-making as an autonomous business of arranging shapes and colours on canvas. Some contemporary art historians developed the technique of formal analysis to such a point that it became like an X-ray machine into which the paintings were fed in order to reveal the inner anatomy of their corporeal structure.

The machinery is witnessed in its most developed form in Sidney Freedberg's *Painting of the High Renaissance in Rome and Florence*, first published in 1961. Freedberg is discussing Leonardo's *Adoration of the Magi* as the founding image of High-Renaissance compositional principles:

The figures of the picture are disposed, around the central image of the Virgin, in an instantly sensible, containing geometric pattern. This pattern is composed of two main interlocking shapes: the broad-based triangle made between the Madonna and the foremost older men, and the semicircle that embraces all the rest. The semicircle is more explicit in its form than any earlier painting of the Renaissance, but it is startling to realize that the triangle of the composition, in its most clearly defined shape, is quite unprecedented in the history of painting. The triangle has the affect of an unshakable solidity of shape, but a solidity that contains and controls the implication of a movement: above its base its upper sides converge in equal and balancing directions on each other. The shape of the semicircle, oppositely, first implies movement, which then is contained by the disciplinary clarity and symmetry of the form . . . The two main motives of design play against each other, at once reinforcing their identity and demonstrating their community of basic kind and, as they interlock, the union between them is flexible and vibrant. The life of the design is of course not merely a function of this geometric framework but of the human images that it contains. Their vitality, literally inhabiting this energy of abstract shape, at once takes from and gives to it.[395]

This kind of formalism found its underpinning in Modernist theory, such as the doctrine of 'significant form' advocated by Roger Fry in *Vision and Design* (1928).

The system of formal analysis favoured by Freedberg was intended to establish an objective – even scientific – method of saying how a picture works. However, the machinery of analysis never became entirely detached from the cultivation of subjective visual skill – from the necessity of acquiring an 'eye' – which presupposes some kind of superior sensibility of a more-or-less innate kind. It is the 'eye' – Bernard Berenson's 'sixth sense' – which lies at the foundation of connoisseurship and which promises to provide the framework of attribution and dating without which the history of Renaissance art could hardly proceed. Typically, the exercise of the sensibility of the connoisseur is associated with writing, which itself aspires to some literary style. Kenneth Clark's 1939 monograph of Leonardo shows the system at work. Writing about Leonardo's work in Milan, Clark is faced with the problem that none of Leonardo's portraits are signed and dated, and indeed with the difficulty that we cannot be absolutely certain that any surviving portrait is actually by the master:

> Several portraits dating from this period have survived with ancient inscriptions to Leonardo, but their authenticity has always been open to doubt, chiefly on account of a prosaic quality which the amateur is reluctant to associate with him. Leonardo's drawings show that he could be prosaic, or rather objective, if occasion demanded, and these portraits need a liberal and patient examination.
>
> Most modern critics believe that the picture at Cracow, of a 'Lady with an Ermine', represents Cecilia Gallerani, and is Leonardo's original . . .
>
> The Cracow picture must date from the first years after Leonardo's arrival in Milan. Those parts which are well preserved are still in the clear colours of the Florentine *quattrocento* tradition. Parts of the picture are in bad condition. The whole background is new and the left side of the figure has been repainted. But certain parts are intact – the ermine, the lady's face, and her hand, all but the tips of the two lower fingers. These parts alone are sufficient evidence that the picture is by Leonardo. The face has lost a little subtlety through the repainted background sharpening the original outline, but the drawings of the eyes and nose still have all the beautiful simplification which we find in the early silverpoint drawings. Although the outline of the shoulder has been hardened, we can still recognise Leonardo's sense of form, which we find again, twenty years later, in a red chalk drawing for the 'Madonna with the Yarn Winder'. The hand shows an understanding of anatomical structure and a power of particularisation none of Leonardo's pupils possessed. But most convincing of all is the beast. The modelling of its

head is a miracle; we can feel the structure of the skull, the quality of the skin, the lie of the fur. No one but Leonardo could have conveyed its stoatish character, sleek, predatory, alert, yet with a kind of heraldic dignity. The serpentine pose of the ermine gives, in epigrammatic form, the motif of the whole composition and it is this movement, quite apart from the details, which distinguishes it from other portraits of this date attributed to Leonardo, such as the 'Belle Ferronnière' in the Louvre.[396]

The most characteristic vehicle for the exercise of such skills is the monograph, backed up by scholarly essays on works by particular artists and by the more general survey of artistic developments by period or place. The genre of the monograph, typically presented with a generous suite of high-quality illustrations and sometimes with a full catalogue of works, refuses to die, even at a time when its rationale has come under severe challenge. Shortly before his death in 1994, John Pope-Hennessy, the English art historian who spent most of his career in the museum profession, published his long-awaited book on Donatello. At the start, he lays out his aims:

> My intention, when I started working on this book, was to describe what is conventionally known as an artistic personality. But ineluctably, the artistic personality became an individual. With Donatello the relation between art and life is very close. . .
>
> This book is about one of the greatest artists who has ever lived. Artists are private people whose identities are hidden in their work, but it is possible, by looking closely at Donatello's sculptures, to establish some of the respects in which his mind and aspirations and the work that he produced differed from those of his contemporaries. His style was subject to constraints imposed not only by personal convictions, but by the social role his sculptures were expected to fulfil, by the intellectual climate in which they were produced, and by the velleity of the patrons by whom he was employed. Unless these can be hypothetically reconstructed (hypothetically, since they are matters on which there is little direct evidence) his achievement cannot be satisfactorily explained.[397]

Again, like Clark and Wilde, the role of historical context is acknowledged, but the centre of the endeavour is identified as being about art as the thing we know as 'Art', and indeed about the exposition of one of the canonical heroes of artistic innovation and of a personal style, who is seen as forging a level of human communication that somehow transcends time and place. The subsequent analyses in Pope-Hennesssy's monograph exemplify style analysis, connoisseur's word-painting and aesthetic appreciation of a very high order.

Broadly speaking, the kind of endeavour represented by Wilde, Clark and Pope-Hennessy has come to define what art history is publicly seen as being, above all in the minds of the increasing numbers who attend exhibitions and provide the market for the well-illustrated art book and the audience for the public lecture. It is an endeavour inseparable from the ideas of aesthetic pleasure and being a cultured person. None of the texts could be mistaken for writing from the Renaissance itself, and they work with words in relation to images in intricate ways that cannot be adequately paralleled in Renaissance sources. What status does this kind of writing have with respect to the primary texts? Are the authors simply being wise after the event? Are they basically reading back current preconceptions about how art works into a period during which such preconceptions were unthinkable and inappropriate?

That any historian's writing indelibly bears the marks of when and where it was written is self-evident. Freedberg's high formalism would be unthinkable without developments in twentieth-century abstraction. Clark's connoisseurship derives in a more-or-less direct chain of descent from the nineteenth-century tradition of 'art for art's sake', represented in Britain by Walter Pater, whose famous account of the *Mona Lisa* – 'beauty wrought out from within upon the flesh little cell by cell' and 'by what strange affinities has the dream and the person grown up thus apart and yet so closely together'- he quoted with open admiration.[398] And Pope-Hennessy's espousing of the monograph as a central genre of art history is locked into the system of values through which the nineteenth and twentieth centuries have defined the worth of art and the majesty of the great artist. But all of the authors attempt to make their critical framework adhere to greater or lesser degrees to the researched documentation of the artist and the artefacts. The notions embedded in their writings – the convictions that one of the merits of good art is that it exhibits formal composition of a high order, that it takes a special sensibility to detect the very best, and that artists are the heroes of the business – can all be seen *in nuce* in the Renaissance texts we have studied.

In itself such ancestry does no more than demonstrate that we have in some way inherited the values of the period, for good or for ill, and that we have taken them to extremes, either by exaggeration or by concentrating on one set of values rather than another. However, there is a positive side to this ancestry, in that we can reasonably aspire to refine our tools to operate increasingly in keeping with values recognisable in the period itself. It seems to me that one of the historian's central tools is the exposure of mechanisms by which selective or skewed modes of viewing have progressively developed, not in such a way as to make the past carry the blame for attitudes that we may now be inclined to question, but so as to enrich our appreciation of the necessarily partial dialogues of successive ages, including our own, with the past. Thus Freedberg's high formalism looks at Renaissance art through specially attuned eyes, and involves a particular skewing of Renaissance values, but it is not wholly arbitrary in relation to these values. Explaining his stance, or even questioning its claims, is not to dismiss its potential power in pointing to one facet of Renaissance art.

Running parallel to the traditions of style analysis, and standing in opposition to formalism, was the content-based study known as iconography, by which the narrative, allegorical and symbolic meanings of the works might be subject to exegesis, much as if the artefact is a text. It is identified particularly with a method of reading cultural signs pioneered during the period from the late 1880s to the 1920s by Aby Warburg, of the Hamburg banking family, and embodied in his remarkable library which transferred to London in 1933. Iconographical analysis relies upon a cultural foundation in the great European traditions of humanist education in the ancient and Christian classics, as realised in the context of a growing interest in 'symbolic forms' in the first quarter of the twentieth century. The interest not only fed upon the latest concepts of human psychology and on the artistic tendencies collectively known as Symbolism, but also drew upon the increasing study of cultures outside the Western 'mainstream'. Just as an African mask must be understood in terms of its ritual function and its expression of deep beliefs, so a Botticelli painting must be seen as locked into the most profound nexus of contemporary cultural systems. Iconography has often been regarded (and indeed exploited) as an elaborate method for the unravelling of the symbolic content of works of art. The historian operates as a kind of cultural detective, becoming an expert in the reading of the visual and textual clues to tell us what meanings lie behind appearances. However, for the founders of the discipline, and for its highest practitioners, the technical exposition of symbolic content was a means towards the higher end of revealing cultural mentalities. For Warburg, the historian is required to explore 'the uncanny vaults where we found the transformers which transmute the innermost stirrings of the human soul into lasting forms', even if 'the solution to the enigma of the human mind' ultimately lay elsewhere – in 'a new formulation of the eternal question as to why fate consigns any creative mind to the realm of perpetual unrest where it is left to him to choose whether to form his personality in the Inferno, Purgatorio or Paradiso'.[399] Comparably, Erwin Panofsky defined the final aspiration of iconographical analysis as the revelation of the 'essential tendencies of the human mind'.[400]

High practitioners of the iconographer's art, like Panofsky and Edgar Wind, brought dazzling arrays of learning to bear upon works by the great Renaissance masters. During the course of a fifteen-page exegesis of the *Primavera*, Wind works towards how we might understand the role of Mercury:

> The crux of any interpretation of the *Primavera* is to explain the part played by Mercury. By tradition he is 'the leader of the Graces'; but while that would seem to explain his place next to them, it is hard to reconcile with his disengaged – not to say indifferent – attitude. Mercury is also the 'guide of souls' (*Psychopompos*) whom he conducts to the Beyond; but although he is here represented as nostalgic and bears on his cloak a symbol suggestive of death (inverted flames), there is nothing funereal about this youth, who seems too relaxed, in his quiet contrapposto, to suggest a ghost-like journey. His detachment and poise also seem to contradict an important passage in Virgil that might otherwise explain his action. 'With his staff', we read in the *Aeneid*, 'he drives the wind and skims the turbid clouds.'. . .
>
> Not only was Mercury the shrewdest and swiftest of the gods, the god of eloquence, the skimmer of clouds, the psychopompos, the leader of the Graces, the mediator between mortals and gods bridging the distance between earth and heaven; to humanists Mercury was above all the 'ingenious' god of the probing intellect, sacred to grammarians and metaphysicians, the patron of lettered enquiry and interpretation to which he had leant his very name (*ermeneia*), the revealer of secret or 'Hermetic' knowledge, of which his magical staff became a symbol. In a word, Hermes was the divine *mystagogue*.
>
> Because 'he calls the mind back to heavenly things through the power of reason', Ficino assigned to him the first place in the 'converting triad which leads back to the upper world': *trinitas conversoria sive ad supera reductoria in qua primum Mercurius tenet gradum animos per rationem ad sublimia revocans.*

The removal of the clouds would indeed be a proper occupation for a god who presides over the reasoning soul . . .

Even so, one may doubt whether Mercury's concern with clouds is to be understood in the *Primavera* in a negative sense, as if he were purging the mind or the air of an obstruction. For that his gaze is too contemplative, his bearing too poetical. He plays with the clouds rather as a Platonic hierophant, touching them but lightly because they are beneficent veils through which the splendour of transcendent truth may reach the beholder without destroying him . . . The transcendent secret is kept hidden, yet made to transpire through the disguise. 'Nec mysteria quae non occulta,' wrote Pico in the *Heptaplus*; or, in his Commentary on Benivieni's *Amore*: 'Divine things must be concealed under enigmatic veils and poetic dissimulation.' As *interpres secretorum* (Boccaccio's phrase for Mercury), Mercury looks upward and touches the clouds. 'Summus animae ad Deum ascendtis gradus caligo dicitur atque lumen.' The highest wisdom is to know that the divine light resides in clouds.[401]

Discovering Panofsky and Wind in succession to my adherence to Fry, I did not fail to be dazzled – not least because the distant Latin of my obstinate schooldays stood at a remote distance from such an awesome mastery of the classics. But, as will have been apparent in chapter V, doubts about the relevance of such mastery subsequently crowded in. As I came to know more about the proclivities of actual artists, so it was harder to see them as the Renaissance predecessors of Panofsky's and Wind's ways of thinking – not that the great iconographers were overtly claiming that this was the case. The problem with such iconography was, and is, to know exactly where it is located as a mode of explanation in relation to the more practical businesses of the genesis and reading of Renaissance artefacts.

The great merit of iconographical study, compared to formal analysis, is that it centres more concentratedly upon the embedding of art in its highest cultural context through contemporary and earlier texts. I became aware that the main alternative way by which we might embed artefacts in the values of their environment was through the social history of art. The driving force behind such histories has been a predominantly Marxist conception of class structures and cultural products. A representative text is provided by Arnold Hauser's *The Social History of Art* (1951).

[Giotto] was really the master of simple, sober, straightforward middle-class art, the classical quality of which sprang from the ordering and synthesising of experience, from the rationalization and simplification of reality, not from idealism abstracted from reality . . . His conception of art is rooted in a still comparatively unpretentious middle-class world, although it is a world already firmly grounded on capitalistic foundations. His activity falls into the period of economic prosperity between the formation of the political guilds and the bankruptcy of the Bardi and Peruzzi, into that first great period of middle-class culture, in which the finest buildings of medieval Florence, the churches of S. Maria Novella and S. Croce, the Palazzo Vecchio and the Cathedral with the Campanile, were created. Giotto's art is austere and objective, like the character of those who commissioned his works, men who wished to be prosperous and to exercise authority, but who attached not too much importance to outward show and lavish expenditure.[402]

A similar equation between style and the taste of a specific class is made when Hauser talks about the High Renaissance:

The ruling class will look to art, above all, as the symbol of the calm and stability it wished to attain in life. For if the High Renaissance develops artistic composition in the form of the symmetry and correspondence of the separate parts, and forces reality into the pattern of a triangle or circle, then that does not imply merely the solution of a formal problem, but also the expression of a stable outlook on life and on the desire to perpetuate the state of affairs which corresponds to this outlook. It places the norm above personal freedom in art and considers the norm here, as in life itself, to be the most certain way to perfection.[403]

With respect to the notions of 'art', its evolution, and the formal analysis of artistic style, Hauser shares much with the formalist Freedberg. But for Hauser the triangles and circles speak of social imperatives. The difficulty is not so much that the equations seem implausible at an obvious level of artistic expression, but that a detailed study of artistic patronage in the Renaissance undermines the dependability of the equations at a social level. Whether or not the Bardi and the Peruzzi, the leading banking families in Florence who provided Giotto with important patronage, can really be seen as promulgating 'middle-class' taste, there is no doubt that Giotto's art found an eager market in the courts, not least in Naples, where Giotto was well rewarded for his services. We have also seen that members of the same social stratum, like Palla Strozzi and Felice Brancacci in Florence, might exhibit quite different preferences when commissioning, say, paintings for their family chapel, with Palla preferring the lavish naturalism of Gentile da Fabriano to the more austere Masaccio. And, if we consider the equations from the standpoint of artists' careers, the pioneers of what is called the High Renaissance, Leonardo and Michelangelo, forged the new style in such diverse environments as Medicean and Republican Florence, Sforza Milan and Papal Rome. If Leonardo's *Adoration*, commissioned by monks as the result of a saddle-maker's bequest in Florence, and his *Last Supper*, painted on the command of the Duke of Milan, are both seminal works in the founding of the High Renaissance, it is difficult to see how their formal structures can be considered as direct expressions of patrons who occupied such different social positions.

I have referred to the formal, iconographical and social methods to which I was introduced as 'alternatives', but in reality they only function as strict alternatives in a doctrinaire framework in which one mode expresses the absolute belief of the person who espouses it – that art is about formal arrangement, that art reveals the deepest motives of the human mind, that art is part of a capitalist production within the class system . . . or whatever. Generally, art history has taken over and mingled together something of the various types of analysis without the substance of the underlying beliefs. My own teaching and writing, not atypically, has tried to build outwards from the documentation to deal with the content, the patronage and the visual power of the works within a set of assumptions about art. It is this kind of vaguely agnostic compound that has come to make up the art history to which the interested public is generally exposed. Let me give two examples, one originating from the tourist industry in the 1960s, when I first visited Florence, and the other directed at the press at the opening of the Leonardo exhibition at the Hayward Gallery in 1989. The first comes from a ponderously translated guidebook which I bought in 1965:

> Masaccio was the great innovator of the fifteenth century who brought art to a human conception, adherent, that is to say, to a real vision, in which situations and sentiments acquire a dramatic value and the figures appear powerfully blocked in their monumentality. In his brief life, as he died when he was hardly twenty-eight (1401-28), Tommaso Guidi called Masaccio brought with his expressive power a real revolution in the field of art and influenced in this way successive generations. The actual period has also taken from this great maestro its lesson. The decoration of the chapel of the Brancacci family was entrusted to Masolino da Panicale, who is presumed to be Masaccio's teacher, but who has some Gothic in him and paints figures that are full of grace with a pleasant and narrative taste. Called to paint in Hungary, the work was continued by Masaccio who gave us his masterpiece with the 'Payment of the Tribute'. As Masaccio left unfinished his cycle of frescoes, his work was completed by Filippino Lippi who tried not to be less great than his predecessor, but without a doubt, he remained in a field of narrative grace and of documentation with numerous portraits of personages his contemporaries who were found in the frescoes.[404]

And the Leonardo press release:

> Painter, sculptor, architect, engineer, stage designer, musician, writer, student of the physical sciences, mathematician, geologist, anatomist, natural historian . . . Despite the range of his activities, it was Leonardo's work as an artist that shaped his career. Yet our knowledge of him as an artist is incomplete – a few finished masterpieces, a tragically deteriorated mural, a series of unrealised projects and a number of lost works. The surviving drawings and manuscripts represent the core of his legacy. The diversity of this legacy is the key to the exhibition, which opens with an outline of his career through drawings associated with artistic projects. In later sections, the conventional classification of his work is ignored. The drawings are presented in such a way that the characteristic patterns of his creativity emerge, revealing the magnificent coherence of his vision of man in nature and his sense of the inter-relatedness of all things wthin the context of the laws which govern the world . . .
>
> None of Leonardo's ambitions lay closer to the heart of his vision of man's ability to create a 'second world of nature' than his desire to achieve man-powered flight. He wanted to create a mechanical organism which would work in perfect concord with the physical laws of the universe to overcome the very elements themselves. He was also keenly aware that the legendary status would be accorded to the first modern inventor who was successful in teaching man to fly. Leonardo had no doubt as to where the solution lay. If he could arrive at a full understanding of how birds sustain themselves in the

air, particularly mighty birds such as the eagle, he would be able to apply these principle to manned flight.[405]

The publicity officers involved in the industry of promotion which is needed to support such major exhibitions try to anticipate what will capture media attention. The making of the flying machine had the advantage that it was a 'story'. It was picked up, amongst others, by the *Evening Standard*:

> Leonardo da Vinci's 500-year-old-dream of manpowered flight will take spectacular shape at his first major exhibition in Britain for 30 years. The showing will feature the greatest range of the artists's drawings ever assembled – 88 of them lent by the Queen from her unrivalled collection at Windsor castle. But the exhibition will be dominated by a replica of one of Leonardo's flying machines with a 36ft wing span . . . The flying machine, designed to flap its wings . . . is being built of materials available to Leonardo in the 15th century, such as beechwood, iron, brass, hemp and leather. "This thing weighs as much as a grand piano", explained Mr. Wink [responsible for recreating the flying machine]. "I worked out that it would take 30 horse power to make the wings flap fast enough, and then it would probably fall apart".[406]

The underlying assumption behind such publicly oriented literature, and more generally behind the kinds of organisation which generate them – the galleries and museums, the tourist authorities, and the industries of cultural education – is that the great culture of the past provides uplifting human experiences. It is one of the ways through which a civilised person expresses his or her cultivation. Huge industries of cultural travel and institutions for the display of art have grown up in this climate. The great works still *in situ* have come under siege. The Brancacci Chapel, following its restoration, is now

112.   The *Assunta* by Titian in the Frari on a Sunday

entered via paying turnstiles and a room packed with guides, slides, postcards, videos and so on, in such a way that it takes a positive act of will to remind ourselves that it was once a family chapel opening off a Carmelite church. The great Titians in the Frari in Venice have become objects of artistic devotion for cultural pilgrims. On those occasions when the high altar beneath the *Assunta* is actually used for the saying of the Mass, the visitors lurk in disgruntled groups behind the shut iron railings at the centre of the Renaissance screen, wondering when the service will finish (fig. 112). Even when viewed in its original setting, the 'authentic' experience of such a work is excluded by present circumstance and by the field of shaping assumptions we bring to the act of viewing.

Matching the transformation of churches into galleries of art, has been the construction of galleries as temples of aesthetic devotion. In the case of the Sainsbury Wing of the National Gallery in London, designed by Robert Venturi and Denise Scott-Brown and opened in 1991, the displays have responded to the increasing emphasis in art history upon the envisaging of works in their physical contexts by the establishing of a generally Renaissance and somewhat church-like interior (fig. 113). The display of some altarpieces above shallow grey boxes make a kind of generic reference to the original altar. Thus the paintings by Piero della Francesca are housed in a 'chapel' devoted to his art, with the *Baptism* displayed in the altarpiece mode – though in a very different kind of frame from its original setting (fig. 114). If the visitor prepares for his or her exploration of the galleries devoted to Renaissance art by using the computerised access in the Micro Gallery, located in a room off the grand staircase, it is easy to find such a painting via various routes, including through the name of the artist and through the category of 'Altarpieces' (fig. 115). The main system of classifying paintings

113.   Robert Venturi and Denise Scott Brown, View of the main axis with Cima's *Incredulity of St Thomas*, London, National Gallery

114. Room 66 with Piero's *Baptism*, London, National Gallery

115. *Altarpieces*, print-out from the Micro Gallery, London, National Gallery

Altarpieces

Altarpieces provided a pictorial addition to the furnishings of an altar, which would also include a crucifix, candles and saint's relics. The earliest altarpieces date from the 12th century and developed from the altar front or retable

Altarpieces could be painted and/or sculpted, and varied from the very small-scale with a single figure, to a very large, multi-panelled, complex structure.

Altarpieces were single-sided, if the altar was set against the wall, or they could be double-sided if the altar was free-standing and it was possible to celebrate the *Mass before either side.

Polyptychs

Small-scale Altarpieces and Dipcychs

Single Panel Altarpieces

Central Panels

Side Panels and Wings

Predellas

Pinnacles and Pilasters

in the Micro Gallery is based on four broad categories in the introductory index: '*Artists*'; '*General Reference*' (by key terms and subjects such as 'Cassone', 'Charles I', 'Chastity', and 'Copper'); '*Picture Types*' (initially by 'Still Life, Portraits, Religious Imagery, Views, Stories and Allegories, and Everyday Life', and subsequently by subdivisions of these 6 categories); and '*Historical Atlas*' – grouped into the major art centres, such as Florence or Paris.

The categories in the Micro Gallery belong to the same conceptual framework as those that have determined how the Piero is shown. Thus the picture is in an art gallery, in a wing devoted to the Renaissance, adjacent to works of similar date, in company with other paintings by the great master, Piero della Francesca, and set up approximately in terms of the type of picture it was in its original setting. How we see the painting, and what we notice in it, are deeply affected by what kind of thing we consider it to be. In spite of the visual reference to it as an altarpiece and the category in the Micro Gallery, there is little doubt that the majority of visitors still predominantly regard it as 'a Piero della Francesca' – which, again, can be related authentically to a Renaissance motive, namely a growing embryonic sense of the worth of the artefact in terms of the esteem of its individual maker. A brief survey has been revealing in this respect. A minority of inquirers exploited the 'Historical Atlas', while 93 per cent of users availed themselves of the 'Artists' facility, much in line with the emphasis upon individual artistic personality in the culture of which the Sainsbury Wing is part. However, the relatively high use of 'Picture Types', at 74 per cent, does suggest that the increasing emphasis on the functions of types of pictures in scholarly and even in popular presentations of art history has exercised some influence on the expectation of the kind of visitors who use the Micro Gallery.[407]

What kind of thing we think a work of art is conditions the demands we make on it, and these demands in turn affect not only display but also conservation. If our emphasis is on the unique qualities of a work by a great master, our efforts will be directed towards the restoration of those aspects which are believed to exemplify those qualities. Recent emphasis, increasingly insistent in the last half of the twentieth century, has been that the aim of restoration is to show the 'real', the 'authentic' survival, stripped of all later accretions, to reveal the 'original' effect, much as musical compositions are now played on period instruments. The confidence that we can indeed discern and recover what is truly original from later additions is fuelled by the battery of scientific techniques of analysis which have been developed, including pigment analysis, microscopic paint sections and examination by non-visible emissions, most notably infra-red and ultraviolet light and X-rays. My intention here is not to explain the techniques in themselves but to note that the aspiration to recover the 'original' is underpinned not only by a faith that we can now define what is original in absolutely objective terms but also that the scientific tenor of the exercise of modern conservation makes our choices superior to those of earlier ages. In as much as we do possess powerful new tools which tell us much about the physical composition of Renaissance artefacts, we are in a superior position, but our choices are no less founded upon sets of aesthetic assumptions than those of earlier restorers and their audiences.

The rendering of the *Last Supper* such that all the very extensive areas of paint loss are laid bare (fig. 116) would have appeared barbaric to the spectators who

116. Leonardo da Vinci, *St Thaddeus and St Simon*, during restoration

117.   The Refectory of S. Maria delle Grazie, Milan, in 1900

visited the refectory around 1900, when it was set up as a veritable academy of art, with copies on easels and hanging from the walls (fig. 117). Retouchings by successive generations of restorers had been largely devoted to the recovery of something like the original pictorial effect of the picture as a vivid narrative – or what they considered to be such an effect. Current campaigns of restoration, most especially the great public events of the cleaning of the *Last Supper* (fig. 118) and the Michelangelo frescoes in the Sistine Chapel, play towards the revealing of vivid details under strong spot-lighting and close-up photography, and towards a brightness of impact which speaks of an age intolerant of poorly illuminated spaces and the patina of time. Above all they play to the revealing of the 'true Leonardo', in keeping with our conception of the artist as cultural hero (fig. 119).

This conception of the great artist as provider of a great human experience manifests itself not only in the 'higher' end of elite culture but also in the more 'vulgar' ends of mass tourism and the proliferation of popular artefacts that bowdlerise the 'original'. An object like a jigsaw puzzle (fig. 120) of the *Last Supper* (actually based on an engraving rather than the deteriorated painting) may seem very removed from the dedicated professionalism and extreme discrimination of the conservator, and from the sober researches of the academic historian, but the programmes of conservation and research are ineluctably as much part of the same system of cultural values as the jigsaw. These values are responsible for the demands that we make on pictures. Without demands there would be no imperative to conserve artefacts of past ages, no passion, and, in the final analysis, no finance for conservation and research. Our demands are not necessarily wrong, and we have seen that they do reflect values apparent in the

118.   The *Last Supper* under restoration

119. *Leonardo and Pupils* outside the Banca Commerciale Italiana, Milan

120. *'Last Supper'* jigsaw

period itself, but they are as selective and partial as those of other post-Renaissance eras. Leonardo took immense care over the details of light, shade, form and colour in his paintings, and modern techniques can reveal such details in a literally new light. However, generally speaking, an artist who ran a Renaissance studio, as Leonardo certainly did, is likely to have found the idea of other hands intervening to make his picture whole and entire as a narrative less unsettling than its transformation into a series of authentic fragments.

The great public restorations, in which the act of conservation becomes a spectator sport, with resulting television programmes, videos, CD-ROMs, slides, books and postcards, are locked into the system of cultural resources which has increasingly involved sponsorship as an integral part of the funding of projects large and small. The Renaissance wing at the National Gallery in London was financed by John and Lisa Sainsbury, whose fortune was acquired through supermarkets. The *Last Supper* restoration was initially sponsored by Olivetti, while Nippon TV of Japan struck a financial deal with the Vatican, which gave them both prestige and a stranglehold over reproduction rights for Michelangelo's frescoes. For a corporate sponsor to be associated with great art brings cultural prestige, no less than it did to earlier patrons of the kind we have studied and to the later collectors of Renaissance art, whose appetites were met by such dealers as Joseph Duveen and by associated art historians, most notably Bernard Berenson. In 1992, an exhibition centred upon Leonardo's *Madonna of the Yarnwinder* at the National Gallery of Scotland, received financial support from the Italian drinks company, Martini. The announcement in *Sponsorship News* (fig. 121), the magazine devoted to stories of sponsors' activities, reflects some of the motives of the act of corporate patronage – no less than the correspondence associated with the original patron of the picture reflected some of his motives:

121. *Sponsorship News,* cover, vol. XI, no. 4, April 1992

David Rutherford, Director of External Affairs – Martini & Rossi UK, comments: 'Martini, as an Italian company, is delighted and honoured to be sponsoring this intriguing and magnificent Leonardo da Vinci exhibition at the National Gallery of Scotland in May. This coincides with the launch, in Scotland, of our new quality spumante Martini Brut. We are all confident that the exhibition will be a great success.'

Timothy Clifford, Director of the National Galleries of Scotland, welcomed the involvement of Martini Brut: 'We thank Martini for their generous support, and wish them well with the launch of Martini Brut. We look forward to raising our glasses in celebration at the opening of the exhibition'.[408]

I deliberately said '*some*' of the motives. Although it is easy to explain what has happened in terms of Martini's interest in a prestigious way of supporting the launch of a new Italian product in Britain and of the necessity for underfunded galleries across the world to court wealthy sponsors, the reality of the motivations are a good deal more complex. A whole series of intersecting personal tastes, enthusiasms, contacts, friendships, power relations and decision-making processes are involved, ranging in a seamless manner from the overtly self-interested to the altruistic. Like the original genesis and early uses of the artefacts, their subsequent exploitation is located in a richly human nexus of action and reaction, of conscious and unconscious values, which we oversimplify at our peril.

Inseparable from the concept of the cultural value of art is its designation as a form of cultural capital, translatable into actual financial worth. Again, this form of value has been seen *in nuce* in the period itself, though our sense of the value of the cultural product that we call art has radically outstripped that of most other kinds of material possessions. The recent history of the only Leonardo codex in private hands gives a good idea of the flavour of the kind of cultural competition which has driven prices to such huge extremes.

In 1980 money was urgently needed to maintain the estates of the Earl of Leicester, and it was decided to realise the financial value of the codex which had been in the family's hands since 1717. It was determined that it should be sold at auction to maximise its price. The story of its 'capture' is recounted in the co-written autobiography of the petroleum mogul, Armand Hammer:

> I sat quietly in the front row [in Christie's auction house]. . . . Only I knew my reason to be at the sale: I intended to purchase the Codex. As I told the press later, 'Not even Mrs. Hammer knew why we were there.' When the gavel fell on the final bid, I had won the Codex. With the Christie's commission included, I had spent nearly six million dollars to get what is now not only the last Leonardo manuscript in private hands, but the only one in the Western hemisphere.

Hammer's subsequent dismembering of the codex, its mounting as separate sheets, and its many exhibitions in various prestigious locations around the world – as a kind of travelling *Wunderkammer* – speak of at least one of his prominent motivations:

> The Codex has now travelled the world . . . Renamed the Codex Hammer by [Carlo] Pedretti, Leonardo's work was scheduled for exhibition in Florence in 1982. I took the Codex on my plane, flying to Pisa, since it was the only nearby airport large enough to accommodate Oxy One. When I left the plane, I was followed by security guards armed with sawed-off shotguns and Uzi machine guns: they carried the Codex to Italian soil after an absence of 265 years . . .
>
> Four hundred thousand people viewed the Codex in Florence. I was made an honorary citizen of Vinci, and I was honored by the presence of the President of Italy, Sandro Pertini, at the exhibition's opening ceremony. He also presented me with Italy's highest honor to a foreigner, the order of the grand Officer to the Merit of the Republic. I promised to return the Codex for exhibition and study no less than every five years. . .

But even here, with such apparently blatant transparency of motive, we should not necessarily assume that self-advertising magnificence was all that drove Hammer as a collector:

> The Armand Hammer collections were created for the public – to share the love of art and to promote international peace and goodwill. Those are the true motives – but I have to admit that there is another one as well.
>
> Collecting pictures is also one of the best games in the world. It combines the satisfactions of detailed scholarship with the thrill of the hunt and the excitement of business. It is an ideal recreation for me. The art world is a jungle, echoing to the calls of vicious jealousies and ruthless combat between dealers and collectors; but I have been walking in the jungles of business all

my life, and fighting tooth and nail for pictures comes as a form of relaxation for me.[409]

Clearly, a contemporary source such as this, is a potential field for critical analysis no less than the historical sources we have been examining. And some of Hammer's motives can be recognised in the more agressive Renaissance collectors of antiquities.

Subsequently Hammer passed the codex with his art collection to the gallery he endowed in California, as an adjunct to the office block of Occidental Petroleum. However, the financial aspect of the endowment proved insufficient for the needs of the gallery after the donor's death, and it was decided once again that the manuscript was the most appropriate and valuable item to sell in order to secure the future of the remainder of the collection. Auctioned in a rerun at Christie's in 1994, the manuscript was purchased for $32,000,000 by the computer multi-millionaire, Bill Gates, who redesignated it as the Codex Leicester – the name it had assumed during the period of more than two-and-a-half centuries in which it had been in the possession of the Earls of Leicester – rather than retaining its short-lived name as the Codex Hammer or renaming it as the Codex Gates. The renaming by Hammer and Gates's reversion to the older designation signal that the two collectors' motives are not entirely comparable, and it is perhaps not too difficult to see why a modern master of computer software should be drawn to a mind like Leonardo's in a different way from Armand Hammer.

In the light of such huge monetary dealings, it is ironically appropriate that the monumental Leonardo of stone stands beside the Banca Commerciale Italiana in Milan (fig. 119), while facing La Scala opera house – a cultural god located between potent symbols of culture and finance.

The complex art world into which students were introduced in the 1960s and the subsequent extension of many of the trends – record prices, institutional ambitions, cultural prestige, blockbuster exhibitions, commercial pressures on public bodies, sponsorship, publicly paraded connoisseurship, the spread of art history as a discipline, the broadening of 'art appreciation' into wider realms of society, and the great underpinning notions of 'Art' and the 'Artist' – can be seen as related in a more-or-less continuous line of succession from the Renaissance. This is hardly surprising, given that many of the great societal notions which dominated cultural thinking in Western countries in their period of world domination arose in the late Middle Ages and Renaissance. I am thinking of such notions as progress, civilisation, culture, science, religion, technology, capital, deficit finance, systems of mass governance and the state. Art is not so much a simple product of the attitudes and social forces within these conceptual fields but is an active participant in the complex and kaleidoscopic dialogues which have appeared in many different guises over the course of some six centuries. Clearly it is only in the context of a wholesale challenge to the system of cultural values that it becomes possible to speak as something other than an insider – that is to say with the advantage of a historical perspective which looks at things from an entirely different angle from that possible within the system.

Leaving aside the question as to whether even the most apparently radical challenge can actually avoid being a product of the system itself, we can witness the establishing of a series of 'outsider' stances that purport to define what the production and power of art was and is really about. The two dominant challenges have come from Marxist political theory and from Freudian psychology, both of which have posited fundamental motivations hidden behind the screen of declared intentions which covers the surface of conventional narrative history. For the Marxist, art works are a symptom – albeit a particularly potent one – of the huge shaping forces in society, and, in terms of the Renaissance, of the economic impetuses which have forged the class structures of modern society. For the Freudian – to continue in a vein of heavy generalisation – art taps deep into our psyche, expressing our inner fears, dreams and sexuality in a way that may be apparently masked by the ostensible subject matter and functions of art in a particular period. In Renaissance studies, the classic Marxist examples available to English-speaking students in the 1960s were the social analyses by Arnold Hauser (as we have already noted) and Frederick Antal's classic *Florentine Painting and its Social Background*, originally published in 1947-8.[410] The *locus classicus* for the placing of an artist on the psychoanalyst's couch was Freud's analysis of Leonardo's childhood in *Ein Kindheitserinnerung des Leonardo da Vinci*, which appeared in 1910.[411] Aspects of both doctrines penetrated the practice of art history, and found some specialised adherents, but I think it is true to say that neither became central to mainstream practice in art history on an international basis.

More recently, new kinds of Marxist-oriented and psychologically-directed approaches have impinged widely on the discipline, as they have upon other studies in the humanities. Broadly speaking, the new approaches – or perhaps we might better say revived and extended approaches under the banners of a new critical vocabulary – aim to tunnel under the publicly declared intentions of the kinds of historical witnesses we have been quoting. The main tendencies are the semiotic study of signification identified with Ferdinand de Saussure, the structuralism inspired most particularly by Claude Levi-Strauss, the social and philosophical methods identified with Michel Foucault and Jacques Derrida, theories of the psychology of seeing pioneered by Jacques Lacan, and the revisionist histories generated by feminism. Diverse though the tendencies are, they share in common the conviction that cultural history should aspire to reveal the real, hidden forces concealed behind the immediate evidence, behind not only the picture but also behind all the conscious and unconscious actions and values which brought it into being and (in some styles of analysis) the motivations of those involved in its reception. It is not my intention here to review these approaches in their own rights, or to outline a critical history of their often diluted and muddled impact on art history. Rather, I am concerned to define how the *type* of strategy that they represent stands in relation to the kind of functional treatment of contemporary documents with which I have been concerned in this book. For this purpose, I am deliberately taking two texts of an 'extreme' kind in the Freudian tradition – that is to say operating with the underlying belief systems fully in place – before looking at an example of the way in which such approaches tend to be integrated within the more catholic embrace characteristic of academic art history.

The first does not specifically address the Renaissance, but exemplifies the kind of grand, overarching, post-Freudian theory that can be taken into any period, since it assumes a fundamentally common structure of psychological motivation which finds expression in various ways across temporal and geographical boundaries. It is drawn from an essay on collecting by the French philosopher and cultural sociologist, Jean Baudrillard:

> If it is true that, in terms of object choices, perversion manifests itself classically in the form of fetishism, we can hardly overlook the fact that, throughout the system, the passion for, and possession of, an object are conditioned by comparable purposes and modalities, and can indeed be seen as what I would call a *discreet variety of sexual perversion*. Indeed, just as possession is coloured by the discontinuity of the series (be it real or virtual) and by the targeting of just one privileged term, so sexual perversion consists of the inability to grasp the partner, the supposed object of desire, as that singular totality we call a person. Instead it is only able to operate discontinuously, reducing the partner to an abstract set made up of various erotic parts of its anatomy, and then exercising a projective fixation on a single item. Whereupon a given woman stops being a woman and becomes no more than a vagina, a couple of breasts, a belly, a pair of thighs, a voice, a face – according to preference. Henceforth she is reduced to a set whose separate signifying elements are one by one ticked off by desire, and whose true signified is no longer the beloved, but the subject himself. For it is the subject, the epitome of narcissistic self-engrossment, who collects and eroticizes his own being, evading the amorous embrace to create a close dialogue with himself. . .
>
> Whatever the orientation of a collection, it will always embody an irreducible element of independence from the world. It is because he feels himself alienated or lost within an alternative discourse that is for him entirely amenable in so far as he is the one who dictates its signifiers – the ultimate signified being, in the final analysis, none other than himself . . . Indeed we are bound to ask: can objects ever institute themselves as a viable language? Can they ever be fashioned into a discourse oriented other than towards oneself?[412]

It would not be too hard to envisage a treatment of Medicean collecting predicated upon such preconceptions – drawing in elements of portraiture, the collecting of maps, the portrayal of the nude female body, and so on. My worries as a historian, confronted with such a treatment, do not only concern its rightness or wrongness – there are plentiful examples of efficacious histories founded on premises which I cannot accept – but also involve my growing conviction that there seems to be no way of demonstrating whether it is right or wrong. Its level of generality means that it does nothing to explain individual or collective acts and styles of collecting in specific cultural contexts. It becomes a 'so what?' kind of history – when it is considered as *history* and not as collective psychoanalysis. The same problem arises, to my mind, when alternative explanations, such as the dominance of power or gender relations, are driven like cultural bulldozers across the complex and sensitive landscape of human motivations. Indeed, I believe in general that for any human activity, such as collecting, to be sustainable at a high level of priority, the motivations must be polyvalent and continuously adaptable for both groups and individuals within general frameworks of constraint.

The second text, or rather two passages from the same source, is drawn from an essay by Julia Kristeva, feminist literary critic and psychoanalyst:

Freud could maintain that Leonardo's 'artistic personality' was formed, first, by the precocious seduction he was supposed to have experienced at the hands of his mother (the vampire tail of his dreams would represent the tongue of his mother, passionately kissing the illegitimate child); second, by a double motherhood (taken from his mother, Leonardo was raised in his father's family by his stepmother, who had no children of her own); and finally, by the impressive authority of an office-holding father. The father finally triumphed over the drawing power of the mother, which determined the young man's interest in art, and near the end of his life, Leonardo turned toward the sciences. Thus, we have a typical configuration of a homosexual structure. Persuaded by precocious seduction and double motherhood of the existence of a maternal phallus, the painter never stopped looking for fetish equivalents in the bodies of young people, in his friendships with them, in his miserly worship of objects and money, and in his avoidance of all contact with and access to the feminine body. His was a forbidden mother because she was the primordial seducer, the limit of an archaic, infantile jouissance that must never be reproduced. She established the child's diffident narcissism and cult of the masculine body which he ceaselessly painted, even when a mother figures at the centre of the painting. Take for example Leonardo's Virgins: *Madonna with the Carnation* and *Virgin and Child with St Anne.* There we find the enigmatic smile, identical with that of the *Mona Lisa,* herself furtively masculine; with naive tenderness, face and torso turn toward the male infant, who remains the real focus of pictorial space and narrative interest. The maternal figure is completely absorbed with her baby; it is he that makes her exist. 'Baby is my goal, and I know it all' – such is the slogan of the mother as master. But when Narcissus is thus sheltered and dominated, he can become the privileged explorer of secondary repression. He goes in quest of fantasies to ensure the group's cohesion; he reveals the phallic influence operating over everyone's imaginary . . .

And on Bellini:

Anna's last will, dated November 25, 1471, does not list him among the children heirs, Nicolosia and Gentile. So it seems that Anna Rinversi did not recognise herself as Giovanni's mother, giving credence to speculations concerning an illegitimate birth or obscure marriage . . .

Anna does not appear to have replaced the 'real' mother, as the honorable Leonardo's wife [*sic*] replaced Leonardo's real mother. Anna knew nothing of the painter of Madonnas. But even if we do remain incredulous in the face of biographical lack and commentators' perplexity, let us also behold the distance, if not hostility, separating the bodies of infant and mother in his paintings. Maternal space is there, nevertheless – fascinating, attracting and puzzling. But we have no direct access to it. As if there were a maternal *function* that, unlike the mother's solicitude in Leonardo's paintings toward the baby-object of all desire, was merely ineffable jouissance, beyond discourse, beyond narrative, beyond psychology, beyond lived experience and biography – in short beyond figuration. The faces of his Madonnas are turned away, intent on something else that draws their gaze to the side, up above, or nowhere in particular, but it never centres it in the baby. Even though the hands clasp the child and bodies sometime hug each other, the mother is only partially present (hands and torso), because, from the neck up, the maternal body not covered by draperies – head, face, and eyes – flees the painting, is gripped by something other than its object. And the painter as baby can never reach this elsewhere, this inaccessible peace colored with melancholy, neither through the portrayed corporeal contact, nor by the distribution of colored blocks outlining corporeal volumes.[413]

It would not be hard for the historian of Renaissance art to dismiss Kristeva's analysis in the face of its historical inaccuracies: the tail in Leonardo's dream, made famous by Freud, was not that of a vampire; Leonardo did not just turn to science at the end of his life; and so on. But to do so would be to miss the point of what she is trying to do, since it would be possible to adapt even the right facts to her story. The problem for the historian is more profound than the odd factual error. It involves the way in which the mode of explanation necessarily negates the documented imperatives and demonstrable traditions for the generation of Renaissance Madonnas. For example, the 'double mother' of the Madonna-and-St Anne compositions did not arise because of Leonardo's psychological imperatives. The Madonna and Child with St Anne was an established type of picture, and the choice of this subject resided in patronal concerns. In Florence, St Anne was a specifically republican saint, since it was on her day in 26 July 1343 that the tyrannical Duke of Athens had been expelled from the city. For another of Leonardo's patrons, Louis XII, the Virgin's mother would have been appropriate as the name saint of his wife, Anne of Britttany. In the case of Bellini, the painter and his brother were both working in close juxtaposition to the formal tradition of Byzantine Madonnas, in which stiffer decorums persisted longer than in Florence.

In the face of such criticism, we might attempt to rescue the Freudian mode by saying in a more constrained way that the manner in which the individual artist depicts his subjects within the parameters of the historically possible is still psychologically determined. However, a broader knowledge of, say, Venetian Madonnas of the period would show that they generally obey similar rules of decorum – even when the painters were blamelessly legitimate. Leonardo does indeed show the intimacy of mother and child with a new intensity, but this is part of his overarching reform of the way in which symbolic meaning and narrative content are related in all the genres of religious art which he tackled. Kristeva's *reading* – and it is a 'reading' of a predominantly literary and anecdotal kind – has a genuine power, but it is the power of a reading from her particular stance at a particular moment which is unconcerned with the intentionalist and functional explanations which gave a specifically historical dimension to the highly partial stances of the art historians we encountered earlier in this chapter.

As happens almost invariably within the mainstream of a cultural activity, the inevitable pursuit of careers in institutional contexts – academic organisations, art galleries, the publishing industry, and so on – favours a compromised absorption of the 'extreme' views as part of a broadly catholic practice. The way that this absorption occurs can be seen conveniently in one text, from a recent book on schemes of political decoration, written collaboratively by an art historian, Randolf Starn, and a historian, Loren Partridge. The two selected passages concern Mantegna's *Camera degli Sposi* (figs 24 and 103), which we have already encountered on a number of occasions:

> Of course no amount of critical alchemy can turn Mantegna's pictures into flesh and blood. The absence of actual bodies is, after all, a condition of their representation as images, and the closest we are likely to come to a real corporeal presence in the Camera Picta are the physical traces of the artist's instruments. Yet it is the very elusiveness of the corporeal as such that enables us to recover the political side of the Renaissance equation of politics and art in the human form. Since Marcel Mauss's pioneering essay on 'the techniques of the body,' anthropologists and sociologists have shown how conceptions of the body are socially formed (Mary Douglas) or dramatically performed in the encounters of everyday life (Erving Goffman). Patterns of control exercised on the body by different political systems have been closely analysed (Norbert Elias, Michel Foucault), and we have a magisterial history of the intervention of the fictive body of the state to figure the continuity of the political order beyond the transitory body of any particular ruler (Ernst Kantorowicz). It may well be that some physical expressions – for example, of fear, pain and pleasure – are transcultural. The bodies painted in the Camera Picta are bound to be at least twice removed from nature in any case; once because they are already representations, then again because bodies are sites where social and political ideologies and interests are defined and contested.[414] . . . .
>
> What we can see clearly enough is the semiotics of courtly dependency and subordination played out in these figures. Legs are parted, tilted or turned, arms are cocked, all in service and on elegant display. The show of sinuous leg and tunics of brocaded cloth of gold with white trim exhibit the red, silver-white, and gold-yellow heraldic colors of the Gonzaga. From top to bottom the higher figures upstage those beneath them; the more elaborate costumes and privileged attributes – a dagger worn at the side, gloves carried in the hands – are reserved to the figures at the top of the stairs.[415]
>
> Alberti advised painters to include in their pictures figures that seem to look at the viewer, as if drawing attention to the scene, offering a knowing commentary, and inviting a response. Mantegna's trio could be cited as an illustration, but we can follow their glances beyond the text along a familiar trajectory of Renaissance courtly culture that leads art to aestheticize epistemology and both art and epistemology to practice politics. . .
>
> Of course if we knew for certain that the painted glances on Mantegna's ceiling were playing courtly games, they would not be playing to perfection. The courtier's finesse sweeps clear meaning beneath the threshold of easy recognition; the absence of transparent intelligibility arouses the desire to be let in on some inside knowledge that we imagine is being withheld from us as outsiders. Whether or not there is actually a secret to fathom hardly matters. The glance will check our credentials to share an invitation to intimacy in any case, and those who do not know or cannot guess how to pass the test will be excluded from the privileges they have been incited to desire.

That the looks (in all senses) of what seem to be female figures produce such effects genders these courtly arts of seeing and being seen. . .

The offer was safe enough – a painted invitation, teasingly enigmatic, 'merely' feminine, and like other courtly games, a play on the creative licence that the court wished to see in itself . . . In the Camera Picta the feminine realm of the oculus is still sustained by the walls beneath, and the figures we see above seem to have no more obvious function than preening to invite their own obliging submission to whatever the viewer wishes to make of them.[416]

It is difficult to imagine a more succinct demonstration of the ingenious eclecticism of recent art-historical practice, founded upon a belief that other disciplines have 'shown' certain truths about the way that society uses 'sign systems' and that these findings have to be accommodated by art historians. The explicit name-dropping, including that of the almost inevitable Foucault, and the implicit references to other recent theorists of culture, testifies to the way that the authors and their intended audience belong to a certain kind of academic club, as does the succession of loaded terms – of apparently normal or more-or-less normal words that signal an approved framework in academic cultural theory. I am thinking of such terms as 'bodies' (human figures advertently and inadvertently shaped to convey social meaning); 'control' (social and political repression); 'to figure' (to give visual form to a socio-political concept); 'site' (any visual location for the embodiment of social meaning); 'ideology' (any belief system other than the authors' own); 'to contest' (to dispute ideological dominance over sites for meaning and action); 'to privilege' (to show covert bias towards things or ideas characteristic of a particular ideology); 'glance' (the psychological direction of looking according to gender relations and power); 'to aestheticize' (to conceal a social value in 'art' by hiding it within the conventions of beauty); 'to gender' (to render any representation in such a way that it carries sexual bias and reflects inequalities of power); and 'power' (the dominant value behind all apparently objective and disinterested activities). Also characteristic is the final indeterminacy of the 'reading' on the grounds that a picture is an 'ambiguous text' which cannot be interpreted according to authorial intention and will be read differently by each spectator.

The problem with such writing is not that it fails to draw effective attention to the way that various visual features of the work carry meaning. And its claims as 'New Art History' to operate in fields which lie outside the scope of earlier techniques have some justification. Rather, the immediately obvious problem is that the language carries so much theoretical baggage and requires so thorough an initiation into various kinds of interpretative theory that it is difficult to disentangle the historical rationale of the arguments from the imperatives of the academic industry of art history. The layering of analyses of meaning suffers from the same difficulties that beset the most complex forms of earlier iconography, namely that the status of the arguments are unclear because their different kinds of adherence to contemporary evidence about the making and reading of pictures is nowhere made systematically apparent. It is difficult to know how and to what extent the various kinds of 'reading' can hope to achieve more than a contemporary 'reading in' of implicit narratives and covert motives according to the authors' personal and institutional concerns in the present.

Compared to the grand cultural eclecticism of Starn and Partridge, or the great schemes of Marxist and Freudian analysis, the present book has aspired to undertake a limited task in looking at what we might do in a preliminary way with the primary sources available to us. It is my belief that our embarking on this limited job is a prerequisite for a responsible level of historical humility in the face of the legacies of the past. This book has been motivated by a belief that it is possible to create an open dialogue between primary sources from the period itself and the cultural values of our own society in such a way that we can claim to be working systematically towards a reconstruction of how artefacts functioned then, in relation to how they might work for us now. The dialogue is intended to be clear in its premises and to permit an open scrutiny of the mechanisms through which it is constructed. The analyses have been founded on the determining of the functions of the sources and, through these, the discerning of the functions of the artefacts themselves. These functions rely upon a complex blend of conscious intentions and frameworks of assumptions of a less conscious kind, and can be seen to be refracted in various ways through the lenses of differently equipped observers. I believe that the kinds of meaning which emerge from a functional study bear a non-arbitrary relationship to the values of the period itself and exhibit a robustness which makes them accessible to us in greater or lesser measure. This accessibility should not be seen in terms of a total reconstruction of the 'authentic' experience, which is forever elusive. We can never inhabit the same mental worlds as contemporary observers, and the works themselves have inevitably undergone physical transformations to lesser or greater degrees. Rather, we can aspire to help the period voices speak to us in their own accents of things which are humanly communicable across the centuries and across cultures. The help provided by the historian is necessarily active and selective, but I believe that it can be offered in a sufficiently sensitive and diplomatic manner to avoid gross distortions of the voices that have come down to us.

I would, therefore, define what the historian can best aim to accomplish in attempting to fill the 'gap' between the narration of contemporary sources and the visual experience as the provision of judicious guidance in enabling period voices and eyes to enter into a responsive interchange with present observers, in such a way that the values of the past and present remain constantly open to re-definition. There is no set formula for the evaluation of the help that is being provided, and the choice of what kind of help we offer is ultimately a matter of intuition. However, it is my conviction that a campaign of naturalisation in the sources that lie closest to the business of the work's generation will inform our intuitions in such a way that our preconceptions can be progressively refined to provide sympathetic frameworks for the interpretation of the products of other cultures. This book has been a plea for such naturalisation. The only means to this end are sustained looking and listening. If the Renaissance voices we have heard in this book have helped us to see better what lies behind the pictures, and to stand in front of them with eyes better attuned to the kinds of object we are looking at, a modest but worthwhile goal will have been achieved.

And, in the final analysis, the experience of the artefacts of past and present cultures provides for me a sense of joy of a specifically visual kind. Such visual experience touches areas of conscious and unconscious thought in which words are able to act only as very coarse filters.

1 Pliny (2), XXXV, 85.

2 Leonardo, BN 2038 27r (R 587); Urb. 50v-1r (McM 276); Kemp and Walker (43), p. 203.

3 Pliny (2), XXXV, 85-6.

4 Alberti (22 and 24), § 62, pp. 104-5 and p. 95.

5 Pliny (2), XXXV, 96.

6 Pliny (2), XXXV, 87-8.

7 1492 Inventory (30), fol. 13v, pp. 25-6 and fol. 18r, p. 36.

8 1492 Inventory (30), fol. 39r, p. 73 and fol. 15v, p. 29.

9 1498 Inventory in Shearman (79), pp. 17-18 and p. 25, no. 38.

10 Shell and Sironi (46), pp. 96-7.

11 John VIII, 3-11

12 1498 Inventory; Shearman (79), pp. 17-19 and p. 25, no. 39.

13 Hope (204), p. 125.

14 Virgil, *Aeneid*, VIII, 803, xi.

15 Filarete (28), fol. 148v, pp. 254-5.

16 Chastel (65), p. 217.

17 Lucian (1), 2-5.

18 Gilbert (12), pp. 111-12 and pp. 84-7.

19 Leonardo, BN 2038 19v; Urb. 9r (McM 30); Kemp and Walker (43), p. 33.

20 Leonardo, Urb. 13r (McM 33); Kemp and Walker (43), p. 28.

21 Pico della Mirandola, *Opera omnia*, Basle, 1601, vol. 1, p. 248.

22 L. Martin, "'Eskimo Words for Snow': A Case Study in the Genesis and Decay of an Anthropological Example", *American Anthropologist*, LXXXVIII, pp. 418-22 and G. Pullam, "The Great Eskimo Vocabulary Hoax", *Natural Language and Linguistic Theory*, VII, 1989, pp. 275-81.

23 G. P. Badger, *Arabic Lexicon*, London, 1881, 12 vols.

24 Barbaro (60), p. 6.

25 Schofield, Shell, and Sironi (37), pp. 515-16, doc. 8.

26 Schofield, Shell, and Sironi (37), p. 543.

27 Kristeller (184), pp. 515-16, doc. 8.

28 Golzio (55), pp. 7-8.

29 Lightbown (161), pp. 1-2.

30 Gilbert (12), pp. 50-1 and pp. 25-6.

31 Borgo (192), pp. 12-19 and pp. 478-80, doc. 1; pp. 548-51, doc. 24; pp. 556-64, doc. 27.

32 Goldthwaite (104), p. 292.

33 Glasser (67), p. 225 and app. D, doc. IV (pp. 325-7), for Giacomo del Maino's frame; pp. 244-5 and app. D., doc. VI (pp. 345-6), for Leonardo's complaints; pp. 256-9 and app. D, docs. X-XV (pp. 364-90), for the litigation and settlement.

34 Chastel (65), p. 122.

35 See the range of documents cited by O'Malley (68).

36 Chambers (14), p. 191, doc. 116 and Thomas (36), pp. 118, 127, 130, 211.

37 Gilbert (12), p.147-8 and pp. 125-6.

38 T. French, *York Minster. The Great East Window*, Oxford, 1995, app. 3, pp. 153-4.

39 Humfrey (157), p. 137.

40 Chambers (14), pp. 42-4, doc. 22.

41 Chambers (14), pp. 56-7, doc. 28.

42 Eisler (201), p. 33.

43 Eisler (198), p. 67; Chambers (14), pp. 78-80, docs. 39-40.

44 H. Rupprich, *Dürers schriftlicher Nachanlass*, 3 vols., Berlin, 1956-69, vol. 1, p. 109; Warnke (72), p. 72.

45 Chambers (14), pp. 81-2, doc. 42.

46 Chambers (14), pp. 83-4, doc. 43.

47 Gilbert (12), pp. 69-70 and pp. 41-2.

48 Glasser (67), pp. 162-9 and app. D., docs. III-V (pp. 318-43); Sironi (47), docs. IV-XIV.

49 Butterfield (171) pp. 225-8.

50 Kemp and Walker (43), p. 268; Beltrami (39), pp. 7-8, doc. 16.

51 Passavant (168), pp. 31-2 and 229 and Passavant (169), p. 55; Kemp (170).

52 Chambers (14), pp. 11-13, docs. 5-6; pp. 69-70, doc. 34; pp. 183-5, docs. 110-11; pp. 188-9, doc. 113; p. 191, doc. 116; B. Santi ed., *Neri di Bicci, Le Ricordanze 1453-1475*, Pisa, 1976; Thomas (36), *passim.*

53 Callmann (167), p. 77, no. 47 and p. 79, no. 113.

54 Gombrich (77), p. 12 and pp. 26-7, app. I; Gilbert (12), p. 212 and pp. 190-1.

55 Vasari (57), vol. 6, pp. 22-3.

56 Chambers (14), pp. 19-21, doc. 11.

57 Poggi (48), vol. 3, p. 8, no. DXCIV; Ramsden (49), vol. 1, pp. 148-9, no. 157.

58 Beltrami (39), pp. 44, doc. 76.

59 Gilbert (12), pp. 34-5 and pp. 9-10.

60 Santi (38); Gilbert (12), pp. 119-24 and pp. 95-100.

61 Gilbert (12), p. 119 and pp. 95-6.

62 Woods-Marsden (151), pp. 34, 36 and 191-2, note 25.

63 G. Previtalli, *Giotto e la sua bottega*, Milan, 1967, p. 151; Warnke (72), p. 8, note 26.

64 Woods-Marsden (152), p. 36 and p. 194, note 45 quoting A. Venturi, *Le vite dei piu eccelenti pittori, scultori ed architettori scritte da Giorgio Vasari*, Florence, 1890, vol. 1, p. 58.

65 Kristeller (184), pp. 516-17, doc. 11.

66 Beltrami (39), pp. 58-9, doc. 95 and pp. 129-31, doc. 204.

67 Alberti (22 and 24), § 25, pp. 60-1 and p. 60.

68 Kristeller (182), pp. 551-3, doc. 115; Chastel (65), p. 12.

69 Kristeller (184), pp. 536-7, doc. 75.

70 Gilbert (12), p. 152 and pp. 130-1.

71 Kristeller (181), p. 541, doc. 86; Gilbert (12), p. 154 and p. 133.

72 Lightbown (184), p. 121 and pp. 462-3, no. 78.

73 Kristeller (184), p. 561, doc. 140 and pp. 561-2, doc. 141; Lightbown (185), pp. 177-80.

74 Beltrami (39), p. 25, doc. 36.

75 Geiger (177), pp. 45, 47-8, 186-7; Scharf (178), p. 88, doc. VIII; Chambers (14), pp. 22-3, doc. 13.

76 Kristeller (184), pp. 545, doc. 101.

77 Chambers (14), p. 134, doc. 73.

78 Beltrami (39), p. 90, doc. 142.

79 Humfrey (157), p. 216.

80 Humfrey (157), p. 248.

81 Vasari (57), vol. 4, pp. 191-2.

82 Paoletti (149), appendix of documents.

83 Gilbert (12), p. 50 and pp. 25-6.

84 Passavant (168), pp. 227-8; Passavant (169), pp. 24-5, 177-9

85 Pope-Hennessy (141), p. 302.

86 de Tolnay (193), vol. 4, 32-73 (1513 project: pp. 32-3; 1516 project: pp. 44-8; 1525-6 project: pp. 49-52; 1532 project: pp. 53-8; 1542 project: pp. 70-3); Poggi (48), vol, 3, pp. 7-11; Ramsden (49), vol. 1, pp. 148-9, no. 157; Pope-Hennessy (143), pp. 311-24.

87 Chambers (14), pp. 91-6, docs. 46-9.

88 Pliny (2), XXXXV.

89 Pliny (2), XXXXV, 65-6.

90 Leonardo, Urb. 5v (McM 31); Kemp and Walker (43), p. 34.

91 Horace, *Ars poetica*, 9-10.

92 Leonardo, BN 2038 19r (R 653), Urb. 8r (McM 30); Kemp and Walker (43), p. 20; citing Plutarch, *De gloria Atheniensium*, III, 346f-7c.

93 Durandus (9), p. x.

94 Theophilus (11), pp. xv, xxxi-v.

95 Leonardo, BN 2038 19v (R 654), Urb 8v (McM 30); Kemp and Walker (43), p. 46.

96 Cennini (18).

97 Cennini (18), p. 4 and p 1.

98 Cennini (18), p. 3 and p. 1.

99 Durandus (9), p. 3.

100 Cennini (18), pp. 4-5 and p. 2.

101 N. Gramacciani, "Cennino e il suo 'Trattato della pittura'", *Res Republica Litterarum*, X, 1987, pp. 143-51.

102 Cennini (18), p. 27 and p. 15.

103 Cennini (18), p. 28 and p. 15.

104 Cennini (18), p. 97 and p. 57.

105 Cennini (18), p. 96 and p. 57.

106 Cennini (18), p. 35 and pp. 20-1.

107 Cennini (18), pp. 197-8 and p. 123.

108 Alberti (22 and 24), p. 3 and pp. 1-2.

109 Leon Battista Alberti, *Della famiglia*, trs. by R. N. Watkins as *The Family in Renaissance Florence*, Columbia, South Carolina, 1969, pp. 133-4.

110 Alberti (22 and 24), pp. 32-3 and pp. 34-5.

111 Leon Battista Alberti, *Profugiorum ab aerumna*, in Grayson (23), vol. 2, pp. 107-83.

112 Manetti (20), pp. 42-6.

113 Alberti (22 and 24), pp. 32-3 and p. 35.

114 Alberti (22 and 24), § 35, pp. 72-3 and p. 71.

115 Alberti (22 and 24), §§ 37 and 42, pp. 74-5, 82-3 and pp. 73, 78.

116 Alberti (22 and 24), § 52, pp. 94-5 and p. 87.

117 Alberti (22 and 24), § 53, pp. 96-8 and p. 88.

118 Alberti (22 and 24), § 62, pp. 104-5 and p. 95.

119 Alberti (22 and 24), pp. 34-5 and p. 36.

120 Piero della Francesca (27).

121 Daly-Davies (180).

122 Piero della Francesca (27), p. 63.

123 Piero della Francesca (27), pp. 64-5.

124 Piero della Francesca (27), pp. 76-7.

125 Barbaro (60), p. 61

126 Ghiberti (25).

127 Ghiberti (25), p. 5.

128 Ghiberti (25), p. 4.

129 Ghiberti (25), p. 45; Gilbert (12), p. 109 and pp. 83-4.

130 Ghiberti (25), pp. 37-9; Gilbert (12), pp. 104-5 and pp. 78-9.

131 Ghiberti (25), pp. 40-1; Gilbert (12), p. 107 and pp. 80-1.

132 Ghiberti (25), pp. 48-9; Gilbert (12), p. 111 and p. 86.

133 Baxandall (61), p. 19.

134 Bergdolt (26).

135 Bergdolt (26), p. 26.

136 Leonardo, Trattato (42).

137 Leonardo, Codice atlantico f. 360 (100 4r).

138 Leonardo, BL 1r; Kemp and Walker (43), p. 1.

139 Leonardo, BN 2038 20v; Urb. 4v-5r (McM6); Kemp and Walker (43), p. 13.

140 Leonardo, BN 2038 22v (R23); Urb. 160v (McM 427); Kemp and Walker (43), p. 16.

141 Leonardo, BN 2038 19v; Urb. 9r (McM 30); Kemp and Walker (43), p. 33.

142 Farago (44).

143 Leonardo, Urb. 14v-15r (McM 28); Kemp and Walker (43), pp. 24, 26.

144 Leonardo, CA 3r (R 50); Kemp and Walker (43), p. 52.

145 Leonardo, CA 203 (ra 543r) (R13); Kemp and Walker (43), p. 49.

146 Leonardo, Winsdor 12665v (R608); Kemp and Walker (43), p. 236.

147 Ruda (166), pp. 515-18; Chambers (14), p. 195, doc. 119.

148 Banker (34), p. 648.

149 Chambers (14), pp. 193-4, doc. 118.

150 Chambers (14), pp. 11-13, doc. 5, pp. 69-70, doc. 34, pp. 183-4, doc. 110; B. Santi ed., *Neri di Bicci, Le Ricordanze 1453-1475*, Pisa, 1976; Thomas (36).

151 Humfrey (157), pp. 154-5.

152 Humfrey (157), pp. 151-7.

153 B. Berenson, *Lorenzo Lotto*, London, 1956, p. 31.

154 Gilbert (12), pp. 146-7 and pp. 124-5.

155 Scharf (178), p. 95, doc. XVII and pp. 97-100, doc. XXII.

156 Kemp and Humfrey (145), p. 18.

157 Chambers (14), pp. 42-4, doc. 22.

158 Gilbert (12), pp. 31-2 and pp. 7-8.

159 Goldthwaite (105), pp. 317-350.

160 Warnke (72), p. 33.

161 Strupp (156), pp. 7-32.

162 Pope-Hennessy (143), pp. 256-7.

163 Butterfield (171), pp. 228, 233.

164 Pope-Hennessy (143), pp. 262-3.

165 Wackernagel (64), p. 239, note 31.

166 Gilbert (12), pp. 176-8 and pp. 148-52.

167 Theophilus (11), p. 79.

168 Gombrich (76), pp. 38-9.

169 Vespasiano (32), pp. 218-19.

170 1494 Inventory (30), p. 1.

171 Cegia (31).

172 1492 Inventory (30), fol. 6r, p. 11.

173 1492 Inventory (30), fol. 6r, p. 12 and fol. 13v, p. 26.

174 1492 Inventory (30), fol. 6v, p. 12.

175 1492 Inventory (30), fol. 8r, p. 16.

176 1492 Inventory (30), fol. 8v, p. 16.

177 1492 Inventory (30), pp. 54, 88-98.

178 1492 Inventory (30), pp. 128-9.

179 1492 Inventory (30), p. 27.

180 1492 Inventory (30), pp. 28-34.

181 1492 Inventory (30), p. 22.

182 1492 Inventory (30), pp. 124-5.

183 1492 Inventory (30), pp. 236-45.

184 1492 Inventory (30), pp. 34-43.

185 Filarete (28), fol. 187r, p. 320.

186 1492 Inventory (30), p. 34.

187 1492 Inventory (30), p. 36.

188 1492 Inventory (30), p. 36.

189 1492 Inventory (30), pp. 44, 47-50.

190 1492 Inventory (30), p. 53.

191 Fusco and Corti (83).

192 Vespasiano (32), p. 399.

193 Bergdolt (26), pp. 32-4.

194 Bober and Rubenstein (74), p. 123.

195 1492 Inventory (30), p. 39.

196 Kristeller (184), pp. 581-2, doc. 183.

197 Kristeller (184), p. 577, doc. 174; Gilbert (12), p. 38 and p. 14.

198 J. M. Fletcher, 'Isabella d'Este, Patron and Collector', in *Splendours of the Gonzaga* (150), pp. 51-2, and p. 168, no. 118.

199 A. Radcliffe, 'Antico and the Mantuan Bronze', in *Splendours of the Gonzaga* (150), pp. 47-8.

200 Gilbert (12), pp. 191-2 and pp. 167-8.

201 Filarete (28), fol. 187r, p. 320.

202 Gilbert (12), pp. 192-3 and p. 169.

203 Rucellai (33).

204 Rucellai (33), pp. 24-6.

205 Rucellai (33), pp. 20-3.

206 Rucellai (33), pp. 23-4.

207 Rucellai (33), p. 55.

208 Rucellai (33), pp. 60-1.

209 Rucellai (33), p. 61.

210 Rucellai (33), pp. 68-9.

211 Rucellai (33), pp. 28-34.

212 Rucellai (33), pp. 120-2.

213 Gilbert (12), pp. 158-9 and pp. 136-7.

214 Vasari (57), vol. 2, p. 122.

215 Baxandall (62), pp. 117-18.

216 C. Frey, *Il libro di Antonio Billi*, Berlin, 1892, pp. 73-5.

217 Alberti (22 and 24), § 49, pp. 92-3 and p. 85.

218 Filarete (28), fol. 187r, p. 320.

219 Gilbert (12), p. 34 and pp. 9-10.

220 Eisler (201), p. 33.

221 Warnke (72), p. 44.

222 Woods-Marsden (151), pp. 36-7.

223 Kristeller (181), pp. 516-17, doc. 11 and p. 542, doc. 88; Lightbown (185), pp. 119-21.

224 Pope-Hennessy (144), pp. 308-10. pl. 12 and pp. 310-11, pl. 14; Poggi (48), vol. 3, pp. 7-9; Ramsden (49), vol. 1, pp. 148-9, no. 157.

225 de Tolnay (193), vol. 2, p. 241, doc. 70.

226 Chambers (14), pp. 25-9, doc. 15.

227 Scharf (178), pp. 90-1, doc. XI; Wackernagel (64), p. 340, note 7; Chambers (14), pp. 24-5, doc. 14.

228 Butterfield (171), p. 227.

229 Golzio (56), pp. 29, 112.

230 Golzio (56), pp. 31-3.

231 Golzio (56), p. 107

232 Hirst (203), p. 69, note 21; Poggi (48), vol. 2, pp. 206-7.

233 Golzio (55), pp. 60-2.

234 Golzio (55), pp. 69-70, 108-12.

235 Golzio (55), p. 32.

236 Golzio (55), pp. 113-14.

237 Poggi (48), vol. 3, pp. 12-13 and 17-18.

238 Poggi (48), vol. 3, pp. 22-3; Ramsden (49), vol. 1, pp. 280.

239 Poggi (48), vol. 3, pp. 22-3; Ramsden (49), vol. 1, pp. 280-3.

240 Ramsden (49), vol. 1, pp. 235-6.

241 Poggi (48), vol. 4, pp. 73-4; Ramsden (49), vol. 2, p. 266.

242 Beltrami (39), p. 154, doc. 244.

243 Beltrami (39), pp. 150-1.

244 Warnke (72), p. 137.

245 de Tolnay (192), vol. 1, p. 47; Ramsden (49), vol. 2, pp. 266-8 and 285-6.

246 Ramsden (49), vol. 2, p. 268.

247 Hartt (200), p. 73, doc. 69.

248 Hartt (200), p. 73, doc. 104.

249 Hartt (200), p. 80, doc. 201.

250 Vasari (57), vol. 5, p. 76.

251 Chambers (14), pp. 149-50, doc. 91; Pignatti (203), pp. 8, 10 and p. 166.

252 Pliny (2), XXXV, 62.

253 Beltrami (39), pp. 152-4, doc. 244; Kemp and Walker (43), pp. 276-7.

254 Shell and Sironi (46), p. 96.

255 Humfrey (157), pp. 85 and 324, note 107.

256 Aretino (56), vol. 1, pp. 78-9.

257 Vasari (57), vol. 4, pp. 44-5.

258 Matthew, 3. 10.

259 *Song of Songs*, 4.12.

260 D. C. Lindberg (ed.), *Roger Bacon's Philosophy of Nature: A Critical Edition of De multiplicatione specierum and De speculis comburentibus,* Oxford, 1983, p.131.

261 Leonardo, Urb. 158v-9v (McM 546); Kemp and Walker (43), pp. 171-2.

262 Gilbert (12), pp. 136-8 and pp. 114-16.

263 *De modo orandi*, ed. S. Tugwell, 'The Nine Ways of Prayer of St Dominic: A Textual Study and Critical Edition', *Medieval Studies*, XLVII, 1985, pp. 1-124.

264 H. I. Roberts, 'St Augustine in "St Jerome's Study": Carpaccio's Painting and its Legendary Source', *Art Bulletin*, XLI, 1959, pp. 283-97, esp. 296-7.

265 St Augustine, *Confessions*, 170-1.

266 Gilbert (12), pp. 72-8 and pp. 42-7.

267 Richter (40), vol. 2, pp. 366-9; Pedretti (40), vol. 2, pp. 353-68.

268 Chambers (14), pp. 47-8, doc. 24.

269 Baxandall (61), pp. 89-90.

270 Chambers (14), pp. 133-4, doc. 73.

271 Poggi (48), vol. 3, pp. 7-9; Ramsden (49), vol. 1, pp. 148-9, no. 157.

272 Vasari (57), vol. 6, p. 38.

273 Condivi (53), p. 58.

274 de Tolnay (193), vol. 3, p. 73.

275 Clements (52), p. 3.

276 Michelangelo (50), p. 83, no. 151; Gilbert trs. (51), p. 100, no. 49; Summers (127), pp. 203-33.

277 Michelangelo (50), p. 16, no. 30; Gilbert trs. (51), p. 19, no. 28.

278 Michelangelo (50), pp. 10-11, no. 20; Gilbert trs. (51), pp. 11-12, no. 18.

279 Michelangelo (50), pp. 4-5, no. 5; Gilbert trs. (51), pp. 5-6, no. 5.

280 Michelangelo (50), pp. 48-9, no. 85; Gilbert trs. (51), pp. 58-61, no. 83.

281 Michelangelo (50), p. 133, no. 277; Gilbert trs. (51), p. 156, no 275.

282 Michelangelo (50), p. 47, no. 83; Gilbert trs. (51), pp. 57-8, no. 81.

283 Michelangelo (50), pp. 123-4, no. 260;

Gilbert trs. (51), p. 145, no. 258.

284 Michelangelo (50), p. 127, no. 266; Gilbert trs. (51), p. 149, no. 264.

285 Michelangelo (50), p. 83, no. 151; Gilbert trs. (51), p. 100, no. 149.

286 Summers (128), p. 212.

287 Michelangelo (50), pp. 135-6, no. 285; Gilbert trs. (51), p. 159, no. 283.

288 Pope-Hennessy (144), pp. 309-10; Hartt (195), pp. 132-3, 136-7, 139-55.

289 Chambers (14), pp. 42-4, doc. 22.

290 Sperling, (162), pp. 218-19.

291 Eisler (201), p. 67.

292 Gilbert (12), pp. 130-1.

293 Apuleius, *Metamorphoses*, X, 31.

294 Shearman (79), pp. 18, 25; Smith (80), pp. 37-8.

295 Gombrich (135), p. 42.

296 Ovid, *Fasti*, V, 195-211.

297 Seneca, *De Beneficiis*, I, iii.

298 Dante, *Convivio*, II, 1, commenting on his own second canzone.

299 Cicero, *De oratore*, I, 5.

300 Cicero, *Pro archia*, VIII, 18.

301 Seneca, *De tranquillitate animi*, XVII, 10-12.

302 Thomson and Nagel (88), p. 69.

303 Baxandall (61), p. 16.

304 Spencer (123), p. 27.

305 Alberti (22 and 24), § 56, pp. 98-9 and pp. 90-1.

306 Seneca, *Ad Lucilium epistulae morales*, 84.

307 Vitruvius (3), I, 1.3.

308 Ghiberti (25), p. 5; Francesco di Giorgio (29), vol. 1, 37.

309 Francesco di Giorgio (29), vol. 2, 489.

310 Baxandall (61), p. 51.

311 Baxandall (61), pp. 67-8.

312 P. Bracciolini, *Epistolae*, ed. F. de Tonellis, Florence, 1815, IV, 15 and 21.

313 L. Valla, *De vero falsoque bono*, ed. M. de Panizza Lorch, Bari, 1970, as *De voluptate*, II, 36 in *Opera*, Basle, 1540, p. 953; Cf. Cicero, *De oratore*, III, 7.

314 Alberti (22 and 24), pp. 32-3 and 34.

315 Baxandall (61), pp. 99, 104-9 and pp. 163-8, text XVI.

316 Ghiberti (25), pp. 38, 41; Gilbert (12), p. 107 and pp. 77, 80-1.

317 Alberti (22 and 24), pp. 32-3 and 35.

318 H. Saalman, *Filippo Brunelleschi. The Cupola of Santa Maria del Fiore*, London, 1980, p. 12.

319 Rucellai (33), p. 55.

320 Baxandall (61), pp. 90-3 and pp. 155-7, text. XI.

321 Eisler (201), pp. 38, 512 and 531, app. E, doc. 1441.

322 Eisler (201), pp. 196, 515.

323 Cicero, *De inventione*, I, 7.

324 Baxandall (61), pp. 101-4 and pp. 163-4, text XVI.

325 Vitruvius (3), IX, preface, 6-9.

326 Manetti (20), p. 42 and Baxandall (62), pp. 124-6; O Morisani, "Art Historians and Art Critics-III: Cristoforo Landino", *The Burlington Magazine*, XCV, 1953, pp. 267-70.

327 Prager and Scaglia (21), p. 129.

328 Ghiberti (25), p. 36; Gilbert (12), p. 104 and p. 77.

329 Baxandall (61), pp. 70-1 and pp. 146-8, text V.

330 Alberti (22 and 24), § 53, pp. 94-5 and p. 88.

331 Filarete (28), fol. 184v and p. 315.

332 Filarete (28), fol. 69v and pp. 201.

333 Filarete (28), fol. 143r and p. 246.

334 Chambers (14), pp. 124-50, docs. 64-92.

335 Philostratus the Younger, *Imagines*, proemium, 6.

336 Quintillian, *Institutio oratoria*, VI, 2.29.

337 Dante, *Paradiso*, X, 43-4.

338 Cennini (18), p. 4 and p. 2.

339 Cennini (18), p. 27 and p. 15.

340 Filarete (28), fol. 7v, and pp. 15-16.

341 Filarete (28), fol. 142v and p. 246.

342 Filarete (28), fol. 143r and p. 246.

343 Filarete (28), fol. 114r and p. 200.

344 Filarete (28), fol. 151v and p. 260.

345 Filarete (28), fols. 108v -10v and pp. 190-3.

346 Cennini (18), p. 27 and p. 15.

347 Petrarch, *Prose*, ed. G. Martelloti et al., Milan and Naples, 1955, p. 1018.

348 Matteo Palmieri, *Della vita civile*, ed. F. Battaglia, Bologna, 1944, p. 4.

349 Gilbert (12), p. 207 and pp. 185-6.

350 Ghiberti (25), pp. 41-2; Gilbert (12), p. 107 and pp. 80-1.

351 Baxandall (61), pp. 104-9, 164-8; Virgil, *Aeneid*, VI, 848.

352 Baxandall (62), p. 118.

353 Gilbert (12), pp. 161-2 and pp. 138-9.

354 Alberti (22 and 24), § 60, pp. 102-3 and p. 93.

355 Valla, as in note 313 above.

356 Gilbert (12), p. 207 and pp. 185-6.

357 G. Cavalcanti, *Storie fiorentine*, quoted by U. Procacci, "Di Jacopo di Antonio e delle compagnie di Pittori del Corso degli Adimari nel XV secolo", *Rivista d'arte*, XXXV, 1963, pp. 3-70.

358 Savonarola *Sermon on Ezekiel* in Gilbert (12), p. 185 and p. 159.

359 Leonardo BN 2038 20v, Urb 4v-5r; Kemp and Walker (43), p. 13.

360 Leonardo Urb 5v (McM 31).

361 Leonardo Urb 13r-v (McM 33).

362 Leonardo Urb 33v-4r (McM 93); Kemp and Walker (43), pp. 201-2.

363 Leonardo Urb 15v (McM 28); Kemp and Walker (43), p. 46.

364 Leonardo Windsor 19045; MacCurdy (41), vol. 1, p. 137.

365 Leonardo Urb 28r, BN 2038, 24v (McM 53).

366 Leonardo Urb 8v, BN 2038 19v (McM 30) and Urb 5r (McM 35).

367 Leonardo Urb 24v (McM 48).

368 Leonardo Urb 157r (McM 437).

369 Leonardo Windsor 19030v; MacCurdy (41), vol. 1, p. 116.

370 Leonardo Urb 36r (McM 280).

371 Leonardo Urb 50r-v (McM 102).

372 Leonardo Urb 12r-v (McM 42); Kemp and Walker (43), p. 32.

373 B. Bellincioni, *Le Rime*, ed. P. Fanfani, Bologna, 1876, p. 106, LXXVII.

374 G. Visconti, *I Canzonieri per Beatrice d'Este e per Bianca Maria Sforza*, ed. P. Bongrani, Milan, 1979, pp. 117-18, CLXVIII.

375 Bellincioni, *op. cit.*, pp. 72-3, XLV.

376 Richter (40), vol. 2, p. 387.

377 Richter (40), vol. 1, p. 45, note 2.

378 Pacioli (45), fol. 2r, pp. 47-8.

379 Luca Pacioli, *De viribus quantitatis*, CXV.

380 Pacioli (45), letter of dedication.

381 Beltrami (39), pp. 115-16. doc. 184.

382 A. De Beatis, *Die Reise des Kardinals Luigi d'Aragona durch Deutschland, die Niederlande, Frankreich und Oberitalien, 1517-1518*, ed. L. Pastor, Freiburg im Breisgau, 1905, p. 143.

383 B. Cellini, *Della Architettura* in *La letteratura italiana*, XXVII, Milan and Naples, n.d., p. 1111.

384 Kristeller (183), p. 488, doc. 1.

385 Kristeller (184), pp. 489-90, doc. 4.

386 Gilbert (12), p. 155 and p. 131.

387 Gilbert (12), pp. 201-2 and pp. 179-81; Kristeller (185), pp. 523-34, doc. 34.

388 Kristeller (184), pp. 489-90, docs. 3 and 6.

389 Kristeller (184), p. 493, doc. 11.

390 Lightbown (185), p. 157; B. Fiera, *De Iusticia pingenda*, ed. J. Wardrop, 1957, pp. 18-24.

391 Kristeller (184), p. 538, doc. 79.

392 Santi (38), XXII, pp. 668-9; Kristeller (184), pp. 493-5, doc. 12; Gilbert (12), pp. 119-22 and pp. 95-6.

393 Kristeller (184), pp. 551-3, doc. 115; Chastel (65), p. 112.

394 Wilde (154), pp. 43-4.

395 Freedberg (142), p. 7.

396 Clark (188), pp. 98-100.

397 Pope-Hennessy (160), pp. 7, 11.

398 Clark (188), pp. 172-4, 175.

399 Gombrich (138), pp. 258-9.

400 Panofsky, 'Iconography and Iconology: An Introduction to the Study of Renaissance Art', in Panofsky (130), table on p. 66.

401 Wind (134), pp. 121-4.

402 Hauser (99), vol. 1, p. 287.

403 Hauser (99), vol. 1, p. 348.

404 Edoardo Bonechi, *Florence. A Complete Guide for Visiting the City*, c. 1965, n.p.

405 Press release for the *Leonardo da Vinci* exhibition, Hayward Gallery, 26 January-16 April 1989.

406 *Evening Standard*, 5 July 1988, p. 17.

407 V. Mellor, *The Micro Gallery. An Evaluation of the Hypertext System in the National Gallery*, M.Sc. thesis, The City University, London, 1993.

408 *Sponsorship News*, XI, no. 4, 1992, p. 13.

409 Hammer (71), pp. 445-7.

410 Antal (102).

411 Freud (187).

412 J. Baudrillard, 'The System of Collecting' in Elsner and Cardinal (70), pp. 19 and 24.

413 J. Kristeva, 'Motherhood According to Bellini', in *Desire in Language. A Semiotic Approach to Literature and Art*, ed. L. S. Roudiez, trs. T. Gora, A. Jardine and L. S. Roudiez, Oxford, 1981, pp. 244-7.

414 Starn and Partridge (85), refer to M. Mauss, 'Les techniques du corps', *Journal de la psychologie*, XXXI, 1936, pp. 177-93.

415 Starn and Partridge (85), pp. 93-4.

416 Starn and Partridge (85), pp. 119-21.

(References in the notes are given by the authors' or editors' names with the number of the item in the bibliography in brackets. Items have been arranged in sections and grouped within the sections in a way that I hope might be helpful for anyone who wishes to explore certain themes. The groupings inevitably overlap, and some of the items that appear in one place could also feature in another. The bibliography concentrates on books used directly by the author and on a selection of works which provide an entry into the issues discussed.)

SOURCES

(in chronological and thematic groups)

1) Lucian, *Calumniae non temere credendum*, vol. 1, trs. A. M. Harmon, Loeb Classical Library, 1913.

2) Pliny, *Historia naturalis*, trs. H. Rackham, W. H. S. Jones and D. E. Eichholz, Loeb Classical Library, 1938-62.

3) Vitruvius, *De architectura*, trs. F. Granger, Loeb Classical Library, 1931-4.

4) J.-P. Migne, *Patrologiae cursus completus. Series latina*, Paris, 1844-64.

5) J.-P. Migne, *Patrologiae cursus completus. Series graeca*, Paris, 1857-66.

6) H. van der Waal, *Iconclass: An Iconographic Classification System*, 17 vols., Amsterdam, 1973-85 .

7) J. Schlosser, *Die Kunstliteratur. Ein Handbuch zur Quellenkunde der neueren Kunstgeschichte*, Vienna, 1924; Ital. trs. F. Rossi, as *La letteratura artistica*, Florence, 1964.

8) E. Holt ed., *A Documentary History of Art*, vol. I, *The Middle Ages and the Renaissance*, Princeton, 1981.

9) W. Durandus, *Rationale divinorum officiorum*, book I, trs. J. M. Neale and B. Webb, as *The Symbolism of Churches and Church Ornaments*, London, 1906.

10) C. R. Dodwell ed., *Theophilus: The Various Arts (De Diversis Artibus)*, Oxford, 1986.

11) Theophilus, *On Divers Arts*, trs. J. G. Hawthorne and C. S. Smith, Chicago and London, 1963.

12) C. Gilbert ed., *Italian Art 1400-1500* (Sources and Documents in the History of Art), Englewood Cliffs, New Jersey, 1980 (repr. 1992); in Italian as *L'Arte del Quattrocento nelle testimonianze coeve*, Florence-Vienna, 1988.(Italian ed. page nos. precede trs. ed. in notes.)

13) R. Klein and H. Zerner eds., *Italian Art 1500-1600* (Sources and Documents in the History of Art), Evanston, Illinois, 1989.

14) D. Chambers ed., *Patrons and Artists in the Italian Renaissance*, London, 1970.

15) G. Milanesi, *Documenti per la storia dell' arte sienese*, 3 vols., Siena, 1864-6.

16) G. Gaye, *Carteggio inedito d'artristi dei secoli XIV, XV, XVI*, 3 vols., Florence, 1839-40.

17) H. Schultz, *Denkmäler der Kunst des Mittelalters in Unteritalien*, 4 vols., Dresden, 1860.

18) C. Cennini, *Il libro dell'arte*, ed. F. Brunello, Vicenza, 1971; trs. D.V. Thompson, as *The Craftsman's Handbook: the Italian "Il libro dell'arte" by Cennino D'Andrea Cennini*, New York, 1954.

19) *Mariano Taccola, De Machinis. The Engineering Treatise of 1449*, ed. G. Scaglia, 3 vols., Wiesbaden, 1971.

20) A. Manetti, *Life of Brunelleschi*, ed. H. Saalman and trs. C. Enggass, University Park, Pennsylvania and London, 1970.

21) F. D. Prager and G. Scaglia, *Brunelleschi. Studies of his Technologies and Inventions*, Cambridge, Mass., 1970.

22) C. Grayson ed. and trs., *Leon Battista Alberti: On Painting and On Sculpture. The Latin Texts of De Pictura and De Statua,* London, 1972.

23) C. Grayson ed., L. B. Alberti, *Operi Volgari*, 3 vols., Bari, 1960-73.

24) M. Kemp ed., *Leon Battista Alberti on Painting*, trs. C. Grayson, London and New York, 1991.

25) J. Schlosser ed., *Lorenzo Ghiberti's Denkwürdigkeiten. I commentarii*, Berlin, 1912.

26) K. Bergdolt ed., *Der dritte Kommentar Lorenzo Ghibertis: Naturwissenschaften und Medizin in der Kunsttheorie der Frührenaissance*, Weinheim, 1988.

27) Piero della Francesca, *De prospectiva pingendi*, ed. G. Nicco-Fasola, Florence, 1942; new ed. with notes and bibliography by E. Battisti, F. Ghione and R. Paccani, Florence, 1984.

28) A. Filarete, *Trattato di Architettura*, ed. A. M. Finoli and L. Grassi, 2 vols., Milan, 1972; trs. J. Spencer, New Haven and London, 1965 (references in the text are to the Spencer edition).

29) C. Maltese and L. Maltese Degrassi eds., *Francesco di Giorgio, Trattati de architettura civile e militare*, 2 vols., Milan, 1967.

30) M. Spallanzani and G. Bertelà eds., *Libro d'inventario dei beni di Lorenzo il Magnifico*, Florence, 1992.

31) F. Cegia, *Libretto sagreto (1494-6)*, ed. G. Pamplooni, 'I ricordi segreti del mediceo Francesco di Agostino Cegia', *Archivio storico italiano*, CXV, 1957, pp. 188-234.

32) Vespasiano da Bisticci, *The Vespasiano Memoirs. Lives of Illustrious Men of the XVth Century*, trs. W. George and E. Waters, London, 1926.

33) A. Perosa and F.W. Kent ed., *Giovanni Rucellai ed il suo Zibaldone*, 2 vols., London 1960-81.

34) J. Banker, 'Piero della Francesca's S. Agostino Altarpiece: Some New Documents', *The Burlington Magazine*, CXXIX, 1987, pp. 645-51.

35) J. Beck with G. Corti eds., *Masaccio. The Documents*, Florence, 1978.

36) A. Thomas, *The Painter's Practice in Renaissance Tuscany*, Cambridge, 1995.

37) R. Schofield, J. Shell and G. Sironi eds., *Giovanni Antonio Amadeo. Documents / I documenti*, Como, 1989.

38) G. Santi, *La vita e la gesta di Federico di Montefeltro, Duca d'Urbino*, ed. L. M. Tocci, 2 vols., Vatican City, 1985.

39) L. Beltrami, *Documenti e memorie riguardanti la vita e le opere di Leonardo da Vinci*, Milan 1919.

40) J. P. Richter ed. *The Literary Works of Leonardo da Vinci*, 2 vols., London and New York, 1970; with *Commentary* by C. Pedretti, 2 vols., Oxford, 1977.

41) E. MacCurdy ed., *The Notebooks of Leonardo da Vinci*, 2 vols., London, 1938.

42) A. P. McMahon ed. and trs., *Treatise on Painting by Leonardo da Vinci*, 2 vols., Princeton, 1956.

43) M. Kemp ed., *Leonardo on Painting*, trs. M. Kemp and M. Walker, London and New Haven, 1989. (All references to Leonardo's manuscripts are abbreviated as in this edition, pp. 317-28).

44) C. Farago ed., *Leonardo da Vinci's Paragone. A Critical Interpretation with a New Edition of the Text in the Codex Urbinas*, Leiden, New York, Copenhagen and Cologne, 1992.

45) Luca Pacioli, *De Divina proportione*, Milan, 1509; facs. ed. repr. 1982 with an introduction by A. Marinoni; French trs. by G. Duchense and M. Giraud, Paris, 1980.

46) J. Shell and G. Sironi, 'Salaì and Leonardo's Legacy', *The Burlington Magazine*, CXXXIII, 1991, pp. 95-108.

47) G. Sironi, *Documenti inediti per la storia della "Vergine delle Roccie" di Leonardo da Vinci*, Milan, 1981.

48) G. Poggi ed., with P. Barocchi and R. Ristori, *Il Carteggio di Michelangelo*, 5 vols., Florence, 1965-83; *Carteggio indiretto*, ed. P. Barocchi, K. Loach Bramanti, R. Ristori, 2 vols., Florence, 1988-95.

49) E. Ramsden ed., *The Letters of Michelangelo*, 2 vols., Stanford, California, 1963.

50) Michelangelo, *Rime*, ed. E. N. Girardi, Bari, 1960.

51) R. Linscott ed., *Complete Poems and Selected Letters of Michelangelo*, trs. C. Gilbert, Princeton, 1963.

52) R. J. Clements, *The Poetry of Michelangelo*, London, 1966.

53) A. Condivi, *Vita di Michelangelo Buonarrotti*, ed. H. Wohl and trs. A. Sedgwick Wohl, Oxford, 1976.

54) G. Vasari, *La vita di Michelangelo nelle redazioni del 1550 e del 1568*, ed. P. Barocchi, 5 vols., Milan-Naples, 1962.

55) V. Golzio, *Raffaello nei documenti, nelle testimonianze dei contemporanei e nella letteratura del suo secolo*, Vatican, 1936.

56) P. Aretino, *Lettere sull'arte*, ed. E. Camesasca, with a commentary by F. Pertile, 4 vols., Milan, 1957-60.

57) G. Vasari, *Le vite de'più eccelenti pittori, scultori e architettori nelle redazioni del 1550 e 1568*, 9 vols., ed. R. Bettarini and P. Barocchi, Florence, 1966-87.

58) G. Vasari, *Le vite de'più eccelenti pittori, scultori e architettori nelle redazioni del 1550 e 1568*, 9 vols., ed. G. Milanesi, Florence, 1878-85.

59) K. Frey, *Giorgio Vasari. Der literarische Nachanlass*, 2 vols., Munich, 1923-30; *Neue Briefe*, vol. 3, Munich, 1940.

60) D. Barbaro, *La pratica della perspettiva*, Venice, 1569.

STUDIES OF WRITTEN EVIDENCE AND THE BUSINESS OF ART

61) M. Baxandall, *Giotto and the Orators. Humanist Observers of Painting in Italy and the Discovery of Pictorial Composition 1350-1450*, Oxford, 1986 (corrected repr.).

62) M. Baxandall, *Painting and Experience in Fifteenth-Century Italy*, Oxford, 1988 (2nd ed.)

63) M. Baxandall, *Patterns of Intention. On the Historical Representation of Pictures*, New Haven and London, 1985.

64) M. Wackernagel, *The World of the Florentine Renaissance Artist. Projects and Patrons, Workshop and Art Market*, trs. A. Luchs, Princeton, 1981.

65) A. Chastel, *A Chronicle of Italian Renaissance Painting*, trs. L. and P. Murray, Ithaca, New York, 1984.

66) B. Cole, *The Renaissance Artist at Work from Pisano to Titian*, London, 1983.

67) H. Glasser, *Artists' Contracts in the Early Renaissance*, New York and London, 1977.

68) M. O'Malley, 'The Business of Art. Contracts and Payment Documents for Fourteenth- and Fifteenth-Century Italian Altarpieces and Frescoes', Ph.D. diss., Warburg Institute, London, 1994.

PATRONAGE AND COLLECTING

69) J. Alsop, *The Rare Art Traditions. The History of Collecting and its Linked Phenomena*, London, 1982.

70) J. Elsner and R. Cardinal eds., *The Cultures of Collecting*, London, 1994.

71) A. Hammer with N. Lydon, *Hammer. Witness to History*, London, 1987.

72) M. Warnke, *The Court Artist. On the Ancestry of the Modern Artist*, trs. D. McLintock, Cambridge, 1993.

73) A. Cole, *Virtue and Magnificence. Art of the Italian Renaissance Courts*, New York, 1995.

74) P. P. Bober and R. Rubenstein, *Renaissance Artists and Antique Sculpture. A Handbook of Sources*, London and Oxford, 1986.

75) F. W. Kent and P. Simons eds., *Patronage, Art and Society in Renaissance Italy*, Oxford, 1987.

76) E. H. Gombrich, 'The Early Medici as Patrons of Art', in *Norm and Form*, London, 1966, pp. 35-57.

77) E. H. Gombrich, "Apollonio di Giovanni: A Florentine Cassone Workshop seen through the Eyes of a Humanist Poet", in *Norm and Form*, pp. 11-28.

78) M. Bullard, 'Heroes and their Workshops: Medici Patronage and the Problem of a Shared Agency', *Journal of Medieval and Renaissance Studies*, ed. L Rice, XXIV, 1994, pp. 179-98.

79) J. Shearman, 'The Collections of the Younger Branch of the Medici', *The Burlington Magazine*, CXVII, 1975, pp. 12-27.

80) W. Smith, 'On the Original Location of the "Primavera"', *Art Bulletin*, LVII, 1975, pp. 31-9.

81) C. Elam, 'Art and Diplomacy in Renaissance Florence', *Journal of the Royal Society of Arts*, CXXXVI, 1988, pp. 813-26.

82) J. Cox-Rearick, 'Sacred to Profanne: Diplomatic Gifts of the Medici to Francis I', *Journal of Medieval and Renaissance Studies*, ed. L. Rice, XXIV, 1994, pp. 239-58.

83) L. Fusco and G. Corti, 'Giovanni Ciampolini (d. 1505), a Renaissance Dealer in Rome and his Collection of Antiquities', *Xenia*, XXI, 1991, pp. 30-46.

84) C. Clough, 'Federigo da Montefeltro's Patronage of the Arts', *Journal of the Warburg and Courtauld Institutes*, XXXVI,

293

1973, pp. 129-44.

85) R. Starn and L. Partridge, *Arts of Power. Three Halls of State in Italy, 1300-1600*, Berkeley, Los Angeles and Oxford, 1992.

86) M. Hollingsworth, *Patronage in Renaissance Italy. From 1400 to the Early Sixteenth Century*, London, 1994.

GENERAL AND REGIONAL
(grouped thematically)

87) J. Bowen, *A History of Western Education*, vol. II, London, 1975.

88) D. Thompson and A. F. Nagel eds., *The Three Crowns of Florence. Humanist Assessments of Petrarca, Dante and Boccaccio*, New York, Evaston, San Francisco and London, 1972.

89) R. Weiss, *The Renaissance Discovery of Classical Antiquity*, Oxford, 1988.

90) P. Burke, *Tradition and Innovation in Renaissance Italy: A Sociological Approach*, London, 1974.

91) P. Burke, *The Italian Renaissance Culture and Society in Italy*, Oxford, 1993.

92) L. Martinez, *Power and Imagination. City-States in Renaissance Italy*, London, 1983.

93) G. Holmes, *Art and Politics in Renaissance Italy*, London, 1993.

94) G. Holmes, *The Florentine Enlightment, 1400-1450*, Oxford, 1992.

95) L. Jardine, *Worldly Goods*, London, 1996.

96) J. R. Hale, *Florence and the Medici. The Pattern of Control*, London, 1977.

97) D. Herlihy and C. Klapisch-Zuber, *Tuscans and their Families. A Study of the Florentine Catasto of 1427*, New Haven and London, 1985.

98) F. W. Kent, *Household and Lineage in Renaissance Florence. The Family Life of the Capponi, Ginori and Rucellai*, Princeton, N.J., 1977.

99) D. Weinstein, *Savonarola and Florence. Prophecy and Patriotism in the Renaissance*, Princeton, 1970.

00) A. Hauser, *The Social History of Art*, 2 vols., trs. S. Godman, London, 1951.

101) M. Camille, *The Gothic Idol. Ideology and Image-Making in Medieval Art*, Cambridge, 1991

102) F. Antal, *Florentine Painting and its Social Background. The Bourgeois Republic before Cosimo de' Medici's Advent to Power: XIV and Early XV Centuries*, London, 1947.

103) R. A. Goldthwaite, *Wealth and the Demand for Art in Italy, 1300-1600*, Baltimore and London, 1993.

104) E. Welch, *Art and Society in Italy 1350-1500*, Oxford, 1996.

105) R. A. Goldthwaite, *The Building of Renaissance Florence. An Economic and Social History*, Baltimore, 1990.

106) R. A. Goldthwaite, *Banks, Palaces and Entrepreneurs in Renaissance Florence*, Aldershot, 1995.

107) F. D. Prager and G. Scaglia, *Brunelleschi. Studies of his Technology and Inventions*, Cambridge, Mass. and London, 1970.

108) P. Galuzzi ed., *Prima di Leonardo. Cultura delle macchine a Siena nel Rinascimento*. Milan, 1991.

109) N. Rubinstein, *The Palazzo Vecchio, 1298-1532. Government, Architecture and Imagery in the Civic Palace of the Florentine Republic*, Oxford, 1995.

110) J. K. Lydeker, 'The Domestic Setting of the Arts in Renaissance Florence', Ph.D. diss., John Hopkins University, Baltimore, 1987.

111) J. K. Lydeker, 'Il patrizio fiorentino e la commitenza artistica per la casa', in *I Ceti dirigenti nella Toscana del Quattrocento*, ed. F. Papafava, Florence, 1987, pp. 209-21.

112) P. Thornton, *The Italian Renaissance Interior, 1400-1600*, London, 1991.

113) J. A. Levenson ed., *Circa 1492. Art in the Age of Exploration*, exh. cat., Washington, 1991.

114) E. Kris and O. Kurz, *Legend, Myth and Magic in the Image of the Artist. A Historical Experiment*, trs. A. Laing and rev. L. M. Newman, New Haven and London, 1979.

115) A. Martindale, *The Rise of the Artist in the Middle Ages and Early Renaissance*, London, 1972

116) B. Kempers, *Painting, Power and Patronage. The Rise of the Professional Artist in Renaissance Italy*, trs. B. Jackson, London, 1994.

117) D. Summers, *The Judgement of Sense. Renaissance, Naturalism and the Rise of Aesthetics*, Cambridge, 1987.

118) M. Barasch, *Theories of Art from Plato to Winckelmann*, New York and London, 1985.

119) M. Kemp, *The Science of Art. Optical Themes in Western Art from Brunelleschi to Seurat*, New Haven and London, 1992.

120) J. Gage, *Colour and Culture. Practice and*

Meaning from Antiquity to Abstraction, London, 1993.

121) S. Fermor, 'Studies in the Depiction of the Moving Figure in Italian Renaissance Art, Art Criticism and Dance Theory', Ph.D. diss., Warburg Institute, London, 1990.

122) M. Kemp, 'From "Mimesis" to "Fantasia": the Quattrocento Vocabulary of Creation, Inspiration and Genius in the Visual Arts', *Viator*, VIII, 1977, pp. 347-98.

123) J. R. Spencer, "'Ut rhetorica pictura'. A Study in Quattrocento Theory of Painting", *Journal of the Warburg and Courtauld Institutes*, XX, 1966, pp. 24-44.

124) C. Gilbert, *Poets Seeing Artist's Work. Instances in the Italian Renaissance*, Florence, 1991.

125) C. Gilbert, 'Grapes, Curtains, Human Beings: the Theory of Missed Mimesis', *Künstlerischer Austausch* (Acts of the XXVIII International Congress for Art History, Berlin, 1992), ed. T. Gaehtgens, Berlin, 1994, pp. 413-19.

126) D. Cast, *The Calumny of Apelles. A Study in the Humanist Tradition*, New Haven and London, 1981.

127) J. M. Massing, *Du texte à l'image. La Calomnie d'Apelle et son iconographie*, Strasbourg, 1990.

128) D. Summers, *Michelangelo and the Language of Art*, Princeton, 1981.

129) P. L. Rubin, *Giorgio Vasari. Art and History*, New Haven and London, 1995.

130) E. Panofsky, *Meaning in the Visual Arts*, London, 1970.

131) E. Panofsky, *Studies in Iconology. Humanistic Themes in the Art of the Renaissance*, New York, 1962.

132) E. Panofsky, *Idea. A Concept in Art Theory*, trs. J. J. S. Peake, New York, 1968.

133) E. Panofsky, *Renaissance and Renascences*, New York, 1972.

134) E. Wind, *Pagan Mysteries in the Renaissance*, Harmondsworth, 1967.

135) E. H. Gombrich, *Symbolic Images*, London, 1972.

136) E. H. Gombrich, *The Heritage of Apelles*, London, 1976.

137) E. H. Gombrich, *New Light on Old Masters*, Oxford, 1986.

138) E. H. Gombrich, *Aby Warburg. An Intellectual Biography*, Oxford, 1986.

139) E. H. Gombrich, *Norm and Form*, London, 1966.

140) J. Shearman, *Only Connect . . . Art and the Spectator in the Italian Renaissance*, Princeton, 1992.

141) W. S. Sheard and J. Paoletti eds., *Collaboration in Italian Renaissance Art*, New Haven and London, 1978.

142) S. J. Freedberg, *Painting of the High Renaissance in Rome and Florence*, Cambridge, Mass., 1961.

143) J. Pope-Hennessy, *Italian Renaissance Sculpture*, Oxford, 1986.

144) J. Pope-Hennessy, *Italian High Renaissance and Baroque Sculpture*, Oxford, 1986.

145) M. Leithe-Jasper, *Renaissance Master Bronzes from the Collection of the Kunsthistorisches Museum Vienna*, exhib. cat., Smithsonian Institution, Washington, 1986.

146) M. Kemp and P. Humfrey eds., *The Altarpiece in the Renaissance*, Cambridge, 1990.

147) R. Starn and L. Partridge, *Arts of Power. Three Halls of State in Italy, 1300-1600*, Berkeley, Los Angeles and London, 1992.

148) L. Andrews, *Story and Space in Renaissance Art. The Rebirth of Continuous Narrative*, Cambridge and New York, 1955.

149) J. Paoletti, *The Siena Baptistry Font. A Study of an Early Renaissance Collaborative Program, 1416-1434*, New York and London, 1979.

150) D. S. Chambers and J. Martineau eds., *Splendours of the Gonzaga*, exhib. cat. London, Victoria and Albert Museum, 1981-2.

151) J. Woods-Marsden, *The Gonzaga of Mantua and Pisanello's Arthurian Frescoes*, Princeton, 1988.

152) G. L. Hersey, *Alfonso II and the Artistc Renewal of Naples, 1485-1495*, New Haven, 1969.

153) E. S. Welch, *Art and Authority in Renaissance Milan*, New Haven and London, 1995.

154) J. Wilde, *Venetian Art from Bellini to Titian*, Oxford, 1974.

155) P. Fortini-Brown, *Venetian Narrative Painting in the Age of Carpaccio*, New Haven and London, 1988.

156) P. Humfrey, *Painting in Renaissancce Venice*, London and New Haven, 1995.

157) P. Humfrey, *The Altarpiece in Renaissance Venice*, London and New Haven, 1993.

158) J. Strupp, 'The Color of Money. Use,

Cost and Aesthetic Appreciation of Marble in Venice ca. 1500', *Venezia Cinquecento*, III, 1993, pp. 7-32.

ARTISTS
(geographically and chronologically)

159) H. Janson, *The Sculpture of Donatello*, Princeton, 1963.
160) J. Pope-Hennessy, *Donatello Sculptor*, London, New York and Paris, 1993.
161) R. W. Lightbown, *Donatello and Michelozzo: an Artistic Partnership and its Patrons in the Early Renaissance*, 2 vols., London, 1980.
162) C. M. Sperling, 'Donatello's Bronze "David" and the Demands of Medici Politics', *The Burlington Magazine*, CXXXIV, 1992, pp. 218-24.
163) P. Joannides, *Masaccio and Masolino. A Complete Catalogue*, London, 1993.
164) P. L. Roberts, *Masolino da Panicale*, Oxford, 1993.
165) W. Hood, *Fra Angelico at San Marco*, New Haven and London, 1993.
166) J. Ruda, *Fra Filippo Lippi. Life and Work with a Complete Catalogue*, London, 1993.
167) E. Callmann, *Appollonio di Giovanni*, Oxford, 1974.
168) G. Passavant, *Andrea Verrocchio als Maler*, Dusseldorf, 1959.
169) G. Passavant, *Verrocchio. Sculptures, Paintings and Drawings*, London, 1969.
170) M. Kemp, 'Verrocchio's *San Donato* and the Chiesina della Vergine di Piazza in Pistoia' (forthcoming)
171) A. Butterfield, 'Verrocchio's Christ and St Thomas: Chronology, Iconography and Political Content', *The Burlington Magazine*, CXXXIV, 1992, pp. 223-35.
172) R. W. Lightbown, *Sandro Botticelli. Life and Work*, 2 vols., London, 1989.
173) C. Dempsey, *The Portrayal of Love. Botticelli's 'Primavera' and Humanist Culture at the Time of Lorenzo the Magnificent*, Princeton, N.J., 1992.
174) M. Kemp, 'The Taking and Use of Evidence; with a Botticellian Case Study', *Art Journal*, XLIV, no. 3, 1984, pp. 207-215.
175) R. Stapleford, 'Intellect and Intuition in Botticelli's *Saint Augustine*', *Art Bulletin*, LXXVI, 1994, pp. 69-80.
176) R. Bagemihl, 'On Reading (into) Botticelli's St Augustine', *Source*, XVI,

1997, pp.16-19.
177) G. L. Geiger, *Filippino Lippi's Caraffa Chapel; Renaissance Art in Rome*, Kirksville, Missouri, 1986.
178) A. Scharf, *Filippino Lippi*, Vienna, 1935.
179) R. W. Lightbown, *Piero della Francesca*, London and New York, 1992.
180) M. Daly-Davies, *Piero della Francesca's Mathematical Treatises. The "Trattato d'abaco" and "Libellus de quinque corporibus regularibus"*, Ravenna, 1977.
181) M. Kemp, 'New Light on Old Theories: Piero's Studies of the Transmission of Light' *Piero della Francesca tra arte e scienza*, Atti del Convegno Internazionale di Studi, Arezzo (1992), ed. M. Dalai Emiliano and V. Curzi, Venice, 1996, pp. 33-46.
182) M. A. Lavin, *Piero della Francesca's Baptism of Christ*, New Haven and London, 1981.
183) G. Paccagnini, *Pisanello*, London, 1973.
184) P. O. Kristeller, *Andrea Mantegna*, Berlin and Leipzig, 1902.
185) R. W. Lightbown, *Mantegna*, Oxford, 1986.
186) J. Martineau ed., *Andrea Mantegna*, exhib. cat., London and New York, 1992.
187) S. Freud, *Ein Kindheitserinnerung des Leonardo da Vinci*, Vienna, 1910; trs. by A. Tyson as *Leonardo da Vinci and a Memory of his Childhood*, London, 1963.
188) K. Clark, *Leonardo da Vinci. An Account of his Development as an Artist*, Cambridge, 1939; ed. by M. Kemp as *Leonardo da Vinci*, London, 1988.
189) M. Kemp, *Leonardo da Vinci. The Marvellous Works of Nature and Man*, London, 1989.
190) M. Kemp, 'Looking at Leonardo's *Last Supper*', in *Appearance, Opinion, Change: Evaluating the Look of Paintings*, (Papers given at a conference held jointly by the United Kingdom Institute for Conservation and the Association of Art Historians, June 1990), London, 1990, pp. 14-21.
191) M. Kemp, 'Science and the Poetic Impulse', *Journal of the Royal Society of Arts*, CXXXIII, 1985, pp. 196-214.
192) L. Borgo, *The Works of Mariotto Albertinelli*, New York and London, 1976.
193) C. de Tolnay, *Michelangelo*, 5 vols., Princeton, 1943-60.
194) C. Seymour, Jr., *Michelangelo's "David":*

A Search for Identity, Pittsburgh, 1974.

195) F. Hartt, *David by the Hand of Michelangelo. The Original Model Discovered*, London, 1987.

196) K. Weil-Garris Brandt, 'Michelangelo's Early Projects for the Sistine Ceiling. Their Practical and Artistic Consequences', *Michelangelo Drawings*, Washington, 1992, pp. 57-87.

197) M. Hirst, *Michelangelo and his Drawings*, New Haven and London, 1988.

198) W. Wallace, *Michelangelo at San Lorenzo. The Genius as Entrepreneur*, Cambridge, 1994.

199) R. Jones and N. Penny, *Raphael*, New Haven and London, 1983.

200) F. Hartt, *Giulio Romano*, 2 vols., New Haven, 1958.

201) C. T. Eisler, *The Genius of Jacopo Bellini: the Complete Paintings and Drawings*, London and New York, 1989.

202) P. Humfrey, *Cima da Conegliano*, Cambridge, 1983.

203) T. Pignatti, *Giorgione*, trs. C. Whitfield, London, 1971.

204) C. Hope, *Titian*, London, 1980.

205) H. Wethey, *The Paintings of Titian*, 3 vols., London, 1969-75.

206) M. Hirst, *Sebastiano del Piombo*, Oxford, 1981.

312

The index has been provided by Frederika Adam.

Photographic Credits

All the illustrations in this book come from the archives of the cited museums, or from the author's collection, apart from those listed below:

Alinari 99

Nicolo Orsi Battaglini © 35, 60, 84, 85

The Bridgeman Art Library, London 21

Antonio Quattrone 34

RMN, Paris © 26, 29, 96

The Royal Collection © Her Majesty Queen Elizabeth II 25, 50, 92

Scala 3, 13, 19, 24, 108

Musei Vaticani, photo A Bracchetti/P Zigrossi 71